MARCHING TO A DIFFERENT DRUMMER

Unrecognized Heroes of American History

Robin Kadison Berson

GREENWOOD PRESS
Westport, Connecticut • London

Library of Congress Cataloging-in-Publication Data

Berson, Robin Kadison.
  Marching to a different drummer : unrecognized heroes of American
history / Robin Kadison Berson.
    p. cm.
  Includes bibliographical references and index.
  ISBN 0–313–28802–X (alk. paper)
    1. Social reformers—United States—Biography. 2. Dissenters—
United States—Biography.   I. Title.
HN57.B467 1994
303.48'4'0973—dc20   93–49533

British Library Cataloguing in Publication Data is available.

Library of Congress Catalog Card Number: 93–49533
ISBN: 0–313–28802–X

First published in 1994

Greenwood Press, 88 Post Road West, Westport, CT 06881
An imprint of Greenwood Publishing Group, Inc.

Printed in the United States of America

The paper used in this book complies with the
Permanent Paper Standard issued by the National
Information Standards Organization (Z39.48–1984).

10 9 8 7 6 5 4 3 2 1

CONTENTS

Acknowledgments   ix

Introduction: Why This Book Exists   xi

Subject Lists   xix

William Apess   1
  Native American rights leader

Sara Josephine Baker   12
  children's health reformer

Smedley Darlington Butler   20
  anti-imperialist military reformer

George Washington Cable   33
  human rights and civil rights advocate

Tunis G. Campbell   44
  African American community organizer

Luisa Capetillo   56
  labor organizer, women's rights advocate

Edward Coles   67
  abolitionist, human rights advocate

vi   Contents

Anna Julia Cooper   75
  educator, women's rights advocate

Angie Debo   86
  historian, Native American rights activist

John Lovejoy Elliott   95
  humanist, community organizer

Elizabeth Freeman   106
  abolitionist

Laura S. Haviland   113
  abolitionist, educator, human rights advocate

Thomas Hazard   121
  abolitionist

Lugenia Burns Hope   127
  community organizer, civil rights activist

Myles Horton   135
  educator, civil rights and labor rights activist

Jovita Idar de Juarez   150
  Mexican American rights, women's rights activist

Florence Kelley   158
  women's and children's rights activist, labor reformer

Thomas Kennedy   168
  activist for religious freedom

Susette La Flesche   176
  Native American rights activist

Lucy Craft Laney   186
  educator, civil rights advocate

Benjamin Lay   195
  abolitionist, pacifist, penal reform advocate

Belva Ann Lockwood   202
  women's rights activist

Seth Luther   211
  labor organizer

Vito Marcantonio   218
  civil rights and freedom of conscience advocate

Tanya Zolotoroff Nash   226
  activist for Deaf rights

Mary White Ovington   234
  civil rights activist

Jeannette Rankin   243
  women's rights activist, pacifist

John Swett Rock   255
  abolitionist, civil rights activist

Ernestine Louise Rose   265
  abolitionist, women's rights activist, free-thinker

Rose Schneiderman   277
  labor organizer

Tye Leung Schulze   288
  Chinese American community activist

David Walker   294
  abolitionist

George Henry White   303
  civil rights and anti-lynching activist

Carola Woerishoffer   313
  women's and labor rights activist, philanthropist

Minoru Yasui   324
  civil liberties activist

Index   335

ACKNOWLEDGMENTS

Working on this book, assembling this cast of remarkable characters and discovering their astonishing lives, has been a rare privilege; without the imagination and vision of Barbara Rader of Greenwood Press, I would never have had this opportunity, and I am deeply grateful to her. In addition, a wide variety of scholars and librarians has helped me gather documentation on lesser-known lives: Lennie Draper of the University of Oklahoma Press; Carmen Fontán, Center for Puerto Rican Studies, Hunter College; Margo Gutierrez, Chicano Studies Librarian, University of Texas at Austin; Natalie Koretz, Archivist of the American Ethical Union; Professor Lauren Kessler, University of Oregon School of Journalism; Louise Schulze Lee of San Mateo, California; Heather Lloyd, Head of Special Collections and University Archives, Oklahoma State University; Elizabeth Mager, Keeper of Records, Haviland Records Room, New York Friends Yearly Meeting; Glenn Omatsu, Asian Studies, UCLA; John Tateishi, Kentfield, California; Ruthe Winegarten, Austin, Texas; True Yasui of Denver, CO and Dr. Homer Yasui of Portland, OR; Judy Yung, Chinese Cultural Foundation, San Francisco; Joel Ziev, Director, New York Society for the Deaf. My family provided support, patience, and humor—and ate a lot of cold food.

Finally, I am deeply indebted to Milton Meltzer, who offered encouragement, suggestions, and his own luminous example of historical writing as a profoundly ethical exercise.

INTRODUCTION: WHY THIS BOOK EXISTS

Even a superficial look at history shows that social progress never
rolls in on the wheels of inevitability. It comes through the tireless
effort and the persistent work of dedicated individuals.

Martin Luther King, Jr., Commencement
address at Lincoln University, 1961

All significant moral change springs from people who are in some
sense deviant, at least insofar as they are willing to suffer the risk of
continuing unpopularity.

David Brion Davis, *The Problem of Slavery
in the Age of Revolution*, p. 14.

It could be argued that this is a book about dedicated deviants. The
women and men discussed here all defied the social and moral conventions of their times. Those who were among the despised and denigrated
refused to accept the limitations and negative images society sought to
impose upon them; those of them among the safe and privileged rejected
the comfort of easy ignorance and knowingly thrust themselves into are-
nas that were fraught with difficulty and danger. At one time or another
in their lives, all of the people in this book were out of step with their
neighbors, a position as misunderstood as it is honored in American
tradition.

"If a man does not keep pace with his companions," mused Henry
David Thoreau, "perhaps it is because he hears a different drummer. Let
him step to the music which he hears, however measured or far away"

(Thoreau, 290). Thoreau is a prime example of the moral maverick, the individual for whom conscience transcends all other loyalties. "It is not desirable to cultivate a respect for the law, so much as for the right," he wrote in *Civil Disobedience*. "The only obligation which I have a right to assume is to do at any time what I think right" (Thoreau, 637).

This devotion to conscience is sometimes bought at a fearful cost. In a choice example from literature, Huck Finn, Mark Twain's magnificent moral maverick, confronts the choice of either returning his friend Jim to slavery or helping him escape to freedom. Huck is well aware that his friendship and respect for Jim violate all the conventions and standards of his society:

> Well, I tried the best I could to kinder soften it up somehow for myself, by saying I was brung up wicked, and so I warn't so much to blame; but something inside me kept saying, "There was the Sunday school, you could a gone to it; and if you'd a done it they'd a learnt you, there, that people that acts as I'd been acting about that nigger goes to everlasting fire" (Twain, 270).

In a desperate attempt to demonstrate his loyalty to the system of slavery, Huck writes a letter to Miss Watson, Jim's owner, telling her where Jim is. He tries to convince himself that he has done the honorable, "Christian" thing: "I felt good and all washed clean of sin for the first time I had ever felt so in my life, and I knowed I could pray now." But as he stares at his letter and painfully recalls his deep love for Jim, his seemingly irrational conscience takes over in one of the most ringing moral moments in American literature:

> But somehow I couldn't seem to strike no places to harden me against him, but only the other kind . . . and then I happened to look around, and see that paper.
> It was a close place. I took it up, and held it in my hand. I was a-trembling, because I'd got to decide, forever, betwixt two things, and I knowed it. I studied a minute, sort of holding my breath, and then says to myself: "All right, then, I'll *go* to hell"—and tore it up (Twain, 272).

Poor Huck has been so indoctrinated by his society that he perceives his courageous decision as profoundly immoral. Unable to articulate his reasoning, he is nonetheless compelled to obey a different law, to "step to the music which he hears." The people profiled here are luckier than Huck in that their difficult stances are taken with a full awareness of their justness.

The figures in this volume share more than their moral defiance. They are linked by a common thread of unshakable decency, an empathic capacity to embrace the entire human family, a willingness to accept the individual responsibility to act against injustice. As scattered in time, place, class, and ethnicity as they may be, this thread of decency binds them together. Their lives intersect again and again in multiple shared concerns, weaving a proud tapestry of integrity, compassion, and commitment.* Martin Luther King, Jr. wrote, "We are caught in an inescapable network of mutuality; tied in a single garment of destiny. Whatever affects one directly, affects all indirectly" (King, 210).

In a strange kind of human dialectic, the specific injustices and outrages of American history seem to elicit specific ethical heroism. Slavery; economic and political abuses; the particular urban desperation born of rapid industrialization and unprecedented immigration; the cruel, poisonous cancer of racism and segregation—each crisis has been met by individuals whose dedication and intelligence have responded to desperate need. Within the first decade of substantial Spanish settlement in the Caribbean, for example, the horrors of slavery inspired one of its most passionate opponents, the eloquent priest Bartolomé de Las Casas. Las Casas chronicled in sickening detail the abuses inherent in slavery and excoriated the men involved in all aspects of the trade. Later, the assumption that injustice necessitates outspoken condemnation motivated the late 17th-century Quakers of the Germantown, Pennsylvania Meeting, who published the first recorded English protest against American slavery.

Like the struggle against slavery, political and economic repression in America has produced thousands of heroes. We must acknowledge the stature of countless anonymous, ordinary wage-earning men and women who labored under brutal, dehumanizing conditions for twelve to sixteen hours a day and who still managed to educate themselves and their children. Any worker in 19th-century America who dared to envision an effective union deserves to be called heroic. In the context of a power structure deeply inimical to workers' goals, even middle-class supporters of the union cause risked much. For example, on May 4, 1886, labor organizers in Chicago called a mass meeting in Haymarket Square to protest unprovoked police brutality; when police moved to break up the meeting, a bomb was thrown, and in the resultant panic, several policemen as well as numerous demonstrators were killed. Although the actual bomb thrower wasn't identified, the eight strike organizers were blamed, subjected to a blatantly unfair trail, and sentenced to hang. Four were hanged and one committed suicide in prison. When John Peter Altgeld became governor of Illinois in 1893, one of his first acts was to pardon the three surviving Haymarket martyrs. Public sentiment, manipulated by the press, ran high against him; the courageous act effectively sabo-

---

*In recognition of these intersections, an asterisk will be used to identify figures who are mentioned in other subjects' chapters and as well are profiled in depth themselves.

taged his political future. Still, when the Haymarket convictions were first handed down and all the men were still alive, Altgeld, then a judge for Cook County, was silent. How much more courageous were those who defied public rage and retaliation directly after the trial, in the atmosphere of hatred and fear, when few were willing to speak out in the name of real justice and decency. William Salter, the leader of the Chicago Ethical Culture Society, and the reformer Henry Demarest Lloyd worked frantically to try to save the lives of men who had been condemned not for their actions but for their unpopular beliefs. They failed, and Salter's notoriety almost destroyed his thriving humanist congregation. Nonetheless, they represent the finest American tradition of principled protest.

The grotesqueness of racism and segregation has elicited some of the most admirable actions in our history. Rosa Parks is well known for refusing to give up her seat on a segregated bus in Montgomery, Alabama, triggering a sequence of events that eventually desegregated public transportation in her city. But who today realizes that Rosa Parks was heir to the courage of Elizabeth Jennings? Jennings, a teacher and church organist in New York City, was thrown violently from a segregated horse car in 1853. She sued the horse car company, ably represented by a young white lawyer named Chester A. Arthur, who would one day become president of the United States. Jennings won her case and desegregated the trolleys of New York. Similarly, Mary Tape, a Chinese-born resident of San Francisco, refused to accept second-class citizenship for her American-born children. In 1884 she sued the San Francisco Board of Education in an attempt to force the admission of all children to the same public schools. Tape's legal victory was stripped of immediate impact, however, when the school board created a separate public school for Asian children; but once again, it is Tape's vision and courage, not her material success, that commands attention. The shame of segregation motivated George Washington Cable,* a highly successful and critically acclaimed novelist, to risk his entire career to denounce the evils of segregation and the unspeakable conditions within the convict lease system of the South.

Similarly, the horrifying human cost of uncontrolled industrialization and mass immigration sparked some of the most far-sighted, original, humane innovations in American history. Sara Josephine Baker* revolutionized the practice of infant care and expanded the concept of community responsibility; Rose Schneiderman* offered dignity and a modicum of economic self-determination to young women workers previously considered incapable of organizing; John Lovejoy Elliott* inspired an entire impoverished community to set astonishing goals and to work effectively toward their realization.

It may seem that the people profiled here were idealists—the word usually carries with it connotations of a dreamer's lack of realism. In actuality, all of these people were practical, clear-sighted individuals who educated and equipped themselves appropriately, working to find real methods to bring the real world closer to a more moral, ideal standard. Combining humane goals with practical methodology, Edward Coles* gathered hard data on land prices in slave and free states in his fight to keep Illinois free; Florence Kelley* deliberately utilized middle-class mothers' concern for the health of their own children to fire her campaign against the unsanitary conditions in the sweatshops that produced the undergarments of the middle class; Carola Woerishoffer* went undercover to investigate firsthand working conditions in New York City's laundries; John Lovejoy Elliott* approached the street gangs of Chelsea with a practical offer of gaming space in order to draw them step by step closer to a more self-respecting awareness of their full potentialities; Tunis Campbell* set up practical, functional communities to replace the freedmen's apathy with pride and competence.

One can call these people dreamers only in their refusal to accept the conditions of their times—social, economic, political, ethical—as inevitable and immutable. Their vision of humanity was more inclusive, more just than the "reality" that confronted them. That they found the courage to act in the name of their vision "remains critical evidence that there is far more to human nature than exploitive selfishness, and more to the future than the doom of cyclical repetition" (Oliner, xii). Dr King would see them as magnificently maladjusted, and he would be proud of them:

> [T]here are certain things within our social order to which I am proud to be maladjusted. . . . I never did intend to adjust to . . . segregation and discrimination. I never did intend to adjust myself to religious bigotry. I never did intend to adjust myself to economic conditions that will take necessities from the many to give luxuries to the few. . . . And I call upon all men of good will to be maladjusted because it may well be that the salvation of our world lies in the hands of the maladjusted (King, 216).

This cast of characters is idiosyncratic and unique. Selection was based not on material success or achievement, but on the breadth and quality of the vision that animated these lives. These people had a strong sense of their own as well as others' personal worth and dignity, an honest recognition of injustice and inequity, and a commitment to work in ethical ways against intolerable situations. They project a sense of pioneering bravery, a willingness to take steps others may have seen the need for but feared to take. They are *not* saints: In truth, any attempt to portray them as somehow superhuman would betray the ultimate, awesome realization that principled ethical action is within everyone's capacity. This realization poses an intimidating responsibility, but it is this very acceptance of moral responsibility that is the wonder, the glory of the species.

Research for this collection was a combination of a gleeful detective mentality, serendipity, persistence, and wild loops of imagination. For some lesser-known figures it was like hunting a mysterious animal: catching a fleeting glimpse of a fascinating shape tangential to the work on a different person, tracking faint clues of the elusive creature through other scholars' footnotes back to the lair of original source, finally getting close enough to glean some understanding and appreciation. For example, Carola Woerishoffer* first came into view in a speech by Rose Schneiderman* urging middle-class women to empathize more fully with the exhaustion of their working-class sisters. Schneiderman was relatively well documented; Woerishoffer slipped away and required substantial sleuthing. Regrettably, even the most zealous sleuthing did not produce photos of Thomas Hazard, Seth Luther, or David Walker.

This book, then, is a celebration of the maladjustment that has, small increments at a time, moved American society closer to the ideals we are proud to profess. In many cases, the "unrealistic" goals of these reformers have been absorbed into a casual, commonly accepted notion of what is and therefore must have always been: How many of us can envision a time when the concepts of Social Security, workmen's compensation, universal suffrage, and integrated education seemed radical and unattainable? The men and women who achieved all this and more deserve the honor and immortality we accord them here; it is an act of historical integrity to remember these lives. More immediately, we can hope that examples of moral courage, imagination, and ethical vision will broaden our own definitions of individual possibility and the human capacity for honor, decency, dedication, and compassion. Consider this book an invitation to get maladjusted.

References

Avrich, Paul. *The Haymarket Tragedy*. Princeton, NJ: Princeton University Press, 1984.

Burns, James McGregor, and Stewart Burns. *A People's Charter: The Pursuit of Rights in America*. New York: Alfred A. Knopf, 1992.

Davis, David Brion. *The Problem of Slavery in the Age of Revolution, 1770–1823*. Ithaca, NY: Cornell University Press, 1975.

Derleth, August. *Concord Rebel: A Life of Henry D. Thoreau*. Philadelphia: Chilton Co., 1962.

King, Martin Luther, Jr. *Testament of Hope: Essential Writings of Martin Luther King, Jr.* Edited by James M. Washington. San Francisco: Harper & Row, 1986.

Las Casas, Bartolomé de. *The Devastation of the Indies: A Brief Account*. Baltimore: Johns Hopkins Press, 1992 [1552].

Oliner, Samuel P. and Pearl M. Oliner. *The Altruistic Personality*. New York: The Free Press, 1988.

Thoreau, Henry David. *Walden and Other Writings.* Edited by Brooks Atkinson. New York: Modern Library, 1950.

Twain, Mark. *The Adventures of Huckleberry Finn.* New York: Modern Library, 1985 [1884].

SUBJECT LISTS

CHRONOLOGY

Eighteenth Century

Benjamin Lay
Thomas Hazard

Elizabeth Freeman

Nineteenth Century

William Apess
Edward Coles
Thomas Kennedy
David Walker
Seth Luther
Laura S. Haviland
Ernestine Louise Rose
John Swett Rock
Tunis G. Campbell

Susette La Flesche
Belva Ann Lockwood
Lucy Craft Laney
George Washington Cable
Anna Julia Cooper
Florence Kelley
George Henry White
John Lovejoy Elliott

Twentieth Century

Carola Woerishoffer
Sara Josephine Baker
John Lovejoy Elliott
Anna Julia Cooper
Florence Kelley
Mary White Ovington

Rose Schneiderman
Smedley Darlington Butler
Jeannette Rankin
Tye Leung Schulze
Vito Marcantonio
Myles Horton

Luisa Capetillo
Lugenia Burns Hope
Jovita Idar de Juarez

Tanya Zolotoroff Nash
Minoru Yasui
Angie Debo

GENDER

Women

Sara Josephine Baker
Luisa Capetillo
Anna Julia Cooper
Angie Debo
Elizabeth Freeman
Laura S. Haviland
Lugenia Burns Hope
Jovita Idar de Juarez
Florence Kelley
Susette La Flesche

Lucy Craft Laney
Belva Ann Lockwood
Tanya Zolotoroff Nash
Mary White Ovington
Jeannette Rankin
Ernestine Louise Rose
Rose Schneiderman
Tye Leung Schulze
Carola Woerishoffer

Men

William Apess
Smedley Darlington Butler
George Washington Cable
Tunis G. Campbell
Edward Coles
John Lovejoy Elliott
Thomas Hazard
Myles Horton

Thomas Kennedy
Benjamin Lay
Seth Luther
Vito Marcantonio
John Swett Rock
David Walker
George Henry White
Minoru Yasui

ETHNICITY

African American

Tunis Campbell
Anna Julia Cooper
Elizabeth Freeman
Lugenia Burns Hope

Lucy Craft Laney
John Swett Rock
David Walker
George Henry White

Asian American

Tye Leung Schulze

Minoru Yasui

Hispanic American

Luisa Capetillo   Jovita Idar de Juarez

Native American

William Apess   Susette La Flesche

European American

Sara Josephine Baker   Benjamin Lay
Smedley Darlington Butler   Belva Ann Lockwood
George Washington Cable   Seth Luther
Edward Coles   Vito Marcantonio
Angie Debo   Tanya Zolotoroff Nash
John Lovejoy Elliott   Mary White Ovington
Laura S. Haviland   Jeannette Rankin
Thomas Hazard   Ernestine Louise Rose
Myles Horton   Rose Schneiderman
Florence Kelley   Carola Woerishoffer
Thomas Kennedy

MAJOR FOCUS

Abolition

Edward Coles   Thomas Hazard
Elizabeth Freeman   Benjamin Lay
Laura S. Haviland   David Walker

Civil/Minority Rights

William Apess   Lucy Craft Laney
George Washington Cable   Belva Ann Lockwood
Anna Julia Cooper   Vito Marcantonio
Angie Debo   Tanya Zolotoroff Nash
Laura S. Haviland   Mary White Ovington
Lugenia Burns Hope   Ernestine Louise Rose
Myles Horton   John Swett Rock
Jovita Idar de Juarez   Tye Leung Schulze
Thomas Kennedy   George Henry White
Susette La Flesche   Minoru Yasui

Labor Rights

Tunis G. Campbell
Luisa Capetillo
Myles Horton
Florence Kelley
Belva Ann Lockwood

Seth Luther
Vito Marcantonio
Rose Schneiderman
Carola Woerishoffer

Social Reform–Housing, Health, Children's Rights

Sara Josephine Baker
Luisa Capetillo
John Lovejoy Elliott
Lugenia Burns Hope

Florence Kelley
Tanya Zolotoroff Nash
Carola Woerishoffer

Women's Rights

Luisa Capetillo
Anna Julia Cooper
Jovita Idar de Juarez
Florence Kelley
Belva Ann Lockwood

Jeannette Rankin
Ernestine Louise Rose
Rose Schneiderman
Carola Woerishoffer

Freedom of Conscience

Smedley Darlington Butler
George Washington Cable
Luisa Capetillo
Edward Coles
Angie Debo
Myles Horton

Thomas Kennedy
Vito Marcantonio
Jeannette Rankin
Ernestine Louise Rose
Minoru Yasui

MARCHING
TO A DIFFERENT
DRUMMER

WILLIAM APESS

(January 31, 1798–?)

Native American Rights Leader

In the protracted, bitter, and anguished confrontation between Native Americans and Europeans, isolated voices on both sides called for justice and restraint and spoke the language of brotherhood and decency. One of the least known among these was William Apes (or Apess, as he himself preferred to spell it), who rose from the chaos of poverty and alcoholism to lead one of the few successful Indian rebellions. Virtually self-educated, Apess became an articulate, forceful spokesman for Native American rights and for universal brotherhood. He wrote five books, including the first lengthy autobiography by a Native American. His sense of human worth and dignity, his fully developed use of historical evidence, and his devastating evaluation of European American racism are astonishingly immediate and relevant almost two hundred years after he propounded them.

Mr WILLIAM APES,

A NATIVE MISSIONARY OF THE PEQUOT TRIBE

OF INDIANS.

William Apess
Courtesy, American Antiquarian Society.

William Apess was born into a shattered, desperate society. Although the Wampanoag and Massachusetts tribes initially welcomed and even assisted the English settlers in New England, most whites perceived the natives as a threatening, bestial species. As "children of nature," natives represented everything untamed, sensual, and potentially uncontrollable to a rigid society obsessed with control. Indians were impediments to the nascent theory of Manifest Destiny, the smug, comforting notion that God intended the settlers to conquer this new continent to fulfill his divine plan.

For most English settlers, there was never any intention of peacefully sharing the new land with the Indians. In 1615, only one year after John Smith first explored the region around Plymouth, the first slave ship arrived. It carried away kidnapped Indians, and it left behind the small-pox virus, against which the natives were utterly helpless. Within five years, the Wampanoag had lost over two-thirds of their people; the death toll among the Massachusetts was closer to 90%. One Puritan historian saw the hideous plague as "the Wonderful Preparation of the Lord Jesus Christ by His Providence for His People's Abode in the Western World"; he was especially grateful that most victims of the plague were "chiefly young men and children, the very seeds of increase" (Chronicles, 7).

Apess's tribe, the Pequot, struggled under special hardships. In 1637 they were the target of the first deliberate genocidal war launched by the English in America. Settlers from Plymouth, Connecticut, and Massachusetts Bay attacked the main Pequot town on the Mystic River, set fire to it, and shot most of the residents attempting to escape the flames. Over fifteen hundred men, women, and children were killed. The survivors, fewer than three hundred people, were forced to sign a treaty declaring themselves extinct; they were forbidden ever to use the name Pequot again, and most of them were sold into slavery.

By the time William Apess was born in 1798, the remnants of the Pequot were the weakest, poorest, most dispirited tribe in New England. They lived on two small reservations in southeast Connecticut or in small towns across southern New England. Many young men had been killed fighting with the colonists in the French-Indian War and the Revolution, and many others went to sea for years at a time on whaling ships; the resultant gender imbalance encouraged a high rate of intermarriage with the blacks, free and slave, of the region. The father of William Apess was the product of a Pequot and white intermarriage. Apess wrote that his mother was the full-blooded descendant of Pequot chiefs, although very few Native Americans in New England could claim unadulterated blood lines.

Apess was only three years old when his parents separated, leaving him and his siblings with his maternal grandparents. By his own account, his grandparents were alcoholics who abused each other and the children. Life was chaotic; the children were usually hungry, cold, and neglected. When Apess was four or five, his grandmother beat him so severely that his arm was broken in three places. Rescued by a young uncle, Apess was made a ward of the town of Colchester, Connecticut, which paid his doctors' bills and bound him out to a kind white neighbor. Despite his grandparents' horrendous treatment, Apess was careful in his autobiography to blame their moral collapse and alcoholism on a greedy white civilization that seduced the natives with its vices but denied them access to its advantages.

Apess lived with his white foster family, the Furmans, for the next six years. They treated him reasonably well and encouraged his interest in their Baptist faith. The six winters of schooling the Furmans allowed Apess were to be the only formal education he ever received. As he approached adolescence, Apess seems to have resented the restrictions of his servile position. He ran away several times, and in disgust, the Furmans sold his indenture contract to a prominent family in New London.

In New London Apess was exposed to a Methodist revival campaign, and he was riveted by its fiercely egalitarian perspective. Many Congregationalists and Episcopalians regarded Methodism as a dangerous, disreputable religion that agitated the lower classes to inappropriate attitudes; the elite, conservative family that "owned" Apess concurred, and they forbade him from attending any Methodist meetings. But Apess had been formally converted to Methodism on March 15, 1813—a date so significant to him that he recorded it years later in his autobiography. The boy's defiant attendance at revival meetings earned him repeated beatings, and he soon ran away again.

This time Apess escaped bondage permanently, finding a menial job in New York City. At the age of fifteen, Apess enlisted as a drummer boy in the militia during the War of 1812. During the long march north to Lake Champlain and Montreal, so many troops deserted that the boy was forced to take part in active combat. More important for his future, Apess, discharged from the army in 1815, found a temporary home with the Ojibway of Ontario. This was his first experience of tribal life, his first opportunity to observe the mutuality and moral strengths of a relatively intact native culture; for the first time, he was offered some reason to feel positive about his racial identity.

Still a deeply troubled, lonely young man, Apess drifted south with a vague notion of going "home" to his family in Connecticut. He had become a heavy drinker in the army, and the voyage south, punctuated by odd jobs, periods of oblivion, and attempts at detoxification, took almost eighteen months. Finally, in 1818, he found himself in Colchester, reasonably sober, staying with an aunt, Sally George, who was a tribal leader and a healer widely respected by whites as well as by natives. Aunt Sally preached in the Pequot language, and she wove strength and dignity from equal strands of passionate Methodism and traditional Pequot spirituality. She had a profound impact on Apess; he recalled feeling a sense of harmony and contentment whenever she preached.

In Colchester Apess worked for a local farmer. When the farmer refused to pay Apess the agreed-upon amount due him and threatened to beat him, some ember of self-respect and dignity ignited inside the young Pequot. He stood up to the abusive farmer, physically and psychologically, and demanded—successfully—what was owed him. The moment was a kind of epiphany for Apess, a turning point he recognized clearly. "I had been cheated so often that I determined to have my rights this time, and forever after" (McQuaid, 611).

Strengthened in his commitment to Methodism, Apess was baptized in December, 1818. Methodism offered him a way to be both Indian and Christian, while still rebelling against the controlling forces of white society. As he explained,

> I thought I had no character to lose in the estimation of those who were accounted great. For what cared they for me? They had possession of the red man's inheritance and had deprived me of liberty; with this they were satisfied and could do as they pleased; therefore, I thought I could do as I pleased, measurably. I therefore went to hear the *noisy Methodists* (Apess, 1x).

With his baptism, Apess accepted responsibility for his life. The following year he went back to Coltrain, the town in northwest Massachusetts where he was born, to visit his father and to learn from him the shoemaker's craft. Apess married a fellow Methodist, Mary Wood, whom he described as "a woman nearly the same color as myself"; the couple had three children. Increasingly, Apess felt called to preach. In April, 1829, he was formally ordained a minister in the radically egalitarian Protestant Methodist Church, and he became a circuit-riding missionary among the scattered Pequot. His sermons always concentrated on the universality of the Gospel, on the message of total equality before God. He spoke of egalitarian brotherhood, of the intrinsic dignity and worth of all human beings. It was a vision not widely promulgated by most white churches in America.

In 1833 Apess came to preach in Mashpee, on Cape Cod, the last surviving Native American town in the entire state. He found a town in crisis, a small but determined and coherent tribe with a long and honorable history. The town of Mashpee ("Marshpee," in most contemporary accounts) was established in 1667 as an unalienable reserve of more than ten thousand acres for Christian Indians, through the will of the Reverend Richard Bourne. Colonists destroyed many such protected Indian towns in 1676 in a vengeful wave after King Philip's War, but Mashpee survived. During the Revolution, Mashpee sent a higher percentage of its eligible men than any other town on Cape Cod to fight with the Continental Army. Ironically, the new state of Massachusetts deprived the Mashpee, descendants of the Wampanoag, of rights the Crown had accorded them: Mashpee's own freely elected officers were replaced by three non-resident white overseers appointed by the governor. The overseers had broad powers and enormous opportunities for exploitation and corruption. Valuable grazing, haying, and logging rights were leased to neighboring whites; the overseers could legally send into bound service anyone in town. Significantly, the overseers now controlled all rights to entry and residence in Mashpee. Throughout the 18th century, when the Mashpee themselves voted on who was invited into the town, they had extended a generous welcome to numerous African Americans, as well as to Hessian mercenaries deserting from the British army; by 1832, only 8 of 315 official residents of Mashpee could claim to be of "pure" Mashpee blood.

The complex intermingling of races and cultures had produced a people with a proud tradition of individuality, self-reliance, and defiance. When Apess arrived in the spring of 1833, he precipitated an open rebellion in a situation already saturated with resentment. Since 1809 the Mashpee had endured the questionable attentions of the Reverend Phineas Fish, an arrogant, bigoted Congregationalist imposed on them through a fund administered by Harvard College. Fish was aloof, lazy, and generally contemptuous of the Indians. Most of the Mashpee ignored him and attended informal Baptist services run by a native preacher, Blind Joe Amos. Nonetheless, Fish occupied a spacious home in town and assumed the rights to valuable acres of town farm and forest land. The Mashpee were ripe for the leadership and inspiration Apess provided.

Apess arrived in Mashpee in mid-May, 1833. The community welcomed him and his family: they were formally adopted into the tribe only days later, given a house, and assigned farming and fishing rights. Apess soon called a public meeting to discuss the situation. Out of this meeting grew the Mashpee Resolutions, a set of radical declarations addressed both to the governor and to the corporation of Harvard College. Couched in the ringing language of egalitarian constitutionalism, fervent in the spirit of reform and temperance, the opening resolution declared boldly, "We as a tribe, will rule ourselves, and have the right to do so; for all men are born free and equal, says the Constitution of the country" (Apess, 175). The Resolutions warned that as of July 1, 1833, the Mashpee would resume full control of their own forests and fields: no white man would be permitted to cut wood or hay without their prior consent. In addition, they demanded the removal of Phineas Fish. In June a delegation headed by Apess went to Boston to see Governor Levi Lincoln; they came away from this meeting under the mistaken impression that Lincoln supported them. On the strength of that assumption the reformers returned home, elected a tribal council, ordered the overseers to leave, and suggested strongly to Fish that he find another home. They specifically condemned the racist, discriminatory attitude that permeated his religious services:

> We do not be Lieve in your trying to Make us be Lieve that we have not as good Rights to the table of the Lord as others, that we are kept back merely because our skin is of A Different Complexion and we find nothing in so doing to Justify you in the Scripture. . . . We are for peace rather than anything else but we are satisfied that we shall never injoy it until we have our Rights (Nielsen, 410).

Most of white New England reacted with disbelief to the Mashpee's assertiveness; the governor and local officials were stunned by the calm assumption of moral, cultural, and religious equality that underlay all the Resolutions. Governor Lincoln threatened to use state militia to put down what he perceived as an incipient insurrection. Phineas Fish clearly held Apess responsible for all the unrest. In late June he wrote to Governor Lincoln, claiming that the Mashpee had been perfectly docile until Apess arrived: "certainly from the moment of his coming among them, there has been a marked change in the temper and conduct of a large number of Indians." Similarly, the governor's appointed investigator, Josiah Fiske, saw Apess as the ringleader: "Apess has got the entire control and confidence of nearly all the tribe, and they suppose that the Government is fully with him in all his movements" (Nielsen, 411).

On July 1, Apess and several Mashpee confronted a group of white men cutting wood on Mashpee land. When the whites ignored the natives' warning, Apess and his men seized all the wood on their cart and forcibly escorted them to the town boundary. White reaction was nothing short of hysterical. Both sides braced for armed conflict. On July 4, Fiske arrested Apess on charges of rioting, assault, and trespass, all based on the July 1 incident. Apess sternly rebuffed several Mashpee offers of rescue, anticipating loss of life and heavy government retribution. He served thirty days in prison. On his release, he was fined $100 and forced to post an additional $100 as bond for refraining from further agitation. The fines, a staggering amount for that time, were paid largely by a local white reformer.

After his release, Apess composed and published "An Indian's Appeal to the White Men of Massachusetts," detailing the history of Mashpee and the eminent reasonableness of the Indians' demands. His language was invariably precise, patriotic, and imbued with Jeffersonian republicanism. Fiske's condemnation of Apess may strike the reader as inadvertently complimentary:

> [I]t was the settled purpose of Apess to establish in the minds of the natives a belief that each generation had a right to act for itself, and that the guardianship laws which had been imposed by the consent of one generation could not be enforced against the will of another (Apess, lxxiii).

Apess and Blind Joe Amos planned a sophisticated publicity campaign for the Mashpee cause. They won significant allies in Benjamin Franklin Hallett, Barnstable-born editor of the *Boston Daily Advocate*, and William Lloyd Garrison, incendiary editor of the abolitionist *Liberator*. Both newspapers repeatedly endorsed the Mashpee Resolutions and covered the situation sympathetically. Hallett, a lawyer as well as a journalist, appeared with Apess and several Mashpee before the Massachusetts State Legislature in the spring of 1834. Apess argued eloquently that a people could scarcely be blamed for falling into degradation when they were systematically deprived of all opportunity to exercise self-determination.

Astonishingly, the state legislature agreed with Apess. It ratified an act allowing the Mashpee to incorporate their town, elect officials, hire an independent attorney, and generally manage their own affairs. The victory was stunning, small, localized, and lacking in drama though it may have been. Problems remained, largely in the unwelcome person of Phineas Fish. Harvard College, increasingly embarrassed by Fish's truculent behavior, refused to admit its error publicly. In 1836 the college cut Fish's salary in half but permitted him to keep his position. In 1840, disgusted Mashpee changed the locks on the meetinghouse door, symbolically as well as practically articulating Fish's isolation from the spiritual community. Despite growing pressure from reform forces at Harvard, Fish hung on doggedly until 1846, when he finally sold the house he had been given and staged a graceless withdrawal from town.

William Apess lived on in the newly liberated Mashpee for another year or so. In 1835 he published *Indian Nullification of the Unconstitutional Laws of Massachusetts Relative to the Mashpee Tribe; or, The Pretended Riot Explained*, a lengthy, detailed compilation of commentary and documents about the Mashpee crisis. White public opinion continued to vilify him, to cast him as an "outside agitator" who had manipulated the naive Mashpee for his own nefarious purposes. Obviously, Apess achieved no personal financial gain from the Mashpee Rebellion, since Barnstable court records cite him as seriously in debt in 1836 and 1838. Sometime in 1838 Apess, presumably with his family, left Mashpee; he may have accepted another ministerial post somewhere else. No further documentary evidence of any sort has been uncovered on Apess; there is no clue as to what happened to him or his family.

Apess would no doubt be entirely lost to history were it not for his distinctive writings. His voice is clear, rich, informed, incisive. He deliberately used the proud American rhetoric of self-congratulatory patriotism and constitutionalism to focus attention on the grotesque moral inconsistencies implicit in American history and society. He was determined to reconstruct a Native American history that whites were much more comfortable ignoring. He saw the Indians' past as a precious birthright, a necessary foundation on which to erect coherent native identities strong enough to coexist with whites in the pressured, hectic world of the mid-19th century. Apess was no romantic: he saw clearly the present disintegration of his people. While he blamed white society for the natives' despair, he also recognized that things could never again be as they had been. Much of his writing is a search for tools with which to build a valid new Indian society. With a stunningly far-sighted global perspective, Apess recognized, even in the face of the overwhelming European dominance of North America, that whites were nonetheless a worldwide minority: "If black or red skins, or any skin of color is disgraceful to God, it appears that [God] has disgraced himself a great deal—for he has made fifteen colored people to one white, and placed them here upon this earth" (McQuaid, 613).

In his early writings, Apess appealed to whites' sense of justice and Christian brotherhood to inspire recognition of Native American as well as African American rights. By the time of the Mashpee Rebellion, he had despaired of such gentle persuasion; he wrote more forcefully that human rights were universal and unalienable, and that oppressed peoples were responsible for actively uniting against injustice. His critique of white racism grew deeper and sharper. In *An Indian's Looking-Glass for the White Man* (1833), he suggests assembling all the races of the world in one place:

> Now suppose these skins were put together, and each skin had its national crimes written upon it—which skin do you think would have the greatest? . . . Can you charge the Indians with robbing a nation almost of their whole continent, and murdering their women and children, and then depriving the remainder of their lawful rights, that nature and God require them to have? And to cap the climax, rob another nation to till their grounds and welter out their days under the lash with hunger and fatigue under the scorching rays of a burning sun? I should look at all the skins, and I know that when I cast my eye upon that white skin, and if I saw those crimes written upon it, I should enter my protest against it immediately and cleave to that which is more honorable (Apess, 157).

The *Eulogy on King Philip*, Apess's last published work, represents the culmination of all his study and thought. The eulogy was delivered twice in January, 1838, in the Odeon Club of Boston, to observe the 160th anniversary of King Philip's death. In this detailed, impassioned, daring essay, Apess analogized one of white America's most hated and feared enemies to George Washington. He deliberately turned standard American patriotic images upside down to highlight the deep racist contradictions implicit in early American republicanism. He exposed the rigid class distinctions of a society that cherished an image of classless egalitarianism; he excoriated the cruelty and hypocrisy of a society smug in its righteousness and Christianity.

Philip, or Metacomet, was the grandson of Massasoit, the Wampanoag chief who had welcomed and aided the Pilgrims in 1620. By the time of Massasoit's death in 1622, he may have regretted the comfort he had provided the Pilgrims: bigotry, racial discrimination, and officially sanctioned corruption were already steadily reducing Wampanoag territory. King Philip, whom Apess likened to the biblical prophet Isaiah, foresaw the total destruction of Native Americans throughout America. In 1675, having gathered almost twenty thousand allies from tribes throughout New England, Philip launched a desperate attempt to restore Indian control to the land. In the most destructive war in New England history, fifty-two towns were attacked, twelve destroyed completely, and almost one thousand whites were killed. The Indians, however, were vastly outnumbered by whites with a seemingly endless supply of superior weapons. Philip's wife and son were captured and sold into slavery in the West Indies, and in 1676 Philip himself was betrayed and killed in an ambush. His hand was sent as a trophy to Boston; his severed head remained on display on a pike in Plymouth for over twenty years. Across New England, whites engaged in an orgy of violent revenge, destroying many Indian towns, massacring indiscriminately, selling hundreds into brutal slavery.

Audaciously, Apess praised Philip as a hero, a brilliant, visionary leader:

> [A]s the immortal Washington lives endeared and engraven in the hearts of every white in America, never to be forgotten in time—even such is the immortal Philip honored, as held in memory by the degraded yet grateful descendants who appreciate his character; so will every patriot, especially in this enlightened age, respect the rude yet all-accomplished son of the forest, that died a martyr to his cause, though unsuccessful, yet as glorious as the *American* Revolution (Apess, 277).

Apess argued that he was not glorifying war itself. He would not compromise on the issue of basic human rights, nor would he in any way minimize the extent of abuse and exploitation for which whites must accept responsibility. Still, he continued to hope, to believe in the power of moral redemption, to offer a vision of a harmonious society cleansed of poisonous racial prejudice:

> What, then, is to be done? Let every friend of the Indian now seize the mantle of Liberty and throw it over those burning elements that has [sic] spread with such fearful rapidity, and at once extinguish them forever. . . . We want trumpets that sound like thunder, and men to act as though they were going to war with those corrupt and degrading principles that robs [sic] one of all rights, merely because he is ignorant and of a little different color. Let us have principles that will give everyone his due; and then shall wars cease, and the weary find rest (Apess, 307).

Apess was never heard from again. His meticulously researched, carefully wrought, tightly argued chronicles of cruelty and his resonant pleas for recognition and simple justice fell silent, forgotten and unused. European Americans' inexorable drive to the west continued, as the land's original tenants were driven ever further into poverty and loss. Racial relations on this continent still fall far short of the standards of universal shared humanity, of basic decency and cooperation articulated so incandescently by William Apess.

References

Apess, William. *On Our Own Ground: The Complete Writings of William Apess, a Pequot*. Edited with introduction by Barry O'Connell. Amherst: University of Massachusetts Press, 1992.

Chronicles of American Indian Protest. Compiled and edited by The Council on Interracial Books for Children. Greenwich, CT: Fawcett Publishing, 1971.

Forbes, Jack D. (ed.). *The Indian in America's Past*. Englewood Cliffs, NJ: Prentice-Hall, 1964.

McQuaid, Kim. "William Apes, Pequot: An Indian Reformer in the Jackson Era." *New England Quarterly* 50 (December, 1977): 605–625.

Nielsen, Donald M. 'The Mashpee Indian Revolt of 1833." *New England Quarterly* 58 (September, 1985): 400–420.

Woodson, Carter G. "Relations of Negroes and Indians." *Journal of Negro History* 5 (Spring, 1920): 45–57.

SARA JOSEPHINE BAKER

(November 15, 1873–February 22, 1945)

Children's Health Reformer

As a prominent, respected, influential adult, Sara Josephine Baker once described herself as a daughter determined to make up to her father for the inconvenience of having been born a girl. From strands of compassion, self-discipline, humor, skepticism, and practicality learned from various members of her large family, Baker wove the cloth of her life: a courageous, imaginative, innovative life that profoundly affected the entire field of public health and child welfare. Her efforts changed the texture of tens of thousands of other lives around the world.

Sara Josephine Baker
Courtesy of the Library of Congress.

Sara Josephine Baker, the third daughter born in quick succession to a prosperous Quaker couple in Poughkeepsie, was an adventurous, sensitive tomboy throughout a happy rural childhood. Her awareness of social inequities and of personal responsibility developed early. In her witty, incisive autobiography she described a pivotal occasion:

> My impulse to try to do things about hopeless situations appears to have cropped out first when I was about six years old, and it should be pointed out that the method I used was characteristically direct. [Beautifully dressed for a special outing, she wandered outside to wait for her family, hoping someone would come by to admire her. A poor African American child, thin and ragged, did in fact stop to stare, and Baker's response was not what she had planned.] I have never seen such dumb envy in any human being's face before or since. . . . I could not bear the idea that I had so much and she had so little. So I got down off the horse block and took off every stitch I had on . . . and gave everything, underwear and all, to the little black girl . . . .Then I walked back into the house, completely naked, wondering why I had done it and how to explain my inexplicable conduct. Oddly enough both Father and Mother seemed to understand pretty well what had gone on in my mind. They were fine people, my father and mother (Baker, 2).

Baker grew up playing baseball and climbing trees with her younger brother, going fishing with her father, and acquiring almost accidentally a few "female" accomplishments like embroidery and cooking. She devoured her brother's stirring Victorian boys' literature, the sort in which plucky heroes overcome seemingly insurmountable odds through honesty, bravery, and clean living. Through her grandparents' circle of intellectual friends in upstate New York, she met Louisa May Alcott, creator of Jo March, after whom Baker consciously modeled herself.

A major, lasting, and truly memorable influence on Baker was her great-aunt Abby, a wealthy, seemingly pious old Quaker who in reality offered Baker her first exposure to skepticism and nonconformity. When Baker and her cousins visited Aunt Abby, she would gather them in her study to read Bible stories to them. After the story, Abby would say gently,

> Now, children, that is a very silly story. I am an old, old lady and I want all of you to remember what I am saying. It is a silly story and there is not a word of truth in it. Don't ever let anyone tell you that stories like that are true (Baker, 19).

The children never betrayed Abby's confidence; all their parents perceived was the sentimental image of elderly Abby reading the Bible to her beloved grand-nieces and nephews. Much later, Baker credited Aunt Abby with teaching her to question the innate morality of all accepted doctrines.

When Baker was sixteen and preparing to enter Vassar, her warm, generous, hospitable family was torn by tragedy. Her thirteen-year-old brother died suddenly, and only three months later, devastated by the boy's death, her father died as well. Baker had been exceptionally close to them; she felt robbed of her closest companions. Numbed by grief, she abandoned the idea of Vassar (and the anticipated conventionally proper marriage) and decided to go into medicine to help support her mother. There was no special significance to her choice, no medical tradition on either side of her family, no mentoring local woman doctor; it seemed at the time a fairly straightforward path to independence and a decent income. The opposition of her mother and sister brought out her "native stubbornness" and served only to strengthen her determination.

In 1894, after a year of intense private tutoring, Baker passed the state regents' examination and entered the Women's Medical College of the New York Infirmary for Women and Children, founded by Elizabeth Blackwell and her sister Emily. Baker was younger than most of her classmates and somewhat intimidated by them. In her second year she took an innovative course on "The Normal Child," taught by Dr. Annie Sturges Daniel. Although at first the concept of normality did not seem to her a fit subject for rigorous study, she became fascinated and later credited this course with opening her to the whole notion of preventive medicine; she acknowledged that Dr. Daniel had inspired her thirty-year struggle for children's health reform.

Graduating second in a class of eighteen in 1898, Baker spent the following year as an intern at the New England Hospital for Women and Children. The New England Hospital had been founded in 1862 by the great Maria Zakrzewska expressly to train women physicians and to provide superlative care for female patients; once again, Baker was enriched by the example of competent, confident professional women.

After her internship, she returned to New York City with another young woman doctor and set up a private practice. The first year, Baker's income was $185. Despairing, she took the civil service examination in 1901 and signed on as a medical inspector for the Department of Health; the salary of $30 a month seemed splendid.

Baker came into a corrupt, lax, unprofessional bureaucracy, fueled by no coherent sense of mission, no public sense of urgency, no standards of self-respect. All that changed—or at least, presented the possibility of change—with the election of reformer Seth Low as mayor in 1902. In the midst of a major departmental overhaul, Baker was offered a summer position hunting out and caring for sick babies in the West Side slums known as Hell's Kitchen. The area was densely populated, at that time largely by Irish immigrants, with a growing African-American contingent along the northern fringes of the district. The tenements were four-to-six storey tall "dumbbell" tenements built around fetid air shafts; railroad flats of two to five rooms provided no hallways, no ventilation or light, and no private bathrooms. The better sort had a public toilet on each floor, but it was more common to have a privy in the rear courtyard. The inhabitants were poor, sick, tired, discouraged, and maddeningly fatalistic. Over and over, at a time when the infant death rate reached over 1,500 per week, Baker heard the numb refrain, "Babies always die in the summer." She was deeply shaken, and her innate sense of decency and fair play revolted. Although she was far from sentimental about the degrading life of the slums, she felt profoundly that such hopelessness must be assaulted.

But the end of this dreadful summer, Baker was appointed assistant to the Chief of Inspectors. The scope of injustice and indifference that she confronted was so vast that, to avoid feeling totally overwhelmed, Baker was forced to focus her energies: she decided to fight for the babies.

Baker always believed in the power of education; she was convinced that beneath their chronic exhaustion, the immigrant mothers were fiercely devoted to their children and needed only gentle advice and support. At a time when fully one-third of New York City's fatalities were children under five and one-fifth were babies less than a year old, Baker came to a revolutionary realization—it was far easier to prevent an illness than to attempt to cure it:

> That sounds like a completely absurd and witless remark, but at that time it really was a startling idea; at any rate it seemed so to me. And I found that it was when I tried to convince the authorities that something might be done about teaching people how to stay well (Baker, 85).

Baker's chance to prove her theory finally came in 1908, when she was appointed chief of the newly created Division of Child Hygiene. She had no staff and no budget, but she was determined to demonstrate the value of preventive medicine. That summer she created a team of thirty school inspection nurses, trained them carefully, and deliberately picked an especially loathsome Lower East Side district with an appalling infant death rate. Each day the team received lists of new birth certificates, so that they could get to new babies right away. Nurses visited each home, welcoming the new mother and infant, teaching the crucial safety factor of breastfeeding; frequent bathing; thin, airy clothing; copious ventilation; and periods of time out of doors. In most cases, the immigrant mothers were flattered by the courteous attention from well-educated American women and took the instruction seriously. By the end of the summer, infant deaths in Baker's district had plummeted from the anticipated 1,500 to 300, while adjacent districts' rates were unchanged. The value of prevention had been demonstrated beyond Baker's wildest expectations. Exultant, she reported, "We had saved more babies than there are men in a regiment of soldiers" (Marshall, 5). As a result, the Board of Estimates treated her with new respect and fully funded her Bureau of Child Hygiene; it was the world's first such agency. Baker saw this as the real beginning of her life's work.

The first crisis Baker faced in her new bureau was the revolt of the six male doctors assigned to work under her. Initially refusing to take orders from a woman, they submitted their resignations en masse. She was able to talk them into a month's trial run, and she flattered tender male egos by creating titles for each of them. Baker had a genius for organization and an exciting, innovative agenda; by the end of the month all the resignations had been withdrawn.

Liberated by the total lack of precedent, Baker was able to pioneer a number of important programs: licensing and training midwives; designing and distributing multilingual health care pamphlets; setting up "baby health stations" to distribute safe, pasteurized milk; training nurses and inspectors in successful home visitation techniques; and many other programs aimed at improving the lives of children.

The Bureau of Child Hygiene and its Baby Health Stations proved astonishingly successful: thirty Brooklyn doctors protested to the mayor's office, claiming the stations kept so many babies well that their practices were suffering. By 1913 Baker was in charge of 152 inspectors, all physicians; 263 trained nurses; 55 nurse's assistants; and a support staff of over 50. Her bureau was the largest division within the entire Department of Health.

Baker's handling of the "little mother" situation offers a good example of her magnificent blend of practicality and compassion. In the desperate economy of the slums, many working mothers were forced to leave their older daughters—girls as young as eight or nine—at home in charge of infants. The children were ignorant, tired, impatient, and careless; accidents and disasters were far too frequent. In his famous exposé, *The Bitter Cry of the Children*, muckraking journalist John Spargo condemned the "little mother" syndrome outright. Baker, however, approached the situation differently. Practical as always, she recognized that she could not afford the luxury of simply condemning the situation. She opted rather to work within the limitations of the girls' real lives and their families' desperate economic situations. Baker's bureau worked with schools and settlement houses to create "Little Mothers Leagues," which provided support and training for the young girls; in addition, the Little Mothers

Leagues offered compensatory education to children who were forced to give up their own school years. The program was so well received that newly confident Little Mothers became effective community ambassadors for the baby health stations and other advances they learned of in their meetings.

Baker was a tireless organizer and coordinator. She helped found the Babies Welfare Association, the American Child Hygiene Association, the Children's Welfare Federation, and the College Women's Equal Suffrage League. She lectured on child hygiene at New York University-Bellevue Hospital Medical School for fifteen years, and earned there the first doctorate in public health awarded to a woman. She published voluminously—three monographs and several hundred articles. By 1923 all forty-eight states had bureaus of child hygiene, most modeled after her own agency. This was a goal she had set for herself, and having met it, she retired.

Throughout the 1920s Baker served as a consultant to the federal Children's Bureau and the New York State Department of Health; from 1922 to 1924 she represented the United States on the Health Committee of the League of Nations. With deepening concern for the world situation, she bitterly attributed the spurt of concern for child welfare to a heightened awareness of the child as a potential soldier. A nation either at war or *planning* to be at war, she wrote presciently in 1939, "must look to its future supplies of cannon fodder" (Baker, 165).

In 1934 Baker spent several months traveling throughout the (former) Soviet Union to observe a comprehensive, centralized system of child welfare. Once again, she evaluated the situation with clinical objectivity. She saw chaotic conditions, a casual brutality and indifference that appalled her, and a joyless, obedient passivity among Soviet children that saddened her. The only two groups she saw that were adequately fed were the soldiers and the children. Despite all this, she came away impressed by the effort being made, and confirmed in her belief in state medicine. In her vision, state-sponsored medicine could provide both decent incomes for doctors and affordable health care for all citizens. "In any case," she wrote, "a civilization which insists upon compulsory education must logically insist upon compulsory health for the children it educates" (Baker, 237).

Most of Baker's later years were spent on a small farm in New Jersey. Her vision of a society's responsibility to its children never faltered. In an interview only a few years before her death, she reiterated her belief that universal health care—especially prenatal care—was every citizen's right. Baker died of cancer at the age of seventy-five and is buried with her family in Poughkeepsie. The defining passions of her life are movingly articulated toward the close of her autobiography: "I have faith in the ultimate decency of mankind. I believe that this salvaging of human life has been worth while."

References

Baker, Sara Josephine. *Fighting for Life*. New York: Macmillan, 1939.

James, Edward T., ed. *Notable American Women*. Cambridge, MA: Belknap Press, 1971.

Kihss, Peter. "Woman Doctor a Fighter, Campaigns to Reduce Infant Mortality Rate." *New York World-Telegram*, January 21, 1942, 12.

Marshall, Edward. "A Regiment of Babies' Lives Were Saved Here in 1912." *New York Times* 5,5 (January 12, 1913): 1.

Whitman, Alden, ed. *American Reformers*. New York: H. W. Wilson, 1985.

SMEDLEY DARLINGTON BUTLER

(July 30, 1881–June 21, 1940)

Anti-Imperialist Military Reformer

Teddy Roosevelt called him "the ideal American soldier." The Navy Department, seven years before it tried to court-martial him, described him as "one of the most brilliant officers in the United States." In the midst of the 1931 court-martial controversy, a popular magazine declared, "he still remains as a shining symbol of the glitter, the gorgeousness and the romance that once was war" (Tucker, 292). This flamboyant son of Quakers was awarded two Congressional Medals of Honor (one of which he tried to refuse); he seemed to represent everything dashing, heroic, and slightly outrageous in the best American military tradition. His conversion to passionate antiwar activism remains one of the most stunning recantations in American history, a wild, unpredictable example of uncompromising, solitary conscience in action.

Smedley Darlington Butler
Courtesy, National Archives, photo no. 127–N–519528.

Smedley Darlington Butler was born into a prominent, highly political family in West Chester, Pennsylvania, in 1881. The Butlers had come to Pennsylvania in 1710; the Smedleys and the Darlingtons were no less rooted and respected in Quaker Pennsylvania. Butler's grandfathers ran two of the major banks in West Chester. His maternal grandfather served in Congress, and his father, Thomas Butler, held the same seat after him from 1896 to his death in 1928. Butler was sent to Haverford Friends School, attended Meeting twice weekly, and spoke "plain speech" ("thee" and "thy") with his family. But it would seem that the family was never totally reconciled to all of Quaker doctrine: both grandfathers served in the Union Army during the Civil War, contrary to the deeply held tenet of pacifism.

In this privileged, prosperous environment, Butler grew up on stories of his grandfathers' exploits. At the age of twelve he joined the Boys' Brigade, a youth preparedness movement and precursor of the Boy Scouts. Young Smedley was a slender if not scrawny teen-ager who somehow, through determination and nascent charisma, managed to become both captain of the school baseball team and quarterback of the football team. Butler was only sixteen when the United States declared war on Spain in 1898. He was an indifferent student, restless and resentful of the proper, careful path already laid out for his life. He attempted unsuccessfully to enlist in the army; shortly thereafter, with his mother's full cooperation, he lied about his age, was commissioned as a second lieutenant in the Marine Corps, and shipped out to Guantanamo, Cuba.

While Butler saw no combat during the Spanish-American War, he braved other dangers. As a skinny, intense, outspoken youth, he was initiated with brutal hazing and humiliations he never forgot. Years later, as a commanding officer in Vera Cruz, Mexico, he wrote that two new young second lieutenants who had just joined his command were "nice looking boys and pretty well scared—not of the enemy but of their own seniors. They remind me of myself sixteen years ago when I reported for duty in Cuba and I shall certainly see that these boys are not as much teased as I was" (Schmidt, 8). When Butler mustered out of the Corps a year later, he refused to return to school. He was profoundly affected by the fierce egalitarian anti-intellectualism of the men he had come to trust and respect; for the rest of his life he consciously allied himself with the rank-and-file and distanced himself from the officer elite.

The Spanish-American War, with American acquisition of Cuba, Puerto Rico, and the Philippines, signaled the emergence of the United States as a major imperialist power. Recognizing the realities of international military commitments, in 1900 Congress authorized a 300% increase in the Marine Corps. A delighted Smedley Butler reenlisted, passed the officers' examination brilliantly, and was sent as a first lieutenant to the Philippines.

The Philippines had been under Spanish control since the 16th century. Filipino nationalists, led by the daring young Emilio Aguinaldo, had been struggling against Spanish oppression for years. American forces were happy to use the Filipino insurrectionists against the Spanish, but they had no intention of honoring Filipino hopes for self-government. The American attitude was tainted by the pervasive racism of American society; the military had more in common with the Spanish oppressors than with the courageous but dark-skinned rebels. Butler saw action in several small encounters with Filipino guerrilla units. Although only seventeen years old, he proved an excellent commander of troops and acquitted himself admirably under fire.

From the Philippines, Butler was sent to China, where the Boxer Rebellion was endangering the large foreign populations in Peking and Tientsin. The so-called Boxers were more formally the "Society of Righteous and Harmonious Fists," a nationalist uprising originally aimed at the corrupt dowager empress and the exploitative foreign business "spheres of influence." Unable to contain the Boxers, the Chinese government joined the movement against all foreigners; by the time the Marines landed, several hundred aliens and Chinese Christians had been slaughtered and the foreign legations in Tientsin and Peking were under siege.

Severely wounded outside Tientsin, Butler still managed to carry a wounded comrade miles back to the safety of their own lines. Several enlisted men with him in this incident were awarded Medals of Honor, but as an officer, Butler was ineligible; for the same reason he was unable to accept a Victoria Cross offered by the British. His commanding officer reported glowingly on "the fine qualities of Mr. Butler, his control of his men, courage, and excellent example in his own person of all the qualities most admirable in a soldier" (Schmidt, 17).

In 1902, bracing for future interventions throughout Central America, the United States established a permanent military base on the Puerto Rican island of Culebra. From that base, Butler and his Marines bolstered a pro-United States president in Honduras, where the United Fruit and Standard Fruit companies had major interests. In 1903 he helped maneuver a rebellion against Colombia that resulted in nominal independence of Panama; coincidentally, less than two weeks after declaring its independence, Panama ceded to the United States the ten-mile-wide strip that would become the Panama Canal Zone.

By 1909 Butler was in command of the Marines' Panama battalion, which made frequent incursions into Nicaragua to meddle in national politics there. In later life, Butler would recall most shamefully the American manipulation of blatantly corrupt presidential elections in 1912. Butler's intrinsic personal honor was deeply offended by the growing interference of the American military in the economic and political life of Central America; he was beginning to recognize exploitative connections that would become increasingly inescapable as he matured. "It is terrible that we should be losing so many men," he wrote to his wife, "all because Brown Brothers [a leading New York banking house] have some money down here" (Schmidt, 54).

In 1914 the president of Mexico, Victoriano Huerta, ordered the arrest of several United States Marines who had entered a restricted area in Tampico. The United States government, which neither trusted nor officially recognized Huerta, demanded that he apologize and salute the American flag. When Huerta refused, President Woodrow Wilson sent an American fleet to Vera Cruz, to intimidate him, to protect one billion dollars in American investments, and to prevent possible German interference. The American military action was poorly conceived, badly run, and generally pointless; its major result was a deep reserve of bitter anti-American feeling among most Mexicans. In the midst of all this, Butler did some clever reconnoitering that came close to spying and concocted a fairly far-fetched scheme (never activated) to kidnap Huerta.

Despite–or perhaps because of—the disappointing, unfocused, nature of the Vera Cruz expedition, it produced a veritable orgy of medal-giving. More Congressional Medals of Honor were awarded after Vera Cruz than in any other comparable action before or since. Butler himself was offered one (new regulations had made officers eligible), but he tried to refuse it, insisting that he had done nothing worthy of such recognition:

> I've no more courage than the next man, but it's always been my job to take my fellows through a mess the quickest way possible with the loss of the fewest men. . . . I've been scared plenty, but if I'd ever let my men know it, *they'd* have been scared (Archer, 62).

Butler's next station was the tortured island nation of Haiti, the first independent black country in the western hemisphere and a constant source of concern and anger to the United States. Haitian slaves led by Toussaint L'Ouverture had defeated French forces and declared their independence in 1798. Tormented by a legacy of internecine racial hatreds, Haiti had floundered through the 19th century, its government almost always precarious. Multiple European imperialist designs on Haiti in the early 20th century rendered the government even more unstable: in 1914 alone, four successive presidents were overthrown. When the next president was dragged from sanctuary in the French legation and murdered by an enraged mob, France prepared to avenge its offended diplomatic dignity. Germany rumbled about its own economic interests in the island. President Wilson, fearful of a German presence so close to the Panama Canal, sent a force of two thousand Marines to seize control of the island. The mountainous northern half of the island was still dominated by guerrilla rebels known as *cacos*. The Marines' mission was to suppress the cacos, impose and maintain order, and see to it that a government friendly to American interests was installed.

The fighting in Haiti was fierce and bloody. The terrain in the north was difficult, and the cacos initially stunned the Marines by their ferocity and determination. The United States, officially and unofficially, had always had an uneasy relationship with the free black republic; in the racist assumptions of both the president and the military, small, dark-skinned peoples were not expected to be competent soldiers. It took months of difficult warfare before the rebels were finally cornered and their resistance shattered. Butler's troops led the final assault on the rebel command at Fort Rivière; he was awarded his second Congressional Medal of Honor for his conduct there.

After the rebellion was subdued, martial law was declared and Butler received command of the newly organized military police force. Butler ran this *gendarmerie* as a model professional law enforcement unit. He created a loyal, multi-ethnic, stable police presence; during the course of his contact with these men Butler grew from his previous attitude of casually racist contempt to a proud if paternalistic respect for his police. He hoped to train native officers to lead the men, but his superiors objected to the idea of black officers. Despite Butler's good record with the *Gendarmerie Haitien*, the political situation around him, infected by both American interference and the backstabbing manipulations of the light-skinned Haitian elite, bordered on chaos. By early 1918, when Butler left the island, he was in all practicality running the country; he was in charge of over fourteen thousand men working in the police force, on road construction, in prisons, schools, a coast guard, and plantations.

To his great chagrin, Butler saw no action in World War I. He was put in charge of the major American debarkation camp at Pontanezen in France, a filthy, inefficient mudhole that was losing more men to influenza than to wounds. As far as conditions allowed, Butler turned the camp into a model of organization and efficiency. As always, he was energetic, innovative, unorthodox, and more unsparing of himself than of his subordinates. He was always willing to sacrifice military protocol when the well-being of his men was at stake. At one point, in desperate need of supplies and frustrated by the indifference of the army to his urgent requisition requests, he simply took matters into his own hands. As he related later,

Finally I got sick and tired of waiting. . . . One afternoon I marched down
to the docks with 7,000 men and burst into the warehouses. As long as we
were invading the sacred premises, I thought we might as well make a
clean sweep. We needed shovels, axes, picks and kettles as well as duck-
boards [lumber] (Butler, *Old Gimlet Eye*, 254).

The terrible suffering Butler witnessed among returning American troops
at Pontanezen fed the growing seeds of disillusionment and antimilitarism within him. He commented, "Gradually it began to dawn on me to
wonder what on earth these American boys are doing getting wounded
and killed and buried in France" (Archer, 80).

After the war, Butler spent several years as commandant of the new
Quantico Marine Base in Virginia. He took a leave of absence in 1924 to
accept the post of Director of Public Safety in Philadelphia, where he
attempted to redesign the profoundly corrupt police force along military
lines and to crack down on bootlegging and other vice crimes. Blunt,
impulsive, spontaneous, and tactless, Butler came up against a tangled
political environment he could neither deal with nor defeat. While he
increased vice-related arrests six-fold, the politically appointed magistrates refused to support him, and the conviction rate showed almost no
increase. Butler was manipulated and excoriated by politicians and jour-
nalists whenever his reforms seemed likely to affect the real power structure and economy of Prohibition. Bitter, he complained, "I was hired as
a smoke screen. The politicians were buying the reputation I had earned
in twenty-six years' service as a Marine" (Archer, 92). When he left Philadelphia after two years, he commented, "I have learned to believe nothing that anybody says about me and to say nothing that I mean"
(Schmidt, 155).

In 1927 Butler and his Marines were sent to China to deflect a rising
sentiment of violent nationalism. The mission was largely intended to
intimidate without precipitating any incidents; Butler found himself
walking a diplomatic tightrope trying to balance the demands of Chiang
Kai-shek's Nationalist bullies in the south and other warlords' local bullies in the north. Butler concluded that all sides of the conflict were
equally brutal. He maintained the required Marine presence, which he
referred to deprecatingly as "traffic duty," for two years.

Butler resumed command of Quantico in 1929. At the age of forty-
eight, he was the youngest major general in the American armed forces.
He had a presentable wife, three children growing toward college, an
enviable service record, and a need for funds beyond his Marine salary.
He turned to public speaking. A colorful, dramatic, evocative speaker,
he became a popular figure on the lecture circuit. His two set topics were
law enforcement and his own heroic exploits. He gave no advance warning of the radical transformation that was at work within him.

On December 5, 1929, in an after-dinner speech before a large gathering at the Pittsburgh Builders' Exchange, Butler detailed how the Marines had rigged elections in Nicaragua in 1912 and controlled politics in Haiti. Press coverage of Butler's charges was generally sympathetic, but his superiors were furious. Increasingly, Butler's conscience chafed at the limitations imposed by his role within the Marine hierarchy. He must have known before he gave the speech that he would thereby jeopardize his chances for promotion to Marine corps commandant; although Butler was the ranking candidate for the job, his two rivals were both Naval Academy graduates with upper-class backgrounds and State Department support Butler had never courted or enjoyed. The following summer Secretary of the Navy Charles Adams made a formal inspection visit to Quantico; Butler sensed from Adams's steadily disparaging remarks that the whole visit was designed to provide a rationale for the rejection of his candidacy, and his temper was pushed beyond its limits. Introducing Adams to a group of officers, Butler growled, "Gentlemen, I want you to meet the secretary of the goddam Navy" (Tucker, 293).

That fall, denied the commandancy, a disgruntled Butler decided to retire from the corps. Before he could act on the decision, he was once more embroiled in a spectacular public controversy. In a January, 1931, speech arguing that men like Mussolini could not be trusted to honor bilateral disarmament treaties, Butler stated that an acquaintance had been driving in Italy with Mussolini when *Il Duce*, racing through a mountain village, ran over a peasant child and drove on without stopping. Mussolini exploded with indignation, the Secretary of State apologized profusely, and Butler was arrested in anticipation of a full court-martial. Support for Butler in Congress and the press was overwhelming. New York Governor Franklin Delano Roosevelt and former Secretary of State Josephus Daniels offered to testify on his behalf. *Il Nuovo Mondo*, an Italian antifascist newspaper in New York City, investigated Butler's charges, identified Cornelius Vanderbilt, Jr. as the informant, and confirmed the incident. Embarrassed, Mussolini began to argue that the whole unpleasant affair was best forgotten, and the United States government began a hurried operation of what might be called damage control. In a bitter slapstick parody, Butler achieved total control; in the end, all charges were dropped, Butler retained his command at Quantico, and he and his lawyer wrote his own mild reprimand. Butler's decision to retire had been strengthened by the sour experience. When he bid his men at Quantico farewell, he gave out maps to his home in Pennsylvania and assured the men that he would welcome any of them at any time and do the best he could to help with any problems.

Butler hit the lecture circuit full time. He donated half his fees to the Salvation Army and to unemployment relief in Philadelphia. Increasingly, Butler came to see the Depression as a moral turning point for all

America. He urged raising taxes on the wealthy to finance relief through national school and road building projects. Butler was growing steadily more radical. Cut loose from whatever restraints the Corps had imposed, increasingly alienated from the comfortable, conventional politics with which he had grown up, Butler became a defiant loner, a crusading outsider who could call on the loyalty of thousands of insiders. The fierce, joyful egalitarianism of his military life became the cornerstone of his moral stance.

On his lecture tours, Butler began visiting veterans' hospitals across the country, and he was appalled and enraged by what he saw there. Fifty thousand disabled, disfigured, emotionally shattered young veterans were existing in overcrowded, poorly equipped, understaffed nightmare hospitals. Butler became an outspoken advocate for veterans' needs, and as the Depression deepened, he championed the Veterans' Bonus. In July of 1932 he was the honored guest of the twenty thousand impoverished veterans camping near the White House to pressure Congress for early payment of their World War benefits, originally scheduled for full payment in 1945. He called the veterans' gathering "the greatest demonstration of Americanism ever seen," and he insisted that the veterans had as much right to lobby Congress as did the United States Steel Corporation. A few days later, under orders from President Hoover, Army troops under General Douglas MacArthur attacked the veterans' camp, destroyed their tents, and drove most of the unarmed veterans out of Washington.

Disgusted, Butler commented that the real treasury thieves were the industrialists who had made millions from the war. Butler was haunted by the connections he now saw between the government and the capitalists, and by the self-serving purposes to which they both twisted the armed forces. A few years later, he commented in an interview,

> I helped make Mexico safe for American oil interests in 1914. I helped make Haiti and Cuba a decent place for the National City Bank boys to collect revenues in. . . . I helped purify Nicaragua for the international banking house of Brown Brothers. . . . I brought light to the Dominican Republic for American sugar interests in 1916. I helped make Honduras "right" for American fruit companies in 1903. In China in 1927 I helped see to it that Standard Oil went its way unmolested. Looking back on it, I feel I might have given Al Capone a few hints (Butler, "America's Armed Forces," 11).

Ironically, this principled man, driven to analogize his long military career to gangster activities, became the pivotal character in a gangster plot of monstrous proportions. In the spring of 1933, in an effort to stimulate the economy, Franklin Roosevelt took the country off the gold standard; in other words, the government no longer had to back every paper dollar with a gold dollar. In practical terms, he could pay for new jobs for the unemployed and loans for farmers and homeowners, and the citizens paying back their loans would pay in paper money worth less than what the banks had originally loaned. Conservatives, among them the major industrial and banking giants, were outraged. They saw Roosevelt as a socialist undermining private enterprise to subsidize the lower classes.

In response, leading conservatives formed the American Liberty League in September, 1934; founders included Robert S. Clark, heir to the Singer sewing machine empire; the Pitcairn family (Pittsburgh Plate Glass); Mellon Associates; Rockefeller Associates; E. F. Hutton (brokers); the Pew family (Sun Oil); and William Knudsen (General Motors). The stated goals of the League were "to combat radicalism, to teach the necessity of respect for the rights of persons and property, and generally to foster free private enterprise" (Archer, 30). The League was aligned with two openly fascist affiliates: the Sentinels of the Republic, also backed by Pitcairns and Pews, which praised Adolf Hitler and called the New Deal "Jewish Communism"; and the Southern Committee to Uphold the Constitution, which had close ties to the Ku Klux Klan.

The powers behind the Liberty League were determined to destroy what they saw as the socialism of the New Deal. As early as the summer of 1933 an intermediary group approached Butler with the plan that he rally the American Legion behind him and use the Legionnaires to force Roosevelt out of power. The group intended not to depose Roosevelt but to outflank him by forcing him to name Butler as "Secretary of General Welfare"; presumably, Butler would then become the front man for whatever decrees the cabal promulgated. The group's representative confided to Butler that they felt "you are the only fellow in America who can get the soldiers together" (Archer, 158). Butler was assured that millions of dollars had already been raised and that gathering arms for half a million men would be no problem. Although Butler rejected the offer outright and at first dismissed the entire plot as the fabrication of a few men's wishful thinking, events of the following year gradually convinced him otherwise. The creation of the Liberty League itself had been foretold by Butler's contact. Butler knew that Grayson Murphy, a leading broker who was both a founder of the Liberty League and one of the conspirators named by the intermediary, had founded the American Legion in 1919; since then, the Legion itself had compiled a shabby record as an extralegal strike-breaking force: Legion posts were readily aroused by the specter of "communist" agitators and were frequently armed and urged to attack strikers and picket lines.

Butler could see a pattern emerging; he approached John MacCormack, chair of the House Un-American Activities Committee, which in the early 1930s was as concerned with fascist as with communist activities in America. MacCormack tried to conduct a thorough investigation, but it seemed as though the power and prestige of the conspirators worked against him. The prominent figures whose names came up in the testimony of Butler and others were never subpoenaed, and despite clear evidence, no charges of perjury were ever brought. In February, 1935, the committee reported to the House of Representatives, "There is no question that these attempts were discussed, were planned, and might have been placed in execution when and if the financial backers deemed it expedient . . . your committee was able to verify all the pertinent statements made by Gen. Butler" (Archer, 193).

Despite this unequivocal confirmation, the mainstream press, owned largely by the very conservatives supportive of the Liberty League, pilloried Butler and called the plot a ridiculous hoax. Congress itself refused to extend the life of the committee, which officially disbanded in January of 1935; no action of any sort was ever taken against the alleged conspirators. Almost forty years later, MacCormack reminisced, "If General Butler had not been the patriot he was, and if they had been able to maintain secrecy, the plot certainly might well have succeeded" (Archer, 214).

Butler's radicalism mounted in the coming years. As events unfolded in Europe, he grew desperate to prevent American involvement. He understood only too well the infectious momentum of a militaristic patriotism. In a 1935 Armistice Day speech, he reminded his audience that the Spanish-American War had been caused by the journalism of William Randolph Hearst; he accused Hearst of trying to arrange yet another war: "We must work against war now. Wait until the war drums beat and you'll go half crazy. You'll march up Broad Street and raise Liberty Loans to help Europe pay off its debts to the House of Morgan" (Archer, 224). As a prominent speaker for the League Against War and Fascism, Butler insisted that Wall Street and "Big Business" used the same tactics as the European dictators to keep capitalism in power. In his 1935 pamphlet, *War is a Racket*, he cited damning data on war profiteering in World War I; he despaired of ever avoiding war while such monstrous profits could be made:

But there is a way to stop this racket. It cannot be smashed by disarmament conferences, by peace parleys in Geneva, by resolutions of well-meaning but impractical groups. It can be effectively smashed only by taking the profit out of war.

The only way to stop it is by conscription of capital before conscription of the nation's manhood. One month before the government may order the young men of the nation to be killed, it must serve notice of conscription on the country's capital.

Let the officers and directors of our armament factories, our gun builders and munitions makers and shipbuilders all be conscripted—to get $30 a month, the same wage paid to the lads in the trenches. . . .

Give capital thirty days to think it over and you will learn by that time that there will be no war. That will stop the racket—that and nothing else (Butler, *War is a Racket*, 39).

Butler's anti-imperialism, antimilitarism, and anticapitalism were grounded in no sophisticated theory; they grew out of his unyielding egalitarianism and a quintessentially American sense of fair play and decency. Far from a pacifist, Butler advocated a strong national defense and supported reasonable military preparedness. But his disavowal of interventionist war was absolute; as anguished as he was by the tragedy of the Spanish Civil War, he refused even then to advocate military support for the Loyalists. It is a bitter irony that the antifascist Butler was forced to watch his anti-interventionist position exploited by American isolationists—by the late 1930s a largely fascist crowd.

Frustrated, saddened, and despairing, Butler spent the last years of his life struggling to shatter the mystique of militarism and to prevent the sanctification of war. He spoke from a profound insight into his own experience:

As a youngster, I loved the excitement of battle. It's lots of fun, you know, and it's nice to strut around in front of your wife—or somebody else's wife—and display your medals, and your uniform. But there's another side to it, and that's why I have decided to devote the rest of my life to "pulling off the whiskers" (Archer, 133).

The rest of his life, sadly, was not a long time. By 1940 Butler, exhausted and discouraged, was still touring and speaking out against the country's inexorable slide toward war. In May of that year, debilitated and losing weight, he checked into the Philadelphia Navy Yard hospital; one month later, he died there, most probably of stomach cancer.

It seems somehow fitting that Butler's eulogies in the national press were slanted and disingenuous. There was no mention made of the fascist plot; *The New York Times* managed to publish a three-column obituary without a single reference to the antiwar activities that had consumed the last decade of his life. Butler, irreverent, theatrical, cocky, courageous, and self-mocking, would probably have preferred to be remembered by the words of an earlier report, which dubbed him a "profane and spectacular rebel" (Tucker, 293).

References

Archer, Jules. *The Plot to Seize the White House*. New York: Hawthorn Books, 1973.
Butler, Smedley D. "Amendment for Peace." *Woman's Home Companion* 63 (September, 1936): 4 ff.

————. "America's Armed Forces," pt. 2. *Common Sense* 4 (November, 1935): 7 ff.

————. *Old Gimlet Eye: The Adventures of Smedley Darlington Butler as Told to Lowell Thomas.* Quantico: Marine Corps Association, 1981 [1933].

————. *War is a Racket.* New York: Round Table Press, 1935.

Schmidt, Hans. *Maverick Marine: General Smedley D. Butler and the Contradictions of American Military History.* Lexington: University Press of Kentucky, 1987.

Spiller, Roger J., ed. *Dictionary of American Military Biography.* Westport, CT: Greenwood Press, 1984.

Tucker, Ray T. "The Bad Boy of the Marines." *Outlook and Independent.* (February 25, 1931), 292 ff.

GEORGE WASHINGTON CABLE

(October 12, 1834–January 31, 1925)

Human Rights and Civil Rights Advocate

At the height of his fame and popularity, novelist George Washington Cable was frequently compared to Mark Twain. His short stories were eagerly awaited, his novels sold well, his reading tours were sold out to enthusiastic crowds. After his novel The Grandissimes *was published in 1884, a critic hailed him as "the first Southern novelist . . . who has made a contribution of permanent value to American literature" (Rubin, 97). Cable was also a man of uncompromising integrity, painful compassion, and a towering sense of direct moral responsibility to act against injustice. His lonely campaign for the rights and dignity of African Americans cost him his income, his reputation, and ultimately his artistic freedom. Vilified or ignored by most of his contemporaries, he stands today as a brilliant beacon of reason and decency in one of the shabbiest periods of American history.*

George Washington Cable
Courtesy, Historic Northampton, Northampton, MA.

George Washington Cable's family had settled in Virginia in the early 18th century. His father moved to Pennsylvania, freed his slaves, and headed west into Indiana: Cable's mother, born in Indiana, was from an old New England Puritan family. In 1837 the Cable family settled in New Orleans, where George was born in 1844.

New Orleans was an exotic, unique environment within the South. It had come under American control as part of the Louisiana Purchase of 1803. Two generations later, its population was a strange mix of French Catholics, assorted Anglo-Protestants, Germans, Jews, Indians, and Africans, many from the French West Indies. A large portion of these were "Free Men of Color" who had achieved a delicate, tormented legal status. The culture and atmosphere of New Orleans was vibrant, vivid, almost tropical.

In this environment, George Cable grew up in a prosperous, loving home, served at one point by as many as eight slaves. In the late 1840s his father's business collapsed, and the family never again approached economic security. When the senior Cable died in 1859, young George withdrew from school and found work as a marker at the custom house. Denied access to further formal education, Cable was determined to educate himself. He read hungrily, and in his spare time he explored his strange city and its throbbing waterfront. His writer's attention to detail and nuance developed early.

During the Civil War New Orleans was blockaded by Union ships; in 1862 the United States Navy came upriver and the city surrendered. Cable's mother refused to take the oath of allegiance to the United States required of all residents, and she was forced to leave the city with her children. George, her only son, was technically eligible to be drafted into the Union army, but he was slender and short and looked younger than his age.

In 1863 Cable enlisted in the Confederate Army and served bravely with the Mississippi Cavalry through some of the hardest fighting of the western theater. Despite his boyish appearance and the gentle cheerfulness that illuminated his letters home, he was a toughened soldier who had suffered two serious wounds before the end of the war.

After discharge, Cable returned to New Orleans virtually penniless; he owned no clothing but his shabby gray uniform. As the sole support of his mother and older sisters, he worked on the waterfront for tobacco and cotton merchants. A serious, gentle young man, he married a deeply religious local girl, Louise Bartlett, in 1869. Their first child was born the next year.

Comfortable and settled within his new family, Cable turned some of his energies to writing. He began to publish a monthly column in the

Picayune, a leading New Orleans newspaper. He frequently turned to scenes of local color and impact: Mardi Gras celebrations, yellow fever, school affairs, women's issues, lovingly rendered discussions of mundane items like walking canes and kites. His writing was so well received that in 1871 he accepted a full-time position with the newspaper. That summer he wrote disapprovingly of a training institute for teachers at which black and white teachers sat together. Other New Orleans newspapers seized the story as an opportunity to criticize the hated Reconstructionist Republicans; faced by their scathing descriptions, Cable himself suddenly retreated from the story, torn by personal doubts. His editors were angered by his withdrawal; shortly afterwards, when he refused because of his strict Calvinist upbringing to review a theatrical production, he was fired. He returned to the cotton business and quietly continued his own fiction writing.

Cable's first attempt at getting a serious story published met with failure. The popular late Victorian magazines were fascinated by the "genteel tradition," which romanticized the antebellum South and alleged the corruption of Northern "carpetbagger" politicians and the gross incompetence of African American politicians. Cable's story, a dark tale of the sufferings of an African prince kidnapped and destroyed by slavery, did not fit the definitions of the genteel tradition, it was rejected everywhere. Cable learned to adjust his focus, to turn for material to the picturesque, exotic Creole culture of New Orleans. By 1875 he was being published regularly and had developed a reputation as an author of Southern "local color."

Cable had begun doing historical research for his first stories in the early 1870s. He had read—and been outraged by—the city's antebellum Black Code. He joined a debating club, in which his own unforgiving logic forced him to question the racial assumptions he had grown up with. Cable's research was exhaustive and far-reaching. By the end of the decade he could discuss in great detail various Southern state constitutions, both from before the war and from different moments in the course of Reconstruction; he could cite statistics on taxes, revenues, crime rates, illiteracy, school attendance, criminal sentences, property evaluations, and so on. All these data would become ammunition for his reform campaigns in the coming years.

In 1880 Cable, a valued and respected author, made his first visit to New York to meet with publishers, editors, and literary friends. He was exhilarated by the atmosphere in the North; the following summer he brought his family to spend the summer in New Hampshire. Traveling through New England, he became friends with both Samuel Clemens (Mark Twain) and Harriet Beecher Stowe, author of *Uncle Tom's Cabin*. In the coming years, with no compliment intended, some Southern newspapers would link Cable's name with Stowe's.

Back in New Orleans, Cable served as the secretary of a grand jury investigating conditions in local asylums and jails. What he discovered horrified him. He had seen jails and asylums in New England the previous summer, and the contrast startled him. He launched a campaign to have the city appoint a non-paid Board of Prisons and Asylums Commissioners, and he became the new board's first secretary. When he broadened his research to include Southern state penitentiaries, the picture that emerged was even more appalling.

Reconstruction, the post-war occupation of the defeated South, had involved the presence of federal troops and thus some minor protection for the newly freed slaves. But when the last Northern troops were withdrawn in a twisted political deal in 1877, embittered white Southerners turned against the freedmen with a vengeance. The criminal "justice" system was a major component in the New South's control of its barely tolerated black population. What Cable discovered was a vicious system that used the penitentiaries as a form of social and economic control. African Americans who spoke out or who managed to step beyond the subservient economic roles intended for them were frequently imprisoned on trifling offenses; they were then literally rented out to assorted mines, lumber camps, turpentine camps, road gangs, or railroads. This was the infamous convict lease system, a grotesquely biased arrangement that served in effect to reinstate slavery.

Cable was incapable of silence in the face of this evil. In 1882, addressing the National Conference of Charities and Corrections in Louisville, Kentucky, he condemned the Southern prison system and its racial imbalances, citing irrefutable data state by state and comparing these shameful data to analogous figures from Northern prisons. As a major reform spokesman, Cable was elected vice-president of the National Prison Association. But throughout the Southern press, he was blamed for humiliating the South in public and, worse yet, for demanding justice for blacks.

In June, 1883, as commencement speaker at the University of Louisiana in New Orleans, Cable called for a Southern literature that dared to challenge old beliefs and attitudes. Moving ever closer to direct confrontation with the South's treatment of African Americans, Cable declared that literature "must be free; free to study principles for themselves; to present and defend truth; to assert rights; . . . to rectify thoughts, morals, manners, society, even though it shake the established order of things like an earthquake" (Rubin, 119).

The following year, still nationally popular, Cable undertook a long reading tour of the Northeast and Midwest. The more he saw of the rest of the country, the less willing he was to countenance and indulge the peculiar regional fantasies of the South. "The South makes me sick," he wrote to his wife, "the West makes me tired, the East makes me glad. It is the intellectual treasury of the United States" (Rubin, 154).

On June 18, 1884, Cable abandoned any pretense of compromise and confronted the race question head on. On that day, in an address to the American Social Science Association in Tuscaloosa, Alabama, he argued bluntly that slavery had damaged Southern society by producing arrogance and weak morality among the masters. He urged an end to the horrors of terrorism unleashed by the end of Reconstruction, to

> murder, too, and lynching at its heels, the turning of state and county prisons into slave-pens, the falsification of the ballot, night-riding and whipping. . . . From one end of this land to the other there shall be lifted against these crimes an outcry of shame and condemnation. . . . We have been silent long enough (Cable, *Negro Question*, 20).

The outcry of shame and condemnation was raised against Cable himself. Cable could scarcely have launched his civil rights crusade in a more hostile atmosphere. Throughout the South, Democratic white power structures were seizing control and systematically stripping African Americans of any vestige of real rights or protection. Nationally, the eugenics movement, loosely based on misunderstood and distorted Darwinism, focused on the racial inferiority not only of African Americans but also of the flood of Southern and Eastern European immigrants. In 1883 the Supreme Court ruled that the 1875 Civil Rights Act, the major social monument of Reconstruction, was unconstitutional. The popular press published endless articles arguing that Southerners understood "their Negroes" and "their problem" and that the North should leave them alone to handle things. The *New York Tribune* declared that blacks had been given "ample opportunity to develop their own latent capacities," but that "as a race they are idle, ignorant, and vicious" (Woodward, 216).

In January, 1885, *Century Magazine* published "The Freedman's Case in Equity," an expanded version of Cable's Tuscaloosa speech. Cable wasted no time sounding his challenge:

> The greatest social problem before the American people today is, as it has been for a hundred years, the presence among us of the Negro.
> No comparable entanglement was ever drawn round itself by any other modern nation with so serene a disregard of its ultimate issue, or with a more distinct national responsibility. The African slave was brought here by cruel force, and with everybody's consent except his own. Everywhere the practice was favored as a measure of common aggrandizement. When a few men and women protested, they were mobbed in the public interest, with the public consent. There rests, therefore, a moral responsibility on the whole nation never to lose sight of the results of African-American slavery until they cease to work mischief and injustice (Cable, "Freedman's," 409).

Cable gave a short history of race relations in the South, delineating the daily humiliations endured by freedmen. He repeated his charges of racial bias within the convict leasing system; he demanded full integration in all public facilities and institutions—including schools. Without true freedom to motivate him, Cable reasoned, the freed black would remain an economic liability and prevent the full resurgence of a proud, modern, industrialized South. His vision was both prescient and frightening:

> There are those among us who see that America has no room for a state of society which makes its lower classes harmless by abridging their liberties, or, as one of the favored class lately said to me, has "got 'em so they don't give no trouble." There is a growing number who see that the one thing we cannot afford to tolerate at large is a class of people less than citizens. . . . One of the marvels of future history will be that it was counted a small matter, by a majority of our nation, for six millions of people within it, made by its own decree a component part of it, to be subjected to a system of oppression so rank that nothing could make it seem small except the fact that they had already been ground under it for a century and a half. . . . We have shown the outrageousness of these tyrannies in some of their workings, and how distinctly they antagonize every state and national interest involved in the elevation of the colored race. Is it not well to have done so? For, I say again, the question has reached a moment of special importance (Cable, "Freedman's," 418).

The response to "The Freedman's Case" was thunderous and vituperative; the press across the South vilified Cable. The *Century* was deluged with outraged letters, and agreed to publish a rebuttal by Henry Grady, editor of the *Atlanta Constitution* and a respected "moderate" on the race question. Grady stated that neither race wanted integration, that "separate but equal" worked very well, and that everyone in the South, black and white, was completely content. "Nowhere on earth is there kindlier feeling, closer sympathy, or less friction between two classes of society than between the whites and blacks of the South today" (Rubin, 180). In reality, the year during which Grady penned his glowing description of racial harmony had seen the brutal lynchings of 211 African Americans in the South.

In the wake of all this furor and tension, Cable made the decision to move his family north. He had missed them terribly during his long speaking tours, and he had come to believe that the moral environment in the Northeast was better for the whole family. He moved his wife, six children, mother, two sisters, and assorted nieces and nephews first to a small town outside Hartford, Connecticut, and then to Northampton, Massachusetts. Northampton, a lovely town with a vital cultural life, was the home of Smith College, which admitted the daughters of town residents free of tuition; this was a major consideration to a man with five daughters. Cable would never again live in the South.

Cable responded to Grady's article in the *Century* with a series of essays entitled *The Silent South*. He tried to soothe Southern fears of social chaos, to assure white Southerners that political and public equality would not lead inevitably to the dreaded "race mingling." He was concerned, he said, with common, impersonal individual rights, which were violated every day in every Southern setting. Anticipating by seventy years the Supreme Court's reasoning in *Brown v. Board of Education*, he reiterated that the doctrine of "separate but equal" involved an implicit mark of degradation and shame; worse yet, the stated goal of separate but equal was simply not being met. The life of the African American was dominated by the constant daily humiliation of grossly inadequate schools, homes, hospitals, railroad cars, and other accommodations.

By this point, despite his brave title, Cable must have despaired of the "silent South" whose conscience he fought so hard to awaken. As commencement speaker at Vanderbilt University in 1887, he maintained his lonely focus on civil rights and the national moral sense. Now he blamed Northern silence and indifference as well as Southern racial attitudes for the fact that seven million Americans were denied their most basic rights as citizens. While it was fashionable to portray Reconstruction as a failure, Cable declared that the South had never given Reconstruction a chance to succeed, that the races could—must—learn to live in dignified, equitable peace, and that the true prosperity of the entire country depended on it.

Still searching for the ethical pulse of the South, Cable organized the Open Letter Club in 1887. The club was intended to be an open forum for enlightened discussions throughout the South; it attracted several hundred prominent lawyers, clergy, and educators of both races. Published debates and critiques included topics like "Shall the Negro be Educated or Suppressed?" Whatever good the club might have accomplished over time was denied it when Cable himself brought it unacceptable notoriety by breaking one of the oldest social taboos in the South: in 1889, after lecturing at all-black Fisk University, Cable met with black leaders in the home of John C. Napier, a wealthy local black figure; unforgivably, he stayed on after the meeting and ate a meal at Napier's dining table. The white press saw this as an example of the "social integration" they hated and feared; coverage of the event was utterly hysterical. Members of the club were either angered themselves or frightened away by the public outcry, and the Open Letter Club disintegrated rapidly. Cable was disgusted. "I tell you," he wrote to a friend, "this soothing and pacifying and conciliating these people intoxicated with prejudice and political bigotry is helping neither them nor any worthy interest. I am glad my record is made and that I stand before them as unclothed with any reservation as a swimmer" (Rubin, 203).

Throughout the decade after publication of "The Freedman's Case," Cable struggled to keep civil rights and the issue of racial attitudes before the public. In *Forum Magazine* in 1888, he advocated full suffrage for African Americans; he ridiculed the Southern version of Reconstruction history that portrayed black politicians as corrupt buffoons. For Cable, the question came down to the sanctity of individual rights. As might be expected, his early rigid Calvinism had matured into a commitment to the Social Gospel's doctrine of Christianity enacting itself through justice and good works. His profound faith was in the Declaration of Independence and the Constitution of the United States; full rights for African Americans were to him utterly consistent with the living Constitution, and compliance with its stipulations the only honorable path for a true American.

In reality, Cable was almost totally alone in his faith. The situation of African Americans in the South deteriorated throughout the 1890s. Sharecropping mired them hopelessly in debt; state laws disenfranchised them; and across the South blacks became a convenient focus for populist rage and frustration. The mounting racism of the decade targeted the immigrant population as well; the argument was that blacks and immigrants were too easily manipulated and susceptible to corruption, and that in the name of "Pure Government" they must be disqualified from voting. Typically, Cable excoriated this notion: "No man is good enough to govern another without his consent" (Rubin, 207).

Cable was still the sole support of his large family; his financial life was always precarious, and he desperately needed to publish more popular fiction. In 1895 he published a major new novel, *John March, Southerner*. He used his fictional forum to vent his burning frustrations; to expose the hypocrisy of narrow, selfish evangelical religion; to reveal the corruption of "Lost Cause" romanticism and Confederate nostalgia; to argue for the positive potential of blacks in a really new South.

Cable had to break off relations with his regular publisher in order to get the book published; he was fighting for his integrity as a writer as well as for the integrity of his beliefs. When the book produced no meaningful reaction, Cable felt crushed and defeated. To support his family and to spare himself further pain and controversy, he retreated from serious writing; for the next decade he wrote conventional "costume romances" that sold well and meant nothing to him. He had wanted to convince the South of the injustice of segregation; he had hoped to write the best fiction of which he was capable. He was defeated in both hopes: forced to realize that there was no "Silent South" waiting to join him, artistically betrayed by the artificiality of Victorian gentility. The critic Edmund Wilson, mourning Cable's lost potential, wrote, "The influence of the Northern editors was to prove in the long run as lethal to Cable's career as the South's hostility to his views on race" (Wilson, *Patriotic Gore*, 579). Wilson, among this century's most insightful critics, considered Cable "one of the clearest-minded Americans of his time, and in the South after the Civil War, so detached and realistic an intelligence was uncommon and unwelcome. It was not common or welcome anywhere" (Wilson, "Citizen of the Union," 353).

In 1909 Cable revisited New Orleans and saw his worst fears for race relations realized. The city was more rigidly segregated than ever; it had endured a hideous three-day race riot in 1900, and the black middle class had been utterly crushed economically. Only menial jobs were open to them; there was no secondary school for African Americans in the entire city.

A few years later, Andrew Carnegie offered Cable a yearly stipend of $1,000 to ease his burdens and allow him more freedom in writing. Reinvigorated, in 1918 Cable produced a new novel, *Lovers of Louisiana*, in which he revived and updated his old concerns and passions. The novel speaks with an eerily prophetic quality: at one point, a Scotsman visiting New Orleans asks his Creole host about the race issue and is told that that is "the deadest question in America." The Scotsman disagrees passionately:

> No, Mr. Durel, it isn't dead, it's merely 'possuming. . . . Lorrd! Ye can't *neglect* it to death; the neglect of all America can't kill it. It's in the womb o' the future and bigger than Asia, Africa, and America combined. . . . Wi' war and a swarrm o' lesser things on yon side, and preparedness and a swarrm o' lesser things on this, it's pitifully out o' fashion; but fashions have an uncanny trick o' coming back, and there's a day ahead, whether far or near God only knows, when that question—and they that are out o' fashion wi' it—will come round again, as big an' ugly as hoop-skirrts" (Rubin, 270).

The last years of Cable's life were spent in genteel poverty in Northampton. His children grown and gone, his siblings dead, he spent summers in the South and the rest of the year in Northampton. In 1919 Carnegie willed Cable an annuity of $5,000; for the first time, at the age of seventy-five, he was finally free of financial anxiety. His wife died in 1923, and Cable found himself increasingly ignored by a literary scene that had passed him by. Once compared favorably to Henry James, Ivan Turgenev, and Mark Twain, Cable died in 1925 and was largely forgotten.

Cable's crusade was one of incredible courage and loneliness. At monumental cost to his career, his reputation, and his family, he fought for his vision of justice and decency. He had offered a moderate, intelligent, meticulously documented moral alternative to an atmosphere of vicious racial hatred. It was his tragedy—and ours—that American society was not ready to hear him.

References

Cable, George Washington. "The Convict Lease System in the South." *Century Magazine* 28 (February, 1884): 582–599.

———. "The Freedman's Case in Equity." *Century Magazine* 29 (January, 1885): 409–418.

———. *The Negro Question: Selections of Writings on Civil Rights in the South*. Edited by Arlen Turner. Garden City, NY: Doubleday & Co., 1958.

Frederickson, George M. *The Black Image in the White Mind: The Debate on Afro-American Character and Destiny, 1817–1914*. New York: Harper & Row, 1972.

Rubin, Louis D. Jr. *George Washington Cable: The Life and Times of a Southern Heretic*. Pegasus, NY: Western Publishing Co., 1969.

Williamson, Joel. *The Crucible of Race: Black-White Relations in the American South Since Emancipation*. New York: Oxford University Press, 1984.

Wilson, Edmund. "Citizen of the Union." *New Republic* 57 (February 13, 1929): 352–353.

———. *Patriotic Gore: Studies in the Literature of the American Civil War*. New York: Oxford University Press, 1962.

Woodward, C. Vann. *Origins of the New South, 1877–1913*. Baton Rouge: Louisiana State University Press, 1951.

Wynes, Charles E., ed. *Forgotten Voices: Dissenting Southerners in an Age of Conformity*. Baton Rouge: Louisiana State University Press, 1967.

TUNIS G. CAMPBELL

(1812–December 4, 1891)

African American Community Organizer

History is written by the winners. Losers rarely get to tell their side of the story. This observation was perhaps never more true than in the case of Tunis G. Campbell, a dedicated, principled, practical crusader for the rights of freedmen in Reconstruction Georgia, whose competence and success earned him the hatred, fear, and contempt of the local white power structure. Conventional historiography of Reconstruction has accepted the poisoned white image of Campbell; his memory— and historical integrity—have paid a fearsome price.

Tunis G. Campbell
Courtesy, Moorland-Spingarn Research Center, Howard University.

Tunis George Campbell was born free in New Jersey in 1812. His father was a blacksmith who had many white customers, and at an early age Tunis was accustomed to dealing with whites on fairly equitable terms. When the boy was only five years old, a wealthy white friend of the family financed his education at an Episcopal boarding school in Babylon, New York. Campbell, the only African American student in the school, remembered many moments of kindness and encouragement from his teachers; he graduated from the school in 1830. His teachers hoped he would become an Episcopal missionary in Liberia, but young Campbell was reading abolitionist literature and had come to disapprove of the entire colonization movement. The American Colonization Society, founded in 1816 by Henry Clay, claimed to offer blacks new hope and freedom in the artificially created country of Liberia; increasingly, African Americans in the 1830s and '40s saw emigration as a cowardly surrender of their rights in America, and many black spokesmen feared the involuntary expatriation of all free blacks. Young Campbell rejected not only his teachers' plans for him but also their religion. He moved into the more socially progressive Methodist Church, lived with his parents, and spent the next several years voluntarily helping to set up schools for black children and African Methodist Episcopal churches in the slums of Brooklyn and Jersey City. He established a reputation as an effective abolitionist speaker and became more active in the growing opposition to colonization; in 1832 he established an anticolonization society in Brooklyn.

For most of the next thirty years, Campbell worked as a hotel steward and head waiter in various hotels in New York and Boston. He wrote the first manual published in America on hotel management. He was organized, independent, successful, and unintimidated by whites. Campbell was a leading speaker, along with Frederick Douglass, at a major anticolonization convention in New York in 1849. At the Colored National Convention in Rochester, New York in 1853, Campbell was one of 114 delegates. When the convention discussed a proposal to work for "a Union of the Colored People of the Free States," Campbell insisted on broadening the vision of the proposal by deleting the word "colored."[1] Never a racist, Campbell had many radical abolitionist white friends, and he genuinely believed that all good people could work together for the common good.

As soon as Lincoln promulgated the Emancipation Proclamation in January of 1863, Campbell wrote to him with suggestions for organizing the education of the future freedmen; Lincoln never responded. In the summer of 1863, supported by several of his influential abolitionist friends, Campbell finally got the opportunity to be of direct service to the freedmen. He was sent by the Department of War to South Carolina to work on the Port Royal Experiment, the first organized attempt to resettle displaced freedmen. Campbell was enthusiastic. He took his own life savings and set out for Port Royal. "I was sent down," he recorded later, "to organize civil government, to improve the colored people in the South wherever I could do it, and . . . to instruct and elevate the colored people" (Duncan, 16). This was Campbell's first contact with Southern blacks. He listened to painful stories of past horrors and mistreatment, to budding hopes and dreams for the future. He watched dedicated teachers and doctors and administrators work with the former slaves, and he saw brazen corruption and venality in action. He learned from everything he saw.

Campbell got a chance to put all his experience to good use in the spring of 1865, when General Rufus Saxton, military commander of Georgia, appointed him Freedmen's Bureau Superintendent of the major islands off the coast of Georgia. The Freedmen's Bureau was in itself a remarkable phenomenon. The great African American historian W.E.B. Du Bois called it "the most extraordinary and far-reaching institution of social uplift that America has ever attempted" (Du Bois, 219). A Bureau of Emancipation had first been proposed less than a month after the Emancipation Proclamation. Union forces were so inundated by a rising tide of frightened, desperate, starving former slaves that military efficiency was imperiled; Congress was inundated by constant petitions from the various voluntary organizations doing vital fieldwork with the escaping slaves. The Bureau of Refugees, Freedmen, and Abandoned Lands was finally established in March, 1865, with the humane, honorable General O. O. Howard as its director. The bureau was designed to function as a government unto itself: it made regulations, it interpreted and executed them, it punished violators of those regulations. The goal of helping four million slaves become citizens was truly revolutionary; radical programs were needed to move toward that goal. When General Philip Sherman marched into Savannah in late 1864, leaders of the jubilant freedmen informed him that their first priority was land of their own. In response, Sherman issued orders creating free black reservations on the Sea Islands off Georgia; freedmen were given exclusive control of the islands and were granted homesteads of up to forty acres, carved from confiscated Confederate plantations.

The rice coast of Georgia and the Sea Islands along the coast had been prosperous before the Civil War. McIntosh County, where Campbell became a controversial figure, had been a wealthy county with a heavy slave concentration—twenty-six slaves per white family, more than twice the state average. The county was socially as well as economically devastated by the war; of the three hundred local boys who marched off to join the Confederate Army, only fifty returned. The Sea Islands were vulnerable to Union naval action, and most of the white population fled inland early in the war. Plantations were left in total chaos, and slaves were abandoned with no warning or preparation. As Campbell himself wrote to the Freedmen's Relief Association when he arrived, "These people want clothing, for they are robbed of everything" (Sterling, 34).

Campbell arrived on St. Catherines Island in April of 1865. He landed several new families and a small inventory of supplies on both St. Catherines and Sapelo, the largest of the islands. Within two months there were more than four hundred adults and two hundred children on the two islands. Campbell believed strongly that the freedmen needed time alone to gather their strength, to educate themselves, to learn democracy and self-respect: the habits and assumptions of citizenship could not be acquired quickly, especially after experiencing for two hundred years a regime specifically designed to deny slaves any trace of responsibility and initiative. Campbell's motif was "separatism for strength." General Rufus Saxton, the regional Union Army commander, understood what Campbell wanted to accomplish and supported him. With the exception of missionaries and military personnel, whites were not permitted on the islands.

Campbell established an island government modeled on the United States Constitution. The islands had a bicameral legislature, a judicial system, and, most controversially, an armed citizen militia of almost three hundred men. By June he had over 140 children enrolled in schools on both islands; he used personal funds to bring his two sons and their wives from New York to teach. He was desperately short of supplies and wrote frequently to various aid associations beseeching more help. The freedmen's eagerness for education was especially compelling. "We cannot take any more at present," he wrote to the American Missionary Association, "as we have not got books for them. There are a great many adults who want to go also but we cannot take them" (Duncan, 25).

Throughout the summer of 1865, families flocked to the islands and the schools expanded. Campbell was a true Jeffersonian republican whose vision of America was, ultimately, color-blind, a land of small farms, free schools, and small towns populated by thrifty, virtuous, respectable citizen farmers. He saw the separatism of the Sea Island communities as a necessary but temporary stage in nurturing the freedmen's self-confidence and pride—qualities he called "human capital" (Duncan, 25). Campbell was carefully creating an environment to sustain the growth of communal responsibility and cooperative effort. The early months of his Sea Island republic were filled with a sense of optimism and possibility. In July, a Union Army colonel on an inspection tour of the islands praised what he saw taking shape and recognized Campbell's guiding presence.

Others also recognized the significance of what Campbell was attempting on St. Catherines and Sapelo, but their reactions were far from favorable. By the end of that summer, the mainland Georgia Freedmen's

Bureau was under the command of David Tillson, a barely moderate Republican with a profound contempt for African Americans and a determination to attract Northern investment to Georgia. Tillson believed that blacks were incapable of disciplining themselves, of setting their own goals, and of working toward those goals without external pressure. The fact that Campbell and his settlements were demonstrating otherwise merely convinced him that Campbell must be removed. Tillson shared these sentiments with Andrew Johnson, the Tennessean vice-president who had succeeded to the presidency when Lincoln was assassinated in April. Johnson opposed and vetoed every significant act the Reconstructionists in Congress passed; several major acts were saved by a vote to override the veto, but Johnson's conciliatory attitude toward the Confederacy undermined the entire effort. In February, 1866, urged by Tillson, Johnson fired General Saxton for refusing to revoke the homestead grants he had made to freedmen. Tillson gained control of the Sea Islands and set out on an inspection tour. He was appalled by what he found:

Influenced by Campbell, the freedmen were unwilling to permit the white owners to return to the islands, even to occupy such portions of their property as had not been assigned to freedmen in compliance with General Sherman's Special Order No. 15. . . . They had all the animals, implements, seeds, and nearly all the food required to enable them to make a crop this year (Duncan, 30).

Clearly, Campbell represented an intolerable contradiction of everything Tillson expounded. He had to be removed. Tillson used federal troops to overwhelm the islands' inadequately armed militia. He invented charges of fiscal mismanagement against Campbell and summarily exiled him from the Sea Islands. With Campbell off the islands, Tillson turned with a vengeance to his program of forcing the freedmen into labor contracts with white investors. The land grants to the freedmen were revoked; the land was either returned to its Confederate owners or leased to Northern entrepreneurs. Acreage the freedmen had planted in food crops was plowed under and replanted with cash crops like rice and cotton, thus further weakening the blacks' hopes for self-reliance and increasing their dependency on their white employers. Freedmen who protested against outrageously unfair contract stipulations and inflated prices at the white-run company stores, or who resisted signing the contracts, were arrested and punished. Tillson saw Campbell's influence in every flicker of black assertiveness, and he forbade Campbell to come near the islands, "there being good reason to believe that he is advising the freed people on Sapelo Island to pursue

a course alike unjust to their employers, and injurious to themselves"
(Duncan, 35).

Frustrated on the islands, Campbell relocated to the mainland. He
found an abandoned plantation outside the county seat, Darien, which
he arranged to buy in installments. He invited families from the island
settlements and other freed families to his new venture, the communal
farm of Belleville. Within weeks over one hundred people joined him on
the land. As he had on St. Catherines, Campbell drew up a detailed
charter for the Belleville Farmers Association, with officers, inspectors, a
treasury, and a corresponding secretary. Circumstances at Belleville were
far less favorable than they had been on the islands. The land had been
disastrously neglected during the war; days of back-breaking labor were
required before any planting could begin, and the season was already
late. The people who followed Campbell knew what they were up
against, and they fully understood how important the fight was. The
Belleville charter concluded with a defiant challenge:

> And we hereby pledge ourselves, our interest and our labor to the suc-
> cessful issue of this first permanent [organization] for our welfare and hope
> thereby to merit the approbation of our friends who have assisted us and
> the disappointment of our enemies who seek our downfall (Sterling, 251).

Belleville was cursed with several years of bad weather and the consequent poor harvests. Aid from the Freedmen's Bureau and from the over-
burdened private agencies was always inadequate. Campbell knew he
would have to broaden his scope if he were to have more meaningful
influence on the lives of freedmen.

By 1867 Radical Republicans had gained control of Congress and were
able to overpower the conservative Johnson. The first Reconstruction Act
of March 1867 passed over Johnson's veto; two more acts in the next
three months defined the shape of Reconstruction. They established martial law throughout the South and enumerated the requirements for read-
mission to the Union. The former Confederate states had to:

—register all qualified voters, under federal supervision;
—elect delegates to rewrite the state constitution into compliance with
  the United States Constitution;
—elect new state legislatures;
—ratify the Fourteenth Amendment, which established full African
  American citizenship.

Heartened by the strength of the Radical Republicans, Campbell decided it might be possible to work within the structures of elected gov-

ernment. He had come to believe that the Belleville farmers were too dependent on his guidance and that it would be better for them if he were not so involved in the daily running of the community. Beyond that, he had gradually built a self-conscious and united black power base in McIntosh County. Campbell had been a prominent delegate at a major A.M.E. Zion Church conference in Augusta, and in the summer of 1867 he was vice-president of the Republican State Convention in Atlanta, where he earned respect and praise from white as well as black delegates.

In the fall of 1867 McIntosh County elected Tunis Campbell its delegate to the constitutional convention required by federal law; he was one of 37 blacks among 170 delegates. Here, too, Campbell was a natural leader who worked to hold the black delegates together in an effective voting bloc; he was able to engineer passage of a bill eliminating imprisonment for debt. He never missed a single meeting throughout the three months of the convention.

When Georgia ratified a fairly liberal new constitution, Campbell became one of three African Americans elected to the state senate; in the same election, he became the justice of the peace for McIntosh County. In the Senate, he served on the committees on education and petitions; he fought for equitably financed public education, for racially impartial juror selection, and for an end to segregation on public conveyances. He and his two colleagues were active, competent, and assertive, and their white counterparts were determined to remove them.

On September 12, 1868, arguing that the right to vote did not imply the right to hold office, the state legislature expelled all black members of both houses. Campbell and his son, who had been elected to the state House of Representatives, went to Washington to protest. Although no direct action was taken at the time, Campbell's eloquent insistence on equal protection for all citizens may have influenced the passage of the Fifteenth Amendment.

In December, 1869, in response to the steady rise of Ku Klux Klan terrorism, the United States Congress restored military rule in Georgia. The expelled black legislators were reinstated, and for what remained of his term Campbell served on committees on education, the penal system, and the military. He introduced fifteen bills furthering black rights, most of which were unsuccessful. His great concerns were access to voting and education.

Campbell lost his senate seat in 1872 in an election mired in fraud. He continued to serve as a justice of the peace; in that capacity he was most prominent defending the rights of black sailors on the ships docking in Darien, an active port. His vigilance on their behalf, and his willingness to fine and imprison the white ships' captains who abused them, incurred the wrath of local whites.

Campbell had been a major irritant to the white power structure for years. They recognized his influence over McIntosh County African Americans, and they despised him for it. William Sessions, a county judge, commented, "When Campbell is away from the county . . . the negroes are peacable [sic] and well disposed; but when he is present the contrary is the case." Angrily, Sessions acknowledged that "there can be no order enforced contrary to the views of Campbell." The *Savannah Morning News* sneered, "Tunis is no common fellow after all, though a precious and anointed rascal and conspirator. . . . [He is] almost worshipped by the ignorant negroes" (Coulter II, 17, 18). Planters claimed that Campbell's opposition to contract labor and his constant advice to the freedmen cost the planters hundreds of thousands of dollars. By the mid-1870s the momentum of national politics was conservative again, and white "Redeemer" forces, dedicated to restoring the "old order," were seizing power throughout the South. Clearly, the time was ripe to bring Campbell down.

The instrument of Campbell's destruction arrived in January, 1874 in the person of Judge Henry Tompkins, a Confederate veteran newly appointed county judge, a man publicly sworn to destroy Campbell. Throughout 1875 Campbell was harassed by repeated indictments on charges of falsely imprisoning white men—the white men in question the abusive ship captains in Darien. After several badly mismanaged attempts, Tompkins succeeded in bringing a new indictment against Campbell and set bail so high that the black community could not meet it.

At the age of sixty-four, Tunis Campbell was sentenced to one year at hard labor. He was caught in one of the most brutal and degraded mechanisms of the post-war South—the convict lease system. Convict leasing had not existed before the war. It was created and utilized as a tool to intimidate, control, and virtually reenslave the freedmen. Leasing had begun in Georgia in 1868 and was firmly entrenched by the mid-1870s. By law, those convicted of vagrancy were subject to being leased out; by intention, virtually all those convicted of vagrancy were black. Any African American who refused to sign a labor contract, however unfair or exploitative, could be arrested as a vagrant. Contract law was rewritten to include severe punishment for anything like "disobedience," "impudence," or "disrespect to the employer"; employers were the only judges of when such violations had occurred.

In 1875 the Redeemer government of Georgia passed a "pig law," which changed hog stealing from a misdemeanor to a felony with stiff prison sentences. Within two years Georgia's penitentiary population had trebled; 95% of the new convicts were African American, and almost all of them could expect to be leased out to private contractors in turpentine and lumber camps, mines, plantations, and railroads.

Conditions in these camps were appalling, and the treatment accorded the men was brutal. In the late 1870s, convicts leased to one railroad company in South Carolina suffered a 45% annual death rate; the death rate across the South averaged between 16 and 25%. There were some attempts at exposure and reform: in one such brave effort, a United States district judge examined the court records of one Georgia county for one month and disclosed that 149 people—almost all of them black— had been sentenced to a total of 19 years at leased labor for crimes no more serious than walking on the grass and spitting on the sidewalk. The maverick Southern reformer George Washington Cable* published and lectured against convict leasing. But the system was too profitable for both the state and the contractor for reform to have a chance. In the mid-1880s Georgia's United States Senator, Joseph E. Brown, held a twenty-year lease on three hundred "healthy" convicts, for which he paid the state the sum of seven cents per man per working day. The convict lease system thrived throughout the South until the depression of 1893, when it became difficult to find contractors willing to take large numbers of convicts. From that point well into the 20th century, the use of forced convict labor gradually shifted from private contractors to public road gangs.

In January of 1876, Tunis Campbell entered this world. The plantation owner who held his contract would pay the state of Georgia $8.25 for a year of Campbell's labor. Even within this nightmare, the power of Campbell's presence asserted itself. His employer came to respect and trust him, removed his leg irons, assigned him light labor appropriate to his age, and permitted him to preach to the other laborers. None of this good fortune blinded Campbell to the realities of life for his brothers. As he recalled,

It is impossible to describe the way in which the prisoners were worked. They were taken out as soon as they could see—both summer and winter— and kept to work as long as it was light, with one hour for dinner . . . they were beaten most unmercifully with a leather strap, or a buggy trace, and given from fifty to one hundred strokes, until they would keep up or die (Campbell, 26).

Repeated appeals for Campbell's release were all rejected; having already been imprisoned for more than eight months while Judge Tompkins manipulated and defeated bail requests, Campbell served the full year of his convict lease.

When Campbell, exhausted and discouraged, was finally released in January, 1877, he moved to Washington to lobby for increased federal protection of African American rights. The new president, Rutherford B. Hayes, had gained the office through a deeply tainted compromise that gave him the electoral votes of key Southern states in return for his promise to withdraw all federal troops and effectively betray Reconstruction. Campbell could expect little support from such a man. Understandably, Campbell deemed it advisable not to move back to McIntosh County: Judge Tompkins had let it be known that he would find excuses to arrest Campbell whenever he could. In 1882 Campbell attended the state Republican convention in Atlanta and campaigned for Republican candidates throughout the state. He visited McIntosh County, where he was surrounded by support and affection. Despite his years of absence, the local newspaper reported,

> The colored people of this county have the greatest confidence in Tunis G. Campbell. . . . He is still strong in the hearts of the colored people and if he were eligible they would not hesitate for one moment to give him any office within their gift. Wonderful magnetism, curious people (Duncan, 116).

After this visit, Campbell never returned to Georgia. His movements toward the end of his life are difficult to trace. He died in Boston on December 4, 1891.

Tunis Campbell, reviled as a troublemaker and corrupt insurrectionist, was no radical. He believed in the innate dignity of all people. He believed profoundly in the American Dream of land ownership and responsible citizenship. All he demanded was that African American citizens be accorded an honorable opportunity to fulfill that dream. Refusing to wait passively or to beg for his people's rights, Campbell patiently constructed a coherent, effective political consciousness among his black constituents. The unity Campbell inspired in the freedmen of McIntosh County gave them a degree of strength and self-control few African Americans could hope for. Even after Campbell's immediate role was terminated by his persecution and imprisonment, his carefully nurtured citizenship strategy continued to bear fruit. Blacks in McIntosh County remained a recognized political power bloc for almost forty years, despite white supremacist state governments and abandonment by Northern sympathizers. McIntosh County returned black delegates to the state legislature in almost every election until 1907, when the state effectively disenfranchised its black citizens. Tunis Campbell was honored and remembered for decades by the people whose rights, hopes, and dreams he had so fearlessly worked to achieve.

References

Bell, Malcolm, Jr. *Major Butler's Legacy: Five Generations of a Slaveholding Family.* Athens: University of Georgia Press, 1987.

Campbell, Tunis G. *Sufferings of the Rev. T. G. Campbell and His Family in Georgia.* Washington, DC: Enterprise, 1877.

Coulter, E. Merton. 'Tunis G. Campbell: Negro Reconstructionist in Georgia." I— *Georgia Historical Quarterly* 51 (December, 1967): 401–424; II—*Georgia Historical Quarterly* 52 (March, 1968): 16–52.

Du Bois, W.E.B. *Black Reconstruction in America, 1860–1880.* Cleveland: World Publishing Co., 1962 [1935].

Duncan, Russell. *Freedom's Shore: Tunis Campbell and the Georgia Freedmen.* Athens: University of Georgia Press, 1986.

Franklin, John Hope. *Reconstruction After the Civil War.* Chicago: University of Chicago Press, 1961.

Novak, Daniel A. *The Wheel of Servitude: Black Forced Labor After Slavery.* Lexington: University Press of Kentucky, 1978.

Sterling, Dorothy, ed. *The Trouble They Seen: Black People Tell the Story of Reconstruction.* Garden City, NY: Doubleday & Co., 1976.

LUISA CAPETILLO

(October 28, 1879–April 10, 1922)

Labor Organizer, Women's Rights Advocate

As a society shaped by conservative, deeply Catholic, rigidly patriarchal Spain, 19th-century Puerto Rico had little sympathy for rebels, religious nonconformists, or outspoken women. Luisa Capetillo was all three. An eloquent, inspiring labor leader and proponent of social justice, Capetillo offered her own life in total dedication to the principles of anarchism and women's rights. She was a highly educated woman, economically and intellectually independent, a single mother, a respected voice in the male-dominated union movement, a passionate advocate for women's control of their bodies and relationships, a rational evangelist for a truly radical Christian vision—a neglected, major voice of immediate, contemporary impact.

Luisa Capetillo
Courtesy, Universidad de Puerto Rico.

Luisa Capetillo's parents were rebels themselves. Her mother, Margarita Perón, had come to Arecibo, Puerto Rico, from France as a governess. Her father, Luis Capetillo Echevarría, was a Basque steeped in that province's tradition of rebellion. Although his family was more than comfortable financially, Luis identified strongly with the island's workers and always supported himself through menial labor. Both Margarita and Luis were proud adherents to the idealistic revolutionary tradition of the great Romantic Jean-Jacques Rousseau, which had inspired the democratic uprisings throughout Europe in 1848. To these youthful romantics, the French author George Sand, a woman who dressed as a man and lived a daringly unconventional life, was the model of the "new woman"; she epitomized individuality liberated from the yoke of political and moral absolutism. This strain of romantic anarchism, which Luisa Capetillo inherited, was intensely moral. It attacked social and religious conventions as hypocrisy; it perceived itself as responding to a higher moral standard.

Margarita and Luis, true to their belief that the state had no authority to sanction their relationship, never married. They were intensely devoted to each other and to Luisa, their only child. They taught her both Spanish and French and guided her education at home with great care. Luisa read the works of the great humanist authors Victor Hugo, Leo Tolstoy, Ivan Turgenev, and Emile Zola; she studied the political philosophy of John Stuart Mill and the anarchism of Peter Kropotkin. Although the child briefly attended a private girls' school in Arecibo, her real education was utterly different from whatever standard curriculum was offered to her there. Luisa was especially influenced by her mother's example of living her daily life in harmony with her professed beliefs. Margarita was a moral inspiration to Luisa, who dedicated her most important feminist thesis to her mother.

Margarita Perón, refusing on principle to accept support form her lover, worked as a laundress. Her daughter worked with her and helped deliver freshly ironed garments to the wealthy homes of Arecibo. In one such home Luisa met Manuel Ledesma, the heir of one of Arecibo's leading political figures; in 1897 they become lovers. Two children, Manuela and Gregorio, were born to Capetillo during the three years this relationship lasted. Despite their great affection, Capetillo felt stifled and limited by Ledesma's insistence on a totally domestic, obedient role for her. In severing her affair with Ledesma, Capetillo learned firsthand the cost of maintaining her individuality and personhood. Ledesma himself may have learned to respect Capetillo in unanticipated ways: he generously aided Margarita, who raised the two children when Capetillo began her labor organizing career.

After their break-up, Capetillo refused for years to accept any funds from Ledesma. To support her family she began writing articles on socialism for Arecibo newspapers; in addition, she worked as a reader in a tobacco processing plant in Arecibo. In a loud, dramatic voice, she read local and foreign newspapers to the workers. She also read the works of Hugo, Balzac, Flaubert, Dumas, Dostoevsky, and Tolstoy; revolutionary political theorists; and contraband anarchist magazines smuggled in from Cuba. The largely illiterate workers were thus exposed to the great liberal thinkers of the West; they memorized whole passages and came together after work in study groups to discuss various aspects of the theories they had heard. Especially among skilled artisans like the type-setters and cigar-makers, the study groups evolved into sophisticated sessions on labor rights and organizing skills; many major labor leaders were shaped within these groups.

Capetillo was becoming part of the labor world at a tumultuous point in Puerto Rican history. In late 1897, frightened by a recent Cuban rebellion and by the threat of war with the United States, Spain grudgingly granted limited autonomy to Puerto Rico. Organizing the island to deal with the political and civil rights of Spanish citizens took months, while Spain's crisis with the United States deepened. Finally, on July 17, 1898, the first elected Puerto Rican legislature convened; one week later, American troops landed on the island.

Separatists in Puerto Rico had argued for independence from Spain, not the kind of servile status they saw in limited autonomy. To the separatists, the Americans seemed at first like deliverers, marching triumphantly to help remove the last vestiges of Spanish oppression. But the United States was adjusting to its own new imperial status, acquired with the annexation of Hawaii in 1895 and the seizure of the Philippines, Cuba, and Puerto Rico as prizes of the Spanish-American War. American politicians subscribed wholeheartedly to blatantly racist assumptions to justify their new position. On a practical level, the new imperial holdings necessitated a strong American presence to protect vital coal stations in the Caribbean and to control access to the Isthmus of Panama, where long-range plans for a canal were already focused. By 1900, it was obvious that the United States had no intention of facilitating Puerto Rican independence.

American business and the politicians it elected saw Puerto Rico as an investment opportunity, a convenient resource to be exploited. The island's population in 1898 was roughly one million, a turbulent mixture of Spanish, African, and Indian cultures. Coffee was the major crop, representing three times the value of sugar or tobacco. The massive influx of American capital shattered the paternalism of the old Spanish agricultural system and shifted the economic emphasis toward sugar. The consequences for Puerto Rican laborers were catastrophic. The old *patrón* system had allowed small subsistence plots on which agricultural workers could grow their own beans, corn, and rice; the new reliance on sugar eliminated these individual plots. Staple food production fell, forcing workers to buy imported food at high prices. Sugar was a high-profit, low-wage industry; as poorly paid rural workers were no longer able to feed their families, they flocked to cities like San Juan, Rio Piedras, and Arecibo, spawning extensive urban slums for the first time in the island's history. When Samuel Gompers, president of the American Federation of Labor, visited Puerto Rico in 1903, he found widespread devastation and despair. "I have never seen so many Human Beings showing so clearly the signs of malnutrition, nor so many women and children with the marks of hunger in their faces," he reported," . . . the conditions existent in Puerto Rico today reflect no honor or credit upon our country" (People's Press, 44).

The economic circumstances were ripe for the development of a real labor movement. There had been some labor agitation even before the American takeover. Local radicals had been galvanized by the arrival in 1897 of Santiago Iglesias, a young Spanish anarchist; Iglesias, who had fled Spain in 1888, had been forced out of Cuba. A charismatic speaker, Iglesias was organized and methodical as well. His success in gathering radicals and labor leaders to him led the Spanish authorities to imprison him. Literally liberated by the Americans, Iglesias guided the Puerto Rican labor movement into close ties with the American Socialist Party. In 1899 Puerto Rican workers founded the Free Federation of Workers (FLT), which coordinated the efforts of its numerous member unions.

Traditionally, Puerto Rican women had worked as domestics, laundresses, or field laborers. The radical changes in the economy drew them into the rapidly expanding tobacco industry, most often in the lowest-paying jobs like leaf-stripping. Their wages were frequently three to four times lower than men's wages; the injustices they endured in industry and their already heavy domestic responsibilities elicited a new spirit of anger and defiance among many women. From the beginning, women were deeply involved in strikes and protests; they gave themselves wholeheartedly to the nascent labor movement, and they expected support and comradeship from their men. "If you volunteer to organize the working man, why not do the same for working women?" demanded one woman in 1904," . . . it is your support which is necessary to help so many deprived women to unite and defend themselves from the exploitation to which they have been subjected" (Hernandez, 32).

Capetillo worked with the FLT contacting tobacco workers throughout the Caribbean. In 1905 she participated as a journalist in the first massive strike organized by the Federation in Arecibo. "I presented myself as a propagandist, journalist, and writer," she recalled, "with no more authorization than my own calling and initiative, with no more than my own recommendation, no more aid than my own effort" (Valle Ferrer, *Luisa Capetillo*, 62). The passion and vigor of her news articles on the strike brought her great prominence and attention; she was quickly recognized as a major force within the movement. From that point on, she dedicated her life to two goals: educating workers and women in the philosophy of anarchosyndicalism; and encouraging them to organize and better their lives through shared strength.

In 1907 Capetillo published her first book, *Ensayos libertarios* (Libertarian Essays), expanding on her thoughts on a just and equal society. Like her beloved mother and like Tolstoy, Capetillo saw anarchism as a way of life, as an individual's living testament of faith in the future. Her anarchism was nourished by a profound confidence in the basic goodness of human nature: human beings, once freed from the corrupting tyranny of organized religion and government, would revert to a natural condition of gentleness, cooperation, and love. Universal brotherhood would be the foundation of all happiness; egalitarian Christian love would flourish. As an anarchist, Capetillo anticipated the collapse of all artificial forms of control and regulation: the Church, government, the police, the court and penitentiary system. When all exploitation ceased and each human being's basic needs were met, there would be no need for any external constraints.

As a syndicalist, Capetillo expected that workers' organizations would provide whatever stability of production and distribution of goods and food necessary in a truly egalitarian, moral society. Syndicalism, the reliance on workers' control through unions (*syndicat* in French), was an elaboration of the frequently violent, nihilistic anarchism of exiled Russian radicals. It was an international, largely spontaneous movement that ignored conventional parliamentary politics and hoped to invest all authority in a federalized order of local trade organizations. Wherever a socialist political thread existed in the late 19th century, syndicalism quickly braided itself into the growing labor movement. A syndicalist general strike on May Day in 1890 paralyzed cities and mines throughout France, northern Italy, Belgium, Sweden, Poland, Portugal, and even England; over 100,000 supporters demonstrated peacefully in London. In America, syndicalism was the guiding philosophy of the Industrial Workers of the World, the "Wobblies," founded in 1905. The intentions of the syndicalist movement were most succinctly expressed by the French representatives at an international syndicalist conference in Amsterdam in 1907:

> The workers' union is not just an instrument of combat, it is the living germ of the future society, and the society of the future will be what we

have made of the *sindicat.* . . . Syndicalism does not waste time promising the workers a paradise on earth, it calls on them to conquer it and assures them that their action will never be wholly in vain (Lichtheim, 222).

Capetillo's public positions were frequently unpopular. She opposed independence for Puerto Rico, believing that the true ideal was no government at all, and that the leaders of the Unionist Party were as guilty as the Americans of exploiting the workers. Nationalism and patriotism are easy to distort and difficult to oppose, but Capetillo would not compromise. "My homeland is Liberty," she wrote in 1913. "My motto, Truth. My hope, universal brotherhood" (Valle Ferrer, *Capetillo*, 84).

Similarly, Capetillo's unflinching anticlericalism was dangerous in a culture descended from the Inquisition and the mass burnings of the *auto da fe.* Capetillo blamed the Church and its priests for perpetuating ignorance and fear, and for collaborating with the parasitic ruling classes in the exploitation of the poor. She held the Church responsible for the subjugation and incomplete lives of so many women. Unlike many other anarchists, Capetillo was deeply spiritual and sought to foster a radical, transcendent Christianity without Church control. "The only thing that I want and hope for you," she wrote to her young daughter, "is that you be a good human being, not a Christian of routine, no. One interprets the maxims of Jesus without hearing mass, without confession, without receiving communion, without accepting any kind of dogma or lies of the materialistic religions" (Valle Ferrer, *Capetillo*, 50).

Capetillo's vision of a loving, harmonious, egalitarian society demanded the emancipation of women. The first step, she insisted, was to offer women the full range of educational opportunities. In traditional Puerto Rican culture, even middle-class and wealthy women were relatively uneducated. The first United States census of the island in 1899 indicated only 1,387 women with more than a primary school education; even the educated elite women tended to stay at home and not to make practical use of their training. Within the liberal community, women's education was one issue that united various reform factions across class divisions.

But Capetillo's definition of meaningful education for women was exponentially more radical and advanced than that of her bourgeois sisters. She insisted on a full, rigorous academic program for girls, including all branches of science and mathematics. More controversially, she called for demanding training in physical education, believing that girls' sense of self-esteem and competence depended in large part on their mastery of their bodies. In the same vein, Capetillo advocated a thorough education for all women in sexuality and contraceptive techniques. She believed such knowledge represented another facet of the self-determination to which women, as independent beings, were entitled. It is no coincidence that another leading female anarchist, Emma Goldman, was also a passionate advocate for birth control. In an era in which many physicians, clergymen, and authors denied that women had any sexuality whatsoever, women like Luisa Capetillo seemed to threaten the very foundations of society.

In her determination to achieve a life pattern closer to the nature idealized by anarchism, Capetillo became a vegetarian and set stiff standards for personal hygiene. Even this position brought her notoriety. When Ledesma put their daughter, Manuela, in a traditional convent school, the nuns regarded Capetillo as a dangerous subversive and censored her letters to her daughter. In the convent only two baths were permitted each week, and the girls were required to wear a muslin shift even while bathing; Capetillo's suggestions to Manuela that she bathe every day, totally unclothed, were treated as "obscenities."

In 1911 Capetillo produced both a second son and her third book. The son, Luis, was born of a brief, unhappy affair in Arecibo; he was closer to her than the older children, and grew to share her principles and faith. He became an active participant in the ongoing labor struggle on the island. The book, *Mi Opinión sobre las Libertades, Derechos y Deberes de la Mujer como Compañera, Madre y Ser Independiente* (My Opinion on the Freedom, Rights, and Duties of the Woman as Companion, Mother, and Independent Being), was the first feminist manifesto published in Puerto Rico. Elaborating on her own experiences, Capetillo described how the traditional social systems perpetuated the ignorance and enslavement of women. She expanded on her educational program for girls, and she discussed at length her concept of "free love."

Free love—the right to form emotional and sexual contracts without the sanction of the state or church—was a logical extension of anarchism's condemnation of all external controls. It was an aspect of anarchism that simultaneously titillated and horrified Victorian society; it was subject to deliberate misunderstanding, abuse, and outright ridicule. Capetillo would accept no double standard of sexual behavior, but she did not endorse promiscuity and sexual exploitation. She called on people to accept total responsibility for their own conduct:

> Acquire habits that are good for yourself and your fellow men, and the rest will be added. The logical consequence of drinking too much is drunkenness; he who curses another curses himself. Don't be fooled: everything comes out of ourselves; we are free to the extent that justice is in us (Capetillo, "Memories of the Free Federation," 46).

Her vision was of competent, independent men and women who entered sharing, mutually respectful relationships based on love alone; when the relationship was no longer mutually satisfying, either partner was entitled to sever the connection. To Capetillo, an economically dependent married woman was little more than a legally sanctioned prostitute.

The movement for women's rights in Puerto Rico split along deep class divisions. Spokeswomen from the middle-class, educated elite supported improved educational opportunities for women, but their major focus was on suffrage for literate women like themselves. Proletarian women's advocates like Luisa Capetillo understood the crushing daily burdens of poor women. Capetillo fought passionately for educational rights and for *universal* suffrage, regardless of literacy, but she never lost sight of the larger economic and social context in which inequities crippled poor men as well as poor women. Her first struggle was always for economic justice. Capetillo took no part when middle-class feminists formed the Puerto Rican Feminist League in 1917; she was busy organizing a strike of agricultural workers. Nonetheless, Capetillo deserves recognition for her role in articulating the demand for suffrage. In 1908 she brought the issue before the Fifth Congress of the FLT. Years later, a union leader recalled, "Women's suffrage was formally discussed, and, at the Congress, the first real suffragist Puerto Rico has ever had, Luisa Capetillo, became a prominent figure, but she never received any credit for this" (Valle Ferrer, "Feminism and its Influence," 40).

In 1912 Capetillo moved to New York City. She lived among the Hispanic tobacco workers, writing for anarchist newspapers and organizing meetings and study groups. Over the next several years she lived with tobacco workers in Tampa, Florida, and in Cuba. In Havana Capetillo was arrested for wearing trousers in public; once again, she was following her anarchist principles in her daily life: trousers were more efficient and comfortable to her, and she would not accept the authority of the state to limit her choice of attire. For her defiance as well as for her support of an explosive strike among Cuban cannery workers, the president of Cuba ordered her deported as a dangerous radical.

In 1918 Capetillo directed a major farm workers' strike in eastern Puerto Rico, which brought out over thirty thousand laborers and enraged the United States government. As America reacted hysterically to the Russian Revolution and the presence of an actual Bolshevik government, radicals of all varieties endured a wave of brutal repression. Capetillo was arrested, roughly handled by police, and subjected to deliberate mistreatment while in jail. Her bail, set at $400, was unusually high for the time.

For several years Capetillo commuted between New York City and Puerto Rico. She opened a vegetarian restaurant in New York, which became a magnet for socialist discussion groups. Characteristically, she was more concerned with supporting the assembled anarchists than with making money; she would frequently feed without charge the impassioned reformers gathered around her.

When writing and organizing in Puerto Rico, Capetillo lived in a half-finished shack in the slums of Rio Piedras. There, enduring the same wretched circumstances as the people she sought to help, she contracted tuberculosis. On April 10, 1922, her eleven-year-old son Luis brought her to the municipal hospital in Rio Piedras; she died there a few hours later, at the age of forty-two.

Luisa Capetillo nurtured a vision of the future grounded in mutuality, love, and trust. Her steadfast adherence to the integrity of her faith frequently brought her condemnation, loss, and disrespect. She dedicated her life to strengthening the poorest and most abused members of her society; in addition to her practical aid in strikes and protests, she offered them her glowing vision of what the future could be. Perhaps her greatest gift was her ability to present the ethical anarchist ideal to illiterate peasants without condescending to them. "I am a socialist because I want all the advances, discoveries and inventions to belong to everyone, and that socialization be established without privileges," she wrote.

> Socialism is not a negation, nor a violence, nor a utopia. It is a real and tangible truth. . . . Socialism persuades with truth and does not offend. Pure reason, harmony among all, gentleness of character—these belong. . . . Let us instruct ourselves to purify ourselves, educate our will to do good; and let reason consume the fire of the passions—a holocaust for the freeing of mankind and the pursuit of spiritual progress (Capetillo, "Memories of the Free Federation," 50).

Controversial in her own time and terribly neglected in the present, Capetillo was the first major woman leader in the Puerto Rican labor movement. A friend and fellow FLT member remembered her as one of "the apostles and leaders of humanity's grand causes" (Valle Ferrer, *Capetillo*, 96).

References

Acosta-Belén, Edna. "Women in Twentieth Century Puerto Rico." In Adalberto López, ed., *The Puerto Ricans: Their History, Culture, and Society*. Rochester, VT: Schenkman Books, Inc., 1980.

Capetillo, Luisa. "Memories of the Free Federation"[1911]. In Angel Quintero-Rivera, ed., *Workers' Struggle in Puerto Rico: A Documentary History*. New York: Monthly Review Press, 1976.

———. *Mi Opinión sobre las Libertades, Derechos y Deberes de la Mujer como Compañera, Madre y Ser Independiente*. San Juan: The Times Publishing Co., 1911.

Carrión, Arturo Morales. *Puerto Rico: A Political and Cultural History*. New York: W. W. Norton Co., 1983.

Hernandez, Isabel. "The History of Women's Struggle for Equality in Puerto

Rico." In Edna Acosta-Belén, ed., *The Puerto Rican Woman*. New York: Praeger Publishers, 1979.

Lichtheim, George. *A Short History of Socialism*. New York: Praeger Publishers, 1970.

People's Press Puerto Rico Project. *Puerto Rico: The Flame of Resistance*. San Francisco: People's Press, 1977.

Quintero Rivera, Angel. "Socialist and Cigar Maker: The Artisans' Proletarianization in the Making of the Puerto Rican Working Class." *Latin American Perspectives* 10, 2 & 3(Spring–Summer, 1983): 19–38.

Valle Ferrer, Norma. "Feminism and its Influence on Women's Organizations in Puerto Rico." In Edna Acosta-Belén, ed., *The Puerto Rican Woman*. New York: Praeger Publishers, 1979.

———. *Luisa Capetillo: Historia de Una Mujer Proscrita* (Luisa Capetillo: History of an Exiled Woman). Rio Piedras, P. R.: Editorial Cultural, 1990.

EDWARD COLES

(December 15, 1786–July 7, 1868)

Abolitionist, Human Rights Advocate

*In his first draft of the Declaration of Independence, Thomas
Jefferson stated that "all men are created equal and independent." In the face of that acknowledgment, the existence, continuation, and expansion of chattel slavery represent the
central paradox of American history. Jefferson himself struggled unsuccessfully throughout his life to deal with the Declaration's implications. Edward Coles, born into the same
world of power and privilege as Jefferson, confronted the di-
lemma and reached a conclusion radically different from Jefferson's. Coles's solution to the conundrum of the moral
slaveholder reveals a conscience of heroic integrity, a compassion grounded in justice, a brutally honest mind that foresaw
the inevitability of the Civil War fifty years before the event.*

Edward Coles
Courtesy of the Illinois State Historical Library.

Edward Coles was the youngest son of Colonel John Coles, who was a cousin of Patrick Henry and one of the most prosperous of the Virginia aristocracy. Coles was brought up to assume his rightful place in a gracious, cultured, powerful society. But his excellent education, combined with a native integrity, forced him to look at his society in the light of unforgiving logic. Years later, Coles related how his life-long commitment to emancipation began in a political science class at the College of William and Mary, taught by Episcopal bishop James Madison. When the discussion focused on natural rights, Coles confronted his teacher: "I asked him . . . if this be true how can you hold a slave—how can man be made the property of man? He frankly admitted it could not be justified on principle, and could only be tolerated in our Country, by our finding it in existance [sic], and the difficulty of getting rid of it." But Coles would not accept the rationalizations:

Was it right to do what we believed to be wrong, because our forefathers did it? They may have thought they were doing right, and their conduct may have been consistent with their ideas of propriety. Far different is the character of our conduct, if we believe we do wrong to do what our forefathers did. As to the difficulty of getting rid of our slaves, we could get rid of them with much less difficulty than we did the King of our forefathers. Such inconsistency on our part, and such injustice to our fellow man, should not be tolerated because it would be inconvenient or difficult to terminate . . . nor ought a man attempt to excuse himself for doing what he believed wrong, because other men thought it right. . . . [I] contended that if the people of the State, forming a social compact, neglected to do their duty, and tolerated a state of things which was in direct violation of their great fundamental doctrines, I could not reconcile it to my conscience and sense of propriety to participate in it; . . . I could not consent to hold as property what I had no right to, and which was not, and could not be property, according to my understanding of the rights and duties of man— and therefore determined that I would not and could not hold my fellow man as a Slave (Coles ms., dated 1844, Historical Society of Pennsylvania).

Thus, before he was twenty years old, Coles's position on slavery was fully articulated; he never wavered from it.

In 1807 Coles returned home from college without revealing his decision to anyone; he was afraid that in response his father might leave him no slaves at all. Shortly after Coles's twenty-first birthday, his father died, and Edward's share of the estate included twenty slaves. His brothers and sisters were appalled by his emancipationist intentions, and they tried to dissuade him by pointing out the hardship that manumission represented for slaves in Virginia; ironically, while insisting that slaves were utterly property and no different from other property, most slave-holding states interfered with the property rights of slaveowners by severely restricting the right to free one's slaves. In Virginia the law required all freed slaves to leave the state within one year of emancipation. In response, Coles made the momentous and painful decision to leave his family and home and to move his entire estate to a free state.

Before he had gone beyond the preliminary planning for this move, events swept him into a very different world. An older brother, Isaac, had been private secretary to Thomas Jefferson during the last years of his presidency, and a first cousin, Dolley Payne, had married James Madison. When Madison became president in 1809, he invited young Edward Coles to serve as his private secretary. Coles served in Washington during the tense years of the War of 1812, as the United States was caught in the worldwide upheavals of Napoleonic confrontation. Even in the midst of this charged atmosphere, his concern for the long-range consequences of slavery never diminished. Years later, he recalled passionate debates with Madison over slavery, and "my surprise that just men, and long sighted politicians, should not, as well in reference to the acknowledged rights of man as to the true and permanent interest of their Country, take the necessary steps to put in train its termination" (Coles ms.).

In the summer of 1814 Coles corresponded with the elderly Thomas Jefferson, hailing Jefferson as the beacon of liberty and urging him to speak out and inspire a new generation to give up the addiction to slavery. Coles considered this a special "duty" for Jefferson, whose articulation of the universality of liberty had ennobled the Revolutionary cause. Coles added that his own repugnance toward slavery was so great that he had decided to leave his home state and all his family and friends. Jefferson's response urged Coles to stay in Virginia and to stir public opinion against slavery through conversation; he argued that he was too old for the great task, and expressed his usual doubts about the possibility of either real independence for slaves or peaceful racial relations in a mixed society.

Disillusioned, Coles proceeded with his own plans. When news of the Treaty of Ghent reached Washington in February of 1815, Coles felt free to resign his position; he promptly set out on a long journey throughout the northwest states to find a suitable site for relocation. He settled on a tract in southern Illinois near the town of Edwardsville, sold his Virginia estate to his brothers, and prepared to draw up manumission papers for all his slaves.

Before he could complete all the necessary arrangements, he was summoned urgently to Washington over a crisis developing in American-Russian relations, caused largely by an insensitive and incompetent ambassador. Reluctantly, Coles accepted the mission of hurrying to St.

Petersburg to soothe an angry Czar Alexander I and to prevent further damage. Three months in Russia gave Coles the opportunity to observe Russian serfdom and to compare it to American slavery. "I found it of an essentially different form of servitude to that of our Negroes," he wrote, "and infinitely of a milder and less oppressive character."

After a leisurely and luxurious return journey, which included long stays in Paris and London, Coles arrived home in the summer of 1817. He made final arrangements for the transfer of his Virginia properties, visited with Jefferson and Madison, spent last days with his large, affectionate, and no doubt thoroughly bewildered family. Then he turned his back on everything he had ever known, on the proud and respected life he had been raised to accept, and set off on his great living experiment in liberty.

When Coles sent his slaves off toward Illinois in the spring of 1819, under the guidance of his trusted mulatto servant Ralph Crawford, they had no idea what his plans for them entailed. They went obediently, as slaves, trustingly, as slaves who had always been well treated. Many of Coles's friends laughed at him for trusting the slave Crawford to lead the expedition. Coles had no such doubts: "I am happy to be able to add, he falsified all their predictions, and conducted the party with as much judgment and economy as anyone, even one of the glorious Saxon race could have done."

Coles followed on horseback and joined them in western Pennsylvania, where he bought several flatboats to complete the journey on the Ohio River. Finally, one beautiful morning when all of spring offered "a scene both conducive to and in harmony with the finest feelings of our nature," Coles called all his slaves together to announce their freedom to them. He handed each person a certificate of freedom, and awarded each head of a family a quarter section (160 acres) of his own land in Illinois, to help them support and sustain themselves. He reminded them that their conduct and success in this endeavor mattered

> not only for their own sakes, but for the sake of the black race held in bondage; many of whom were thus held, because their masters believed they were incompetent to take care of themselves, and that liberty would be to them a curse rather than a blessing. My anxious wish was that they should so conduct themselves, as to show by their example, that the descendants of Africa were competent to take care of and govern themselves, and enjoy all the blessings of liberty, and all the other birthrights of man; and thus promote the universal emancipation of that unfortunate and outraged race of the human family (Washburne, 51).

Clearly, this entire program was for Coles far more than a personal gesture, however necessary that may have been for his own conscience; he hoped in addition to offer proof of the full competence and capacity for self-direction of freed blacks, and thus to destroy apologists' arguments of racial inferiority. Discovering that the state of Illinois also required documents of emancipation, Coles issued these new forms as soon as the party reached Edwardsville (appropriately enough, on the Fourth of July), declaring: "Not believing that man can have of right a property in his fellow man, but on the contrary, that all mankind were endowed by nature with equal rights, I do therefore, by these presents restore to (name of former slave) that inalienable liberty of which he has been deprived" (Washburne, 53).

Coles and his former slaves settled successfully on their new farms outside Edwardsville; he reported proudly years later that, despite the enormous prejudice against free blacks, not one of his freed slaves had ever been in difficulty with the law. Coles himself was appointed registrar of the Land Office in Edwardsville by President Monroe, a position that proved a good starting point for a political career.

Coles's political life in Illinois was, as one might expect, impassioned, spectacular, unconventional, and brief. He arrived and rose to prominence during a pivotal, turbulent time in Illinois history. Originally, Illinois had been a slaveholding territory of the state of Virginia; Virginia ceded the territory to the United States in 1784, with the stipulation that residents who had been citizens of Virginia should have all their titles and possessions (including slaves) honored and confirmed. The Northwest Ordinance of 1787 provided that there be no slavery in the new territories, and states admitted to the Union from the Northwest Territories were required to have antislavery constitutions. But Illinois slaveowners argued that the 1784 deed of cession took precedence over the Northwest Ordinance; although Illinois had indeed entered the Union without slavery, they argued that nothing forbade them from amending the state constitution after admission. Many Illinois settlers were former Kentuckians, and proslavery sentiment ran high throughout the more populous southern half of the state. In 1822 Coles was one of four candidates for the governorship; the other three candidates enjoyed varying degrees of support from the proslavery forces, while Coles was the only antislavery man in the race. By a stunningly narrow margin of fifty votes, Coles won the election. His inaugural speech commented glowingly on the agricultural and commercial potential of the state, but most of it was a fiery exhortation to the state legislature to outlaw slavery fully as required by the 1787 ordinance and to establish better laws to protect free blacks from the horror of kidnapping into slavery.

The battle lines were clearly drawn. Both houses of the state legislature had proslavery majorities, and the goal was set of calling for a convention to amend the state constitution. Through complex maneuvering and deliberate misreadings of the procedural requirements, the proslavery men were able to call for a state-wide referendum on the convention. Coles became the natural leader of the antislavery forces, bringing to this fight the same utterly blunt recognition of long-term consequences that had always marked his moral vision. The rhetoric of the movement bears his stamp:

> In the name of unborn millions who will rise up after us, and call us blessed or accursed for our deeds—in the name of the injured sons of Africa, whose claims to equal rights with their fellow men will plead their own case against their usurpers before the tribunal of eternal justice, we conjure you, fellow citizens, TO PONDER UPON THESE THINGS (Washburne, 68).

However much an idealist Coles might appear, his approach was grounded in a practical appeal to people's enlightened self-interest: He gathered data from across the country on the practical effects of slavery on land prices, costs of produce, and the living standards of non-slaveowners; he analyzed these data to demonstrate the superiority of free over slave labor. (He was aided in this massive research project by Roberts Vaux, a Quaker judge and leading member of the Philadelphia Abolition Society; recognizing the animosity at the time toward Quakers and their prominent role in abolitionism, Vaux urged Coles not to publicize any contact with him or other Quakers.) During the campaign, Coles spent his entire salary and a great deal of his own money trying to reach the citizens of Illinois. Somehow, despite the far greater expenditure and very modern "dirty tricks" of the proslavery men, the referendum in August, 1824 resulted in an overwhelming defeat for the convention. In truth, it was a known assumption that the convention was to have been called strictly to pass a proslavery amendment to the constitution; in effect, the massive defeat of the convention assured Illinois's future among the free states.

This bitter fight cost Coles his political future and much more. In retaliation for his role in their defeat, proslavery men filed suit against Coles for having "illegally" freed his slaves. (A new state law, not yet publicized when Coles and his former slaves entered the state, required Illinois state documentation for all freed slaves. Unaware of the law, Coles failed to apply for the necessary documentation for his former slaves.) The suit entailed fines of $200 for each slave Coles had freed; the case was argued before a proslavery judge who refused to let any witnesses testify for the defense, disallowed all evidence Coles submitted, and fined him over $2,000. Coles appealed, and the case dragged through the courts until 1827, when the State Supreme Court finally overturned the original decision.

Coles's intelligence and energy were focused on many issues beyond the constitutional crisis. He was an effective, far-sighted governor. He supported public education, an organized agricultural policy, lower prices for public land sales, and such long-range improvements as an Illinois-to-Michigan canal. He never lost sight of the monstrous slavery issue; he warned always that the system degraded the oppressor as well as the oppressed, and that in the absence of a peaceful resolution, armed conflict was inevitable. In 1826 Coles's brother-in-law, John Rutherfoord, was elected to the Virginia state legislature. Coles urged him to speak out quickly and forcefully for gradual emancipation:

> The policy of Virginia for some years past has been most unfortunate. So far from acting as if Slavery were an evil which ought to be gotten rid of, every measure which could be taken has been taken to perpetuate it, as if it were a blessing. Her political pilots have acted like the inexperienced navigator, who, to get rid of the slight inconvenience of the safety-valves, have [sic] hermetically sealed them, not foreseeing that the inevitable consequence will be the bursting of the boiler, and dreadful havoc among all on board (Washburne, 226).

Coles did not seek a second term as governor. He did run for Congress in 1832, but was defeated in a wave of Jacksonian reaction against wealthy, highly educated public figures. Coles left Illinois permanently and settled in Philadelphia, where he lived a quiet, scholarly life; he presented several papers at historical societies and maintained a voluminous correspondence. He married in 1833 and fathered two sons and a daughter. In 1868, well into a relatively peaceful old age, Coles died. In a painful example of the heartless ironies of history, his younger son (Roberts, named for Roberts Vaux), committed to the Confederacy, was killed in the Civil War his father had foreseen so clearly and tried so hard to prevent.

References

Dictionary of American Biography. New York: Charles Scribner's, 1957.

Ketcham, Ralph. "The Dictates of Conscience: Edward Coles and Slavery." *Virginia Quarterly Review* 36 (Winter, 1960): 46–62.

"Letters of Governor Coles on the Struggle of Slavery and Freedom in Illinois." *Journal of Negro History* 3 (1918): 158 ff.

Washburne, E. B. *Sketch of Edward Coles.* Chicago: Jansen, McClurg & Co., 1882.

ANNA JULIA COOPER

(August 10, 1859[?]–February 27, 1964)

Educator, Women's Rights Advocate

Throughout a life that stretched from slavery into the civil rights movement, Anna Julia Cooper championed the right of all peoples to dignity, education, and respect. As an educated, competent, independent woman, she faced the double challenge of being African American and female in a society that was profoundly, proudly racist and sexist; with confidence and elegance, she defied that society's assumptions about her. Her life was dedicated to the education of all her people but especially to nurturing the minds of black girls. Through her activist adherence to her ideals, she provided an example of individual excellence rendered incandescent by service to the human community.

Anna Julia Cooper
Courtesy, Oberlin College Archives.

Anna Julia Cooper herself was the product of the sort of exploitative power-based relationship that stigmatized the black woman so severely: her mother was Hannah Stanley, a slave in Raleigh, North Carolina; her father was most probably Hannah's master, Dr. Fabius Haywood. Anna Haywood's mother, whom she idealized, never talked about her father. As an adult, Anna wrote of him, "I owe nothing to my white father beyond the initial act of procreation" (Hutchinson, 187). Cooper credited her mother with great strength and determination; she attributed to Hannah her fierce pride and willingness to sacrifice herself for a principle.

The Emancipation Proclamation of January 1, 1863, freed Anna and her family on paper. Nevertheless, an eager and alert black population in Raleigh was poised for decisive action. Only a month after the surrender of the Confederacy, the newly free African Americans of North Carolina petitioned President Andrew Johnson to restore their voting rights. They had enjoyed suffrage in North Carolina until 1835, when the state constitution was revised in reaction to Nat Turner's bloody 1831 uprising. In September, 1865, Raleigh hosted the Convention of Colored Citizens of North Carolina, a gathering of over five hundred delegates from across the state determined to demand full citizenship, including the right to vote, testify, and serve on juries. For a bright, eager child, Raleigh was an exciting, provocative place to live.

In 1868 the Episcopal Church opened St. Augustine's Normal School in Raleigh to train African Americans as teachers. Ten-year-old Anna Haywood entered St. Augustine's on a full scholarship; she would remain at the school in a variety of capacities for almost fourteen years. Anna was obviously intelligent and thirsty for learning; at the age of fifteen she was already teaching classes of younger children. In 1874, when she received special permission to attend the Greek class offered to theology students, Anna met George Cooper, a West Indian who was studying to become a minister. When she completed her courses at St. Augustine's in 1877, the two were married; they stayed at the school, where both became teachers. Barely two years later George Cooper died suddenly. At the age of twenty-one, Anna Cooper became a widow. In her first grief, she clung to the security of St. Augustine's, where she continued teaching.

Cooper was already educated beyond most women in America, but she wanted more. She applied for admission to Oberlin College in Ohio, the first college in the country to admit women as well as blacks. The town of Oberlin was located near Lake Erie; founded by free thinkers and abolitionists, it had been a major center of Underground Railroad activity. Cooper assured the president of Oberlin that she was adequately prepared for the academic work: in addition to English grammar and literature, algebra, and geometry, she had read Ceasar, Virgil, Sallust, and Cicero in Latin and Xenophon, Plato, Herodotus, and Thucydides in Greek.

Oberlin accepted Cooper with sophomore standing and a full scholarship. A serious, committed student, a widow, and several years older than her classmates, Cooper did not partake much of college social life. She boarded with a Professor Charles Churchill and his family; they welcomed her with warmth and genuine affection. Cooper found the Churchill home stimulating and cultured. She learned from them a life-long habit of generosity and hospitality.

Cooper always intended to return to the classroom. Her faith in the power of education was limitless. "Teaching had always seemed to me the noblest of callings," she wrote years later," and I believe that if I were white I should still want to teach those whose needs present a stronger appeal than money" (Hutchinson, 38). After graduating from Oberlin in 1884, she became head of the department of modern languages and science at Wilberforce College in Xenia, Ohio, named for the dedicated English abolitionist William Wilberforce. Her annual salary of $1,000 was considered excellent at the time, but she accepted substantially lower wages a year later to return to St. Augustine's and be near her mother and family. While teaching mathematics, Latin, and Greek at St. Augustine's, Cooper became active in the North Carolina Teachers' Association, an alliance of black teachers struggling to get state support for the education of black children. In 1887, on the basis of summer courses, Oberlin awarded Cooper a master's degree in mathematics.

That same year, Oberlin recommended Cooper as a teacher for the Washington Colored High School, the only high school in the District of Columbia for black students. The high school had a history of attracting strong teachers, especially among qualified women. Since local law until 1923 required women to leave their teaching posts if they married, the female teachers were by default all single or, like Cooper, widowed. They offered support and strength to each other and devoted their lives to their students. In several different capacities, Cooper would remain at the Colored High School—known as the M Street School—for most of the next forty years. She set high standards for her students, male and female; her own life offered an example of the courageous refusal to compromise.

During her early years at M Street School, Cooper became deeply involved in feminism, especially in the controversy over women's education. Since her own experiences at St. Augustine's, she had criticized the black clergy for failing to encourage the educational hopes of young women and to provide scholarships for them. In 1890 she addressed the American Conference of Educators, a liberal biracial group concerned with improving black education. Preparing her paper, she surveyed

American colleges that admitted black women, and she was appalled by the results. Even the black colleges had only a few women; Oberlin had five, Ann Arbor College (University of Michigan) three, Wellesley three, and Cornell one. Nearly two hundred black women were enrolled in European colleges, where they were more welcome than in the United States.

Cooper's address on higher education for women became part of her first book, *A Voice from the South*, published in 1892. The book was a collection of essays all approaching Cooper's twin passions—feminism and racism—from different angles. Cooper was unsparing, demanding, forceful, and well-armed with the weapons gleaned from a long study of history. She condemned white authors for presuming to understand blacks; she charged that white Southern authors like Joel Chandler Harris "with flippant indifference have performed a few psychological experiments on their cooks and coachmen, and with astounding egotism, and powers of generalization positively bewildering, forthwith aspire to enlighten the world with dissertations on racial traits of the Negro" (Cooper, 186). She was equally critical of black men who failed to understand and support their women:

> while our men seem thoroughly abreast of the times on almost every other subject, when they strike the woman question they drop back into sixteenth century logic. . . . I fear the majority of colored men do not yet think it worth while that women aspire to higher education. . . . The three R's, a little music and a good deal of dancing, a first rate dress-maker and a bottle of magnolia balm, are quite enough generally to render charming any woman possessed of tact and the capacity for worshipping masculinity (Cooper, 75).

Cooper was not exaggerating the extent to which middle-class African American men accepted the ideology of Victorian culture. Mary Church Terrell, a nationally prominent educator and social reformer, had attended Oberlin with her father's support and blessing, but when she decided to work for a living after college, he was enraged: "He disinherited me, refused to write to me for a year because I went to Wilberforce to teach. Further I was ridiculed and told that no man would want to marry a woman who studied higher mathematics. I said I'd take a chance and run the risk" (Giddings, 109).

For Cooper, the women's movement, the "race problem," and even the special situation of black women were all subsumed in the greater cause of seeking justice for all oppressed peoples. Cooper was outraged when prominent white feminist Anna B. Shaw complained that white women received less courtesy than Indians:

Is not woman's cause broader, and deeper, and grander than a bluestock-
ing debate or an aristocratic pink tea? Why should woman become a plain-
tiff in a suit versus the Indian, or the Negro or any other race or class who
have been crushed under the iron heel of Anglo-Saxon power and selfishness? . . . [Women must speak out for all victims of injustice.] Then woman's lesson is taught and woman's cause is won—not the white woman
nor the black woman nor the red woman, but the cause of every man or
woman who has writhed silently under a mighty wrong (Cooper, 123–126).

To Cooper, black women carried a special, exalted mission masked as
a burden. She saw women as the saviors of the race, as the source of
true strength, moral courage, and racial progress. There could be no dignity for the black man while black women were exploited and denigrated: "Only the BLACK WOMAN can say 'when and where I enter,
in the quiet, undisputed dignity of my womanhood, without violence
and without suing or special patronage, then and there the whole *Negro
race enters with me*'" (Cooper, 31).

Ironically, the clearest recognition of this potential for strength and
leadership came from white supremacists, who feared it. Senator Ben
Tillman of South Carolina refused to support women's suffrage because
it would mean that black women could vote, and "Experience has taught
us that negro women are much more aggressive in asserting 'the rights
of the race' than the negro men are." Mississippi Senator J. K. Vardaman
concurred: "The negro woman will be more offensive, more difficult to
handle at the polls than the negro man" (Giddings, 123).

In Cooper's cosmos, every right was grounded in responsibility. The
opportunities she demanded for black girls and boys would provide
them with better tools with which to serve their people. Ultimately, her
proud, demanding feminism offered to black men a stronger comrade in
a partnership struggling to improve the lives of all African Americans.

Throughout the 1890s, Cooper was active in the club movement, the
organizational effort among black women to provide to their communities services and supports that segregated governments denied them.
These women confronted not only devastating needs within their own
communities, but a hostile, demeaning stereotype promulgated by white
popular culture. As one white newspaper commentator wrote in 1902,
"I sometimes hear of a virtuous Negro woman, but the idea is absolutely
inconceivable to me. . . . I cannot imagine such a creature as a virtuous
Negro woman" (Giddings, 82). Even women's rights and service organizations like the YWCA and the Women's Christian Temperance Union
were rigidly segregated; it seemed as if no segment of society was prepared to respect the African American woman. In defiance of such images, educated middle-class black women organized to strengthen each
other and to fight for improved conditions in black neighborhoods. In

1892 Cooper helped form the Colored Women's League of Washington, D.C., with other leading black feminists like Mary Church Terrell and Charlotte Forten Grimké. The League provided a training class for kindergarten teachers, industrial and domestic skills classes, relief work with the poor, and support services for the flood of bewildered rural immigrants lost in the tenements of the city. Cooper helped start the first settlement house for African Americans in Washington, the Colored Social Settlement, of which she was soon appointed supervisor. The Settlement offered free milk distribution for poor babies, day care for the infants of working mothers, a kindergarten, a lending library, a wide range of activities for older children, and an innovative "Big Brother" program in which trusted high school boys mentored younger fatherless boys. Most of these activities replicated existing municipal services supported in part by blacks' taxes but forbidden to them under Jim Crow laws. Anna Cooper was a founder and life member of the Washington Colored Women's YWCA; she started the capital's first chapter of the Camp Fire Girls for black children.

In 1893 Anna Cooper was invited to address the Congress of Representative Women in Chicago; she spoke on "The Needs and Status of the Black Woman," focusing on specifics without losing sight of the transcendent moral goal: "We take our stand on the solidarity of humanity, the oneness of life, and the unnaturalness and injustice of all special favoritism, whether of sex, race, country, or condition" (Hutchinson, 88). Throughout the decade, Cooper traveled and lectured extensively, addressing the first National Conference of Colored Women in 1895, the National Federation of Afro-American Women in 1896, and the first Pan-African Conference in London in 1900. In 1902 she scourged the country's polite hypocrisy before the Friends' General Conference: "A nation cannot long survive the shattering of its own ideals. Its doom is already sounded when it begins to write one law on its walls and lives another in its halls!" (Hutchinson, 115).

Through all this, Cooper continued teaching at the M Street High School. In 1902 she became principal of the school, determined to raise its standards even higher. Her goal was to mold eager students who were ultimately committed to using their knowledge for the benefit of their entire community. Her expectations for her students ran directly counter to the prevailing dogma on African American intelligence and limitations. Late 19th-century social theory was dominated by sociologist Herbert Spencer's misinterpretations of Darwin's evolutionary theories. In Spencer's "Social Darwinism," different races and classes (the two were indistinguishable to many Victorian theorists) competed for survival and dominance. The white Anglo-Saxon Protestant male was tacitly understood as the pinnacle of evolution; the nonwhite races and women of all races were clearly at a lower stage of development, and thus not competent to compete with white men in the industrialized world. African Americans' demands for equal opportunity were dismissed as laughable and inappropriate at best, a threat to divinely appointed white civilization at worst.

In this environment, Booker T. Washington, founder of Tuskegee Institute and chief proponent of "industrial education," offered white society a reassuring image of black aspirations. Washington abandoned any claim to equal rights, insisting that blacks just wanted to be hardworking, clean-living, peaceful, grateful peasants. His concept of industrial education was designed to prepare African Americans to function efficiently in the menial, labor-intensive roles white America permitted them. The Northern industrialists who sponsored most of the philanthropies involved in Southern black education recognized the necessity of maintaining a compliant, inexpensive labor pool; most black schools in the South were forced to accept the framework of industrial education at the expense of academic study.

Anna Cooper understood the real need for industrial education; she knew that the majority of her students could aspire no higher than to a job in the skilled trades. To Anna Cooper, industrial education enabled individuals to earn legitimate wealth, which could provide the leisure time to allow continued intellectual development. She saw no conflict between industrial and classical education, both of which could be utilized for racial uplift; but she refused to limit her school to a Tuskegee-approved curriculum. She was determined to provide the black community with its own lawyers and doctors. White Southern colleges did not accept blacks, and most black Southern colleges were not accredited and in any case were falling in line with the Tuskegee model; of necessity, Cooper encouraged M Street students to apply to Northern colleges, and she worked diligently to find scholarships, grants, and loans for them.

When M Street graduates began receiving scholarships at schools like Harvard, Brown, Oberlin, Yale, Amherst, Dartmouth, Radcliffe, and Williams, the Washington Board of Education took notice. They were furious with Cooper and her embarrassing ability to defy accepted notions of blacks' academic limitations; they determined to remove her from her post. Annette Eaton, an M Street student during the ensuing crisis, recalled that Cooper's real "crime" was the level of academic achievement she expected—and got—from her students: "It was pure heresy to think that a colored child could do what a white child could" (Cooper, xxxiv). The Board of Education charged that Cooper had refused to use a Board-approved textbook; that she was too sympathetic to weak students; that she was unable to maintain tight discipline; that she did not have "proper spirit of unity and loyalty."

Despite resounding support from professional associations and alumni, Cooper was relieved of her principalship in June of 1906. She became a language teacher at Lincoln Institute in Jefferson City, Missouri. Cooper was angry but determined to fight and to give her teaching energies to her new students. In 1909 she wrote in an Oberlin class newsletter, "The dominant forces of our country are not yet tolerant of the higher steps for colored youth; so that while our course of study was for the time being saved, *my head was lost in the fray.*" But her faith in education remained unshaken: "As for me, I stand on the double foundation stone of our Alma Mater—"Labor and Learning" . . . simply, for my people and for all people a man's chance to earn a living not dissociated from man's first and highest prerogative—to live" (Hutchinson, 83).

In 1910 a new school superintendent in Washington invited Cooper back to M Street, not as principal but as a teacher of Latin. Possibly to find an outlet for her frustrated talents, Cooper spent the next three summers studying in Paris at La Guilde Internationale; in 1914, with her French coursework fully credited, she became a doctoral student at Columbia University. Her graduate studies were waylaid by a major family crisis in 1915, when she adopted her brother's five orphaned grandchildren, ranging in age from six months to twelve years. At the age of fifty-six, Cooper was honest and good-humored about her instant family, declaring herself stubborn and foolhardy rather than brave or noble.

While she seemed to cope admirably with the five children and their needs, Cooper's own needs suffered; with five new dependents, she was unable to meet Columbia's one-year residency requirement for the Ph.D. degree. Totally unwilling to accept defeat, Cooper managed to transfer her Columbia credits to the Sorbonne, where another several summers' research enabled her to complete her dissertation. "The Attitude of France on the Question of Slavery Between 1789 and 1848." In the spring of 1925, on her Easter break from teaching, she defended her thesis successfully. At the age of sixty-five, Anna Julia Cooper became the fourth black American woman to receive a Ph.D. Significantly, all three of the other black woman doctorates were also associated with the M Street High School; two were teachers there and one was a graduate.

In 1930 Cooper retired from the M Street School, known since 1916 as Paul Laurence Dunbar High School. Utterly incapable of idleness, she became the president of Frelinghuysen University, a loose conglomerate of assorted adult evening schools for Washington's working black population. Founded in 1906 by a former slave, Frelinghuysen provided religious classes, literacy programs, and various skilled trades classes; its programs were aimed at the city's poorest sector, but Cooper worked fiercely to elicit understanding and financial support from the black middle-class. She was frustrated in this by the Depression. Frelinghuysen spent the 1930s and '40s in a desperate scramble for funds, and a change in standards cost the school its accreditation. Frelinghuysen, as troubled as it was, filled a shameful void in the capital: Of Washington's seven full-time universities, only Howard accepted blacks; of eighty part-time or special training schools, not one enrolled blacks. Cooper was deeply committed to the mission of Frelinghuysen; after the school lost its building during the Depression, she opened her home to its classes, and she willed her property to the school, to be used in some way for the education of African Americans.

Sadly, Cooper's last years were difficult. She had seen her youngest adopted niece, her namesake Annie Cooper Haywood, as a successor, as a protegé who would step in and work for the dreams when Cooper no longer could. But the young woman left school to marry, and died of pneumonia in 1939 at the age of twenty-four. Devastated, Anna Cooper faced the loss of the family continuity and pride she valued so. She retired from the faltering Frelinghuysen in 1942. Cooper continued to study, read, and write well into her retirement; her final publication, in 1951, was a book on the historically prominent family of her dearest friend, Charlotte Forten Grimké. Honored publicly on her one hundredth birthday, Cooper commented quietly, "It isn't what we say about ourselves, it's what our life stands for" (Hutchinson, 175).

In 1964, in her 105th year, Anna Julia Cooper died in her home on T Street in Washington. The list of her accomplishments and achievements is staggering: she helped found major organizations; she shared speakers' platforms with both W.E.B. Du Bois and Booker T. Washington; she inspired generations of students to dream of intellectual excellence, dignity, and stature. By the example of her own life, she taught them that the dreams were worth fighting for, that a life of service, commitment, and self-respect was within their grasp.

References

Cooke, Paul Phillips. "Anna J. Cooper: Educator and Humanitarian." *Negro History Bulletin* 45, 1(January–March, 1982): 5–7.

Cooper, Anna Julia. *A Voice from the South* [1892]. Introduction by Mary Helen Washington. New York: Oxford University Press, in collaboration with the Schomburg Center for Research in Black Culture, 1988.

Giddings, Paula. *When and Where I Enter*. New York: William Morrow, 1984.

Hellerstein, Erna Olafson, et al., eds. *Victorian Women: A Documentary Account of Women's Lives in Nineteenth Century England, France, and the United States*. Stanford, CA: Stanford University Press, 1981.

Hutchinson, Louise Daniel. *Anna J. Cooper: A Voice From the South*. Washington, DC: Smithsonian Institution Press, 1981.

Loewenberg, Bert, and Ruth Bogin, eds. *Black Women in Nineteenth Century American Life: Their Words, Their Thoughts, Their Feelings*. University Park, PA: Penn State University Press, 1976.

Smith, Jessie Carney, ed. *Notable Black American Women*. Detroit: Gale Research, 1993.

Terrell, Mary Church. "History of the High Schools for Negroes in Washington." *Journal of Negro History* 2 (1917): 253–266.

ANGIE DEBO

(January 30, 1890–February 21, 1988)

Historian, Native American Rights Activist

When Angie Debo's family settled in Marshall, Oklahoma Territory, in the fall of 1899, the eastern half of the territory, a vast area of fertile farmland, forests, and untapped mineral resources, was owned by the Five Civilized Tribes—the roughly seventy thousand members of the Creeks, Choctaw, Cherokee, Chickasaw, and Seminole tribes. Within the next twenty years these ancient tribes were forcibly dissolved as legal entities and their members—exploited, robbed, and in many cases murdered for their land—were reduced to humiliating poverty and degradation. Angie Debo became the first historian to document this national shame. Her long, active life was dedicated to scholarly integrity and to correcting the abuses she had revealed. In the course of that life she repeatedly defied massive obstacles, ostracism, and censorship; she profoundly influenced subsequent generations of American historians and directly affected the outcome of court cases and federal hearings. The entire field of Native American studies— and numerous tribes themselves—are in her debt.

Angie Debo
Courtesy, Special Collections and University Archives,
Oklahoma State University Library.

In 1899, nine-year-old Angie Debo arrived by covered wagon in the frontier village of Marshall. Although her parents were largely uneducated and too poor to provide many books for their curious daughter, she received attention and encouragement from a teacher in the one-room school in Marshall. The teacher, Miss Gleason, nurtured Debo's love of reading, lent her books, and urged her parents to buy the child books whenever possible. Later, having justifiably failed the child of a school board member, Gleason was threatened with dismissal and accused of favoring Catholic children. Although she was not actually fired, the incident created so much pain for Gleason that she left the school. Debo was stunned. "I remember saying to my mother and father, 'That wasn't true what was said about Miss Gleason that she was only good to Catholic children. She let me read to her and I'm not a Catholic' " (McIntosh, 165). The child Angie keenly observed both Miss Gleason's adherence to her standards and the price imposed on her by institutional vengefulness. She never forgot either.

At the age of twelve, Debo received her common school diploma. She was eager to go on to high school, but Marshall had none. Frustrated, Debo marked time at home. "There was no library, no magazines, and only the one book our parents managed to buy for each of us children as a Christmas present" (*Angie Debo*, 1). At sixteen Debo took the territorial examination and spent several years teaching in rural schools. In 1910 Marshall was finally able to open a high school. Debo went back to school and graduated with the first class in 1913. She was twenty-three years old.

At the University of Oklahoma, where she enrolled in 1915, Debo studied under one of the major influential figures of her life: historian Edward Everett Dale, a recent Harvard Ph.D. and student of Frederick Jackson Turner. Turner had revolutionized historians' perspective on the role of the frontier in American history, and his protegé Dale passed this new focus on to his student, Debo. In 1918 Debo returned to teaching, saving for graduate school. She received a master's degree in history from the University of Chicago in 1924. As she was completing her degree, thirty colleges and universities contacted the history department at Chicago looking for possible teachers. As Debo recalled, "Twenty-nine of them said they wouldn't take a woman under any circumstances. One of them preferred a man. They would take a woman if they couldn't get a man. One of the thirty. It hit us all pretty hard" (Schrems and Wolff, 187). Debo finally found a position at West Texas State Teachers College, where she taught for about ten years. While there, she entered the doctoral program in history at Oklahoma, working under Dale. Dale urged her to write her dissertation on the Choctaw Indians, using his prestige and authority to give her access to previously unused primary sources like the original Choctaw Council papers. Her dissertation, published in 1934 as *The Rise and Fall of the Choctaw Republic*, won the prestigious John H. Dunning Prize of the American Historical Association and was so praised by reviewers that Debo felt able to risk leaving her teaching job to write and research independently. She went home to Marshall.

In the hopeful afterglow of her well-received first book, Debo decided to expand her investigation of the Indians of Oklahoma to embrace all of the Five Civilized Tribes. "I just thought it would be interesting to find out how the affairs of the Five Civilized Tribes were terminated," she reported years later.

> I didn't know that all of eastern Oklahoma was dominated by a criminal conspiracy to cheat the Indians out of their property and that this corrupted the legislature also. I didn't know those things were so. Nobody had ever written about that history of Oklahoma and when I got into it I couldn't honestly get back out (*Indians, Outlaws*, 5).

What Debo was unearthing, through a scrupulous scouring of tribal records, anthropological reports, and unpublished archival materials, was a massive, deliberate, systematic program that destroyed tribal entities and left individual Indians utterly unprotected from savage white exploitation. The Dawes Act of 1887 was passed largely in reaction to Helen Hunt Jackson's 1881 exposé *A Century of Dishonor*, which chronicled a shabby history of federal violations of tribal treaties. With no understanding or sympathy for the complexities of tribal culture and identity, the Dawes Act stripped tribes of any meaningful legal function and allotted small plots of land to individual Indians; ostensibly, the Indians' title to these 160-acre parcels was supposed to be more protected than their tribal holdings had been. In reality, the tribes were systematically robbed of as much as 90% of their previous reservation acreage; individual plots were assigned in far-flung areas with poor soil and frequently no water; and the Indians themselves were plunged into the morass of white America's legal system with no preparation and no honest guidance.

The first Dawes Commission offices in Oklahoma opened in 1893. Leaders of the Five Civilized Tribes were not impressed with the government's plans for them. They resisted allotment vehemently; in 1898 the Five Tribes met to organize the formation of a separate, all-Indian state. In response, the Curtis Act of that year summarily abolished all tribal government. An underground resistance movement of Indians opposed to allotment, begun among the Creeks, claimed over five thousand Indians by 1905. Enraged by the Indians' rejection of allotment, the federal government, unprovoked, raided the sacred campgrounds where the resisters were living, arrested them, and imposed long prison sentences on outrageous charges.

Allotment and its consequences reduced a proud, interdependent people to a state of confusion, poverty, and despair. In 1906, De Witt Clinton Duncan, a seventy-six-year-old, Dartmouth-educated Cherokee, testified before the Senate on the effects of allotment:

> And I am here today, a poor man upon the verge of starvation—my muscular energy gone, hope gone. I have nothing to charge my calamity to but the unwise legislation of Congress in reference to my Cherokee people. . . . What am I to do? I have a piece of property that doesn't support me, and is not worth a cent to me, under the same inexorable, cruel provisions of the Curtis law that swept away our treaties, our system of nationality, our very existence, and wrested out of our possession our vast territory (Nabokov, 267).

How ironic for the white settlers of Oklahoma, having successfully forced individual allotments on the Five Tribes, to discover shortly thereafter that many of the allotments sat on top of vast reservoirs of oil. Unsophisticated and totally lacking any principled representation, the Indians were defenseless against the feeding frenzy that ensued. As Debo described it,

> The orgy of exploitation that resulted is almost beyond belief. Within a generation these Indians, who had owned and governed a region greater in area and potential wealth than many an American state, were almost stripped of their holdings, and were rescued from starvation only through public charity. . . . It should not be necessary to point out that Oklahomans are no worse than their neighbors, for this is only one episode—although the most dramatic episode—in a process that constitutes an unrecorded chapter in the history of every American frontier. But the reaction of this process upon the ideals and standards of successive frontier communities is a factor in the formation of the American character that should no longer be disregarded by students of social institutions (Debo, *And Still the Waters Run*, x).

Within twenty years of the discover of oil, 80% of Indian allotments was in white hands. Indians were tricked into making their marks on deeds of sale; healthy Indians were declared incompetent and made wards of the state, so that their allotments could be "entrusted" to the management of white guardians. Lists of Indian orphans were sold so that whites could buy their guardianships from the state; in at least several documented cases, Indian parents were murdered so that their orphaned childrens' allotments would be open to trusteeship. By the 1920s, oil had turned Oklahoma into one of the richest states in the country, and many of her leading citizens had made their fortunes on fraudulent allotments. They included Senator Robert L. Owen and Charles Haskell, chairman of the Dawes Commission and later Oklahoma's first governor. Debo was appalled by what she was uncovering, but she was not daunted.

> Those grafters were among the leaders of Oklahoma society in 1934 at the time I wrote this . . . . And so I went ahead and named those prominent people and gave the full story of what they did. . . . When I would write a chapter, I would read it to my mother. She would say, "Nobody will ever publish that book" (*Indians, Outlaws*, 11).

He mother's warning seemed well founded. The completed manuscript, entitled *And Still the Waters Run: The Betrayal of the Five Civilized Tribes*, was submitted to the University of Oklahoma Press in 1936. The director of the fledgling press, Joseph Brandt, was a Rhodes scholar and a man of great integrity. He recognized Debo's book as "one of the most valuable books ever offered to the University Press. . . . There will be some tough problems, I can see, with some of the grafters still living, and if the book passes our readers, I can see that the Wailing Wall of Jerusalem will not have a monopoly on tears" (Schrems and Wolff, 191). One of the readers concurred that "nothing quite so ambitious has been attempted . . . it is a real joy to come across a work of such competence" (ibid., 192). Another reader, a University of Oklahoma law professor, called the book a "masterpiece" and recommended publication, but warned of "certain dangers for the press . . . but these are dangers which inhere whenever one tells the unpleasant truth" (ibid., 192). Ultimately, other voices were raised. The assistant to the president of the university admitted he was afraid of the book and commented in the margin at one point, "This gentleman is a good friend of the University of Oklahoma. Why should we go out of our way to rehash something he no doubt would like for the public to forget?" (ibid., 193). Brandt reacted with outrage to the university president's decision to forbid publication. He insisted that the "obligation to publish is moral. If we fail to publish . . . we have frankly failed to meet a moral issue and with some people in the state we will be as surely damaged as we will be with others if we do publish" (ibid., 194). Nevertheless, the book was rejected by the press. Debo was devastated. She had counted on this book to solidify a reputation well initiated by her first book in 1934. She was no longer teaching and had no reliable source of income. She retreated to her mother's home in Marshall. "This frontier area was so remote from educational institutions and knowledge of such things that I was sort of buried there. The fact that I had done good work didn't count for much. That was a period in which I had plenty to discourage me" (*Indians, Outlaws*, 11).

In 1938, prompted to a great extent by his disgust over the way Debo's manuscript had been handled, Brandt accepted the directorship of the Princeton University Press. One of his first acts was to contact Debo and ask her to submit the manuscript to Princeton. Revision, editing, and concern for libel actions dragged out the processing of the book into 1939. Debo was desperate. She wrote to Brandt that she was "at the end of my financial and spiritual resources. . . . I have spent all my time desperately trying to find something to do—teaching, lecturing, research, *anything*—but I have dropped completely out of the world, and there is no possible way of getting back until I can publish something" (Schrems and Wolff, 202).

In the fall of 1940, Princeton finally published *And Still the Waters Run*. It received favorable scholarly reviews, but was ignored by the academic community in Oklahoma. Coincidentally, the president of the Oklahoma Historical Society, a former governor and federal judge, was himself listed as one of the villains in the book. On the other hand, the Indians were delighted. Sunshine King, director of the Creek Museum, remembered, "We had lots of copies of Angie Debo's book at the tribal library because those books were always checked out. Reading Angie Debo, it was just like at last somebody told the story and there was documentation to back it up" (*Indians, Outlaws*, 14).

Debo continued with her exhaustive research on Native Americans, supporting herself as a substitute high school teacher and, during World War II, as the pastor of her local Methodist church. Finally, in 1947, she was appointed a librarian at Oklahoma State University. She wrote nine books, edited three, and wrote over one hundred articles and book reviews. As a leading expert on Native American history and a woman with a driving sense of justice and responsibility, she was drawn into numerous ongoing battles over Indian rights. She viewed her activism as an inescapable, natural concomitant of her scholarly work. In 1976 she described the process that had led to her lobbying and networking on behalf of the Aleuts and other Alaskan natives struggling to retain title to their lands:

> Although it is fashionable just now to assert that no scholar can be objective, that he slants his findings according to his own bias, I do not admit this. When I start on a research project I have no idea how it will turn out. I simply want to dig out the truth and record it. I am not pro-Indian, or pro-anything, unless it is pro-integrity. But sometimes I find all the truth on one side of an issue.
>
> Once I felt that when this truth was uncovered and made known, my job was done. Later I came to see that after my findings were published I had the same obligation to correct abuses as any other citizen (Debo, "To Establish Justice," 405).

In 1969, at the age of seventy-nine, Angie Debo began actively building an extensive network of sympathetic citizens to support the Alaskans.

She was eventually in direct correspondence with over 250 people, informing them of impending congressional debates and legislation, encouraging them to lobby their politicians, keeping the media informed of their activities. Finally, in 1971, the natives' claims were confirmed by Congress. Although the act of Congress represented some serious compromises, Debo could nonetheless call the settlement "the most important victory ever won by the natives of this continent since the white man found it almost five centuries ago" (ibid., 409). Debo was launched on a new career as an Indian rights activist. She was instrumental in securing land claims for the Pima and for the tiny Havasupai tribe as they struggled to regain title to ancient ancestral lands on the rim of the Grand Canyon. Her books are frequently cited as compelling evidence in court, where their reliability is accepted by both sides. As indigenous peoples throughout the world learn to fight legally for their rights, Debo's work is beginning to achieve international impact.

Debo served throughout the late 1960s and 1970s on the Board of Directors of the Oklahoma American Civil Liberties Union (ACLU). She was a vehement and outspoken defender of freedom of speech and frequently represented the ACLU in debates and panels. She was something of a surprise to her opponents, as reported by a long-time friend:

> I think perhaps they expected a scruffy, long-haired, bearded hippie type, and in walked this wonderful woman with a grand-motherly appearance, incredible knowledge, superb credentials, and a sense of humor. Her adversaries simply did not know how to deal with such a knowledgeable and dignified hell-raiser (Gloria Valencia-Weber, in *Angie Debo*, 11).

Debo's active scholarly life continued well into her eighties. Her last book, *Geronimo: The Man, His Time, His Place*, was published by the University of Oklahoma Press in 1976. In true Debo style, it utilized previously untapped primary sources and Indian testimony to debunk the myth of Geronimo as a bloodthirsty monster; Debo portrayed a brave, passionately loyal defender of his tribe against overwhelming odds.

In an interview shortly before her death, Debo mused over her long life. She spoke of her determination, her drive, her need to be useful:

> When I was eleven years old, I was thinking about the life that would stretch out before me. I didn't expect it to last until I was ninety-five. But I did think it would last a long time and I decided to commit that life. And I decided that service and integrity were the important things.
>
> That did dominate my choices and I still think that that is the creative use of a life rather than to try to grab what one can (*Indians, Outlaws*, 91).

References

Angie Debo. College of Arts and Sciences and Department of History, Oklahoma State University. Includes autobiographical sketch and eulogy by Gloria Valencia-Weber. Stillwater, OK, 1988.

Debo, Angie. *And Still the Waters Run: The Betrayal of the Five Civilized Tribes.* Princeton: Princeton University Press, 1940.

———. "To Establish Justice." *Western Historical Quarterly* 7 (October, 1976): 405–412.

Indians, Outlaws, and Angie Debo (video transcript). Boston: WGBH, 1988.

McIntosh, Kenneth. "Geronimo's Friend: Angie Debo and the New History." *Chronicles of Oklahoma* 66, 2 (Summer, 1988): 164–177.

Nabokov, Peter, ed. *Native American Testimony.* New York: Viking Press, 1992.

Schrems, Suzanne H. and Cynthia J. Wolff. "Politics and Libel: Angie Debo and the Publication of *And Still the Waters Run.*" *Western Historical Quarterly* 22 (May, 1991): 185–202.

JOHN LOVEJOY ELLIOTT

(December 2, 1868–April 12, 1942)

Humanist, Community Organizer

Seldom in American history have the ideal and the practical blended as magnificently as they did in John Lovejoy Elliott, founder of one of the most innovative and successful settlement houses in the country. A towering figure in Progressive New York, Elliott was a dynamic humanist spokesman who fell in love with one of the city's worst neighborhoods and dedicated his life to its denizens. Never fully comfortable with abstractions, Elliott took the ennobling concepts of the Ethical Culture religion and brought them resoundingly, tumultuously to life in the streets and tenements of Chelsea. He touched thousands of lives with loving energy and benevolence; his influence on major institutions and urban policy was profound, enormous, and lasting.

John Lovejoy Elliott
Courtesy, Ethical Culture Archives,
New York Society for Ethical Culture.

Born to a struggling farm family in rural Princeton, Illinois, John Lovejoy Elliott could easily be cast as the archetypically wholesome American boy. His family, however, was anything but typical; his upbringing was, by mid-19th-century standards, unconventional if not downright unsavory. Elliott's mother, Elizabeth Denham Elliott, was a niece of the martyred abolitionist Elijah Lovejoy. Her home was an active station on the Underground Railroad, and she grew up deeply committed to abolitionism and to the concept of individual responsibility—commitments she passed on to her four sons. During the Civil War, Elizabeth became a teacher of newly freed slaves through the Sanitary Commission. After the war, she returned home and married a young Union veteran, Isaac Elliott, a graduate of the University of Michigan. Isaac, already something of a skeptic, had become close friends in the army with Robert Ingersoll, who would become a nationally known humanist, rationalist, and atheist. The two young men were passionate devotees of Thomas Paine and Voltaire, two of Western history's great rationalists and freethinkers. Ingersoll was a frequent guest of the Elliotts throughout John's youth and a lifelong friend; as a grown man, Elliott was the featured eulogist at Ingersoll's funeral.

Elliott grew up in a home comfortable with the evolutionist theories of Charles Darwin and the utopian socialism of Edward Bellamy, connected with no organized church. His parents encouraged broad reading and open discussion. Unaffiliated with conventional church outlets for charity and "good works," Elliott's mother was a compassionate, generous woman who gave willingly of her time, skills, and limited material resources in the small community. Although the family was poor, Elliott idealized his parents and remembered his childhood with a humorous reverence. "[A]nything that reminds me of the farm where I grew up is pleasant," he wrote sixty years later. "One of my brothers said that I was probably the most ignorant boy about work that ever left a farm, and while this is possibly true, I have very pleasant memories if not about work, at least about neglecting it" (Neumann, 110).

In 1888, a somewhat unfocused dreamer and an indifferent student, John Elliott entered Cornell University. Cornell, then twenty years old, had been founded by Ezra Cornell, a Quaker with a decidedly liberal philosophy: the school he founded, which had been denounced as a "godless institution," had no denominational affiliation, no required chapel, an open-minded president, and a liberal, nonclerical faculty. Elliott was in his element. Nonetheless, during his early years at Cornell he felt lost and confused, intimidated by the academic workload and anxious about a future that held no purpose for him. In many ways, his unconventional upbringing represented great freedom at the cost of comforting—if binding—connectedness. "My inability to join any of the traditional religious groups, or to be satisfied with the nation as an object of worship, or with disbelief as a finality, left me with a haunting sense of isolation from the most important associations of men" (*Fiftieth Anniversary*, 95).

During his sophomore year, Elliott attended a lecture that changed his entire life. He came under the spell of one of the most dynamic, original, and creative figures in American reform history—Felix Adler, founder of the Society for Ethical Culture. The son of a prominent Reform rabbi in Germany, Adler came to the United States at the age of six, when his father was appointed rabbi of New York's prestigious Temple Emanu-El. Adler graduated from Columbia University and received a Ph.D. in Aramaic and ancient religions from the University of Heidelberg in 1873. His comparative study of religions convinced him that the true goal of all religion was to foster compassionate, principled, moral conduct toward other human beings—and that this goal was far more vital than the details of theology and dogma that separated the world's religions and had caused such suffering and anguish throughout human history. He had been expected to take over his father's congregation, but their reaction to his first sermon, entitled "The Judaism of the Future," convinced both the congregants and Adler that he was no longer ideally suited to the job.

In 1876, supported by a number of reform-minded liberal Jews and Protestants, Adler founded the Society for Ethical Culture, a humanist religion grounded in the belief that righteous conduct—ethical behavior—needs no supernatural source or sanction. Ethical Culture was born in a critical year for America, a year of fraudulent national elections, extensive labor unrest and strikes and their shockingly brutal suppression, a point at which middle-class America began to see the dark, exploitative underside of industrial growth. The new religion's motto, "Diversity in creed, unanimity in deed," struck a resonant chord for many educated urban citizens. By the time Elliott heard Adler at Cornell, there were Ethical Societies in New York, San Francisco, Chicago, Philadelphia, St. Louis, and even London. The Society had started the first free kindergarten in New York City, which quickly grew into the Ethical Culture School; the Visiting Nurse Service; the Tenement House Building Company, which erected revolutionary model low-income housing and group homes for orphans; the Good Government Club, which fought against political corruption; the first settlement house in the United States; the Mothers' Society to Study Child Nature, which became the Child Study Association; the Visiting and Teaching Guild for Crippled Children; the Bureau for Justice, later known as the Legal Aid Society. Adler described a movement dedicated to working for the best potentialities in human beings, and he urged the students to join in the work.

"They who make this creative ethical task their object will never be distracted with the doubt whether life is or is not worth living" (Hohoff, 18).

Elliott was electrified. He felt that Adler was speaking directly to him, offering him the community and purpose he knew he lacked. He approached Adler, who responded enthusiastically. It was Adler who arranged Elliott's doctoral studies at the University of Halle, one of the oldest universities in Germany and the first German university to teach in the vernacular rather than in Latin. Prophetically, Elliott's dissertation was entitled "Prisons as Reformatories."

In 1894, fresh from two years of exhilarating study in Germany, Elliott was hired as Adler's assistant in the New York Society for Ethical Culture. He was drawn into the volatile, cultured, energetically optimistic world of Progressivism. He formed friendships with leading social workers like Mary Simkhovitch of Greenwich House and Lillian Wald of Henry Street Settlement; he renewed his affectionate relationship with Robert Ingersoll.

One of Elliott's responsibilities was the Society's program that sent teachers into the homes of poor, house-bound crippled children. Accompanying the teachers and the district nurses who helped select the children, Elliott was exposed to a degree of urban poverty and need beyond his worst imaginings. Some of the city's worst slums were in Chelsea, the West Side region from 14th to 34th Streets. In the 1890s Chelsea was a hideously crowded, violent neighborhood, largely Irish. It was dominated by the hectic, frequently corrupt life of the Hudson River docks, the looming skeleton of the Ninth Avenue elevated train, and the constant danger of the grade-level New York Railroad tracks.

Elliott was appalled by the desperation and needs that he saw, but his reactions were more complex than that. Quintessentially midwestern, rural, profoundly skeptical John Elliott fell in love with pulsating, raucous, violent, fiercely Catholic Chelsea. He was especially drawn to the street toughs, the poorly educated, purposeless young men of the numerous gangs; he could see their rootlessness and the fear of a pointless future beneath the swagger and bravado. In the chill of March, 1895, Elliott rented a room in Chelsea and invited the members of a local gang, the Hurley Burlies, to use it as a safe, dry place to talk, play cards, and shoot dice. After considerable initial resistance, distrust, and vandalism, Elliott's rented room became so popular that he had to find a larger space. He located a large loft on Ninth Avenue; with assistance from Ethical Society members, he bought some athletic equipment and games. Clubs and activities for girls as well as boys proliferated rapidly. Elliott's own boisterous, humorous, nonjudgmental style welcomed the suspicious adolescents; they were intrigued as much by his willingness to take them seriously as by his ability to laugh at himself. Significantly, he rented a cold-water flat in the neighborhood and committed himself to living as his neighbors did. Decades later, one of those teen-agers recalled Elliott as "a man with the body and attitude of a prizefighter and the soul of a saint" (Radest, 115).

Many more conventional authority figures in the neighborhood were suspicious of Elliott's casual, nondogmatic approach to the gangs. One local minister reported to the police that the Hurley Burlies were "a menace to neighborhood morality" (Munzer and Vogel, 29). But for the most part, Chelsea's response to Elliott was overwhelmingly positive. In 1895 he coordinated all the various activities in the loft as the Hudson Guild, a settlement house that incorporated formally two years later. By then it was housed in a rented four-story house on 26th Street, providing clubs, educational activities, and services for mothers and young working women as well as for children and adolescents.

In this experiment Elliott was guided not only by his own instincts but by the pioneering traditions of the Ethical Culture Society. The revolutionary nature of the settlement house lay in the recognition of shared humanity with the poor and in the commitment of the educated volunteers to "settle,"—to live in the midst of the urban squalor they were attempting to ameliorate. The first such settlement was Toynbee Hall, opened in 1884 in London's Whitechapel district, a residential hall staffed by highly educated young men who paid dues for the privilege of organizing educational and cultural activities for the neighborhood. Toynbee Hall drew many international visitors, among them a young American social worker named Jane Addams and an idealistic young Ethical Society leader, Stanton Coit.

It was Stanton Coit who established the first settlement house in the United States, the Neighborhood Guild, opened on New York's Lower East Side in 1886. Industrial America was struggling to deal with a monumental tidal wave of poverty-stricken, largely rural immigrants who simply overwhelmed already inadequate social services. In this critical situation, the settlement house concept appealed to a small but dedicated and capable educated elite. In 1888 seven young women opened the College Settlement in New York, and the next year, Jane Addams founded the better known Hull House in Chicago. In 1891 there were six settlement houses in the United States. By 1897 there were 74; barely ten years later there were over four hundred.

Although Elliott was at first dependent on the generosity of the wealthier "uptown" Ethical Society members, he refused to portray the Hudson Guild as a charity. Felix Adler's profound modification of the Golden Rule was "Act so as to elicit the best in others, and thereby in yourself." This reciprocity was the spiritual foundation of everything Elliott built through the Guild. He insisted on active neighborhood participation in all levels of planning and operation. At first, most staff members were Ethical Society volunteers, but Elliott always encouraged the confidence and organizational skills that would allow an indigenous leadership to develop. The Guild's constitution cites as one objective "the establishment of a neighborhood center and the encouragement of united activity for social and educational betterment" (Hohoff, 71). Beyond the activities themselves, Elliott sought for the Chelsea community development, mutuality, and self-respect through self-government. He was especially attentive to the women in the community, respectful of their loyalty to traditions but consistently supportive of their right to articulate their own needs and to help shape programs responsive to those needs. He formed the House Council, a functional board of directors with representatives of all the various clubs, which established and enforced basic rules. The clubs paid minimal rents to the Guild: no one had to feel the subtly undermining weight of charity.

Through all the exciting chaos and tumult of organizing the Hudson Guild, Elliott continued his work with the Ethical Society, teaching ethics classes at the growing Ethical Culture School, running adult education programs, officiating at weddings and funerals. Tall, outgoing, affectionate, and intensely practical, Elliott seems to have complemented the slender, cerebral, philosophical, somewhat aloof persona of Felix Adler. "I feel very proud, as Felix thinks I am working too hard," Elliott scribbled in his diary in 1899. "It makes me grin because I am not, but am quite willing that he should think so," (Radest, 115).

In 1908 the Hudson Guild was able to move into its own new building on 27th Street. It offered gymnastics classes, piano lessons, sewing and carpentry classes, and instruction in the folk dances of the neighborhood's varied ethnic groups. A growing employment service emphasized vocational guidance and paid special attention to job opportunities for the handicapped. In addition, there was an expanding library, an after-school homework support center, and a print shop that taught basic skills and handled all the printing jobs for the Ethical Culture Society as well as the Guild.

The history of that print shop epitomizes Elliott's hoped-for symbiosis of ethics and practicality. Elliott had advertised for a printing teacher. Arthur Blue, a retired master printer, a lonely widower with grown children, responded. Blue turned out to be an inspired teacher. The eager but ignorant boys in the class gave his life a new focus and purpose; he gave the boys self-discipline, standards, and hope. Blue brought in teachers to provide a grounding in English grammar, economics, and history; he tried to give his students the cultural background they were almost totally lacking. Elliott and Blue worked persuasively with both employers and the powerful printers' unions to get funding for the school and to establish consistent standards. Soon the five printers' unions in New York began requiring that their apprentices attend Blue's classes; by the time Blue died in 1924, the School for Printers' Apprentices was the largest printing school in America.

While much of Elliott's inexhaustible energy was devoted to the Guild, he was deeply committed to other important humane endeavors. On February 12, 1909, the centenary of Abraham Lincoln's birth, Elliott signed the "Call" for a renewed commitment to racial justice that led directly to the founding of the NAACP. Of the sixty prominent reformers and educators, black and white, who signed that ringing proclamation, four were leaders in the Ethical Culture Society: John Lovejoy Elliott, Anna Garlin Spencer, William Salter, and Henry Moskowitz.

In the years before World War I, the Guild responded to a rapidly changing neighborhood. English language classes were offered to new Greek and Italian immigrants; a cooperative buying club raised the quality of food available; a strenuous campaign forced the demolition of the worst tenements and helped create a public bath house on 28th Street in an era when most apartments had no bathtubs. The Guild ran three summer camps and acquired a 500-acre farm in New Jersey, run on a rotating basis by Guild families. The farm offered inexpensive family vacations and served as a conference site for organizations like the Ethical Society and the radical Teachers' Union. This emphasis on cooperation did not sit well with some authorities. A life-long Chelsea resident recalled, "The Church always thought the Guild was Communist" (Kisselhoff, 51).

Elliott brought further notoriety to the Guild through his pacifist stance before and during the war. Elliott, with many other reformers like Jane Addams, Lillian Wald, and even Thomas Edison, advocated negotiation rather than armed conflict. As the chairman of the Bureau of Legal Advice, Elliott worked with young men seeking conscientious objector status within the draft system. This was a daunting job in an America dominated by the 1918 Sedition Act, which punished the willful printing, writing, publishing, or speaking of "any disloyal, profane, scurrilous, or abusive language about the form of government of the United States"— or about its constitution, its flag, or even the uniforms of its armed forces. Since it was also against the law to "declare war contrary to the teaching of Christ" (Hohoff, 90), more than four hundred conscientious objectors without conventional religious affiliation received long prison sentences. Eugene V. Debs was sentenced to ten years in prison for blaming the war on capitalism. In 1918 the Department of Justice raided the offices of the Bureau of Legal Advice, hoping (unsuccessfully) to gather evidence on which to indict Elliott, Roger Baldwin, and others for treason. After the war, the Bureau was absorbed into what became the American Civil Liberties Union. A founding member, Elliott served on the board of the ACLU for the rest of his life.

Elliott never lost the concern for prison reform and rehabilitation first articulated in his doctoral dissertation. He understood the frustrations and lack of focus that could result in criminal violence; he worked with delinquent boys and their families; he testified in court for them; he worked to improve the juvenile justice system. When his boys went to prison, he would spend days traveling upstate to visit them and to keep them in touch with their families; he helped them apply for pardons; when they were released, he worked to find them shelter and jobs. The Guild employed a number of former convicts.

Elliott's faith in the redeemability of Chelsea's petty criminals survived direct assaults on his own life. An elderly resident recalled from her childhood in Chelsea that Elliott was frequently robbed:

> See, he would always leave his door open. So the fellas in the neighbor-hood who needed a few dollars would go in and take his suits, bring 'em up to the hockshop and get a couple of bucks. Then Dr. Elliott . . . would have to go there and get them back. He never caused a fuss. He never said a word (Kisselhoff, 52).

Elliott was well aware that 94% of the boys in Elmira Reform School had no job training, and that many of them were not academically inclined or intelligent enough to learn a skilled trade. He opened the Guild's industrial class to provide manual training and some psychological treat-ment to boys already identified as troublemakers in school. The class was plagued by theft and vandalism until Elliott turned it into an ex-periment in cooperative self-government; treated with respect for the first time in their lives, most of the boys began to accept some respon-sibility for themselves. On one occasion Elliott received a large package with the following scrawled note:

> Dear Dr. Elliott, a few months ago some tools was stolen from the shop but the boy who is writing this letter asks you to please accept the tools which he is sending you the tools the boy took were not so much but the boy wants to make up for what he did so he is sending back what he can remember what he stole he is sending you more than he got from your shop. Yours truly Unknown. PS Please take them it will pay up for a little anyway. PSS Remember you are getting more back than I stole from you Thank you (Hohoff, 140).

Elliott was always determined to improve the housing available in Chelsea. In the early 1920s the Guild built a model tenement on 28th Street, the six-story Chelsea Homes, which actually boasted a private bath in each of its thirty-four apartments. He fought constantly to force the city to recognize its moral responsibility to provide decent, affordable housing for its citizens. He saw all his settlement, housing, and prison reform work in the larger context of the ethical challenge he had accepted

at the age of twenty-two from Felix Adler. On the fiftieth anniversary of
the Ethical Society, he wrote:

> Although these occupations are varied and may seem disconnected, they
> have a common source and a single purpose—the attempt to perceive "the
> uncommon good in the common man," and to give that good new ways
> of expression . . . .Nothing has meant more to me than finding that the truth
> in the Ethical faith has its immediate effect on existing institutions. To have
> seen a spiritual ideal . . . acting upon individual men and women and mov-
> ing in the life of communities has given me perhaps the deepest ground
> of hope in the present, and conviction and faith for the future (*Fiftieth
> Anniversary*, 99).

The Depression devastated Chelsea and strained the resources of the
Hudson Guild. Elliott was working desperately hard; in addition to his
work with the Guild, he had taken over as senior leader of the Ethical
Society after Adler's death in 1933. Despite a constant scramble for funding to meet escalating demands, Elliott pursued his long-range goal of
improved housing. In 1937 he founded the Chelsea Association for Planning and Action, which coordinated all the neighborhood organizations
in a united drive for large-scale affordable housing. In 1941 clearance
was begun for a major housing development, but America's entry into
World War II sidelined all domestic projects during the war years. Elliott,
who died in 1942, did not live to see the 1946 opening of the John Lovejoy Elliott Houses, four twelve-story residential buildings designed as a
community, with open gardens, walks, and spacious playgrounds. Elliott
Houses, providing homes for more than six hundred families, was New
York's first city-aided low-rent housing project.

Elliott's devotion to humane causes was always grounded in a direct
commitment to individuals. In 1938, at the age of seventy, he rescued
the leaders of the Vienna Ethical Society, who had been imprisoned by
the Gestapo shortly after Hitler occupied Austria. Armed with petitions,
affidavits, and bribe money, Elliott spent several months shuttling between Vienna and Berlin, negotiating with the Gestapo, before the two
men were released and permitted to emigrate with him to New York.
As America faced a new wave of refugee immigrants, Elliott galvanized
New York to effective, sympathetic action. He founded the Good Neighbor Movement, which coordinated a broad range of support services and
responded to the need for language classes, children's services, housing,
psychological counseling, and other adjustment services.

Overworked and exhausted, Elliott suffered from a chronic cough that
developed into pneumonia; he died in the spring of 1942. He had found
a spiritual home in a lifetime of practical idealism and service. "I am
filled with the sense of wonder and awe in the presence of the spiritual

nature as it manifests itself in the daily lives of men and women," he wrote (*Fiftieth Anniversary*, 100). Roger Baldwin remembered him as "a witty saint who laughed to cover his loneliness, a bachelor married to a whole community, . . . a teacher who taught from life and learned from kids, a man who so loved people that no task to aid them was too small." (Hohoff, i). The Guild he founded is one of New York City's most effective, innovative social service agencies. In the 1990s, with a multimillion-dollar budget and a full-time staff of almost one hundred, it provides over ten thousand people each year with services from day care, counseling, parenting, youth and elder support, to a successful art gallery and a highly respected performing arts program. As one of Elliott's boys recalled, "Dr. Elliott always thought of the dignity of the people. . . . He made you feel like you had something worthwhile in you which you should try to develop. . . . Most important, I think somehow he gave you a feeling that you should believe in yourself" (Kisselhoff, 52).

References

Davis, Allen F. *Spearheads for Reform: The Social Settlements and the Progressive Movement, 1890–1914*. New Brunswick, NJ: Rutgers University Press, 1984.

Elliott, John Lovejoy. "Interdependence." In *Ethical Religion: Its Basis and Possibilities*. New York: American Ethical Union, 1940.

The Fiftieth Anniversary of the Ethical Movement, 1876–1926. New York: D. Appleton and Co., 1926.

Friess, Horace L. *Felix Adler and Ethical Culture*. New York: Columbia University Press, 1981.

Hohoff, Tay. *A Ministry to Man: The Life of John Lovejoy Elliott*. New York: Harper & Brothers, 1959.

Kisselhoff, Jeff. "On the Waterfront." *New York Post*, April 23, 1989: 49–54.

Munzer, Martha E. and Helen W. Vogel. *Block By Block: Rebuilding City Neighborhoods*. New York: Alfred A. Knopf, 1973.

Neumann, Henry. *Spokesmen for Ethical Religion*. Boston: The Beacon Press, 1951.

Radest, Howard B. *Toward Common Ground: The Story of the Ethical Societies in the United States*. Garden City, NY: Fieldston Press, 1987.

ELIZABETH FREEMAN

(ca. 1744–December 28, 1829)

Abolitionist

Elizabeth Freeman was born a slave. She had no education; she could neither read nor write. She lived through the wild, exhilarating era of the American Revolution, when ringing, glorious phrases about rights and equality became part of people's everyday vocabulary. And what Elizabeth Freeman heard, she took seriously and literally. By the stunning act of insisting in court on her humanity and therefore her equality under the new constitution of the state of Massachusetts, Freeman helped destroy slavery in the state. Her story is a shining example of the real power of "self-evident" truth— and of the loving, lasting bonds sometimes formed when good people work together for a just cause.

Elizabeth "Mumbet" Freeman
Courtesy, Massachusetts Historical Society.

Elizabeth Freeman, whose slave name was Bett, grew up a slave in the household of Pieter Hogeboom in Claverack, New York, near Albany. Hogeboom's daughter, Hannah, married John Ashley, the heir of a prominent family in western Massachusetts. Pieter Hogeboom died in 1758; it was probably at this point that Hannah Ashley inherited both Bett and her younger sister, Lizzie. John Ashley had become a dominant figure in Sheffield, Massachusetts. He had represented Berkshire County in the colonial legislature since 1750; in addition, he was a justice of the peace and a judge in the Court of Common Pleas. In 1773 he was appointed the chairman of a committee of Sheffield leaders drawn together "to take into consideration the grievances which Americans in general and Inhabitants of this Province in particular labor under" (Swan, 52).

The meetings of this committee were held in the Ashley home. The clerk of the committee, Theodore Sedgwick, was a brilliant, spirited, compassionate young lawyer who would play a crucial role in Bett's future. The committee produced a document known as the Sheffield Declaration. It included the following resolution:

> Resolved that Mankind in a State of Nature are equal, free and independent of each other, and have a right to the undisturbed Enjoyment of their lives, their Liberty and Property (Swan, 52).

The Sheffield Declaration was unanimously approved at the next town meeting; eventually, its sentiments were incorporated into the final 1780 state constitution.

The constitution that the citizens of Massachusetts ratified in 1780 was not the first submitted to them. The first constitution, drawn up in 1778, denied the vote to "Negroes, Indians, and Mulattoes." It was defeated overwhelmingly across the state, in part because of the suffrage restriction and in part because it did not include a Bill of Rights; several towns specified that they had rejected it because "it wears a very gross complexion of slavery" (Higginbotham, 90). John Adams himself drafted a revised constitution, which called for unrestricted male suffrage and articulated a Bill of Rights thirty articles long. Article I reads: "All men are born free and equal, and have certain natural, essential, and unalienable rights; among which may be reckoned the right of enjoying and defending their lives and liberties" (Commager, 107). Although the constitution contained no explicit emancipation clause, the seeds of "self-evident truth," germinating in Bett since the Sheffield Declaration, were further nourished.

In the spring of 1781 a single domestic crisis served as a catalyst for all Bett's frustrated musings and longing. Both Bett and Lizzie were working in the kitchen with Mistress Ashley; in the relatively benign structure of New England slavery, such shared labor was not unusual. As Sedgwick's son related years later,

> In this state of familiar intercourse, instances of cruelty were uncommon, and the minds of the slaves were not so much subdued but that they caused a degree of indignation not much less than if committed upon a freeman.
>
> Under this condition of society, while Mum Bett resided in the family of Col. Ashley, she received a severe wound in a generous attempt to shield her sister. Her mistress in a fit of passion resorted to a degree and mode of violence very uncommon in this country: she struck at the weak and timid [Lizzie] with a heated kitchen shovel: Mum Bett interposed her arm, and received the blow; and she bore the honorable scar it left to the day of her death (Sedgwick, 15).

Outraged, Bett left the Ashley house and went to consult with a man whose convictions and principles she remembered well—Theodore Sedgwick. She was convinced that she need not suffer such treatment any further; she cited the revolutionary doctrine of equality. Harriet Martineau, a British writer and friend of the younger Sedgwick, recounted that first conference between Sedgwick and Bett. Bett said that she had learned about liberty

> "by keepin' still and mindin' things." But what did she mean, she was asked, by keeping still and minding things? Why, for instance, when she was waiting a table, she heard gentlemen talking over the Bill of Rights and the new constitution of Massachusetts; and in all they said she never heard but that all people were born free and equal, and she thought long about it, and resolved she would try whether she did not come in among them (Martineau, 105).

Bett's sentiments were in keeping with a rising flood of egalitarian expectation among African Americans. Although the concept of involuntary servitude was written into Massachusetts's Body of Liberties in 1641, the conscience of the colony seemed always ambivalent toward slavery. In 1771 the colonial legislature passed a bill outlawing slavery, but Governor Hutchinson refused to sign it. As the Revolution approached, the constant talk of rights, of rights violated, of one people unjustly oppressed by another, permeated the thinking of African Americans as well. A 1773 petition to a legislator from slaves in Boston declared,

> We expect great things from men who have made such a noble stand against the designs of their *fellow-men* to enslave them. We cannot but wish

and hope Sir, that you will have the same grand object, we mean civil and
religious liberty, in view in your next session. The divine spirit of freedom,
seems to fire every humane breast on this continent (Aptheker, 7).

The following year a group of slaves offered to fight for the British in
exchange for their freedom. As they explained to General Thomas Gage,
"[W]e have in common with all other men a natural right to our free-
doms without Being depriv'd of them by our fellow men as we are a
freeborn Pepel and have never forfeited this Blessing by aney compact
or agreement whatever" (ibid., 9). There is no record of a response from
Gage.

When the colonists discovered the offer, they were outraged. Abigail
Adams, however, saw the situation in a different light, as she wrote to
her husband: "It always appeared a most iniquitous scheme to me to
fight ourselves for what we are daily robbing and plundering from those
who have as good a right to freedom as we have" (Higginbotham, 88).

The rhetoric of slave protest escalated during the war. A 1777 petition
to the state legislature repeated the claim of a "Natural and Unalienable
Right to that freedom which the great Parent of the Unavers hath Be-
stowed equalley on all menkind." Two years later, a slave petition declared:

> [W]e perceive by our own Reflection, that we are endowed with the same
> Faculties with our masters, and there is nothing that leads us to a Belief,
> or Suspicion, that we are any more obliged to serve them, than they us,
> and the more we are Convinced of our Right . . . to be free (Aptheker, 11).

In Massachusetts, where slaves had never lost the right to petition the
courts for redress of grievances, a number of slaves had sued their masters for their freedom. Bett's proposed suit differed from these prede-
cessors in a profound way: previous suits had involved claims of broken
promises of manumission, failure by heirs to free slaves in accordance
with wills, or some other flaw in the title by which the slave was held.
But Bett made no such claim. Her argument was directly with the legality
of the institution of slavery in the state of Massachusetts.

Theodore Sedgwick agreed to take on the case. He obtained a writ of
replevin—an action taken for the recovery of property, from the Berkshire
County Court of Common Pleas, in behalf of Bett and another Ashley
slave, a man named Brom, who has otherwise disappeared from history.
The property of which Bett and Brom had been deprived, according to
the writ, was their own persons. Colonel Ashley refused to relinquish
what he considered his valid title to his slaves, and the case went to
court on August 21, 1781. The plaintiffs declared that they were being
detained in illegal bondage; Colonel Ashley insisted that they were in-

deed his "servants for life." The jury found that Bett and Brom were *not* Ashley's servants; they ordered him to pay thirty shillings in damages to the plaintiffs and over five pounds in court costs as well. There can be little doubt that Sedgwick drew upon the Massachusetts Bill of Rights in making his clients' case; frustratingly, the court records provide no summary of the arguments and no explanation of the jury's verdict. Ashley filed an appeal, but subsequently dropped it when a series of related cases in 1783 clearly implied the unconstitutionality of slavery in Massachusetts.

After the trial, Mum Bett renamed herself. The last name she chose, fittingly enough, was Freeman. She rejected Colonel Ashley's request that she return to his household; instead she became a loving and much-loved nurse to Theodore Sedgwick's growing family. The widow of a Revolutionary War soldier, she never remarried; she had one daughter and, eventually, a number of grandchildren.

Freeman's honor and bravery were a family legend among the Sedgwicks. In February, 1787, during Shays's Rebellion, she was alone in Sedgwick's Stockbridge home when a roving band of angry farmers, deeply in debt, broke into the house. Anticipating trouble, she had already hidden the family's silver and other valuables in her own shabby trunk. She armed herself with a heavy kitchen shovel and accompanied the mob as it searched the house for goods to steal; when they came to her own room and noticed her trunk, she reportedly jeered at them, "Oh, you had better search that . . . an old nigger's chest! You are such gentlemen, you had better search that—" and humiliated them so that they left the trunk undisturbed (Welch, 52).

When Freeman retired she was able to buy a small home of her own, where she was frequently visited by the grown Sedgwick offspring she had helped raise. One Sedgwick daughter, Catherine, remembered a poignant moment when the elderly Freeman confessed to her,

> Anytime, anytime while I was a slave, if one minute's freedom had been offered to me, and I had been told I must die at the end of that minute, I would have taken it—just to stand one minute, I would have taken it just to stand one minute on God's earth a free woman (Swan, 54).

After her death, when Theodore Sedgwick, Jr. delivered a lecture on abolition in Stockbridge, he used Elizabeth Freeman to refute any theories of racial inferiority:

> If there could be a practical refutation of the imagined natural superiority of our race to hers, the life and character of this woman would afford that refutation. . . . Having known this woman as familiarly as I knew either of

my parents, I *cannot* believe in the moral or physical inferiority of the race to which she belonged (Sedgwick, 18).

Elizabeth Freeman is buried among the Sedgwicks in the Stockbridge cemetery. The epitaph on her tombstone was written by another Sedgwick, Charles. It reads:

> ELIZABETH FREEMAN, known by the name of MUMBET, died Dec. 28, 1829. Her supposed age was 85 years. She was born a slave and remained a slave for nearly thirty years. She could neither read nor write, yet in her own sphere she had no superior nor equal. She neither wasted time nor property. She never violated a trust, nor failed to perform a duty. In every situation of domestic trial, she was the most efficient helper, and the tenderest friend. Good mother, farewell (Swan, 55).

References

Aptheker, Herbert, ed. *A Documentary History of the Negro People in the United States.* New York: The Citadel Press, 1969, Vol. I.

Commager, Henry Steele, ed. *Documents of American History.* New York: Appleton-Century-Crofts, 1963.

Higginbotham, A. Leon Jr. *In the Matter of Color—Race and the American Legal Process: The Colonial Period.* New York: Oxford University Press, 1978.

Kaplan, Sidney. *The Black Presence in the Era of the American Revolution, 1770–1800.* New York: New York Graphic Society in association with the Smithsonian Institution Press, 1973.

Martineau, Harriet. *Retrospect of Western Travel.* London: Saunders and Otley, 1838, Vol. 2.

Sedgwick, Theodore. *The Practicability of the Abolition of Slavery.* New York: J. Seymour, 1831.

Smith, Jessie Carney, ed. *Notable Black American Women.* Detroit: Gale Research, 1992.

Swan, Jon. "The Slave Who Sued for Freedom." *American Heritage* 41 (March, 1990): 51–55.

Welch, Richard E. *Theodore Sedgwick, Federalist.* Middletown, CT: Wesleyan University Press, 1965.

Zilversmit, Arthur. "Quok Walker, Mumbet, and the Abolotion of Slavery in Massachusetts." *William and Mary Quarterly* 25 (October, 1968): 614–624.

Laura S. Haviland

(1808–1898)

Abolitionist, Educator, Human Rights Advocate

Laura Haviland lived through times of tremendous challenge and change. She was a dynamic synthesis of contradictory elements: personal serenity set against an enormous capacity for moral outrage; visionary idealism laced with hard-nosed practicality; gentle dignity willing to undertake flamboyant schemes in the face of great danger. Haviland was a legend on the Underground Railroad. Her life, moving from the excitement of the Underground Railroad to the exhaustion, hardship, and drudgery of relief work in refugee camps long after the Civil War, demonstrates a sustained commitment to the implementation of justice.

Laura S. Haviland
Courtesy, Lenawee County Historical Museum.

Born in 1808, Laura S. Haviland was the oldest child of active Quakers. She grew up in isolated farm country around Cambria, New York. There was no school available, and the children were educated at home. A voracious reader, Haviland consumed the contents of her father's library; she remembered most vividly John Woolman's condemnations of slavery. At the age of seventeen Haviland married a young farmer, Charles Haviland. Shortly thereafter, her parents headed west to Michigan Territory, where rich farmland was selling for $1.25 per acre. In 1829, already the parents of two babies, the Havilands joined Laura's family, settling on the Raisin River in southern Michigan. For many years, their lives were absorbed by the work of establishing a frontier community and caring for a rapidly growing family. Even in these first years, Haviland acquired a reputation as an effective, tireless, and generous nurse and midwife.

Haviland's life took on a new focus in the early 1830s with the arrival in the community of Elizabeth Margaret Chandler. Chandler, a committed Quaker abolitionist, had worked with Benjamin Lundy on his newspaper, *The Genius of Universal Emancipation*, and had written a book on abolition. Her moral energy inspired both the Havilands, and they collaborated in 1832 to establish Michigan's first antislavery society. By 1837 Laura and Charles were the parents of six children and the operators of the first Underground Railroad station in Michigan. The settlement around them had grown to the point where Laura determined to open a school. Her brother donated land for the school, and assorted neighbors helped put up several cabins as classrooms. The school, called the Raisin Institute, opened in 1837 with fifty students of all ages. The meaning of education, for Laura Haviland, always went beyond the conventions of curriculum. Raisin Institute was open to all children, regardless of race; she saw this school as a vehicle for true moral enlightenment:

> At that day [1837] there was not a school in our young state that would open its doors to a colored person. . . . Hundreds of young people who enjoyed the privileges our school afforded came to us with their prejudices against colored people and our position in regard to them; but they soon melted away. . . . We richly earned the cognomer of "Nigger Den," yet Heaven smiled and blessed our work" (Danforth, 40).

While Raisin Institute grew, so did Haviland's own family: two more babies were born, in 1839 and 1844. Her life was full and focused, balancing the demands of her large family, of the Institute, and of increasing work with runaway slaves on their way to Canada. A virulent epidemic of erysipelas, a staph-like infection, decimated the community in 1845 and tore apart the fabric of Haviland's life: within six weeks, she lost both her parents, a sister, her husband, and her youngest child. Recovering herself from the disease, she faced the future as a 38-year-old widow with seven children and sole responsibility for a school that was deeply in debt. By 1847, Raisin Institute was recognized by the state and incorporated as a tax-free institution; its graduates were highly respected teachers throughout the region. Haviland's oldest children had begun to marry, and she was surrounded by a loving and supportive community. Rather than retire, for the next fifty years she achieved a magnificent balancing act, not only fulfilling the responsibilities she already bore but taking on grave additional burdens, committing her life to the enactment of decency and justice.

Haviland became much more deeply involved in the Underground Railroad. Eventually, her secret travels against slavery would take her into Arkansas, Kentucky, Louisiana, Tennessee, throughout Ohio, Indiana, and into Canada. She would frequently travel alone into the South, posing as a cook and even occasionally managing to pass as a free black, to gain access to plantation kitchens and slave quarters and communicate plans to escaped slaves' families. One enraged slaveowner, after she had helped a slave escape, wrote vicious letters to her as "Laura Haviland, a damned nigger stealer." His family circulated an offer of $3,000 for her capture, dead or alive.

The Fugitive Slave Law of 1850 established brutal penalties—fines and imprisonment—for those found guilty of aiding escaping slaves. In her characteristically straightforward fashion, Haviland confronted a Southern lawyer she met about the inherent illegality of the law. He acknowledged the validity of her argument, and stated fiercely that the slaveowners had fought for the law

> Because we made up our minds to bring you northerners to terms, whether it was constitutional or not. . . . Now we knew that it was an unconstitutional thing before we put it before Congress, but we put it there to let you know we could drive it down northern throats, and we did it, too! (Danforth, 125).

Faced with the punitive provisions of the Fugitive Slave Law, Haviland orchestrated an elaborate network of signals and warnings, in response to which her neighbors would gather to protect her and any escaping slave. If any cases came to court, they would be heard in nearby Detroit, before Judge Ross Williams, a man with abolitionist sympathies; he always postponed the hearing, which gave Haviland time to get the trapped slave safely to Canada.

Haviland was notorious throughout the South. Her gentle, pious, calm demeanor seemed especially infuriating to slaveowners. She never lost her temper; by some accounts, she allowed herself to seem naive and acquiescent. In reality, she never let fear or danger deter her from the path she had chosen. She was a regular visitor at the Cincinnati home of Levi Coffin, one of the leaders of the Underground Railroad; together they engineered the meticulously crafted escape of hundreds of slaves. Haviland frequently escorted the slaves from Cincinnati on to Toledo and beyond; the circumstances of their lives and escape left many of them so weakened and ill that her nursing skills were essential.

Haviland repeatedly placed herself in personal danger in Louisville, Kentucky, trying to help the imprisoned abolitionist Calvin Fairbanks. Fairbanks, who had been caught trying to rescue a slave woman, was being held in appalling conditions in the Louisville jail; Haviland, using her maiden name to avoid her own capture, visited him, bringing food, blankets, and support. When her friends across the Ohio River in Cincinnati urged her not to make the dangerous trip into slaveholding territory, she replied that Jesus had paid no attention to artificial boundaries when visiting those in prison. She made repeated secret trips to Louisville to arrange for Fairbanks's defense with a sympathetic lawyer. In his memoirs years later, Fairbanks recalled, "This very estimable woman, who had for many years given her time and means for the promotion of the highest interests and the protection of the defenseless of all classes, and especially the African people of America, still labored for my rescue" (Fairbanks, 93). (No defense could have convinced a Kentucky jury to forgive Fairbanks: he spent a total of over seventeen years in prison there for his rescue missions.)

In 1852 Haviland and her daughter Anna organized a school for black children in Cincinnati; they moved on to Toledo to initiate a similar project. Although state law required public funding of a "colored school" in any town where there were at least fifteen potential students, Haviland faced an uphill battle against local prejudice and indifference. She appeared repeatedly before the school board, submitting petitions, reminding them of their legal obligations, and simply wearing down their resistance. Within six months, when continued funding was assured, Haviland turned the school over to a dedicated young African American teacher, John G. Mitchell. Mitchell, who was slowly working his way through Oberlin College, would graduate in 1858 and later become a dean at Wilberforce University.

Haviland next turned her energies to the rapidly growing communities of escaped slaves in Windsor, Ontario. She opened a school for the fugitives, both children and adults; she initiated Sunday School classes and helped organize a "Christian Union Church" to emphasize shared goals and maintain harmony among the various Protestant denominations. Her own beloved Raisin Institute, which had been closed in 1849 for financial reasons, was able to reopen in 1856, with an expanded staff and program and an eager new principal from Oberlin College. Haviland designed a program in which fugitive slaves taught the students about slavery and prejudice. Despite several years of relative prosperity, the school closed again in 1864, when half the faculty and many students enlisted in the Union Army.

The nightmare battle casualties and chaotic conditions of the early Civil War demanded a response from Haviland. By the end of 1861 she had independently gathered over twenty thousand garments, blankets, bandages, and other supplies; she managed to contact the Sanitary Commission representatives in Chicago and negotiated a free pass into the refugee camps in Cairo, Illinois. In Memphis she visited a frontline hospital dominated by a brutal, indifferent, alcoholic surgeon; Haviland was incapable of accepting evil as inevitable: she launched a crusade against the incompetent surgeon that took her to the medical director of Memphis and the army's chief of medicine and led to the drunkard's dismissal.

Throughout the war and for years afterward, Haviland traveled almost constantly, going north into Michigan and Illinois to gather supplies, hurrying south to hospitals and refugee camps in places like Natchez and Vicksburg to distribute the desperately needed supplies and to nurse and teach. She made a point of visiting newly "liberated" plantations to collect neck irons, knee restraints, and other instruments of coercion and torture; she was determined that people in the North should learn the full horrors of slavery, and that people in the South should not be permitted to deny them.

In Natchez, she found over four thousand freedmen living in ragged tents, with no organized food distribution; they were dying at a rate of fifteen each day. As soon as she had managed to set up a primitive system for food delivery, Haviland turned her attention to schools. She and a team of dedicated teachers were soon running six day schools and three night schools. Although most of the thirty teachers were white Northerners, two schools were taught by black teachers. One of the former slaves had run a secret school in Natchez for seven years at great personal risk; slaves who had worked from dawn to sundown came to classes held from midnight until two in the morning.

Appointed an agent for the Freedmen's Aid Commission in 1864, Haviland received a salary of $40 per month; it was the first time she had ever been paid for any of her work with former slaves. Her time was spent organizing the collection of supplies, arranging equitable distribution of those supplies, visiting refugee camps, nursing, teaching, writing reports, and lecturing to increase public awareness and sensitivity. She reported constant struggles within the Union Army over the attitudes toward and treatment of black soldiers and freedmen. One of the few bright spots for her was the long-awaited release from prison, on

April 30, 1864, of her old friend Calvin Fairbanks. By the end of 1864 she had been forced to sell Raisin Institute; happily, the Freedmen's Aid Commission purchased it to serve as an orphanage for abandoned African American children.

As the war ended, the South was in chaos. The military occupation by Union troops provided minimal protection and order, but their presence was scattered and unreliable. Former slaves, homeless and destitute, were at the mercy of bitter white Southerners. A special rage was directed at blacks discharged from the Union Army; there were numerous documented incidents of blatant murders and lynchings, and the Union authorities were largely unresponsive.

Into this cruel and despairing situation, Haviland threw herself with astonishing energy. She spent time in refugee camps throughout Kansas; she brought a group of seventy-five orphans to live at Raisin Institute, which had been renamed Haviland Home; she nursed and taught and cleaned and organized in camps in Tennessee and Virginia; she met with President Andrew Johnson to seek pardons for black citizens still in Southern prisons for having helped escaping slaves.

The economic and social upheaval of the war and its aftermath produced an atmosphere of bitterness, distrust, resentment, and fear. Relief workers were frequently harassed and threatened by angry whites. In the spring of 1867, when Haviland went home to Michigan with another band of homeless children, she found herself and her children the target of a vicious, slanderous campaign. She was accused of destroying the economy of southern Michigan by bringing in hordes of shiftless beggars who had become an unbearable public burden on taxpayers. Haviland had to conduct her own investigations into the actual circumstances of those grown orphans who had left the home; she had to launch an intensive lecturing and publicity drive to deflect the rising current of racism.

Returning to Washington for further relief work, Haviland was appalled to learn that the American Missionary Association, which had bought Haviland Home, had arbitrarily decided to shut it down and was literally abandoning the children on the streets of nearby Adrian, Michigan. Exhausted but enraged, Haviland rushed home. She struggled to gather back the scattered children, literally begged for funds, and took over the management of the orphanage herself. She applied for state approval and the funding that would bring, but the next several years were difficult and frightening. Haviland suffered a concussion in a fall; shortly afterwards, she endured a severe stroke from which she never fully recovered. By the end of 1870, the orphanage was down to a two-week supply of food, and a weak, tired Haviland was busy writing urgent letters to supporters asking for supplies. Finally, the state accepted responsibility for the home, renaming it the Michigan Orphan Asylum and assuming its financial management. After teaching at the home for two years, Haviland retired to live with a widowed daughter.

Retirement did not last long. The final withdrawal of federal troops from the South in 1877 signaled the end of Reconstruction and removed whatever feeble protection African Americans had experienced. The intent behind the rise of groups like the Ku Klux Klan was stated clearly in an article in *Mercury*, a popular magazine edited by a former Confederate colonel: "The Negroes in these states will be slaves again, or cease to be. Their sole refuge from extinction will be in slavery to the white man" (Danforth, 249). An epidemic of antiblack violence across the South produced a new wave of desperate refugees escaping north. The Freedmen's Aid Commission was overwhelmed. By 1881 there were more than fifty thousand poverty-stricken African Americans living in appalling conditions in camps in Kansas. Their presence elicited resentment and violence from whites. Haviland knew she had no choice but to respond. With her daughter, she went to Washington to testify and lobby for the Freedmen's Aid Commission; she carried relief supplies into Kansas, and with her own funds bought 240 acres to set up farms for the refugees. The city of Haviland, Kansas, is named in her honor.

Back in Michigan, Haviland helped found the state Women's Christian Temperance Union; she worked to design and initiate a new division of the orphanage: a training school for "wayward" girls. In 1887 she published her memoirs, *A Woman's Life Work*. The book went quickly through five editions; her adventures seemed so incredible to some readers that the later editions supplied documentation of her stories—letters, commendations, newspaper articles. Four days before her death at the age of ninety, she found the energy to write a letter of public appeal on behalf of the old abolitionist Calvin Fairbanks, who was living in poverty. At Haviland's funeral, her coffin was carried by both black and white pallbearers; interracial choirs sang the hymns. She was buried in Raisin, the community from which she had drawn so much strength.

References

Bacon, Margaret Hope. *Mothers of Feminism: The Story of Quaker Women in America*. San Francisco: Harper and Row, 1986.

Danforth, Mildred E. *A Quaker Pioneer: Laura Haviland*. New York: Exposition Press, 1961.

Fairbanks, Calvin. *The Life of the Reverend Calvin Fairbanks During Slavery Times* [1890]. New York: Negro University Press, 1969.

Haviland, Laura. *A Woman's Life Work*. Chicago: C. V. Water & Co., 1887.

Siebert, Wilbur. *The Underground Railroad from Slavery to Freedom*. New York: Russell & Russell, 1898.

THOMAS HAZARD

(September 15, 1720–August 26, 1798)

Abolitionist

Thomas Hazard was born to a family that had played a prom-inent role in Rhode Island since 1638. His direct ancestor, another Thomas, built an estate of over one thousand acres in Narragansett; his own father was one of the area's largest landowners—and slaveowners. Hazard's immediate world did not merely accept slavery: Rhode Island was arguably the col-ony most actively involved in the triangular slave trade (see below). Two of Hazard's cousins were slave-traders. Hazard, his father's eldest son and heir, was expected to step in line and assume his proper place. He could not; he stepped decid-edly out of line, and in so doing helped change Rhode Island history.

Rhode Island was an unusual colony. Founded by the dissident Roger Williams, it offered a haven to Baptists, Ranters, Deists, Jews, and even Quakers (whom Williams defended despite his disapproval of their doctrine of Inner Light). This literally unorthodox atmosphere encouraged an independent, confident spirit, with a rare willingness to rely on individual conscience. Within this context, the Hazard family was itself unusual. They were recognized for their intense individuality and independence, for what a later family historian called "a peculiar decision of character." Eldest sons were invariably named either Thomas or Robert, after the paternal grandfather. As a result, Thomas Hazard was surrounded by no fewer than thirty direct relatives also named Thomas Hazard; they came to distinguish themselves by identifying nicknames: Bedford Tom, Nailer Tom, Fiddlehead Tom.

Thomas Hazard, abolitionist and reformer, was known as "College Tom" because he had spent several terms studying at New Haven College—later Yale University. He came to feel that he could not reconcile the realities and vanities of college life with his Quaker conscience, and he left before completing his degree. Hazard's firm Quaker principles probably came from his mother. His father was by all evidence not a Quaker: his name never appears in the records of local meetings, and he was always referred to publicly as "Robert Hazard, Gentleman"—a title a Quaker would not have utilized.

The growth of slavery in Rhode Island paralleled the struggle of Quakers to face the logical implications of their faith. A 1652 law prohibiting both black and white slavery and setting a ten-year limit on any bondservant's term was in reality ignored. The first shipment of Africans arrived in Rhode Island in 1696. Within a decade, the colony was deeply committed to an economy dominated by the infamous triangular trade, in which New England produced rum from Caribbean sugar, traded the rum in Africa for slaves, and sold the slaves in the islands and the southern colonies for more sugar—and profit. By the middle of the century there were thirty major distilleries in Newport alone, and countless respected Rhode Island families depended for their livings on the traffic in human beings.

Ministers of varied denominations insisted early on that slaves had souls and were entitled to baptism and religious instruction. (One such minister, a Dr. McSparran, tutored the young Thomas Hazard.) In 1716 the careful compromises of Rhode Island Quakers were assaulted by John Farmer, an English-born Quaker who had witnessed personally the brutalities of Barbadan slavery. The particular harshness of the system on Barbados profoundly affected a number of pioneering Quaker abolitionists, including the notorious Benjamin Lay* as well as Farmer. Quakers had been blamed for a slave insurrection on the island in 1675; in consequence, they were forbidden to preach to blacks, to allow slaves to attend their meetings, and to serve as school teachers. Farmer's message was one of uncompromising moral directness, calling for immediate, unconditional liberation. It was not well received by the Newport Meeting, which disowned Farmer. Nonetheless, by the next Yearly Meeting, Friends in Newport were expressing "weighty concern" over the slave trade; ten years later, in 1727, they actually censured the importation of slaves into the colony.

In the midst of all this uneasiness, College Tom came of age. Many years later, he recalled a pivotal moral moment when he was about eighteen years old and home from college for the summer. His father sent him out to the fields to help hay, but it was so unbearably hot that the boy retreated to the shade beneath a tree to read. Finding it so hot that he could not concentrate on his book, he watched the slaves laboring under the merciless sun. He experienced a sudden, transcendent awareness that he had no right to make these other men work under conditions he was free to reject. He never forgot the moment of his awakening.

In 1742 tall, soft-spoken, strikingly handsome young Tom Hazard was recognized as a propertied freeman by the town of South Kensington. The same year, he married a third cousin, Elizabeth Robinson, whose father, William, later became governor of the colony. Hazard's father gave the young couple a large farm and a number of slaves as a marriage gift. Hazard journeyed into Connecticut to buy prime livestock; he arrived there late on a Saturday afternoon and was invited to a friend's home for Sabbath. There he met an elderly Congregationalist deacon who defied him to reconcile Christianity with slaveowning; the man declared that Quakers couldn't be real Christians as long as they owned slaves—and young Hazard found that he agreed. Rushing home, he confounded his father and family by freeing all his slaves and vowing to operate his farm with free labor. Robert Hazard threatened to disinherit his son. Thomas may have had more support and understanding from other members of his family, however. Elizabeth's brother, Rowland Robinson, had invested in one slaving voyage, but when he saw the condition of the slaves on their arrival in Newport, he is said to have wept with horror and shame. He took his entire share of the cargo—twenty-eight men, women, and children—home with him, refused ever to sell any of them, and supported them all decently. At her request, he even sent one woman back to Africa.

By his courageous actions, Thomas Hazard had changed his own life irrevocably. His example inspired his good friend Jeremiah Austin, who freed the single slave he owned—his entire inheritance. But Hazard was driven to convince others. Heartened by a visit from John Woolman in 1747, he determined to work within the formal Quaker structures to effect a radical shift in communal conscience. Incrementally, Hazard labored for the abolition of slavery throughout Rhode Island. In 1757 his South Kensington Meeting began hearing witness from Friends who had freed their slaves; the testimony was used to urge others to release their slaves. In 1765 Hazard steered a committee through an awkward situation in which a Friend, Joshua Rathban, was pressured to free a newly purchased slave; he turned her over to his son, who, while promising to free her, actually sold her out of the community. Under Hazard's guidance, the committee ordered Rathban to sue his son for damages and to use the fee collected to redeem the slave. When Rathban refused, the Meeting disowned him. By 1769 the Rhode Island Yearly Meeting acknowledged that slaveowning as well as slave-trading was unacceptable; Hazard was part of the committee formed to visit slaveholding Friends and attempt to convert them. Within the following two years, the spirit of the Yearly Meeting had shifted so that slaveowning Friends were simply warned to expect expulsion. With typical Quaker organization and precision, Hazard's committee called on such Friends with blank manumission papers and practical details to expedite the process of freeing slaves. The stricture against owning slaves was taken very seriously: Moses Brown, a scion of one of the wealthiest families in Rhode Island, dutifully freed all his slaves before becoming a Friend in 1773; the following year, former Governor Stephen Hopkins was disowned for refusing to free a slave woman.

As the Quakers committed to abolition began to trust a "sense of the meeting" within their own ranks, they directed their energy to the civil hierarchy. In 1774 Hazard helped bring an abolitionist petition before the General Assembly. The petition stated unequivocally:

> Whereas the inhabitants of America are generally engaged in the preservation of their own rights and liberties, among which that of personal freedom must be considered as the greatest; those who are desirous of enjoying all the advantages of liberty themselves should be willing to extend personal liberty to others (Aptheker, 358).

The legislation urged by the petition, forbidding the importation of any slaves, passed the General Assembly. The issue of slavery was subsumed by more immediate concerns during the Revolution, but the Quakers were ready as soon as peace was restored. In 1783 the legislature appointed a committee to consider a Quaker petition for the abolition of slavery. The petition borrowed from the Declaration of Independence to describe slaveholding as "repugnant" and "subversive of the happiness of mankind, the great end of all civil government." By an Act of 1784 Rhode Island opted for the gradual abolition of all slavery, for the education and proper apprenticeship of freed children, and for town-sponsored support of disabled and elderly former slaves. Three years later, guided by the Quakers' ever-wider sense of responsibility, the legislature imposed stiff penalties on imported and exported slaves and on any ships that engaged in "the trade." Thomas Hazard helped design this bill as well as the newly chartered Providence Society for the Abolition of the Slave Trade, which linked its efforts with an interstate movement of rising momentum. Its constitution, generally attributed to Hazard, declared that all human beings are members of one great family and added, "It is therefore the duty of those who profess to maintain their own rights . . . to extend, by the use of such means as are or may be in their power, the blessings of freedom to the whole human race" (Hazard, 256).

On numerous occasions throughout his life, Hazard seems to have articulated the highest ideals of the Meeting in other areas as well. In 1771, rebuking another Meeting that discriminated against its women, he wrote, "neither do we think it Convenient so far to Degrade our women's meeting. . . . Truth admits of none but believing that both male and female are all one in Christ Jesus." Throughout the Revolution, Friends suffered special hardships—fines, confiscations, vandalism—because of their noncombatant stance; in addition, economic woes were compounded by the religious requirement to avoid any profit from any war-related activity. Hazard was deeply involved in an organized social service support network that tried to sustain Friends whose lives were severely disrupted as a consequence of their adherence to principle.

Education was another abiding concern for Thomas Hazard. He was one of the original Fellows of Rhode Island College, founded in 1764. In 1780 he began planning, through the Providence Yearly Meeting, a school that would be open to local poor children as well as Quaker children. In 1785, urged by Hazard, the South Kensington Meeting looked into its own school. After many false starts, the Friends School, well funded by Moses Brown, opened in 1814; it is now the Moses Brown School.

Hazard, by all accounts a loving and well-loved husband and father to three sons, died at the age of seventy-eight. College Tom had moved with unshakable ethical confidence to larger and larger challenges: he had first freed his own slaves, then worked to influence his own Meeting, gone to Yearly Meetings to inform and agitate against slaveholding, and finally taken his struggle successfully to the broader civil government.

References

Aptheker, Herbert. "The Quakers and Negro Slavery." *Journal of Negro History* 25 (July, 1940): 331–362.

Bicknell, Thomas W. *A History of the State of Rhode Island and Providence Plantations*. New York: American Historical Society, 1920.

Dictionary of American Biography. New York: Charles Scribner's, 1957.

Hazard, Caroline. *Thos. Hazard, son of Robt., call'd College Tom.* Boston: Houghton Miflin, 1893.

Whitman, Alden, ed. *American Reformers.* New York: H. W. Wilson, 1985.

LUGENIA BURNS HOPE

(February 19, 1871–August 14, 1947)

Community Organizer, Civil Rights Activist

As the promises and hopes of Reconstruction crumbled into bitter ash with the withdrawal of federal troops in 1877, African American communities across the South were faced with massive challenges. In the face of arrogant official neglect at best and active hostility in most cases; these communities were forced to assume the functions of civil government for their own people. One major element of this effort was the club movement, an extensive network of reformers and activists allied in the attempt to ameliorate the precarious lives of their people. African Americans bore their share of the tax burden, but they were increasingly denied access to hospitals, schools, libraries, recreational facilities, and basic municipal services; in order to survive, the churches and clubs of the black South struggled to provide these services. With the Supreme Court decision in Plessy v. Ferguson *in 1896, "separate but equal" was firmly entrenched as the law of the land; African American leaders knew that for the foreseeable future they couldn't do anything about the "separate," but they were determined to fight relentlessly for the "equal."*

Lugenia Burns Hope
Courtesy, Atlanta University Center, Robert W. Woodruff Library.

Lugenia Burns Hope embodied the highest aspirations of the club movement and reached beyond that to create an internationally recognized model of community-based social service. Assertive and direct, she was forced by the unabashed racism of white society to speak discreetly and to act painstakingly. Acknowledged by her colleagues as a "radical" integrationist and a confirmed feminist, she worked for seemingly small, incremental, achievable goals rather than directly for the truly just society that she knew was the birthright of all people.

Hope was born in St. Louis, Missouri, the youngest of seven children. Her parents were both biracial; her paternal grandfather, William Burns, was the secretary of state of Mississippi during the 1850s. Lugenia's father, Ferdinand, was a prosperous carpenter. Upon his sudden death, her mother decided to emigrate north to give her children better educational and employment opportunities. Wisely, she chose Chicago.

Chicago in the late 19th century had a small, concentrated, activist African American population. The "Black Belt" supported its own hospital, nursing school, YWCA, and newspapers, among them the respected *Conservator*, edited by the husband of Ida B. Wells, Ferdinand Barnett. The community rang with the language of racial pride, self-reliance, and economic solidarity.

Hope received a solid and varied education in Chicago, attending the Chicago School of Design, Chicago Business College, and the Chicago Art Institute. Throughout her many-faceted career she made good use of her arts training, offering sculpture classes to students from Morehouse and Spelman Colleges, teaching millinery classes, and coordinating art instruction for hundreds of children through the Neighborhood Union Association. When the financial difficulties of her older brothers forced her to leave school, Hope found work as a dressmaker and bookkeeper. She was gradually drawn to the work of the "King's Daughters," a charitable organization working among the needy, especially young working girls. Through her work as the first black secretary for the King's Daughters, she became involved with Hull House and met the great Jane Addams. All her life, Hope was inspired by the scope and organization of Hull House. She cited her work with the King's Daughters and Hull House as the source of her visions of community organization. Equally important, she was developing a profound sense of competence, independence, and self-worth, as well as an almost religious conviction that individuals *can* effect meaningful social change.

In 1893 Lugenia met John Hope, a theology student at Brown University who was taking summer courses at the University of Chicago. Their relationship developed quickly, but Lugenia was wary of giving up her independence, and she was working two and three jobs simultaneously to support her mother. They corresponded and debated over the next few years, while John became a classics instructor at Roger Williams College in Nashville and Lugenia's siblings negotiated on sharing the care of their mother. Toward the end of December, 1897, the two finally married and moved to Nashville, where John was still teaching. Less than a year later, John received an offer to teach at Atlanta Baptist College; he accepted eagerly, and the young couple relocated to Atlanta. It would be their home for the next thirty-eight years.

Turn-of-the-century Atlanta was the most completely segregated city in Georgia. Most of Atlanta's 63,000 African Americans were desperately poor. The women worked as domestic servants or laundresses, the men as menial laborers; the tiny upper class produced a few businessmen, lawyers, and among the women, teachers and dressmakers. The black community's overall death rate was 150% higher than that among whites; tuberculosis and pneumonia were common. Black Atlanta had no sanitation, no sewage disposal, no paved streets, no decent housing, no law enforcement. Progressivism in Georgia was sewn from old racist cloth; blacks were blamed for the degradation inflicted upon them, condemned as unworthy of participatory citizenship and susceptible to corruption. On these grounds, major Georgia politicians began a sustained drive to complete the disenfranchisement of all African Americans.

Despite all this, the Hopes were exhilarated by life at Atlanta Baptist College. The school, to be renamed Morehouse College in 1913, boasted a remarkable faculty that included W.E.B. Du Bois, a professor of history and economics. Du Bois and the Hopes became fast friends and allies as "race men" (and women), committed opponents of Booker T. Washington's accommodationist views. In 1899 Du Bois invited Lugenia to participate in a conference on "The Welfare of the Negro Child." The conference offered the middle-class Hope a glimpse of the chaotic, despairing lives of the neglected poor children of black Atlanta. Her response was to form a committee among other faculty wives to organize home day care for the small children of working mothers. The Gate City Free Kindergarten Association opened two kindergartens its first fall, two more the following year, and four more the next year. From this point on, Hope's primary commitment was always to children, to the children as future citizens, as minds and spirits not yet distorted by hopelessness. She was convinced that prevention was far easier and more successful than remediation.

When Hope's first child, Edward, was born in 1901, she became acutely aware that the city of Atlanta provided *no* park or playground where African American children were permitted. Lugenia rallied a group of faculty wives and mothers from the neighborhood around Atlanta Baptist and Spelman and organized a tightly focused ad hoc committee. They persuaded Atlanta Baptist College to let them build a playground on the college campus; they reached into the community to urge donations of equipment and of workmen's time to install it. This sort of highly specific neighborhood networking became the modus operandi of Hope's major creation, the Neighborhood Union.

In 1906 John Hope was inaugurated as the first African American president of Atlanta Baptist College. That same year, the cumulative effects of a virulently racist state-wide gubernatorial campaign and a vicious, lurid newspaper war in Atlanta exploded into a major race riot. The night of September 22, 1906 saw a rash of coordinated, unprovoked attacks on blacks throughout Atlanta. John Hope, armed secretly by an army veteran, patrolled his campus all night long. Militia units were posted at both Spelman and Atlanta Baptist to prevent attacks. After the riot, Lugenia was more than ever convinced that black Atlanta needed to develop a vital sense of community as much as it needed better jobs, houses, schools, streets, and sewers.

In 1908 a single, undramatic incident finally galvanized Hope into action. A solitary young woman, new to the neighborhood, sickened in her home and died because her neighbors were unaware of her condition. The avoidable death shocked the community; in response, Hope called a meeting of local women to discuss ways to improve communication and conditions among African Americans. This group became the Neighborhood Union, and Hope was elected president.

The goals of the Neighborhood Union included the development of playgrounds and educational clubs of various sorts; instructional programs in hygiene, parenting, and cultural heritage; and the creation of an organization cohesive and confident enough to deal forcefully with the city government. Under Hope's guidance, the Union divided the city into zones, districts, and neighborhoods, to establish direct house-to-house contact with the population and gather accurate data on the conditions and needs of their people. This superb delegation of responsibility, meticulous attention to detail, and the ability to elicit the active involvement of her "clients" were hallmarks of Hope's vision. The quality of her organization facilitated effective mobilization for protest and petition throughout the history of the Union.

By 1914 there were Union branches throughout Atlanta, supported by contributions from individuals and churches, and the monthly membership dues of ten cents per family; they provided numerous arts and crafts classes, educational lectures, programs on African American music and culture, informal libraries stocked with good books, and enriching activities for older girls, whose safety and moral development were perceived as a pressing concern.

The major campaigns of the Union focused on the abysmal level of health care and on the inadequacies of the black school system. In 1913 the Union launched a detailed investigation and exposé of conditions within the segregated schools. Members approached every influential white woman in Atlanta for support and bombarded the Board of Education and the City Council with petitions and reports. Their immediate victories—one small new school and a minor increase in teachers' salaries—were small, but their campaign represented the first sustained organizational effort to confront the racism of the city government.

The Union's drive the following year to improve health care was more effective. They conducted a major educational initiative against tuberculosis and set up diagnostic clinics; dental and immunization clinics followed. Throughout these campaigns Lugenia Hope was a dedicated, tireless presence, a figure of unassailable dignity and confidence.

Hope needed all her dignity and confidence in her battle with the racism of the Young Women's Christian Association. Since 1906 the YWCA had organized throughout the South—for whites; they provided no facilities whatsoever for blacks. The next year the national board agreed to allow black student groups to organize informally in the South, but only at the discretion and under the authority of white branches. The idea of a black YWCA was unthinkable. For years Hope fought eloquently against this policy, with no seeming impact; black delegates to the 1913 national convention were seated in a segregated balcony.

World War I represented a watershed in African American attitudes: the sacrifices of black soldiers and the egregious ugliness of the treatment accorded them in the segregated armed forces galvanized the network of black organizations. Despite repeated rebuffs and deliberate slights from the white field secretary for "colored work," Hope was able to demand the establishment of a black YWCA in 1919. "Northern women," she told her colleagues angrily, "thought they knew more about it than Southern women. Colored women believed they knew more than both and that's why they wanted to represent themselves" (Giddings, 158). By 1921, with almost no budget at all, the Phyllis Wheatley branch was providing classes, guidance, and support to over 350 young women. Finally, in 1922, the national board agreed to eliminate the bitterly resented white field secretaries and to deal directly with black branches.

In the 1920s Hope was invited to participate in the newly formed Council for Interracial Cooperation. This "radical" group was founded in 1920 by a liberal Methodist minister, Will Alexander, to encourage enlightened exchanges between the better elements of both races, in order to promote improved race relations. At the first meeting of the women's committee, Hope opened with typical directness:

We have just emerged from a world war that cost the lives of thousands of our boys fighting to make the world safe for democracy—for whom? Women, we can achieve nothing today unless you [who] have met us are willing to help find a place in American life where we can be unashamed and unafraid (Rouse, *Lugenia*, 109).

These first interracial meetings were considered so controversial that they were held in virtual secrecy. There was great mutual distrust and suspicion. White women, accustomed to dealing with black women only as servants, were stunned to meet a group of highly educated, articulate, poised, and determined African American women, many of whom had better organizational experience and credentials. The first black speaker, the dynamic school founder and Wellesley College graduate Charlotte Hawkins Brown, offered a direct challenge to the white South's mythology of lynching:

> We all feel that you can control your men. We feel as far as lynching is concerned that, if the white woman would take hold of the situation, that lynching would be stopped. . . . When you read in the paper where a colored man has insulted a white woman, just multiply that by one thousand and you have some idea of the number of colored women insulted by white men.
>
> I want to ask . . . won't you help us, friends, to bring to justice the criminal of your race, who is just as much criminal when [he] tramps on the womanhood of my race (Rouse, *Lugenia*, 111).

Eventually, the majority of white delegates seemed not brave enough to bridge the enormous gulfs of history and bigotry. Despite surface appearances of understanding, Hope was disillusioned and angry. "Ignorance is ignorance wherever found," she wrote bitterly, "yet the most ignorant white woman may enjoy every privilege that America offers. Now I think that the ignorant Negro woman should also enjoy them to the best of her ability. We learn by doing, and what is good for one race is good for the other (Rouse, *Lugenia*, 113). Ultimately, the all-white Association of Southern Women for the Prevention of Lynching was unwilling to challenge their congressional delegations, and any federal anti-lynching bills died protracted deaths by filibuster.

Hope was a guiding force in the long, slow drive to register black Atlantans to vote. A life member and the first vice-president of the Atlanta NAACP, she concentrated her energies in the Junior Division in an effort to prepare future voters; special classes rehearsed the complex procedures of registering and qualifying to vote. Evening adult classes, taught by professors from Atlanta University, offered American history and government to thousands. In 1919 Hope organized the Social Service Institute at Morehouse College, which the following year became the

Atlanta School of Social Work, the only training school for black social workers. In 1938 the school became a division of Atlanta University.

Hope was developing a national reputation. She was a member of Herbert Hoover's Colored Advisory Committee, designing relief programs to meet the needs of black refugees from the devastating Mississippi River floods of 1927. Throughout the Depression she served as an assistant to Mary McLeod Bethune, director of the Negro Affairs Division of the National Youth Administration. She lectured nationally for the National Council of Negro Women on major topics such as parenting, racism, education, lynching, feminism, and segregation. When she retired from the presidency of the Neighborhood Union in 1933, Hope was honored for her drive, her gift for leadership and organization, and her determination to bring the legitimate needs and desires of African Americans before white America.

When John Hope died in 1936, Lugenia moved to New York City and traveled extensively for her work with Bethune. As long as she was physically able, she attended conferences, meetings, and lectures; she maintained a rich emotional life with her sons' families and with such leading African American figures as W.E.B. Du Bois and Paul Robeson. After suffering a stroke in 1944, she lived quietly with a niece in Chicago, where she died in 1947.

Lugenia Hope gave tirelessly of herself to the causes she cherished: improved education, health care, pride, and self-reliance for her community; honorable laws equitably administered for all people. She combined an idealist's vision with a hard-headed practicality to achieve more lasting concrete betterment than either component could have alone. At her memorial service, her old friend Charlotte Hawkins Brown recalled,

> She despised deceit and camouflage on the part of anyone. . . . I can hear her saying now, "Charlotte . . . we must not let that pass; if we do we shall meet it again." And on through the years, this uncompromising yet kind and tender-hearted woman fought through the night of our experience for some of the . . . ground we have gained in human relations (Rouse, *Lugenia*, 134).

References

Giddings, Paula. *When and Where I Enter: The Impact of Black Women on Race and Sex in America*. New York: William Morrow, 1984.

Lerner, Gerda, ed. *Black Women in White America*. New York: Pantheon Books, 1972.

Rouse, Jacqueline. "The Legacy of Community Organizing: Lugenia Burns Hope and the Neighborhood Union." *Journal of Negro History* 69 (1984): 114–133.

———. *Lugenia Burns Hope: Black Southern Reformer*. Athens, GA: University of Georgia Press, 1989.

Smith, Jessie, ed. *Notable Black American Women*. Detroit: Gale Research, 1992.

MYLES HORTON

(July 5, 1905–January 19, 1990)

Educator, Civil Rights and Labor Rights Activist

Myles Horton was literally born in a log cabin—not in itself an unusual feat: the impoverished hills of western Appalachia were full of log cabins. But Horton, fired with a driving vision of social justice, moved on from rural Tennessee to study in New York, Chicago, and Europe. Armed with new knowledge and insight, he came home to his mountains and established a unique institution: the Highlander Folk School, built out of his religious faith in working people, committed to helping these people recognize and act on their own strengths. Feared, reviled, persecuted and prosecuted, Highlander became one of the major forces for economic and social justice throughout the South. The ultimate tribute to Horton and his conviction that poor people can organize their own salvation may be that so few people have heard of him and his remarkable school.

Myles Horton
Courtesy, Highlander Archives.

Myles Horton's family was of old Scots stock. His ancestors had settled in North Carolina shortly after the Revolution and had pioneered into eastern Tennessee not long afterward. The region had a history of large plantation agriculture and a slave-based economy. By the time Myles was born, the area was sunk in chronic poverty. Standards of living and of education were abysmal. Although neither of his parents had any high school education, they both worked as school teachers until a "modernization" campaign set standards they could not meet and they lost their jobs. Despite their limited education, they were both open-minded and intellectually hungry. They set a high value on education and encouraged their children's reading. More significant for Myles, they respected independence and honesty and denigrated hypocrisy and self-righteousness. His mother offered Myles a religious vision based on love and responsibility rather than dogma. As he recalled,

> From my mother and father I learned the idea of service and the value of education. They taught me by their actions that you are supposed to serve your fellow men, you're supposed to do something worthwhile with your life, and education is meant to help you do something for others (Horton, 2).

The independence of conscience nurtured by his family frequently left Horton at odds with a rigid, repressive educational system. His directness and willingness to challenge accepted authority marked him as a troublemaker, a label he accepted with perverse pride. "I was always getting in trouble for reading in school." Of his early teachers he remarked, "I didn't respect them because I thought they were killing all the creativity, I became very critical of the way things were done" (Horton and Freire, 28).

Local schooling went up only to the eighth grade, so his family sent him to stay with friends in nearby Humboldt, a larger town where he could attend high school. He lived in his host's garage, working odd jobs to pay for his keep while he finished school. Here too, his clear-sighted honesty offended the social conventions that shaped life around him. On one occasion in the Humboldt church, he listened to a visiting missionary boast of his many conversions among African "savages." The missionary acknowledged, however, that many more natives rejected his teachings than accepted them. He described a system in which the totally "unenlightened" soul was spared damnation, but the soul that rejected Christ was utterly damned. Horton commented that the preacher had actually condemned more souls to hell than he had saved; the boy suggested that it might have been better for everyone had the missionary stayed home.

Throughout his long life, Horton remained unapologetic for his icono-clastic views:

> When people criticize me for not having any respect for existing structures and institutions, I protest. I say I give institutions and structures and traditions all the respect that I think they deserve. That's usually mighty little, but there are things that I do respect. They have to earn that respect. They have to earn it by serving people. They don't earn it just by age or legality or tradition (Horton and Freire, 136).

In 1924 Horton entered Cumberland University, a small church-run college in Lebanon, Tennessee, as a literature major. His stay at the school was problematic. He found the rigid classical education totally remote from the world he knew; he came to believe that this formal education was designed to denigrate the life and culture around him, to teach contempt for his own heritage. As a freshman, he organized the other freshmen against the humiliating hazing rites of the school fraternities, which were unable to break the united front the freshmen presented. It was Horton's first experience of the power of numbers. The following year Tennessee was rocked by the Scopes trial, in which Clarence Darrow and William Jennings Bryan debated the literal accuracy of the Bible and the freedom to teach evolution. Horton, who supported Scopes's right to teach as he saw fit, was branded as a heretic by his teachers and classmates. Each of these experiences seemed to liberate him, to strengthen his resolve to live and work beyond the confines conventional society had laid out for him.

As president of the student YMCA, Horton attended a state conference of the organization in Nashville in 1927. For the first time, he met foreign exchange students and African American students. Open and welcoming to these new influences, he soon came up against the wall of Jim Crow regulations he had never even had to think about before. He was not permitted to take a Chinese girl into a restaurant; the black student with whom he had become friendly could not enter the public library with him. Typically irreverent, Horton had no use for traditional explanations of racism and segregation; he was stunned and outraged.

A seminal experience for Horton occurred that summer, when he took a job running summer Bible schools in the Tennessee mountains for the Presbyterian Sunday School Board. The town he worked in, Ozone, was in a desperately poor area. Saccharine reassurances and stern admonishments had no impact on these struggling families, and attendance at the Bible school was sparse at best. It was here that Horton first learned to teach by listening, to hear what people had to say, to let *them* teach *him* what they really needed. He started holding evening adult education meetings, where he encouraged unemployed, disabled miners and textile workers to share their pain and try to arrive at solutions to their common crises. He started each meeting with a singing game or a traditional local story, demonstrating respect for the indigenous culture and hoping the people would come to respect themselves more. Soon he was holding meetings every night, and people were traveling miles to draw strength and support from each other. When he submitted his final report, his superiors criticized him for grossly exaggerating the attendance at these meetings; the locals had been notoriously indifferent to the more formal instructional efforts previously employed. Horton always felt that the seeds of the Highlander School were planted in Ozone, but it would take him years to digest the experience and to incorporate it into his educational philosophy.

After graduation Horton became the secretary for student YMCAs in Tennessee. Still struggling to understand what had worked—and what hadn't—in Ozone, he discovered the great pragmatist philosopher William James, who insisted that change is always possible. He read John Dewey, who spoke passionately of an education relevant to the real life of the student. Horton insisted that the YMCA meetings he organized be interracial; consequently, he was the target of constant complaints and disapproval. In turn, he was disgusted by the hypocrisy of the YMCA officials, and both he and the organization were relieved when he resigned.

Before his resignation, he met a young Congregationalist minister who would become a major mentor: the Reverend Abram Nightingale. It was Nightingale who urged Horton to broaden his education and to arm himself for the massive moral battles he anticipated; Nightingale introduced Horton to the Christian socialism of Harry F. Ward, a professor at Union Theological Seminary in New York City and author of *Our Economic Morality*; Nightingale convinced Horton to apply to Union.

Horton arrived at Union Theological Seminary in October of 1929, only days before the stock market crash precipitated the greatest crisis in the history of capitalism. UTS was a center of radical Christian socialism; the visionary Reinhold Niebuhr was on the faculty, and the courageous anti-Nazi Dietrich Bonhoeffer was a visiting student. A fellow student described Horton's arrival:

> This little hillbilly fellow, and that was what Myles was, wandered up to New York to Union Theological Seminary to get the Word of the Lord. Instead, he ran into Reinhold Niebuhr, who was speaking with almost as much authority as the Lord, and apparently had a greater social conscience (Adams, 11).

Niebuhr was critical of the comforting liberal theory of inevitable progress. He used a Marxian analysis to identify problems and to postulate solutions. His radical critique of capitalism and his bold defense of the rights of working people had a profound impact on Horton. Almost forty years later, Horton wrote to Niebuhr that "it was your inspiration and encouragement which provided the reservoir of strength and commitment that still keeps me going" (Adams, 12).

Under Niebuhr's guidance Horton immersed himself in the history of American socialism. He absorbed the vibrant, proud, angry words of the Harlem Renaissance, especially the works of Langston Hughes, Countee Cullen, Claude McKay, and Jean Toomer. He visited Brookwood Labor College, a workers' school in Katonah, New York run by leading pacifist A. J. Muste; he visited numerous settlement houses in the city slums. Horton was impressed by the achievements of Brookwood and the cooperative interaction of the settlements, but he considered them too urban and structured to succeed in the Appalachian hills to which he was committed.

In 1930 and 1931 Horton studied sociology at the University of Chicago, striving to understand social dynamics, mass movements, and conflict resolution. He became a frequent visitor to Hull House, where the elderly Jane Addams offered him a vision of strength and humor in the face of great difficulties, intimidation, and outright threats. As he read more widely in the field of adult education, he became deeply impressed by the Danish folk schools, and he decided the only way to understand them was to see them firsthand. In the summer of 1931, against the advice of all his friends except Niebuhr, Horton passed up the offer of a teaching assistantship at Chicago and left for Denmark.

The folk schools of Denmark grew from one man's response to his country's despair and demoralization in the mid-19th century. Defeated militarily and dominated by Prussia, many Danes were destitute and alienated from their own culture. Bishop N.S.F. Grundtvig decided to use nontraditional, unstructured adult schools to celebrate the local culture and to revive the people's respect for their own folk wisdom. By 1925 over 300,000 adult Danes were attending independent folk schools where they studied their own language, history, music, and poetry; participants contributed whatever they could—food, fuel, or labor. Denmark had grown into a proud, cohesive society with a strong tradition of trade unions and farmers' cooperatives. Horton was deeply moved by the schools' freedom from convention, participatory democracy, and sense of commitment to social justice. He recognized that the folk school director's real gift was to offer his own capacity to learn, to trust himself to learn from the people. On Christmas Eve, too excited to sleep, Horton entered in his notebook:

I can't sleep, but there are dreams. What you must do is go back, get a simple place, move in and you are there. The situation is there. You start

with this and let it grow. You know your goal. It will build its own structure and take its own form. You can go to school all your life, you'll never
figure it out because you are trying to get an answer that can only come
from the people in the life situation (Horton, 55).

Horton had found the flexibility, pragmatism, compassion, and purpose
that would guide him for the rest of his life. He was ready to come home.

Back at Union Seminary, Horton and Niebuhr planned his folk school.
Horton enlisted two classmates: John Thompson and James Dombrowski, both young Southerners committed to the regeneration of the
South. Through Will Alexander, head of the Commission of Interracial
Cooperation, they found Don West, another Southerner searching for
ways to bring racial and economic justice to the South. With the help of
Horton's old friend Abram Nightingale, the young men found a large,
rambling old house on Monteagle Mountain in Tennessee; the house had
been run as a school by Dr. Lillian Johnson, an elderly, educated local
suffragist and reformer who agreed to give Horton a one-year proba-
tionary lease. The Highlander Folk School was soon ready for business.

Highlander (the name many Appalachian mountaineers used for
themselves) was located in Grundy County, one of the eleven poorest
counties in the entire country. Horton and his friends hoped to train
rural and industrial activists and to conserve and honor the indigenous
mountain culture. They were flexible and pragmatic about the enterprise.
The only two inviolable principles they established were freedom of
speech and social equality—without exception, Highlander would be a
totally integrated social environment, in direct violation of a 1901 Tennessee law forbidding blacks and whites from eating together or sleeping
in the same building. With all their good intentions, the young reformers
had tremendous difficulty learning to transcend their intellectual, academic training. "We were going to bring democracy to the people," Horton recalled decades later, "I mean bring it to them like a missionary
and dump it on them whether they liked it or not" (Horton and Freire,
43). Gradually the Highlander staff struggled to comprehend the largely
nonverbal communication of many poor mountain people; to avoid offering abstract, theoretical solutions; to earn the trust of deeply suspicious people. Classes were offered in cultural geography, revolutionary
literature, psychology, and specific local economic and social problems.
A seminar on social change provided the basic structure for the workshops that would become the core of the school's curriculum.

Within months, Highlander endured a baptism of fire through its involvement in the bloody, anguished miners' strike at Wilder, about one
hundred miles away. Wilder was a grim, corrupt company town. When
the desperate miners struck, the company shut off electricity and tore
the doors off the already wretched shacks. The National Guard was

called in to defend strikebreakers; the Red Cross gave out food parcels to the strikebreakers while the miners' children were starving. Horton launched a nationwide publicity campaign; letters in newspapers across the country described the situation and asked for food and support. When Horton and Thompson brought food into Wilder, they were threatened and arrested. Horton was charged with "coming here, getting information, going back and teaching it" (Peters and Bell, 250). When two hundred miners and their families were evicted from their homes, Horton was able to find work for many of them with the new Tennessee Valley Authority. While the strike at Wilder was defeated, Highlander had demonstrated its commitment and its usefulness.

Throughout the 1930s, Horton and Highlander were active in both major strikes and the smaller strikes the big labor organizations ignored. Highlander trained local activists in strike strategy, negotiating, organizing, and labor law. One striker, an impoverished woodcutter, recalled thirty years later, "At Highlander we learned how to handle our daily problems, to do so by organizing, by sharing our power and our strength. The most important thing the people ever learned from Highlander was what we learned then—how we could help ourselves" (Adams, 38).

Highlander's increasing significance for the poor people of the mountains could always be gauged by the anger of local bosses. John Edgerton, a mill owner who helped start the Southern Manufacturers' Association because he considered the National Association of Manufacturers too liberal, called Highlander "about the boldest and most insulting thing to the Anglo-Saxon South that has yet been done" (Adams, 40). In 1935 Edgerton was able to force the withdrawal of a crucial $7,000 grant offered to Highlander by the Federal Emergency Relief Administration. Despite this, Highlander expanded steadily. It offered six-week residential training programs for potential union leaders; it provided on-site strike support, including practical advice and help, study and singing groups on the picket lines, and invaluable publicity through its national connections with the liberal community; in noncrisis times, it nurtured cultural life in nearby cities, providing outdoor stages with music lessons, folk dancing, and, always, communal singing.

Daily life at Highlander was demanding and hectic. The practical needs of the workers and poor families who were their main clients kept the staff from losing focus in a haze of idealistic well-meaning. They never lost sight of their ultimate goal: educating common people to unite and create massive social change. Horton freely admitted that this was a passionate pedagogy with no room for "objectivity."

As soon as I started looking at that word *neutral* and what it meant, it became obvious to me there can be no such thing as neutrality. It's a code

word for the existing system. It has nothing to do with anything but agree-
ing to what is and will always be. . . . *Neutrality is just following the crowd.*
. . . Neutrality, in other words, was an immoral act. . . . It was to me a refusal to oppose injustice or to take sides that are unpopular (Horton and
Freire, 102).

Music and drama have always been central elements of Highlander.
Between 1935 and 1952, students at Highlander wrote and produced
nearly one hundred plays about their lives and struggles. Folk and protest songs enriched every meeting. In 1935 a young musician and sto-
ryteller, Zilphia Johnson, came to work at Highlander; a coal miner's
daughter, she was deeply committed to the mission of the school. Only
a few months later, she and Horton were married. For twenty years,
until her death in 1956, Zilphia Horton was a creative force at Highlander. She taught the songs she knew, learned songs from the workers
who came to study; she did field work to collect songs from isolated
mountain families. She transcribed, compiled, edited, and distributed the
songs. She performed frequently with the great folk/blues singer Huddy
Ledbetter, known as Leadbelly; he in turn became one of Highlander's
most effective fundraisers. The song that would become the anthem of
the civil rights movement, "We Shall Overcome," was shaped at Highlander. Zilphia had learned it from striking North Carolina tobacco
workers, who had modified an old gospel tune. In 1947 Zilphia further
adapted the words and taught the song to a frequent visitor to Highlander, Pete Seeger. By the late 1950s the song, with its exultant confidence in the eventual triumph of justice and nonviolence, had spread
throughout the South.

In 1937 the Congress of Industrial Organizations, the CIO, was formed
as a working-class response to the elitism of the "skilled trade" emphasis
of the older American Federation of Labor, the AFL. Highlander welcomed the new umbrella organization and functioned for years as the
official training facility for the CIO. By the late 1940s, Horton was disillusioned by the increasing conservatism and corruption within the
CIO's power structure. Many of the basic goals Highlander had shared
with the unions had been won: union recognition, improved pay and
benefits, membership clauses in contracts, and even some racial integration. But Horton's social and political goals went far beyond the middle-
class self-satisfaction into which the CIO had settled. In 1949 the CIO
decided to expel all members with Communist associations; since the
American Communist Party had provided the first and in many cases
the only support for struggling unions in the explosive Depression years,
the expulsion order affected thousands of people. Two entire unions
were expelled for refusing to eject their Communist members. Horton
was disgusted. He refused to accept CIO directives on whom he should

welcome to training sessions. The disaffection was mutual, and the CIO severed its official connection with the proudly unrepentant Highlander. Reevaluating the national climate and the mission of the school, Highlander's staff agreed to turn their major efforts toward the barely budding civil rights movement.

Race relations throughout the South were tense and explosive. In Tennessee a 1901 law forbade blacks and whites to marry or to eat, sleep, or travel together. There were few resident blacks in Grundy County, and Horton's early efforts to bring black workers to Highlander met with little success; fear and distrust were at first too strong. In 1938 Highlander helped organize the Southern Conference on Human Welfare, a huge interracial convention of liberals held in Birmingham, Alabama; delegates including Mary McLeod Bethune, Dr. Benjamin Mays, and Dr. F. D. Patterson, all presidents of black colleges; Supreme Court Justice Hugo Black; and First Lady Eleanor Roosevelt. In 1940 Highlander informed all the unions it served that it would no longer offer training to any union that discriminated in any degree against African Americans. All Highlander workshops were fully integrated.

In the 1950s Horton built on Highlander's foundation of trust and decency to an extent that touched almost every major figure in the civil rights movement. The Reverend E. D. Nixon, president of the Alabama NAACP, was an old friend of Horton's; he had trained at Highlander for his work organizing Alabama's agricultural workers. At Nixon's urging, Rosa Parks, the executive secretary of the Mongtomery NAACP, came to Highlander in 1955, only months before her quiet defiance triggered the Montgomery bus boycott. The experience changed her life—and through her agency, the future of the country. Years later she commented,

> At Highlander I found out for the first time in my adult life that this could be a unified society, that there was such a thing as people of different races and backgrounds meeting together in workshops, and living together in peace and harmony. It was a place I was very reluctant to leave. I gained there the strength to persevere in my work for freedom, not just for blacks, but for all oppressed people (Couto, 304).

Parks remembered Horton with profound affection and respect:

> Myles Horton just washed away and melted a lot of my hostility and prejudice and feeling of bitterness toward white people, because he had such a wonderful sense of humor. I often thought about many of the things he said and how he could strip the white segregationists of their hardcore attitudes and how he could confuse them, and I found myself laughing when I hadn't been able to laugh in a long time (Clark, 17).

In the coming years, thousands of African Americans, some who became famous and many who did not, received inspiration and training in organizing and nonviolent resistance at Highlander. Future leaders Septima Clark, Ella Baker, John Lewis, Robert Moses, Esau Jenkins, and James Bevel were among the dedicated black activists who, in many cases, first came to know each other at Highlander. James Bevel, who organized the children's marches during the Montgomery Boycott, never forgot the impact on him of Horton's uncompromising, unsparing honesty:

> Myles was a guy who'd ask questions about your assumptions. He would challenge you on your inferior feelings. . . . He has arrived at a self-respect and self-appreciation of mankind. He, in that sense, is not a liberal, he's an enlightened man. . . . He, like, destroyed all the false assumptions of the oppressor and made us deal with the fact that we were cowards and that we were lying, and were not serious about being who we said we were (Morris, 148).

Highlander's political and economic goals had long roused the hostility of the traditional South; its growing involvement in the civil rights struggle gave angry whites additional impetus to accuse the school of subversive and "communistic" intentions. In 1954 Horton was called before the Senate Internal Security Subcommittee, run by the rabid segregationist James Eastland. Eastland demanded that Horton name people who had attended Highlander or who had worked with him in various strikes and protests. Horton refused. He based his stance not on the Fifth Amendment clause against self-incrimination, but on his First Amendment right of free speech; as he saw it, the freedom to speak is inextricably bound to the freedom *not* to speak. He told Eastland, "That's the power over which your committee has no jurisdiction. It's just up to me and my conscience." Eastland was livid and threatened to cite Horton for contempt; years later, Horton recalled his response:

> And I said, "I don't see that that will be much of a problem, senator. I'm willing to testify that I'm in contempt of this committee. I'm in contempt of you and everything you stand for." And he said, "Throw him out!" I was picked up by a couple of federal marshals and thrown down on the marble steps of the court of justice (Schultz and Schultz, 29).

Highlander's most far-reaching contribution to the civil rights movement was the Citizenship School movement. A 1955 workshop had drawn both Septima Clark, a Charleston school teacher active in the NAACP, and her friend Esau Jenkins, a community leader on the impoverished Johns Island. Clark and Jenkins were concerned with the extent of illiteracy on the islands off South Carolina and with blacks' consequent inability to pass voter registration examinations. Horton agreed to help them; he spent weeks living on the islands, observing the communities and the unsuccessful adult education attempts that had been made. He saw hard-working, serious adults come to school rooms where they were treated with well-meaning condescension, seated awkwardly at small, children's desks, and offered a demeaning curriculum. In response, Horton made several crucial decisions about the program that would grow into the Citizenship Schools: it would exist outside the formal educational system; it would involve no certified teachers and no white teachers; it would never forget that its pupils were adults entitled to dignity and respect. The immediate goal would be the minimal literacy required for the voter registration test. As Horton described the plan,

> We decided we'd pitched it on a basis of them becoming full citizens and taking their place in society and demanding their rights and being real men and women in their own right. Putting into practice all these religious things they talked about, and the humanitarian things they talked about, and doing something about it. They owed it to the future generations (Morris, 151).

The first teacher, Bernice Robinson, was Septima Clark's niece and an independent beautician. (Such financial independence was important, since any hint of involvement with Highlander could get any African American fired.) She taught her students from the United Nations' Universal Declaration of Human Rights. That first class of fourteen adults, which opened in 1957 with funding arranged by Highlander, was a huge success. Within three months, 80% of the students "graduated": they passed the registration examination and became registered voters for the first time in their lives. Requests for Citizenship Schools poured in from other islands and soon from across the South. Highlander established special programs for recruiting and training teachers, but Horton fulfilled his promise to keep the experts—and whites—out of the schools. He was proud that not a single Citizenship classroom teacher was directly connected to Highlander; rather, the schools were a magnificent example of seeds intelligently planted producing an abundant harvest. By 1961, when Highlander turned the project over to Andrew Young under the auspices of the Southern Christian Leadership Conference, thirty-seven schools had taught almost fifteen hundred students; black voter registration in affected areas was up 300%. By 1963, 26,000 African Americans throughout the South had successfully registered to vote after attending Citizenship Schools. Septima Clark, who coordinated teacher training, estimated in 1970 that roughly 100,000 blacks had learned to read and write through the school network. Typically, Horton's appraisal of Highlander's role was modest and understated: "Movements are not started by educational institutions, I don't care how good they are. We might have been pretty good, at least the enemies thought so. But not that good, you know" (Morris, 157).

Highlander's enemies did give the school a great deal of credit for its place in the early civil rights movement. The Montgomery Boycott had given the school a degree of notoriety; the Citizenship Schools convinced white politicians that Highlander had to be eliminated. The legislatures of Arkansas, Alabama, and Georgia urged the state of Tennessee to destroy Highlander. Attendants at Highlander's twenty-fifth anniversary celebrations in 1957, at which Martin Luther King, Jr. was the main speaker, included an undercover photographer employed by the governor of Georgia. Soon, billboards across the South carried huge photographs of King at Highlander, denouncing the "Communist Training School." The Internal Revenue Service revoked the school's tax-exempt status, an action Horton was able to have overturned on appeal. The Tennessee legislature established a committee to expose the lurking evil at Highlander, and sensationalized hearings were held in February of 1959; evidence of "communist" plots included photographs of blacks and whites folk dancing together. The school's charter was revoked; fortunately, Horton, with good legal advice, had foreseen this move and had already applied for a new charter under the name "Highlander Research and Education Center." The state confiscated the old school and in 1961 auctioned off all the property: 175 acres; 14 school buildings; seven residences, including Horton's private cabin and that of his elderly parents; furniture, bedding, typewriters. The auction netted the state $44,000, but no one from Highlander ever received any compensation for the seizure of private property. Fittingly, the last group to train at the old site was the year-old Student Nonviolent Coordinating Committee, led by the charismatic Stokely Carmichael; SNCC would play a major role in the upcoming sit-ins and freedom marches.

Highlander reopened, first in a derelict mansion in Knoxville and later in its current location, New Market. Horton remained philosophical about his persecution. "You can padlock a building," he commented. "But you can't padlock an idea. Highlander is an idea. You can't kill it and you can't close it in. . . . It will grow wherever people take it" (Adams, 133).

In the later 1960s Highlander turned back to its original regional focus, concentrating on the problems of demoralization, passivity, and welfare dependency. Once again, the first, crucial step was to offer deep human respect so that others could remember to respect themselves. The Center's concern for the environmental exploitation and degradation of Appalachia soon forced it to a broader vision. By the mid-1970s, Horton had come to see an overriding threat from multinational corporations with no national loyalty; he was distressed by the growing power of the military-industrial alliance. Horton resigned from the full-time staff of Highlander in 1973; while he continued to live on the school property, he spent much of his time consulting and designing local programs in Alaska, Asia, Africa, South America, and Australia. In the 1980s Highlander added workshops on toxic wastes and pioneered in the growing grassroots movement for environmental justice; Highlander has provided international networking for chemical workers in West Virginia and Bhopal, India; and for textile workers in Mexico as well as in Tennessee. Horton pooled knowledge and resources with Paulo Freire, the renown Brazilian proponent of adult education. Highlander created "participatory research," in which local citizens are trained to investigate and design solutions to their own complex problems. In the case of Appalachia, the pressing issue has been land ownership. The Appalachian Land Ownership Task Force, designed and trained by Highlander, has conducted a meticulous state-by-state search of local court records, tracing patterns of ownership, holding companies, and hidden titles. The Task Force has proven that over 80% of Appalachia is corporate- and absentee-owned; the tax burden falls disproportionately on the 20% of the land still in private hands. With Highlander's quiet guidance, citizen groups have lobbied successfully for more equitable land taxation and have fought the devastation of strip mining.

In his later years, tired and fighting cancer, Horton admitted to some discouragement. He acknowledged some victories but spoke of the larger goals still unmet. He had always seen his ultimate goals as unattainable; he saw all of life as a continuous struggle to grow ethically and morally, and he saw Highlander as a part of that process. His job, he said, was "to provide a climate which nurtures islands of decency, where people can learn in such a way that they continue to grow" (Horton, 133). When Horton died at the age of eighty-four, *The New York Times* described Highlander as "one of the most stubbornly tenacious instruments for social change in the nation" (Applebome, 14). His good friend, the great educator Paulo Freire, declared, "The history of this man, his individual presence in the world, is something which *justifies* the world" (Horton and Freire, xxxiii).

References

Adams, Frank. With Myles Horton. *Unearthing Seeds of Fire: The Idea of Highlander.* Winston-Salem, NC: John F. Blair, 1975.

Applebome, Peter. "New Market Journal: Nurturing Seeds in a Garden of Hopes." *The New York Times* (January 29, 1990) 1:14.

Clark, Septima. *Ready From Within: Septima Clark and the Civil Rights Movement,* edited by Cynthia Stokes Brown. Navarro, CA: Wild Trees Press, 1986.

Couto, Richard A. *Ain't Gonna Let Nobody Turn Me Round: The Pursuit of Racial Justice in the Rural South*. Philadelphia: Temple University Press, 1991.

Horton, Myles. With Herbert and Judith Kohl. *The Long Haul*. New York: Doubleday, 1990.

Horton, Myles and Paulo Freire. *We Make the Road by Walking: Conversations on Education and Social Change*. Philadelphia: Temple University Press, 1990.

Morris, Aldon D. *The Origins of the Civil Rights Movement: Black Communities Organizing for Change*. New York: Free Press, 1984.

Peters, John M. and Brenda Bell. "Horton of Highlander." In Peter Jarvis, ed., *Twentieth Century Thinkers in Adult Education*. London: Croom Helm, 1987.

Schultz, Bud and Ruth Schultz. *It Did Happen Here: Recollections of Political Repression in America*. Berkeley: University of California Press, 1989.

Wigginton, Eliot, ed. *Refuse to Stand Silently By: An Oral History of Grass Roots Social Activism in America, 1921–1964*. New York: Doubleday, 1991.

JOVITA IDAR DE JUAREZ

(September 7, 1885–June 1946)

Mexican American Rights, Women's Rights Activist

In a chaotic, tumultuous, often brutal era; within a culture that traditionally offered a severely limited role to women; and further, within a larger society that often despised, denigrated, and demeaned her people, Jovita Idar stands as an exemplar of a proud, courageous, principled, generous life. She articulated a vision of justice and cooperative responsibility; she worked throughout her life—she risked her life—to bring her community closer to her vision.

Jovita Idar de Juarez
Courtesy, Jovita Lopez.

Texas had become part of the United States after the Mexican-American War of 1848. The state of Texas joined the Confederacy in March of 1861, but many Mexican-Texans supported the Union, and there were numerous incidents of harassment and sabotage against Confederate operations. Deep angry feelings remained after the war, when roving gangs of bitter Confederate veterans and outlaws preyed freely on struggling farmers in Texas. During the 1870s and 1880s a massive cattle boom and the new railroad network spurred enormous development in Texas. Eighty percent of Anglo immigrants during these years were from the deep South; they brought their racial attitudes with them, regarding Mexicans as black and treating them with contempt and hostility. Tejanos (Mexican-Texans) lost much of their landholdings to Anglo speculators, both legally and illegally. Anglo Texas imposed increasingly broad segregation on the Tejano communities along the Mexican border; incidents of officially sanctioned discrimination and brutal lynch violence rose steadily. Like African Americans and Chinese and Japanese immigrants, Mexican Americans were engulfed by the poisonous growth of casual racism in late 19th-century America.

Jovita Idar was born into this tense, volatile environment. Her father, Nicasio Idar, was the editor of *La Crónica*, an independent weekly newspaper in Laredo. A strong, proud man, Nicasio turned the newspaper into a major voice for justice and Tejano rights. All nine Idar children grew up in an atmosphere where rights, responsibilities, and the circumstances of the Chicano community were constantly discussed. Jovita, the second child, was an imaginative, spirited girl; an eager student, she won prizes for her poetry and enjoyed reciting before an audience. Whenever time permitted, she would bury herself in her father's well-stocked library and read history, poetry, or literature. As a young teen-ager, Jovita worked translating court briefs for several Laredo lawyers; she learned a great deal about the court system and judicial procedure.

In 1903 Idar received her teaching certificate from the Holding Institute in Laredo and became a teacher in the tiny south Texas town of Ojuelos. Throughout her life Idar remained an active teacher in one context or another, and she honored teachers as a major moral force in society. "Sister teacher," she wrote of her fellow teachers years later, "you who have seen flashes of light budding in the eyes of some children and have felt the pleasure of understanding that you have opened the doors to knowledge for a human being" (Idar, n.p.). But the reality of her early teaching was shocking and frustrating. There were never enough textbooks for her pupils, nor enough paper, pens, or pencils; if all her students came to class, there were not enough chairs or desks for them. She could not provide warmth for her students on cold days. The children themselves came to school inadequately dressed and frequently hungry. Like African Americans across the South, Chicanos paid taxes to support decent, well-supplied schools that their children were barred from entering. Idar realized that her best teaching efforts could scarcely touch her students' difficult, precarious lives. She decided that journalism offered more hope of effecting meaningful change, and she returned to Laredo to write for *La Crónica*.

By the time Nicasio Idar assumed ownership of *La Crónica* in 1910, all of Mexico was aflame with the Mexican Revolution, and the Chicanos of the American Southwest were profoundly involved in the conflict. Mexico had been under the ruthless, absolute control of Porfirio Diaz, a former army officer, since 1876. Diaz encouraged foreign investors and pursued policies that drove many Mexicans into desperate poverty; he brutally suppressed any opposition, driving hundreds of militant socialists and labor organizers across the border with thousands of landless peasants. The Chicano communities in Texas and California welcomed these refugees, harboring the socialists and trying to protect them from the increasing hostility of the United States government; most Chicanos were fervent supporters of the *Partido Liberál Mexicano*, the Mexican Socialist Party, founded in the United States by the exiled brothers Enrique and Ricardo Flores Magón. Chicanos' vision of their own rights and expectations was profoundly affected by their devotion to the ideals of the Revolution. The PLM offered a sophisticated program of women's rights and welcomed their participation in all aspects of party organization. Ricardo Flores Magón was especially sensitive to women's needs. He acknowledged that "although women work more than men, they are paid less, and the misery, mistreatment, and insult are today as yesterday the bitter harvest for a whole existence of sacrifice" (Cotera, 67). Jovita Idar was inspired by this sweeping revolutionary image of inclusive, liberating egalitarianism.

In 1910 Diaz jailed Francisco Madero, his opponent in the presidential election, fearing that Madero was taking the electoral process too seriously. Released after Diaz had won yet another election, Madero fled to San Antonio, Texas, where he conferred with other exiled dissidents. All along the Mexican border, Chicanos responded with eager outrage; throughout Mexico itself, decades of smoldering discontent ignited. Led by men like Pancho Villa and Venustiano Carranza, revolutionary armies sprang up and swept across Mexico. The following year Diaz, elderly and ill, resigned and fled to Europe, and Madero became president. The Revolution had barely begun. The coming decade brought horrific violence and chaos, repeated coups and assassinations, and one million casualties to Mexico; it sent almost one million refugees streaming into the American Southwest and severely exacerbated already strained racial tensions. Casual racism reached a level of public respectability in which a Chicano representative could be referred to as "the greaser from Brownsville" in the state legislature (Acuña, 306).

As racial animosities deepened, Chicanos in southern Texas were shocked by several particularly savage lynchings of Chicano suspects wrenched from inadequate police custody. One suspect, Antonio Gomez, had defended himself against a white man's insults and attacks; when the Anglo died, Gomez was charged with murder, dragged from his cell, publicly beaten to death, then dragged through the streets behind a wagon. He was fourteen years old. Nicasio Idar and his children Jovita, Clemente, and Eduardo launched a vigorous investigation of the lynchings, probing into the attitudes, training, and directives of local and state police and court officials. Their reporting provided damning documentation on grotesque inequalities within the educational and economic systems as well.

The Idars became convinced that the only hope of real improvement for Chicanos throughout Texas lay in organization and concerted political focus. Early in 1911 *La Crónica* began calling for a state-wide conference on the issues most distressing to the Mexican American community. Invitations were extended to all the Chicano fraternal, religious, and mutual benefit societies. Consistent with their broad revolutionary ideals, the Idars paid special attention to the needs of women and invited a number of leading Chicano educators to address the conference.

The organizational drive culminated in *El Primer Congreso Mexicanista* (the First Mexican Congress), a gathering of several hundred concerned Mexican Americans in Laredo in September, 1911. Major workshops focused on the worsening economic status of Chicanos; social discrimination; the deterioration of Mexican culture and Spanish language instruction; educational discrimination; and lynchings and police brutality. The *Congreso* greatly strengthened communication and support networks within the Chicano population.

For Jovita Idar, the *Congreso* provided a precious opportunity to share concerns and hopes with other educated Chicanas. Out of these discussions grew *La Liga Femeníl Mexicanista* (Mexican Feminist League), formed in October 1911 by Idar and ten other prominent Chicanas; Idar was elected president. Like Idar, most of these women were trained as teachers; like their counterparts in the equally beleaguered African American community, they had an almost religious faith in the power of education to strengthen their people. The *Liga*'s first project was to provide free kindergarten and elementary school classes for poor children in Laredo. They collected school supplies, food, and clothing to distribute to Laredo's poorest families; they organized study sessions to help educate the adult women of the community.

In March of 1913 Idar's attention was once more drawn to the Revolution. Savage fighting between government and rebel forces had reached Laredo's sister city, Nuevo Laredo, directly across the Rio Grande. The civilian population panicked under the bombardment; in the chaos, soldiers on both sides fired indiscriminately into the hysterical crowds. Across the river, the sounds of war and suffering were unmistakable and unbearable. One woman, Leonor Villegas de Magnon, responded heroically. Magnon, a kindergarten teacher and mother of three young children, was a highly educated, determined woman and a passionate believer in social justice. She called on her close friend Jovita Idar to help her try to treat the wounded. Idar, Magnon, and several other women rushed to Nuevo Laredo, where they risked their lives to carry the wounded from the streets into the hospital; in the hospital they provided crucial assistance to the desperately overworked physicians. Under constant fire, they scurried through the burning city to rescue hundreds of civilians and soldiers who would otherwise have died. Totally humanitarian, they asked no ideological questions; they rescued soldiers on both sides of the conflict. The experience convinced Magnon of the need for a permanent disaster assistance organization. With Idar's help, she established *La Cruz Blanca* (the White Cross), modeled after the American Red Cross, which had been founded in 1881 by Clara Barton to provide disaster relief and emergency medical aid.

When Idar returned to Laredo, her devotion to freedom of the press brought her into direct confrontation with a potent adversary—the United States government. Despite the tortuous political maneuverings in Mexico, many private citizens remained fiercely loyal to the declared, noble objectives of the Revolution. For the first time, peasants throughout Mexico could hope for a chance at better jobs, schools, health care, and futures. The violence and the revolutionary egalitarianism across the border filled the Anglos of Texas with profound anxiety; at their request, President Woodrow Wilson sent United States Army troops to the border to maintain control and to suppress any outbursts of similar revolutionary enthusiasm. The newspaper for which Idar was then writing, *El Progreso*, printed a scathing editorial criticizing Wilson's policy; in retaliation, the Texas Rangers determined to shut down the newspaper. When the gang of angry Rangers reached the offices of *El Progreso*, they were confronted by one slender, fierce young woman. Jovita Idar stood in the doorway of the building, refusing to let the Rangers enter, offering her determined body in defense of the constitutional rights she believed in so passionately. Jovita won that battle, but she could not wage a war alone against the Anglo power structure of Texas. The Rangers returned the next day while Idar was away, destroyed the presses, and arrested the staff. *El Progreso* was never able to reopen.

In early 1914 the battlefronts of the Revolution swept close to Laredo. *La Cruz Blanca* sprang into action. Magnon turned her large home into a hospital that eventually provided emergency care for over one hundred wounded soldiers. The United States government regarded these men as criminals and sent army troops to arrest them. Switching their clothing and identities with civilian visitors, Magnon was able to sneak many ambulatory patients past the army guards outside her home. The men who were still bed-ridden were trapped; thirty-seven wounded men were arrested and imprisoned with no specific charges or provisions for bail. Outraged and unwilling to submit to injustice, Magnon took their case to the courts, to the United States War Department, and directly to Secretary of State William Jennings Bryan, who finally ordered the men released. Afterward, Magnon, Idar, and a small band of volunteer nurses traveled for months in the hills of northern Mexico, following the army of Carranza, caring for casualties in numerous battles.

Idar returned to *La Crónica*. When Nicasio Idar died in 1914, she and her brothers and sisters took over the operation of the newspaper. Under their direction, *La Crónica* was a consistent moral voice for social justice and equal treatment before the law. The Idars fought against assimilation, treasuring true diversity and urging bilingual education and the maintenance of Mexican cultural traditions.

In 1917 Jovita Idar married Bartolo Juarez, the son of a prominent Laredo family. The couple moved to San Antonio, where Jovita opened a free bilingual kindergarten for Chicano children. Deeply committed to her community, she worked within the local Democratic Party; she served as a volunteer interpreter for Spanish-speaking patients at the county hospital. A devout Methodist, Idar co-edited *El Heraldo Cristiano*, a major Spanish-language church publication in south Texas. In 1946, at the age of sixty-one, Jovita Idar de Juarez died in San Antonio.

Throughout her life, Jovita Idar worked to improve the lives of her fellow Chicanos. She combined a deeply affectionate respect for tradition with a far-sighted, logical willingness to innovate. Her considerable learning, her organizational gifts, her eloquence, and her selfless courage were consistently deployed in the service of equity, decency, and an honorable society.

References

Acuña, Rodolfo. *Occupied America: A History of Chicanos*. New York: Harper & Row, 1981.

Cotera, Martha. *Profile of the Mexican American Woman*. Austin, TX: Information Systems, 1976.

Idar de Juarez, Jovita. "The Best Education." *El Heraldo Cristiano* 2, 247 (October, 1940), n.p.

Limón, José. "El Primer Congreso Mexicanista de 1911: A Precursor to Contemporary Chicanismo." *Aztlan* 5, 1 & 2 (Spring/Fall, 1974): 85–117.

Lomas, Clara A. "Mexican Precursors of Chicano Feminist Writing." In Cordelia

Candelaria, ed., *Multiethnic Literature of the United States: Critical Introductions and Classroom Resources*. Boulder: University of Colorado at Boulder, 1989.

Meier, Matt S. and Feliciano Rivera. *The Chicanos: A History of Mexican Americans*. New York: Hill and Wang, 1972.

Mirandé, Alfredo and Evangelina Enriquez. *La Chicana: The Mexican American Woman*. Chicago: University of Chicago Press, 1979.

Rogers, Mary Beth et al. *We Can Fly: Stories of Katherine Stinson and Other Gutsy Texas Women*. Austin, TX: Ellen C. Temple, in cooperation with Texas Foundation for Women's Resources, 1983.

Texas Foundation for Women's Resources Collection, Mss. 20: *Jovita Idar*. Texas Women's University Special Collections Library. Denton, TX.

Winegarten, Ruthe, ed. *Texas Women: A Celebration of History Exhibit Archives*. Denton, TX: Texas Women's University, 1984.

FLORENCE KELLEY

(September 12, 1859–February 17, 1932)

Women's and Children's Rights Activist, Labor Reformer

Florence Kelley was a key member of one of the most dynamic, exciting, influential teams in history: the women reformers of Hull House, Chicago, in the 1890s. Jane Addams brought to the slums of Chicago the concept of a center, a settlement, dedicated to enriching every aspect of its clients' lives. Julia Lathrop, Alzina Stevens, and Dr. Alice Hamilton molded the fields of social research, juvenile justice, and industrial medicine. Florence Kelley conducted the first social statistical survey in the United States, championed the rights of women and children, fought for industrial safety, and articulated the revolutionary concept that government bore a direct responsibility for the conditions under which its citizens lived and worked. Together these women pioneered the professionalization of the field of social work and the vast, slow change of conscience that shifted social responsibility from private charities to public government.

Florence Kelley
Courtesy of the Library of Congress.

Florence Kelley learned as a child to feel a direct relationship to the evils of human society. A beloved great-aunt was Sarah Pugh, a leading Quaker abolitionist and activist for women's rights. When Florence observed that Aunt Sarah used no sugar and wore no cotton clothing, she explained to the child that these items were produced by slave labor and that she refused to participate in any way in the system of slavery. Years later, Kelley would see her National Consumers League boycott of sweatshop garments as the direct moral descendant of Aunt Sarah's self-imposed denial.

Kelley's childhood was solitary and isolated. Five of her seven siblings died in infancy, and Kelley herself was a sickly child; understandably, her mother was an anxious, fearful woman who seldom permitted Kelley to attend school. Most of her education was drawn from the voluminous library of her father, Judge William Kelley, a "self-made" man who knew firsthand the realities of child labor. As Kelley recalled years later, "In Father's library, in the tranquil home in Germantown, in the conscience-searching Fellowship of the Friends, I had divined depths and breadths of human experience in the universe lying beyond our sheltered household life" (Goldmark, 10). An early supporter of Abraham Lincoln, Judge Kelley was a fervent abolitionist and an outspoken supporter of women's suffrage. He treated his daughter's intellect with respect and fully endorsed her decision to enter Cornell in 1876.

At Cornell, one of the few colleges that accepted women, Kelley regarded the exposure to intense learning and dedicated scholars as an almost "sacramental experience." She attracted the attention of a senior student, Martha Carey Thomas, later dean and president of Bryn Mawr College; Thomas's friendship proved invaluable years later. Kelley's senior thesis was entitled "On Some Changes in the Legal Status of Children Since Blackstone." Research for the thesis involved Kelley in the voluminous and detailed reports of British factory inspectors; she never forgot how essential this documentation was to build her case, especially when she realized that such documentation was totally lacking in the United States.

When Kelley graduated from Cornell in 1882, she intended to enter law school at the University of Pennsylvania, but as a woman, she was denied admission. Bitter and frustrated, she threw herself into running a night school for working girls in Philadelphia. Her highly successful school became the core of the New Century Guild, one of the first settlement houses in Philadelphia. The following year, she accompanied her convalescent brother on a tour of Europe. She was feeling isolated and lost until, in Avignon, they were visited by Martha Carey Thomas; vigorous and enthusiastic, Thomas raved to Kelley about her recent studies at the University of Zurich, the first European university to accept female doctoral candidates. Kelley was inspired. Before enrolling at Zurich in the fall of 1883, Kelley took a walking tour of the industrial midlands of England with her father. The poverty and despair of piecework nail and chain makers were Kelley's first exposure to "homework," or sweatshops. The images stayed with her and drove her lifelong crusade against the sweatshop.

Kelley's years in Zurich were pivotal for her. She married a Russian-Polish doctor, Lazare Wischnewetsky, and bore three children in fairly rapid succession. She was introduced to socialism and recognized in it the ethical direction for her life. She became a friend as well as a translator of Friedrich Engels; her translation of *The Conditions of the Working Classes in England in 1844* was published in London in 1887.

The young family settled in New York City in 1886; Kelley, in addition to raising her small children, began gathering data on women and child laborers. Her husband's medical practice did not develop well; he became angry and withdrawn and the marriage deteriorated rapidly. In 1889 Kelley's beloved, supportive father died. She must have felt utterly alone in 1891 when, searching for more equitable divorce laws than New York's, she brought her children to Chicago.

Shortly after her arrival in Chicago, Kelley was directed to Hull House, Jane Addams's settlement house. She depicted vividly her first meeting with Addams:

> On a snowy morning between Christmas 1891 and New Year's 1892, I arrived at Hull-House, Chicago, a little before breakfast time, and found there Henry Standing Bear, a Kickapoo Indian, waiting for the door to be opened. It was Miss Addams who opened it, holding on her left arm a singularly unattractive, fat, pudgy baby belonging to the cook who was behindhand with breakfast.... We were welcomed as though we had been invited. We stayed, Henry Standing Bear as helper to the engineer several months, when he returned to his tribe; and I as a resident seven happy, active years until May 1, 1899, when I returned to New York to enter upon the work in which I have since been engaged as secretary of the National Consumers League (Kelley, "I Go to Work," 271).

The meeting was the turning point of Kelley's life. Within days, Kelley's children had been added to the large, cheerful nursery at the nearby home of Henry Demarest Lloyd, a leading reformer and close friend of Addams; the relationship between Kelley and the Lloyds became loving and lifelong. Freed from immediate responsibility for her own family, Kelley was drawn into the nurturing, energizing circle of reformers at Hull House. These women were among the first generation of college-educated American women. They knew their own competence, and they knew how little it was valued by the official power structure. They understood personally the need to protect the weak from the strong— women from men, children from adult exploitation, *all* workers from unfair burdens—and they were determined to make their own personal understanding an issue of national conscience. Kelley had found the vital core of communal respect and encouragement that would sustain her for the rest of her life. As Kelley wrote to her mother,

> We are all well, and the chicks are happy. I have fifty dollars a month and my board and shall have more soon as I can collect my wits enough to write. I have charge of the Bureau of Labor of Hull House here and am working in the lines I have always loved. I do not know what more to tell you except this, that in the few weeks of my stay here I have won for the children and myself many and dear friends whose generous hospitality astonishes me (Sklar, 110).

Even before her arrival at Hull House, Kelley had begun her determined drive to collect hard data on the conditions of child labor in the United States; in 1889 she had read a paper on her findings at a conference of commissioners of labor statistics. As a direct result, she was appointed by the commissioner of commerce and labor in 1892 to conduct research into sweatshop conditions in the slums of Chicago. Kelley found over 2,500 sweatshops operating in Chicago, dominating the lives of children as young as three; the twelve-hour day and the seven-day week were standard. At the time, no government agency or private organization was especially concerned with the plight of working children. Kelley never saw research as an end in itself; it was a practical weapon in the war on injustice and indifference. A devout believer in the power of education, Kelley was convinced that if enough people could be forced to see the realities of child labor, they would demand changes in the laws.

Networking with the influential Chicago Women's Club and numerous other reform groups, the Hull House team agitated tirelessly for legislation to set minimum standards in factories and sweatshops. The legislation that Kelley submitted to the Illinois investigative committee in February of 1893 was revolutionary. It prohibited all garment making in tenement buildings, prohibited the labor of children under fourteen and regulated the labor of children from fourteen to sixteen, and mandated an eight-hour day for women in manufacturing. Perhaps most significantly, it provided for stringent enforcement by establishing a state factory inspector with a staff of twelve, five of whom were required to be women. Kelley's bill passed the state legislature in June of 1893; on the recommendation of Henry Lloyd, Governor John Peter Altgeld appointed Kelley the chief factory inspector. Kelley, who two years earlier had had to borrow money for her train ticket to Chicago, was now in charge of a state-wide office with a paid staff of twelve.

Kelley and her inspectors took their task very seriously. She enlisted the help of Julia Lathrop, Alzina Stevens, and, among others, union activist Abraham Bisno. The factory inspectors' lawyer, Andrew Bruce, described the circumstances under which the team labored during a devastating smallpox epidemic that first year:

> I knew Florence Kelley at the time of the smallpox epidemic when both she and Julia Lathrop were risking their lives in the sweatshop district of Chicago and were fearlessly entering the rooms and tenements of the west side and not merely alleviating the sufferings of the sick but preventing the sending abroad of the infected garments to further contaminate the community (Addams, 118).

Frustrated by the hostility of business leaders, city authorities, and court officials, Kelley decided to eliminate the necessity of dealing with prosecutors reluctant to handle her cases. She enrolled in Northwestern University Law School, taking classes at night, and received her law degreed in 1894; thereafter, she could present cases in court herself. The reactionary campaign mounted by business interests culminated in 1895, when the Illinois Supreme Court struck down the eight-hour day as an unconstitutional infringement on "freedom of contract." Two years later, when Altgeld was defeated in the gubernatorial race by a Republican, Kelley found herself summarily dismissed. Her replacement as state factory inspector had spent the previous twenty-two years working for Illinois Glass Company, one of the worst offenders against the 1893 law. Kelley spent another two years lecturing and writing at Hull House. In 1899 she was invited to head a new organization in New York City, the National Consumers League. She left Hull House and moved, with her children, into the similar atmosphere of Lillian Wald's Henry Street Settlement in New York.

The National Consumers League was the outgrowth of an eight-year-old movement to enlist consumer power to force improvements in working conditions. It represented a profound, significant step: the middle-class consuming public's recognition of itself as a vital locus in the constellation of industry. With recognition came an awareness of potential power and a growing acceptance of the responsibility to use that power ethically. As Kelley insisted, "To buy a sweated garment is to have someone work for you under sweated conditions as definitely as if she were in your own employ" (Goldmark, 53). The League's weapons were meticulously gathered documentation and blunt, unflinching publicity; Kelley was very much in her element.

The ultimate goals of the League were the elimination of all child labor and the protection of women laborers. Appealing to the self-interest as well as the idealism of the public, League speakers emphasized the possible contamination of garments produced in unregulated, unsanitary conditions. In the words of a young associate, Kelley was "a guerrilla warrior" (Goldmark, 57). She traveled across the country, exhorting, exposing, inspiring. By the end of her first year with the League, there were five new state divisions; within the next several years, sixty-four branches opened in twenty states. Kelley was able to work effectively with both working people and academics. She drew support from some of the leading figures of the time: Louis D. Brandeis served as *pro bono* counsel until he was named to the Supreme Court in 1916; he was succeeded at the League by his young friend Felix Frankfurter.

Kelley's work with the League led to many other interwoven commitments. In 1901 she helped found the New York Child Labor Committee; she served as well on the National Child Labor Committee, founded three years later. She was convinced that only a national child labor law could force the states to face the situation promptly. Critics—manufacturers, the legislators they controlled, even the Catholic Church—accused her of "Bolshevism," of trying to nationalize the country's children, of destroying the authority of parents. Kelley persisted in calling for the establishment of a national commission, an agency dedicated to the well-being of children. She excoriated a society that lavished more communal attention on animal husbandry than on nurturing its children. In 1905 she wrote, in *Some Ethical Gains Through Legislation*:

> If lobsters or young salmon become scarce or are in danger of perishing, the United States Fish Commission takes active steps in the matter. But infant mortality continues excessive, from generation to generation, in perfectly well-defined areas; yet no one organ of the national government is interested in the matter sufficiently even to gather, collate and publish consecutive information about this social phenomenon (Kelley, *Some Ethical Gains*, 101).

In 1909, Mary White Ovington* asked Kelley to help found the National Association for the Advancement of Colored People. Characteristically, Kelley did more than lend her name to the letterhead. She participated actively as a board member and on several major committees, especially those dealing with lynching and with the inequal distribution of school funds. A founding member of the Women's Joint Congressional Committee, a reform lobby, Kelley fought to have the National Association of Colored Women accepted within the organization. Kelley worked fiercely to gather support for federal anti-lynching legislation; she fought against racial segregation in New York City housing projects. Kelley seemed oblivious to the narrowly racist limitations white society imposed on itself. Ovington recounted how, at the 1920 NAACP conference in Atlanta, Kelley hurried into a meeting late and casually sat down next to William Pickens, the African American field secretary; her unthinking action threw the meeting into a panic: she had shattered the assumption of segregated seating tacitly held even within that pioneering group. "It was some minutes before Mrs. Kelley realized what she had done, but when she did, her enjoyment endured all the way to New York" (Ovington, 179). Kelley's stand for civil rights earned her the hatred and distrust of many. Writing after her death, W.E.B. Du Bois stated bluntly, "And of all Florence Kelley's sins against convention, none— not even her socialism and pacifism, her championing of sex equality and religious freedom, her fight for children and democracy—none cost her more fair-weather friends than her demands for the rights of twelve million Americans who are black" (Athey, 257).

Kelley was not concerned with her popularity. Her mission was not to make people comfortable, but to reach into the moral center of average people and to elicit from them the active compassion she believed nascent in all people. She never let private citizens absolve themselves of the actions and failures of their leaders. She declared to the annual meeting of the National Child Labor Committee in 1906:

> It is ultimately the attitude of mind of the nation that decides whether child labor laws shall be enforced after they are enacted. . . . The enforcement of the law depends not only on the quality of the men to whom the work of enforcing it is entrusted; it depends far more largely on the quality of the community in which those men hold office. . . . The community does not insist that the great in New York City shall obey the law for the protection of the children; and no commissioner of health has had the moral courage to do that which his community does not wish done (Kelley, "Obstacles," 88).

Kelley was pleased by the establishment of a National Children's Bureau in 1912, with Julia Lathrop as its director. But child labor was a controversial topic; powerful industrial forces appreciated child labor not only for its low cost and inexhaustible supply, but also for the weapon it represented against adult unions. Kelley's heroic efforts to achieve a constitutional amendment prohibiting child labor were frustrated in her lifetime. The federal government would not deal with child labor until the minimum protection offered by the Fair Labor Standards Act of 1938; this same law also established a national minimum wage, something Kelley had advocated thirty years earlier. Kelley was more successful in her struggle for federally funded maternal and child health-care services. After a difficult and protracted campaign, the Sheppard-Towne Act of 1921 established local maternal and child health stations. These were the first federal funds appropriated for social welfare.

A confirmed pacifist, Kelley was a founding member of the Women's International League for Peace and Freedom in 1919. In addition, she was the vice-president of the National Woman Suffrage Association and an active member of Eugene Debs's Socialist Party. Her energy and concern seemed boundless. In 1924 she investigated the high incidence of cancer-related deaths among young women employed by the U.S. Radium Corporation in Newark; her persistence led to a national conference on industrial health hazards and to the first protective legislation.

Kelley died in Philadelphia at the age of seventy-two after an illness of several months. She had once described herself as "the most unwearied hoper" in America (Goldmark, vi). Jane Addams saw her as a brilliant, imaginative, passionate crusader, possessed by "a kind of fiercely joyous impatience" (Linn, 139). Lillian Wald commented, "She made her generation think! She goaded others with the whips of her wit, her quickness, her bottomless sympathy, her readiness to act wherever new danger menaced the child or the people whom she believed were imposed upon" (Wald, 43). Kelley inspired and helped train an entire generation of dynamic future social workers and civic reformers, some of whom, like Frances Perkins, went on to play major roles in the decades after her death. Kelley's urgent message is as pertinent today as it was when she promulgated it: that industrial evils are man-made and can be remedied by principled human determination if an educated public accepts its communal responsibility.

References

Addams, Jane. *My Friend, Julia Lathrop*. New York: Arno Press, 1974 [1935].

Athey, Louis L. "Florence Kelley and the Quest for Negro Equality." *Journal of Negro History* 56 (October, 1971): 249–261.

Ginger, Ray. *Altgeld's America*. Chicago: Quadrangle Books, 1958.

Goldmark, Josephine. *Impatient Crusader: Florence Kelley's Life Story*. Urbana: University of Illinois Press, 1953.

Kelley, Florence. "I Go to Work." *Survey* 58 (June 1, 1927): 271–274.

———. "Obstacles to Enforcing Child Labor Laws." *Annals of America*. Chicago: Encyclopedia Britannica, 1968, vol. 13.

———. *Some Ethical Gains Through Legislation*. New York: Macmillan, 1905.

Kraditor, Aileen. *Up From the Pedestal*. Chicago: Quadrangle Books, 1968.

Linn, James W. *Jane Addams: A Biography*. New York: Greenwood Press, 1968 [1935].

Ovington, Mary White. *The Walls Came Tumbling Down*. New York: Harcourt, Brace & Co., 1947.

Sklar, Kathryn Kish. "Hull House in the 1890s: A Community of Women Reformers." In Ellen Carol Dubois and Vicki L. Ruiz, eds. *Unequal Sisters: A Multicultural Reader in United States Women's History*. New York: Routledge, 1990.

Wald, Lillian. *Windows on Henry Street*. Boston: Little, Brown and Co., 1941.

THOMAS KENNEDY

(November 29, 1776–October 17, 1832)

Activist for Religious Freedom

Thomas Kennedy, born in Paisley, Scotland, was inspired equally by the rationalism of the Scottish Enlightenment and the sweeping democratic humanitarianism of Scottish poets like Robert Burns. Throughout his life, he reacted to moments of triumph and despair with bursts of his own poetry—florid, melodramatic, not very memorable verse. But Kennedy deserves to be remembered not for his poetry, but for his courageous, principled, tireless efforts to defeat religious bigotry and discrimination in his adopted country, the United States. Thomas Kennedy, who settled in Maryland, became deeply involved in that state's confused and tortured religious history; he made himself the single most influential force for change in an ongoing battle for freedom of conscience.

Thomas Kennedy
Courtesy, Washington County Free Library, Western Maryland Room.

The land that became the colony of Maryland was granted by Charles I to Cecil Calvert, Lord Baltimore, in 1632. Calvert, a Roman Catholic, intended the colony to function as a refuge for Catholics. He knew, however, that he also had to attract Protestant settlers, and he promulgated a policy of religious toleration to make the Protestants feel safe and welcome; in reality, since Catholics were always a minority of the settlers, the policy of religious toleration acted to protect them as well.

The Maryland Toleration Act of 1649 was designed to reassure the Protestants; since it required belief in Jesus Christ and the Trinity and provided the death penalty for blasphemy, it can scarcely be seen as an articulation of true toleration. The mental and moral universe for these 17th-century Englishmen was a limited, sectarian, and very Christian one: no mention was ever made of Jews, and the existence of agnosticism or atheism was either inconceivable to most men or so abhorrent that it was beyond discussion. In 1723 and again as late as 1776, the laws of the colony stipulated boring through the tongue and branding the forehead of anyone who denied the validity of the Trinity; the state of Maryland did not repeal that particular article until 1820.

Maryland ratified one of the earliest state constitutions in 1777. It required a "religious test"—a public declaration of belief in Jesus Christ and the Trinity—before a man could hold any public office or be admitted to practice law in the state. In 1779, in the chaos and fragmented authority of the Revolution, Maryland stipulated the same religious requirement for citizenship; until 1789, when the federal Constitution standardized a uniform naturalization policy, non-Christian residents of Maryland could not become citizens of the United States.

There were few Jews in Maryland, but they felt the discrimination keenly. As early as 1797, several patriarchs of the Jewish community in Baltimore petitioned the state legislature that "they are a set of people called Jews and that they are thereby deprived on many of the invaluable rights of citizenship and praying that they be placed upon the same footing with other good citizens" (Altfeld, 10). There is no evidence that the legislature ever acknowledged the petition. In 1801 and again two years later, similar petitions were submitted to the legislature, with no results whatsoever. Frustrated, the Jews retreated from direct confrontation. The small Jewish community in Maryland had contributed eagerly to the Revolutionary cause; when war broke out with Britain again in 1812, the Jews once again supplied both financial support and soldiers. Reuben Etting, son of one of the community patriarchs, was commissioned a captain in a Federal marine company during the war. It was one of the ironies of life in Maryland that, because of the religious test, Etting, who served with distinction, was forbidden to be an officer in the state militia. The situation was intolerable, especially since the United States Constitution expressly forbade any religious tests whatsoever. After the War of 1812, Reuben Etting's father, Solomon, his anger and determination stiffened perhaps by his son's military service, searched eagerly for some fruitful means of reopening the debate on the issue in the state legislature. Etting's drive and intelligence were soon to be met by the fiery eloquence and moral fervor of a Christian champion.

Thomas Kennedy was the youngest of twelve children born to a devout Scotch Presbyterian family in the Lowland village of Paisley. Kennedy remembered glowingly an early life filled with affection, support, and moral instruction. He recalled his father as a man of strict honor and his mother, who taught him to love literature, as a woman whose Christian spirit expressed itself in individual acts of kindness and generosity. Inspired by both the American and the French Revolutions, twenty-year-old Thomas vowed to live his life "in virtue's service and in Freedom's Cause" (Altfeld, 126). He emigrated to Georgetown, Maryland, where he lived briefly with an older brother, married, and set out on his own as a bridge contractor. His sentiments were fiercely republican. In 1800, when Thomas Jefferson sponsored a bill to establish complete religious freedom in Virginia, Kennedy rhapsodized:

> Acting in a noble cause,
> He abolished cruel laws;
> Set the mind and body free,
> He's the son of Liberty (Altfeld, 17).

In 1817 Kennedy was elected to the state legislature from Washington County. One of his first acts was to request a committee to study the plight of Jews in Maryland, with the goal of resubmitting what became known as the "Jew Bill." His motives, he declared, were strictly humanitarian and ethical:

> And if I am asked why I take so much interest in favour of the passage of the Bill—to this I would simply answer, because I consider it my DUTY to do so. There are no Jews in the county from whence I come, nor have I the slightest acquaintance with any Jew in the world. It was not at their request; it was not even known to any of them, that the subject would be brought forward at this time (Altfeld, 79).

Kennedy declared that he had been, like most other Christian citizens of Maryland, ignorant of the religious test in the state constitution until it was brought to his attention by "a Gentile gentleman." While that may be true, the evidence also indicates that from that point on, Solomon Etting and other leading Jews worked actively if inconspicuously with

Kennedy in his fight on their behalf; they recognized the value and necessity of having a Christian spokesman.

Kennedy and his committee studied other state constitutions and announced that, to their great shame, Maryland was the only state that so discriminated against her citizens. Kennedy's introductory speeches for his Bill are heavily laced with the biblical imagery and examples that he knew would sound familiar and comforting to his audience. His strategy was to present the idea of toleration to the other legislators in a guise they could recognize and accept without fear. Nonetheless, he revealed himself throughout the debates as a passionate believer in the total separation of church and state, in complete freedom of conscience, and, beneath all the religious rhetoric, as an Enlightenment deist in the mold of Jefferson:

> It is a matter of astonishment that Christians, who were so much persecuted themselves during the three first centuries after Christ, should in their turn have also become persecutors of those who differed from them in sentiment, even about matters not in themselves essential to salvation . . . no sooner do we find Church and State united—no sooner do we find the temporal power and authority exercised in favour of Christianity, than we find its original simplicity and purity corrupted by the cunning craft of wicked and ambitious men who made a "gain of Godliness" . . . I profess myself a Christian. . . . And yet I am free to declare that if Christianity cannot stand without the aid of persecution, without the aid of temporal power, let it fall; and let some other system more rational and benevolent take its place (Altfeld, 84).

> Even where Christianity is unknown, is unthought of, we find numerous instances of the most disinterested magnanimity and virtue. The God of nature has implanted in the human heart the noblest, finest feelings, which often leads the most ignorant to perform deeds of benevolence and charity (Altfeld, 98).

The "Jew Bill" required that officeholders, if they could not swear devotion to Jesus and the Trinity, declare their firm belief in an afterlife and a system of rewards and punishments. Kennedy stated bluntly that he would prefer to see a bill that abolished all religious stipulations whatsoever:

> The bill before us does not go to exempt any but Jews from declaring and subscribing their belief in the Christian religion, and they believe in the Scriptures of the Old Testament, and their God is our God. On this point, however, I must candidly declare that were it left to me, I would abolish the religious test entirely without any exception (Altfeld, 105).

Ruefully, he acknowledged that so liberal a bill would have no chance of passing the legislature.

Somewhat to Kennedy's surprise, the bill was defeated. He reintroduced it in 1819 and again in 1820, with no better results. Turning to his poetry for solace, he poured out his anger and hopes in an epic poem, "To the Children of Israel in Maryland," trying to assure himself as well as them:

> Yet faint not—Jacob's God is still your own,
> Nor shall his people e'er be left alone;
> His Peculiar People he shall save,
> While their oppressors all shall find a grave (Altfeld, 25).

In the ensuing debates, his rhetoric began to harden and to bespeak his growing frustration and moral outrage:

> Mr. Speaker, I would not accept the passage of the bill now on your table as a boon or as a favour. I take a higher and more independent ground. I demand it as an act of justice, sheer justice. . . . I claim it as a right recognized by the old Congress . . . as one of those inalienable, and imprescriptible rights of man with which no human power or authority can justly interfere (Altfeld, 141).

As the years passed, Kennedy attracted some formidable allies. One of these was Judge Henry Brackenridge, whose sophisticated open-mindedness made him recoil at the limitations implicit in the word "tolerance":

> Sir, I abhor intolerance, *whether it be political or religious*; and, yet, I can scarcely regard religious *tolerance* as a virtue. What! Has weak and erring man a right to give *permission* to his fellow mortal to offer his adorations to the Supreme Being after his own manner? . . . the idea of such permission, or toleration, is not better than impiety (Brackenridge, 557).

The proponents of the "Jew Bill" were well aware that they were fighting for the rights of a tiny minority (estimated at roughly two hundred in 1820) who were largely unknown to their peers and who seemed alien and threatening. They repeatedly broadened the scope of the debate to confront the nature and evil of all discrimination. Reminding their listeners of the humane goals of the Revolution, Brackenridge insisted,

> Our political compacts are not entered into as brethren of the Christian faith, but as men, as members of a civilized society. In looking back to our struggle for independence, I find that we engaged in the bloody conflict for the RIGHTS OF MAN, and not for the purpose of enforcing or defending any particular religious creed. . . . But sir, all persecution for the sake

of opinion is tyranny; and the first speck of it that may appear should be eradicated as the commencement of a deadly gangrene. . . . Let us sever at once, and forever, the unnatural union between force and opinion, between temporal power and religious faith (Altfeld, 560).

In December of 1822 Kennedy was finally able to get the bill passed, but since it was in effect a constitutional amendment, its passage had to be confirmed by the next session of the legislature as well. At this point Kennedy became the object of a virulently nativist and anti-Semitic campaign in his home county. Dubbing Kennedy and his supporters the "Jewish ticket," one Benjamin Galloway declared himself the head of the "Christian ticket." Opponents of Kennedy claimed that the "Jew Bill" would endanger Christianity and lead to the corruption and downfall of the great state of Maryland. Given the fact that the United States Constitution already prohibited all religious tests, and given the presence of so few Jews in Maryland, the campaign against Kennedy represented the triumph of hysteria and irrational fears over reality. Kennedy was defeated in the 1823 elections, but statewide, public opinion was shifting in support of his bill. The *Niles Register*, a Baltimore newspaper, commented on the implications of his defeat, "It is a shame that in this enlightened day and in this free country, an attempt should be made, by government, to force the consciences of men, in matters of faith to prescribe the duties which they owe to their Creator" (*Niles Register*, October 11, 1823).

The following year the campaign did not recapitulate its shabby excesses, and Kennedy, running as an independent, recaptured the seat he had lost. Predictably, his first act was to reintroduce the "Jew Bill." Buoyed by refreshed support and borne on a tide of impassioned rhetoric, the act giving Jews complete religious freedom finally passed the legislature in December 1824. The real winners, insisted supporter John Tyson, were all the citizens of Maryland: "The people of Maryland did not surrender to the convention who framed their constitution the right to control their consciences. They could not surrender it, because it was an inalienable right" (Altfeld, 202). Tyson gave Kennedy full credit for his years of selfless work:

[H]is name is identified with the "Jew Bill." You cannot think of one without thinking of the other—he was an early champion in the cause; Atlas-like, he bore it upon his shoulders at a time when it was too heavy for all other men—it fell—he raised it—it fell again—he raised it again and again. . . . Let him consummate the work—He began it, it is his right to end it. Let him be both Alpha and Omega (Altfeld, 203).

And indeed, finally, the "Act to extend to the sect of people professing the Jewish Religion, the same rights and privileges that are enjoyed by

Christians" was confirmed by the next legislature in the December 1825 session. It became law in February, 1826. A few months later, Kennedy wrote to a friend,

> I have seen the first of my wishes as a public servant gratified by seeing the principles of civil and religious liberty established in the United States, and in seeing the persecuted Children of Israel placed on an equality with their fellow citizens. This was, indeed, my dearest wish, and, since I have gratified it I am determined henceforth never to murmur in or out of office, but to submit contentedly to the voice and wishes of the people (Altfeld, 15).

Kennedy retired to his home in Hagerstown, where he was appointed postmaster by John Quincy Adams and published a reform-minded newspaper, the *Hagerstown Mail*. Always concerned with bigotry and oppression anywhere, he followed the religious and civil struggles of the Catholics in Ireland with great interest and compassion. In a cholera epidemic in 1832, Kennedy was taken ill and died at the age of fifty-five. Well known and widely respected, he was soon forgotten by most. In 1918, on the centenary of the passage of the "Jew Bill," the Jews of Washington County erected a monument in his honor. He had worked for almost a decade, selflessly and against great odds, to see the principle of freedom of conscience brought to life in his society. In his vigilance and moral courage, he embodied the spirit of active, ethical citizenship.

References

Altfeld, E. Milton. *The Jew's Struggle for Religious and Civil Liberty in Maryland.* New York: Da Capo Press, 1970 [1924].

Boorstin, Daniel J. *The Americans: The National Experience.* New York: Random House, 1965.

Brackenridge, Henry. "A Vindication of the Civil Rights of Jews." *Annals of America.* New York: Britannica, 4: 552.

Brugger, Robert J. *Maryland: A Middle Temperament: 1634–1980.* Baltimore: Johns Hopkins University Press, 1988.

Commager, Henry Steele. *Documents of American History.* New York: Appleton-Century-Crofts, 1963.

Williams, Thomas J. C. *A History of Washington County, Maryland. From the Earliest Settlements to the Present Time.* Hagerstown, MD: John M. Rank and L. R. Titsworth, 1906.

Susette La Flesche

(May 1854–May 26, 1903)

Native American Rights Activist

The history of America is marked by the occasional rise of unusual families whose members make noteworthy contributions in a variety of creative or public fields. Well-known examples include the Adamses, the Roosevelts, and the Kennedys. Far less well known, but representative of even greater triumph over brutal circumstance, is the family of Joseph Iron Eye, chief of the Omaha tribe in the mid-19th century. Iron Eye himself struggled heroically to bring his tribe safely into a semblance of coexistence with the dominant white culture. His daughter Susan, the first Native American woman to graduate from medical school, returned to her people and opened the first hospital available to them. Another daughter, Rosalie, became a highly respected tribal leader after her father's death; her sister Marguerite was a pioneer in educational reform among the Omaha. Iron Eye's son, Francis La Flesche, was a lawyer and a nationally recognized ethnologist. And his daughter Inshtatheamba, "Bright Eyes," became a major force in the movement to focus national attention on the shameful reservation system and to award Native Americans full citizenship. She was herself a delicate mixture of radically different worlds; throughout her life she strove with courage and eloquence to save her Indian world by rendering it comprehensible to the harsh world of Victorian America.

Susette La Flesche
Courtesy, Nebraska State Historical Society.

J oseph La Flesche, known as Iron Eye, was the son of an Omaha mother and a French father. He was brought up in both worlds and spoke fluent French. Confident and comfortable in a variety of societies, La Flesche married a young woman who was also half Omaha; her father was an American citizen. Iron Eye became the designated heir of Chief Big Elk, and he succeeded as chief in 1853.

The Omaha, like most other Plains tribes, were facing desperate problems. The tribe had lived in what is now southern Nebraska, between the Platte and Niobrara rivers, for over 450 years, but in 1854 a "treaty" signed in Washington forced them to cede enormous tracts of their land to the United States government. They moved further north, dangerously close to the aggressive Sioux. They had been promised both protection from the Sioux and payment from the government, but neither promise was fulfilled. The only hopeful note for them was the character of their assigned reservation agent, the Reverend William Hamilton: he was an honorable and dedicated man determined to help his new charges.

Iron Eye struggled to help his people negotiate this difficult situation safely. He worked tirelessly to encourage farming, to build schools, to develop the requisite skills and attitudes among the Omaha. Wary of the temptations of white civilization, he established a tribal police force, trained and uniformed, to prevent liquor sales and abuse in the Omaha villages. Despite his best efforts, the Indians reeled under the impact of denigrated and lost traditions, a terrible shortage of vital supplies, the introduction of white diseases, and the endemic corruption of the reservation system.

Despite all the looming crises, the child Inshtatheamba, Bright Eyes, lived in a loving extended family steeped in tradition. Iron Eye tried to equip his own children to deal competently with the white world he saw as the inevitable victor in this anguished confrontation. Bright Eyes had vivid memories of witnessing buffalo hunts cradled on her father's horse; she recalled his urging her always to face the world as it was, not as she might have wished it to be.

At the age of eight Bright Eyes was sent to the Presbyterian mission school on the reservation; the school was too far away for a daily trip, and she boarded there during the week. Her Indian name was unacceptable; she was arbitrarily assigned the name Susette, dressed in the clothing of a white child, and forbidden to speak her native language. Whatever her private reactions to this denial of her Indian identity, she was an eager student who learned English remarkably fast. By 1868 she was a shy, studious, intense adolescent with an artistic flair. Her delight in reading drew the attention of the teacher, Miss Read, who became a significant mentor in the girl's life. The following year a new reservation agent, a bigoted and corrupt man, closed the mission school; Miss Read departed and Susette faced a life suddenly stripped of its chief focus. William Hamilton, the former agent, defied orders to leave the reservation; aware of Susette's scholarly interests, he opened his own small library to her, and she worked her way through it hungrily.

In 1871 Miss Read, now the principal of the Elizabeth Institute for Girls in Elizabeth, New Jersey, arranged a scholarship for Susette. For the next four years the girl observed sophisticated Eastern culture and society while she received a rigorous academic education. She returned to the reservation at the age of twenty, a gifted, awkward, exotic hybrid who no longer felt fully comfortable in either world. Her family suggested an arranged marriage according to Omaha traditions, but Susette was appalled at the idea. She began to realize the extent of her isolation.

The tribe to which Susette returned in 1875 had settled into a cold apathy of despair. The tribal police were unable to cope with the open sale of alcohol. White settlers encroached steadily on the best farmlands, and the Indians were helpless to protest. The following year all tribes were ordered to remain on their reservations or to face criminal charges. The Omaha gathered for one final buffalo hunt, but they found the plains littered with mutilated, putrid carcasses; in most cases, only the hide and the tongue had been removed. The rest was left to rot. The mass destruction of the buffalo served a double purpose: it provided whites with highly desirable luxuries, and it deprived Native Americans of their most precious resource. General William Sherman, directing the army's western divisions, foresaw and intended the consequences to the Indians. He commented that the extermination of the buffalo was "the only way to bring lasting peace and allow civilization to advance." His attitude toward the Indians themselves was no different. "[T]he more I see of these Indians," he wrote to his brother, "the more convinced I am that all have to be killed or maintained as a species of pauper. Their attempts at civilization are simply ridiculous" (Wilson, 116).

To many whites, all Indians represented an inconvenient, embarrassing impediment to progress. Attempts at "civilization" were ridiculed or actively betrayed. The conscience of the country at large was finally stirred to outrage by the tragic aftermath of the Ponca removal. An 1865 treaty with the United States had guaranteed the Ponca, a small, peaceful tribe, their traditional homeland on the Missouri River "forever." Barely three years later, without so much as notifying the Ponca, the United States gave the entire area to the Sioux, traditional enemies of the Ponca. Unprotected and preyed upon by the Sioux, the Ponca suffered in helpless silence. Protests on their behalf finally convinced the Bureau of Indian Affairs that a grave mistake had been made, but officials were wary of antagonizing the hostile Sioux; the far easier solution was to force the Ponca to leave their threatened homeland. The removal, decided upon in 1877, was carried out with a rigid, arbitrary ruthlessness. Susette, whose uncle White Swan was a Ponca, described the situation to an audience in Boston's Faneuil Hall:

> The whole Ponca tribe were rapidly advancing in civilization, cultivating their farms, and their schoolhouses and churches were well filled, when suddenly they were informed that the government required their removal to Indian Territory [hundreds of miles southwest in Oklahoma]. My uncle said it came so suddenly upon them that they could not realize it at first, and they felt stunned and helpless. He also said that if they had had any idea of what was coming, they might have successfully resisted; but as it was, it was carried rigidly beyond their control. . . . The Poncas had always been a peaceful tribe, and were not armed, and even if they had been they would rather not have fought (La Flesche, 103).

The Ponca were rounded up by armed troops, their homes destroyed, their schools hastily shuttered. They were sent on a forced march of five hundred miles to Indian Territory; fully one-third of the tribe died of disease and starvation during the trek. The survivors, led by their chief, Standing Bear, struggled to create a bearable life on the arid, harsh land they had been assigned.

In early January, 1879, Standing Bear's only surviving son, dying of malaria, begged to be buried where he had been born; weeping, Standing Bear promised to fulfill the boy's wish. The next day, accompanied by thirty-four grieving followers, Standing Bear set out from Indian Territory to take his son's body home. After ten weeks of appalling hardships, the desperate band reached the Omaha reservation, where they were taken in, nursed, and hidden from authorities. When the reservation agent discovered their presence, he called in the army; the weakened, distraught Ponca were arrested and imprisoned in Fort Omaha, while arrangements were made for their return to Oklahoma.

Before the Ponca could be forced back to the wretched Indian territory, their cause was adopted by a dedicated, charismatic, colorful reformer: Thomas Henry Tibbles. He in turn would bring Susette La Flesche into the controversy and change forever the course of her life. Tibbles was then the assistant editor of the *Omaha Daily Herald*; he was a flamboyant, deeply committed reform journalist. In his wildly varied past he had fought with the Free State forces in Kansas; had been almost hanged as an abolitionist; had lived on such intimate and respectful terms among the Dakota that he was initiated into the revered Soldier Lodge, a secret warrior society. He was a close friend of General George Crook, the regional commander of the army and the man assigned to return the Ponca to Indian Territory. Crook himself was disgusted by the injustice of the case; he brought Tibbles in to investigate and publicize what was being done to the Indians.

Perhaps because of Tibbles's position in the Soldier Lodge, Standing Bear trusted and confided in him. Tibbles launched a massive publicity campaign, speaking to churches throughout the area, wiring to Secretary of the Interior Carl Schurz, sending news articles to papers in Boston, New York, and Chicago. When direct protest brought no response whatsoever from Schurz, Tibbles decided to utilize the courts. He would test the Fourteenth Amendment's application to the rights of Native Americans. With the help of several prominent Omaha lawyers who took on the case *pro bono*, Tibbles filed a writ of *habeas corpus* to protest the illegal imprisonment of United States citizens. It was up to the court to determine whether Tibbles was justified in calling the Ponca citizens.

In his efforts to gather background information on the Ponca's epic journey, Tibbles contacted the sympathetic doctor on the Omaha reservation; the doctor recommended Susette as both a witness and an interpreter. Susette, accompanied by her father, received permission to attend the coming trial. She soon became the trusted interpreter for the entire Ponca group.

The government insisted that Indians were like children, wards of the state; they were not to be considered as fully adult persons, and the *habeas corpus* protection against unwarranted imprisonment did not apply to them. Judge Elmer S. Dundy of the Federal District Court was a strict, honorable man. He distilled the case to one essential question: Were Indians "persons" as stipulated by the Fourteenth Amendment? During the trial, Standing Bear, through Susette, spoke with stunning eloquence of common humanity, of shared hopes, of his people's desperate desire to return to their homeland.

While Judge Dundy was obviously moved, he grounded his final decision firmly in the law rather than in sympathy. On May 12, 1879, Dundy announced to the court unequivocally:

> That an Indian is a *person* within the meaning of the law of the United States, and has therefore the right to sue out a writ of habeas corpus in a federal court or before a federal judge, in all cases where he may be confined, or in custody under color of authority of the United States, or where he is restrained of liberty in violation of the Constitution or laws of the United States (Wilson, 197).

He continued that no rightful authority existed to justify the forcible removal of peaceful persons to Indian Territory; Standing Bear and his followers were free. Ironically, because of the complexities of law controlling Native Americans, he was free to go anywhere except onto a reservation. He was exiled from his own people. Dundy's decision was a milestone in the legal treatment of Native Americans, but it stopped far short of resolving many agonizing problems. Tibbles knew that his work had barely begun.

Susette was invited to speak in a large Episcopal church in Omaha. During the trial, she had seemed shy and wary to Tibbles; he attended her first public address with some apprehension. The dignity and power of her appeal shocked him. "Why should I be asked to speak?" she queried.

> I am but an Indian girl, brought up among the Indians. I love my people. I have been educated, and most of them have not. I have told them that they must learn the arts of white people and adopt their customs, but how can they, when the government sends soldiers to drive them about over the face of the earth? (Wilson, 211)

Tibbles recognized the impact Susette could have. He asked her to accompany him and Standing Bear on a speaking tour of the Northeast, both to interpret for Standing Bear and to speak in her own right. Iron Eye insisted that her brother Frank go with them; Susette, Standing Bear, Tibbles, and Frank would be inextricably bound to each other for the rest of their lives.

Dressed in graceful native buckskins, appearing fragile yet courageous, speaking in a low, melodious voice, Susette captivated Boston. Newspapers spoke of her great intelligence, refinement, and grace. "There is unusual dignity and elegance in her talk in private," commented one, "and a sense of the value of words. . . . She is calm, but full of animation and a very deep feeling" (Wilson, 233). While she observed the conventions of Victorian public speaking, Susette never compromised the integrity of her message; she never softened a harsh image or allowed euphemism to distort her vision. She attacked the myths of the West that Easterners had come to believe, among them the notion that the reservations represented some kind of white beneficence.

> I desire to say that all annuities paid to Indian tribes by the government are in payment for land sold by them to the government, and are not charity. The government never gave any alms to the Indians, and we all know that through the "kindness" of the "Indian ring" [bureaucrats and agents who profited from the reservation system] they do not get the half of what the government actually owes them. . . . It is because I know that a majority of the whites have not known of the cruelty practiced by the "Indian ring" on a handful of oppressed, helpless and conquered people, that I have the courage and confidence to appeal to the people of the United States. . . . We are helpless, it is true; but at heart we do not feel that we are a conquered people. We are human beings; God made us as well as you. . . . We have no protection from the law. The Indians all know

that they are powerless. . . . I have come to you to appeal for your sympathy and help for my people. . . . The people who were once owners of this soil ask you for their liberty, and law is liberty (La Flesche, 103).

In response to the lectures of Susette and Standing Bear, leading Boston reformers founded a committee to raise funds and to lobby for protective legislation. Susette's greatest impact may have been on a writer from Colorado who was visiting friends in Boston: Helen Hunt Jackson. Jackson was a conventional writer who had never before identified herself with any cause. She had had no meaningful contact with Indians; in fact, she had criticized Longfellow's *Hiawatha* for employing "silly legends of the savage aborigines." But Susette's unshakable dignity and demand for justice triggered a profound change in Jackson. She abandoned her original plans and traveled with the speakers to New York, Washington, and Philadelphia. She learned to do exhaustive documentary research and became an expert in Indian diplomatic and economic history. Jackson published a barrage of outraged stories in newspapers and magazines across the country; her articles were published in 1881 as *A Century of Dishonor*, the first book to focus national attention on the unjustifiable treatment of Native Americans. At her own expense, Jackson sent a copy of the book to every member of Congress; she received no official acknowledgment.

As Susette and her companions traveled the East Coast, her confidence and eloquence seemed to mature. Driven by increasing urgency for the safety of her family and people, Susette toured and lectured through repeated illnesses and exhaustion. In 1880 she and Tibbles testified on the Ponca removal before the Senate Committee on Indian Affairs, chaired by Senator Henry Dawes. Dawes was deeply moved by Susette's testimony. He introduced a bill to return the Ponca to their original land; crippled by procedural maneuvers, the bill never reached the floor of the Senate.

Tibbles and Susette broadened their efforts to reach the American public. Susette published stories of her Indian childhood, with her own sketches, in the popular *St. Nicholas Magazine* for children. Tibbles wrote several books on the Ponca, one factual and one a fictionalized account of Standing Bear's life. Susette's introduction to Tibbles's nonfiction *Ponca Chiefs* rings with her almost desperate faith in the intrinsic goodness of informed white society:

I wish for the sake of my race, that I could introduce this little book into every home in the land, because in these homes lies the power to remedy the evil shown forth in these pages. The people are the power which move [sic] the magistrates who administer the laws. . . .

For years the petitions of my people have gone up unnoticed, unheeded by all but their Creator, and now at last a man of your race has arisen, who has shown faith enough in humanity to arouse the nation from the sin of its indifference. Thank God, it was only indifference, not hatred, which withheld from an oppressed and unfortunate race, justice and mercy.

May those who read this story, when they think of the countless happy homes which cover this continent, give help to a homeless race, who have no spot on earth they can call their own (Tibbles, 4).

The issue of home, of a "spot on earth they can call their own," was at the heart of the Indian rights controversy. Susette and Tibbles, who were married in 1881, campaigned throughout the 1880s for full citizenship for Native Americans. The growing movement to support and protect the Indians culminated in the Dawes Severalty Act of 1887, which was seen as the best hope for bringing Native Americans into some sort of bearable coexistence with white society.

In reality, the well-intentioned Dawes Act revealed the unbridgeable chasm between Indian and European concepts of ownership and rights. The Act mandated that tribal ownership of land be dissolved and that Indians as individuals be granted title to workable plots of land; full citizenship was offered only to those who abandoned their tribal identities. In addition, the Act provided for greatly expanded educational facilities—all offering a strictly controlled white man's environment and curriculum. Assimilation was seen as the ultimate, desirable goal. In the harsh, competitive world of industrialized America, Indian values of cooperation, consensus, and nonacquisitiveness were viewed with contempt. To a culture increasingly imbued with a Social Darwinian vision of history, Native Americans represented an inferior, primitive stage of development; if they interfered with the ordained progress of Manifest Destiny, they would have to be eliminated.

Susette and Tibbles had supported the Dawes Act as a necessary step toward full citizenship, but increasingly they witnessed the resultant despair of Indians cut off from tribal life and easy prey to voracious whites whose laws were incomprehensible in Indian terms. The burgeoning immigrant population in the late 19th century created a land hunger that no Indians could withstand. Even before the Dawes Act, major "treaties" throughout the 1880s had reduced tribal holdings by 60%; conveniently, land left over after individual allotment was brought by the United States government for pennies and immediately sold to eager white settlers. In 1890 Native despair erupted in the Ghost Dance uprising of the Sioux; the mystic Wovoka assured the Indians that they were immortal, and that if they killed the white men, the buffalo could return. The final act of the Indian Wars was the crushing of the Ghost Dance warriors at Wounded Knee: in a hollow ringed by almost five hundred U.S. troops armed with machine guns, 120 Sioux warriors in the act of surrendering were slaughtered, along with their wives and children. The rage and panic of Wounded Knee produced a spasm of lesser confrontations, in which Indian women and children were the major victims. Wounded Knee destroyed the last hopes of Native Americans for independence on their own terms.

During the 1890s Susette and Tibbles spent several years in Washington as congressional correspondents for a news service run by the Populist Farmers' Alliance. Increasingly tormented by doubts over allotment and fearful that the Indian way of life could not survive, Susette worked with her ethnologist brother Frank to illustrate his scholarly book on the Omaha tribe. As Susette's chronic poor health overtook her, the couple moved to a farm in Nebraska, on what was Susette's allotment acreage. At the age of forty-nine, surrounded by her family, Susette La Flesche died there. She had spent her life and energy struggling to save her people, to portray them with dignity and integrity, and to ignite the conscience of America.

References

Hoxie, Frederick E. *A Final Promise: The Campaign to Assimilate the Indians, 1880–1920*. New York: Cambridge University Press, 1989.

James, Edward T., ed. *Notable American Women, 1607–1950*. Cambridge, MA: Harvard University Press, 1971.

La Flesche, Susette. "The Plight of the Ponca Indians." In Judith Anderson, ed. *Outspoken Women: Speeches by American Women Reformers 1635–1935*. Dubuque, IA: Kendall/Hunt Publishing, 1984.

Nabokov, Peter, ed. *Native American Testimony*. New York: Viking Press, 1992.

Prucha, Francis Paul. *The Great Father: The United States Government and the American Indians*. Lincoln: University of Nebraska Press, 1984.

Tibbles, Thomas H. *The Ponca Chiefs*. Lincoln: University of Nebraska Press, 1972 [1879].

Wilson, Dorothy Clarke. *Bright Eyes*. New York: McGraw-Hill Book Co., 1974.

LUCY CRAFT LANEY

(April 13, 1854–October 23, 1933)

Educator, Civil Rights Advocate

Lucy Laney's life was filled with paradox and the quiet defiance of limitation. Her parents, born slaves, were proud, dignified, free, and even relatively prosperous by the time Lucy, the seventh of ten children, was born in Macon, Georgia. In a time of rising tension and hostility, white people befriended her, exposed her to the riches of Old World culture, and furthered her education. In an era when African Americans were especially vulnerable and the only approved model of education for them was the Tuskegee "industrial" model, Laney insisted on a full, demanding liberal arts curriculum for her students. She worked her entire life to nurture qualities of discipline, self-respect, intellectual excellence, and moral responsibility in her students; her own life offered the best exemplar of the goals she articulated.

Lucy Craft Laney
Courtesy, Moorland-Spingarn Research Center, Howard University.

Lucy Craft Laney's father, David Laney, was born a slave but was able to purchase his freedom while still a young man. A skilled carpenter, he married Louisa Laney and bought her freedom as well. After studying for the ministry, he refused ordination in the Southern Presbyterian Church, which would have permitted him to minister only to blacks; instead, he was ordained in the "Old School" Northern Presbyterian branch of the church. The family was large, and Mrs. Laney continued to work for the family that had owned her. Mutual support and generosity assumed religious significance in this family; in addition to their own ten children, Laney could not remember a time when her parents did not also care for several orphaned or troubled foster children. "And I have wondered, since I have been grown and know what responsibility is, how my mother and father ever did it," she commented years later, "but we always had enough to eat, we were always comfortable, had books to read, and such fun we children had. Pa always said there was enough to share with one more" (McCrorey, 161). Lucy's passion for reading had endeared her to her mother's employer, a Miss Campbell, who opened her own private library to the child and guided her early reading. With the encouragement and financial support of Miss Campbell, Lucy attended Lewis High School in Macon. At this point, Atlanta University was just taking shape with the support of the American Missionary Association, an abolitionist organization responsible for founding many of the South's fine black colleges. Lucy Laney was selected as a member of the first class at Atlanta University. An eager student, she was one of four members of the first graduating class in 1873.

For the next decade Laney taught in the public schools of Savannah, Macon, and Milledgeville. When Laney began her teaching career, the hopeful phase of Reconstruction had been effectively undermined by the betrayal of the federal government and the concomitant rise of white supremacist "Redeemer" politics. The postwar hopes and expectations of freedmen had been cruelly curtailed and belittled. Throughout the entire South, there was not a single public high school for black children; black schools, usually one-room shacks, struggled with grotesquely inadequate supplies and offered a skeletal curriculum barely reaching sixth- or seventh-grade standards. African American teachers were paid far less than white teachers, usually no more than twelve to eighteen dollars a month. Out of every dollar spent on public education, ninety-three cents went to white schools and only seven cents to black education. But budgetary constraints, however distorted, were not really the most basic consideration: if that were the case, Southern whites would have welcomed the teachers who came to the black schools through the Northern philanthropies and freedmen's aid societies, since these teachers placed no financial burden on local school districts. What underlay all of Southern educational policy was a determination not to lose the inexpensive, subservient agricultural labor pool the freedmen represented. Many white racists may have believed that blacks were incapable of benefiting from an academic education. Even more pernicious was the widespread attitude that a liberal education might leave African Americans dissatisfied with the only role in Southern society whites intended to permit them.

Lucy Laney had been raised by proud parents to be herself dignified, demanding, and proud of her people. "I am as good as anybody else," she declared. "God had no different dirt to make me out of than that used in making the first lady of the land" (Griggs, 101). She struggled in the dispirited atmosphere of public education for ten years, and she came increasingly to believe that her only chance to offer black children the sort of education she believed in was to start her own school. She focused on Augusta, which provided no schools whatsoever for its black children. Her petition for funds was rejected by the Presbyterian Board of Missions for Freedmen, but her father encouraged her and the Ladies' Aid Society of his own church raised one hundred dollars for her. Laney rented a room in the basement of Christ Presbyterian Church in 1883 and opened her school with five students. Within two years, she had 234 pupils. Funding was a constant source of anxiety, as it would be throughout the life of the school. Laney's friend, NAACP founder Mary White Ovington,* described the situation with great affection:

> There were children in plenty, but no funds. She had counted on tuitions, but the child who appealed to her most was the child whose parents could do least, or who had no parents at all. With her vivid imagination, she had only to look at a ragged, dirty boy to see a well-set-up, cleanly, clear-eyed figure in his place. Her imagination saw this; it was for her practical self to bring about the metamorphosis (Ovington, 55).

Laney's school offered literature, classics, mathematics, and a required course in African American history. Laney was an early and passionate believer in the centrality of racial and family pride in the education of a confident, competent, humane individual. Her curriculum emphasized the contributions of blacks in a variety of fields. She brought local African American artists and craftspeople to the school to demonstrate and discuss their work. With the assistance of an elderly German immigrant, she launched a school orchestra. All of this ran directly counter to the prevailing trend of "industrial" education for blacks. The accommodationist philosophy of Booker T. Washington was what whites wanted to hear. The prospectus of the Hampton Institute baldly stated that "no classics are taught," and Washington himself assured his white benefactors that he was careful "not to educate our students out of sympathy with agricultural life, so that they would be attracted from the country to the cities, and yield to the temptation of trying to live by their wits" (Sterne, 105). Influenced by Southern politicians and by the rising racism of the era, Northern philanthropies tended to support industrial—manual and menial—education only. In many black schools, determined teachers maintained parallel lesson plans: one involving meaningful academic work, and the other an obsequious parody of white expectations, which they could activate when inspectors from the sponsoring philanthropies arrived to observe class.

In this environment, Lucy Laney was a maverick and a lonely crusader. Her stated goal was to train competent teachers for the black schools of the South, and in addition to equip her students for college. (Ironically, while the American Missionary Association and other groups had helped found a number of black colleges, their short-sighted policy had not provided secondary schools to prepare young African Americans to succeed in those colleges.) Laney's philosophy made fundraising even more difficult for her. As Ovington pointed out, whites could believe that industrial schools like Tuskegee would provide a supply of obedient workers, but Laney refused to participate in that bargain:

> But to give money to teach Negroes algebra and the classics was of no help to the whites, and was considered ridiculous and perhaps dangerous for a newly-emancipated race.
>
> So, when Lucy Laney, dark-skinned, stocky, with cropped hair and plain dress, taught her class to decline Latin nouns and conjugate Latin verbs, she was regarded as foolish and obstinate. But this did not alter her purpose. She knew the value of the education she had had at Atlanta, and she knew also how extremely difficult it was for colored boys and girls in the South to prepare for college. . . . She meant to send out from her school graduates who would have had as good a training as white graduates, and if her students wished to go to college, they should enter thoroughly prepared. This she accomplished (Ovington, 54).

Laney's school was chartered and recognized by the state of Georgia in 1886. Its early years were plagued by disasters—a flood, a fire, terrible illness, and constant financial crisis. In 1887, desperate, Laney paid her own way to Minneapolis to attend the General Assembly of the Presbyterian Church. She had intended to make an urgent plea for funding, but found herself so disillusioned by the politics and competitive feeling that she asked only for her train fare home to Georgia. While the Board of Missions was impressed by her dedication, they declined to finance more than her train ticket. The pivotal moment for Laney was her meeting with Francine Haines, the secretary of the Women's Executive Committee of Home Missions. Haines was so deeply struck by Laney's sense of purpose and determination that she launched her own crusade for the school among her wealthy friends. Eventually, Haines's campaign would bear fruit in the form of major contributions from several Northern women; the buildings erected with these donations were named in honor of the donors, and Laney renamed the entire school, in gratitude to Mrs. Haines, the Haines Normal and Industrial Institute.

But for years before these contributions materialized, Laney ran Haines Institute by exhausting her own meager savings and endlessly appealing throughout the South for small donations from black churches and clubs. She sacrificed any personal comfort or security to the school's needs. Ovington reminisced, "She put all her savings into the school; she begged and borrowed and paid back when she could. She went hungry and she slept cold. She prayed in her chill room at night, trusting that somehow the way would be made for her to pull through" (Ovington, 56). Laney's commitment to her entire race was such that throughout the life of Haines, no matter how precarious the finances, fully one-third of her students paid no fees whatsoever.

Laney was a true educational innovator. She was well read in educational theory and child development, and in the early 1890s she opened a real kindergarten, the first in Augusta and one of the first in the entire South. She believed fervently in the great value of early intervention and childhood character education, and she insisted that educated black women bore a special responsibility to all black children. As she declared at the Hampton Negro Conference in 1899,

> Negro women of culture, as kindergartners and primary teachers, have a rare opportunity to lend a hand to the lifting of these burdens [the poverty, ignorance, fear, and family chaos that she described as the legacy of slavery], for here they may instil lessons of cleanliness, truthfulness, loving kindness, love of nature, and love of Nature's God. Here they may daily start aright hundreds of our children; here, too, they may save years of time in the education of the child; and may save many lives from shame and crime by applying the law of prevention. In the kindergarten and primary school is the salvation of the race (Loewenberg, 300).

Laney also initiated the first nursing education in Augusta. Dedicated to the education of the whole child, she encouraged the development of sports programs as well as academics and arts; Haines Institute fielded the first organized football team in Augusta. In addition to her work with Haines, Laney fought actively to improve the living conditions of Augusta's entire black community.

Laney's loving, proud influence was like a magic stone dropped into still, expectant water: concentric circles of meaning spread from the center throughout the South. Laney herself reported in 1893,

Already in the public schools of this city, in sight of our building, four of our girls are employed as teachers. . . . We are through our students yearly reaching a large number of persons. Through our forty student teachers, with schools now under their care that average 35 scholars each, we are reaching indirectly 1400 children. The three or four hundred added to this that come directly under our care causes us to reach about 1800 young people; but oh, large as this number seems, it is small when we think of the many hundreds to whom scarcely a ray of light has yet come (Laney, 123).

Laney had good reason to be proud of the young teachers she educated and trained. John Hope, later the first African American president of Atlanta University, was a Haines graduate, as would be his own children. Laney gave Mary McLeod Bethune, the founder of Bethune-Cookman College, her first real teaching job. Their relationship was exceptionally close; for years, Laney sent Bethune whatever used textbooks and supplies she could. When Bethune was elected president of the National Association of Colored Women, she named Laney as a major inspiration in her life. Other outstanding protegés were Janie Porter Barrett and Charlotte Hawkins Brown. Barrett founded the first settlement house in Virginia and pioneered in working with delinquent girls; Brown founded another excellent school, Palmer Memorial Institute, in Sedalia, North Carolina, which she directed until her death in 1961. Throughout the South and as far away as New York City, Haines graduates spoke of Lucy Laney with great love and respect approaching adoration. Several graduates in New York formed the Laney League, which held annual benefits to raise funds for the school. Jane Hope, John's sister and fellow Haines graduate, considered Laney "the most unselfish of the women who are engaged in public work. She has labored untiringly for the race, giving all and expecting nothing in return" (Daniels, 25).

In the early years of Haines, Laney's energy and self-confidence intimated and angered many of the conservative African American professional men with whom she had to deal. Undaunted, Laney carried on with her vision. By World War I, Haines had several modern brick buildings, nine hundred students, and more than thirty teachers. As Haines graduates achieved prominent positions in institutions across the South, Laney began to receive the recognition long due her; she received honorary graduate degrees from Lincoln University, South Carolina State College, Atlanta University, and Howard University.

In her last years, Laney was debilitated by nephritis and hypertension. She was impatient with her infirmities; "I want to wear out, not to rust out," she insisted (Griggs, 101). She drew strength and reassurance from the noisy, hectic life of the school where she had lived all her adult life; when she became bed-ridden, she reluctantly agreed to move to the home the school had built for her across the street. Laney died there on October 23, 1933; she was buried on the grounds of Haines. The Institute, by then a college preparatory high school, was hard hit by the Depression. Church funding was withdrawn and private contributions declined; in 1949 the school was finally closed and razed, and a new public high school, named in Laney's honor, was built on the site.

Laney's passing was noted in the national press. *The New York Age* reported, "A simple ritual of burial was performed, attended by dignitaries, educators and leading representatives from every walk of life who came to pay their tribute of respect to one of the greatest Negro women of the twentieth century." W.E.B. Du Bois called her "the dark vestal virgin who kept the fires of Negro education fiercely flaming in the rich but mean-spirited city of Augusta, Georgia" (James, 651). For sixty years she had maintained a fierce, compelling vision of the precious worth of each individual; she had lived with a moral urgency to elicit from each child the personal excellence she believed innate in all people. A fitting eulogy came from her close friend, prominent black clergyman Francis J. Grimké, when he heard of her death:

> How greatly she will be missed. In her death, not only the Negro race, but the human race loses one of the noblest specimens of heroic womanhood. How wonderful has been her record! For fifty years, in season and out of season, with tireless energy, she gave herself with all that she possessed of heart, soul, mind, and strength, with never a thought of self, to the great task of uplifting a poor, struggling, depressed race out of the ignorance and degradation in which three hundred years of slavery had left it. Has the race produced, or any other race, a finer example of loyalty, of sanctified, consecrated, unselfish devotion than we have here in Lucy Laney? (Grimké, 494)

References

Anderson, James D. "Northern Foundations and the Shaping of Southern Black Rural Education, 1902–1935." In B. Edward McClellan and William J. Reese, eds. *The Social History of American Education*. Urbana: University of Illinois Press, 1988.

Daniels, Sadie. *Women Builders*. Washington, DC: Associated Publishing, 1931.

Griggs, A. C. "Lucy Craft Laney." *Journal of Negro History* 52 (August, 1986): 97–102. [First published January 1934.]

Grimké, Francis J. *The Works of Francis J. Grimké*. Edited by Carter Woodson. Washington, DC: Associated Publishing, 1942. Vol. 4.

James, Edward T., ed. *Notable American Women*. Cambridge, MA: Harvard University Press, 1971.

Laney, Lucy. "A Progress Report from the Founder of the Haines School." In Gerda Lerner, ed. *Black Women in White America*. New York: Pantheon Books, 1972.

Loewenberg, Bert James and Ruth Bogin, eds. *Black Women in Nineteenth-Century American Life: Their Words, Their Thoughts, Their Feelings*. University Park: Pennsylvania State University Press, 1976.

McCrorey, Mary Jackson. "Lucy Laney." *The Crisis* 41 (June 1934): 161.

Ovington, Mary White. *Portraits in Color*. New York: Viking Press, 1927.

Sterne, Emma Gelders. *Mary McLeod Bethune*. New York: Alfred A. Knopf, 1957.

BENJAMIN LAY

(November 26, 1681–February 3, 1759)

Abolitionist, Pacifist, Penal Reform Advocate

In the last quarter of the 17th century, a child born deformed and impoverished had little to hope for; survival itself might have seemed an unrealistic goal. How then to explain the unexpected, improbable, theatrical career of Benjamin Lay, who not only survived, but launched a frontal assault on forms of barbarous cruelty most of his society accepted as the norm— the penal system, with its ·staggering number of capital crimes, and the well-established, generally respected system of slavery. In the process he earned the enmity of countless fellow Quakers and the friendship of Benjamin Franklin.

BENJAMIN LAY.

Lived to the Age of 80, in the Latter Part of Which, he Observed extreem Temperance in his Eating and Drinking. his Foundation's a Particularity in Dress and Customs at times Subjected him to the Redicule of the Ignorant, but his Friends who were Intimate with Him, thought Him an Honest Religious man.

Benjamin Lay
Courtesy of the Library of Congress.

Benjamin Lay, born to poor Quaker parents in Colchester, England, in 1681, grew to an adult height of only four and one-half feet; he was hunchbacked, his head too large for his body and his legs so withered that they scarcely seemed able to support him. Lay's parents were devout Friends but could not afford to educate him; he had no formal schooling and was apprenticed as a teen-ager to a glovemaker. But Lay was driven from his youth by a demanding, uncompromising, searching spirit; he left his apprenticeship to farm with an older brother, and at eighteen he left that life to spend the next seven years at sea. He later reported voyages throughout the Mediterranean and the Middle East on a number of different ships. The life of a common seaman was especially rigorous and brutal: once again, Lay's survival seems to defy expectation. Whatever veneer of toughness and indifference Lay acquired during this time, it did not shield him from horror and disgust when shipmates who had also worked on slave ships described their experiences. These early confrontations with slavery, even in his imagination, filled him with anger and shame.

In 1710, restless again, Lay left seafaring, returned to Colchester, and married a woman named Sarah, described as able, intelligent, dedicated—and also dwarfed. The couple moved to London, where Lay worked as a draper and they joined the Devonshire House Meeting. Lay's relationship with his Quaker community was vitally important to him, but neither party was ever at peace with the other. From the outset, Lay objected to what he saw as traces of unacceptable vanity and arrogance in the speakers at Meeting; and from the outset, the more conventional members of the Meeting resented his outspoken criticism and interference. There were years of private rebukes, stronger warnings, attempts at compromise—but by 1720 the London Friends had had enough of the confrontational Lay and officially disowned him. Disgruntled, Lay and Sarah returned to Colchester, but he was soon in as great difficulty with Colchester Meeting as he had been in London. In desperation, Colchester Quakers petitioned the London Meeting for advice on "This Benjamin Lay late of London (who we Suppose is too well known to many of you)" and how to treat "his Dark disordered Condition." (Rowntree, 6). During these years Lay spoke out critically not only at Quaker Meeting but also in the churches of Anglicans, Baptists, Presbyterians, and Independents. He had a gift for provoking unease and anger. His affectionate biographer, Quaker abolitionist Roberts Vaux (see Edward Coles*), wrote that

he appeared rather like the comet, which threatens, in its irregular course, the destruction of the worlds near which it passes, than as one of those tranquil orbs which hold their accustomed place, and dispense their light, in the harmonious order of heaven (Vaux).

Some time in 1730, disowned by Colchester Meeting and aching with frustration and restlessness, Lay relocated to Barbardos, where he opened a small shop and came face to face with the nightmare of West Indian slavery. Lay was a driven ascetic whose compassion flowed more easily to others than to himself. He refused to eat or wear anything that had resulted in the death of an animal; in addition, he would not make use of any item produced with slave labor. Thus, to his already bizarre appearance he added the exotic touches of crude hand-spun, hand-woven tunics and shoes. A long, prematurely white beard completed his striking image.

Both Benjamin and Sarah were overcome with anguish for the slaves and with concomitant contempt for their slaveowning neighbors. They provided as much free food for local slaves as they could; on Sundays they opened their shop to the slaves and tried to offer some religious instruction and basic education. One day Sarah stopped by the yard of a well-respected local Friend, where she found him beating a naked, bleeding slave tied to a tree. He explained that the ungrateful slave had tried to run away. From that moment on, Lay focused his considerable energy and imagination on convincing his fellow Quakers of the monumental sin of slavery. His crusade did not endear him to his neighbors. "In proportion to the steadiness and determination of his testimony against negro bondage was the hostility of those who were enriched by its existence." Reviled, threatened, and despairing, the Lays determined to leave the island. Sarah worried "lest by remaining there she might be leavened into the nature of the inhabitants, which was pride and oppression" (Vaux). Hoping for an environment more morally acceptable to them, the Lays moved to Philadelphia in 1731.

Lay's expectations of Philadelphia were not entirely unreasonable. Although slavery was widespread in Pennsylvania and many Quakers were more than reconciled to it, there was a strong if uneven thread of antislavery sentiment among Friends in the area. The earliest recorded American condemnation of slavery, in 1688, originated in the Germantown Friends Meeting, just north of Philadelphia. In 1693 the Philadelphia Yearly Meeting advised its members to buy slaves only with the intention of freeing them; a few years later, perhaps spurred by the vehement denunciations of a virtually forgotten abolitionist named William Southeby, Meetings in both Pennsylvania and New Jersey recommended that no more slaves be brought into their communities. (In truth, this may have sprung as much from the pervasive fear of unknown slaves as from any moral impulse.) The use of cautious terms like "advise" and "recommend" underscores the ambivalent and hesitant approach of most Friends in the early 18th century. In 1712 the Philadelphia Yearly Meeting inquired of the London Yearly Meeting if Friends should hold slaves; London's response was a masterpiece of carefully worded polite phrases designed to upset no one. Under Southeby's urging, Philadelphia Friends in 1715 "advised" against the slave trade, but when Southeby continued to call for real condemnation and penalties for recalcitrant Friends, the Meeting rebuked and disowned him. Shortly thereafter, Philadelphia Meeting expelled another fervent abolitionist, John Farmer. (See Thomas Hazard.*)

When Lay arrived, Philadelphia Meeting was deeply involved in dealing with Ralph Sandiford, an impassioned young Englishman who had, like Lay, Farmer, and others, witnessed West Indian slavery firsthand and reacted with intense horror. Sandiford had published a ringing denunciation of slavery, which Benjamin Franklin printed. When the chief justice of Pennsylvania threatened Sandiford with legal penalties if he sold his pamphlet, he distributed it free. Outraged, the Philadelphia Meeting disowned him; despondent, impoverished, and in poor health, he died shortly thereafter at the age of forty. Lay visited Sandiford during his last illness; the two may have been friends for some time before that, and Lay had come to look upon the younger man as a protegé. He saw Sandiford's death as the direct result of the Friends' hypocrisy and cruelty; he assumed a moral responsibility to honor Sandiford's dream as well as his own.

Lay was a brilliant practitioner of guerrilla theater. On one occasion he stood outside a meeting house for hours in heavy snow, his entire right leg bared to the cold. When passing Friends expressed concern for his health, he would reply, "You pretend compassion for me, but you do not feel for the poor slaves in your fields, who go all winter half-clad." On another occasion, having befriended the small son of a neighbor, he invited the child into his home and kept him happily occupied—and out of sight—for an entire day. The child's distraught parents searched frantically for their son; Lay finally orchestrated a "casual" meeting with them and observed the extent of their anxiety. He then commented, "Your child is safe in my house, and you may now conceive of the sorrow you inflict upon the parents of the negro girl you hold in slavery, for she was torn from them by avarice."

Lay's most notoriously dramatic episode occurred during one Yearly Meeting in Burlington, New Jersey. He had secretly dressed in a military uniform, with a sword and a wineskin of berry juice hidden in a large, hollowed-out book. Over the entire costume he pulled a drab Quaker cloak. In the silence of the Meeting, he strode forward and declared:

> Oh all you negro-masters who are contentedly holding your fellow creatures in a state of slavery during life, well knowing the cruel sufferings

those innocent captives undergo in their state of bondage, both in these North American colonies and in the West India islands; you must know they are not made slaves by any direct law, but are held by an arbitrary and self-interested custom, in which you participate. And especially you who profess "to do unto all men as ye would they should do unto you"— and yet, in direct opposition to every principle of reason, humanity, and religion, you are forcibly retaining your fellow men, from one generation to another, in a state of unconditional servitude; you might as well throw off the plain coat as I do. [Here he flung off his cloak and revealed his bizarre regalia.] It would be as justifiable in the sight of the Almighty, who beholds and respects all nations and colours of men with an equal regard, if you should thrust a sword through their hearts as I do through this book. [Now he drew his sword, impaling the hollow book and splattering near-by Friends with the blood-red berry juice] (Vaux).

Lay was also an early proponent of Gandhian nonviolent resistance. When his dramatic declarations on slavery discomfited a congregation and got him forcibly ejected from innumerable churches and meeting houses, he would simply lie in the gutter or path where he had been thrown, refusing for hours to rise and frequently forcing people to step over him as they left their church services. "Let those who cast me here raise me up," he remarked. "It is their business, not mine."

In 1737, with the support of Benjamin Franklin, Lay published a summation of all his thinking on slavery, entitled *All Slave-Keepers, That Keep the Innocent in Bondage, Apostates. . . .* His harshest criticism was reserved for clergy who kept slaves:

I know no worse or greater stumbling blocks the devil has to lay in the way of honest inquirers than our ministers and elders keeping slaves; and by straining and perverting Holy Scriptures, preach more to hell than ever they will bring to heaven by their feigned humility and hypocrisy (Lay, 85).

Beyond his vitriolic, apocalyptic denunciations of slavery and slave-owners, Lay offered practical steps toward resolution. Like many other Quakers, including George Fox himself, Lay supported the religious education of all slaves. Moving far beyond the vision of most other reformers, however, Lay believed in total racial equality. He advocated apprenticeships and academic as well as civil education for blacks in preparation for freedom; he looked forward confidently to a new generation of "convinced" African Friends who would become eloquent missionaries to their own countries. He anticipated nothing less than a fully integrated, utterly equitable society.

Lay was passionately opposed to capital punishment and wrote several pamphlets urging penal reform. He advocated sentences based on hard but purposeful labor, with ample education and what would currently be called rehabilitation. Vaux believed that Lay had, seventy-five years earlier, proposed all the prison reforms that by 1815 made Pennsylvania a proud model of "humane" correction.

As both Sarah and Lay aged, their health deteriorated and they were forced to lodge with a neighboring farmer. Deeply stricken by Sarah's death in 1739, Lay turned increasingly for solace to his studies. Totally self-taught, he had amassed a library of over two hundred books. It was not uncommon for him to visit local schools, talk with the children, and present them with free books as an incentive to keep on learning. In 1758, shortly before Lay's death, Pennsylvania Yearly Meeting determined to disown all slaveholding members. "Now I can die in peace," he commented upon hearing the news. Although Lay had requested cremation, his friends could not countenance such an unorthodox step, and he was buried instead in the Friends' Burial Ground at Abington. All his books and manuscripts, preserved by the farmer with whom he had boarded, were seized by the British during the Revolution and have been lost.

Lay is a difficult figure to assess. He was contentious, confrontational, deliberately provocative, incapable of compromise. He had suffered greatly himself; some historians have been tempted to interpret his life with the arrogance of psychohistorical analysis. Such reductionism demeans his fierce personal courage and dedication. He was, in the words of the abolitionist poet John Greenleaf Whittier, "the irrepressible prophet who troubled the Israel of slave-holding Quakerism, clinging like a rough chestnut-burr to the skirts of its respectability and settling like a pertinacious gad-fly on the sore places of its conscience" (Rowntree, 19).

References

Aptheker, Herbert. "The Quakers and Negro Slavery." *Journal of Negro History* 25 (July, 1940): 331–362.

Davis, David Brion. *The Problem of Slavery in Western Culture*. Ithaca, NY: Cornell University Press, 1966.

Drake, Thomas. *Quakers and Slavery in America*. New Haven, CT: Yale University Press, 1950.

Lay, Benjamin. *All Slave-Keepers, That Keep the Innocent in Bondage, Apostates.* . . . Philadelphia. 1737.

Rowntree, C. Brighton. "Benjamin Lay, 1681–1759." *Journal of the Friends Historical Society* 33 (1936): 3–20.

Soderlund, Jean R. *Quakers and Slavery: A Divided Spirit*. Princeton, NJ: Princeton University Press, 1985.

Vaux, Roberts. *Memoirs of the Lives of Benjamin Lay and Ralph Sandiford: Two of the Earliest Public Advocates for the Emancipation of the Enslaved Africans*. Philadelphia: Solomon W. Conrad, 1815.

BELVA ANN LOCKWOOD

(October 24, 1830–May 19, 1917)

Women's Rights Activist

By her own admission, Belva Ann Lockwood was a tomboy, "a little, dirty-faced girl on a farm, like Topsy, not afraid of snakes or rats or 'nothin', as active as a boy" (Winner, 92). She was a supremely self-confident child, adventurous, defiant, a champion of weaker children. A classmate remembered her as "the most daring and generous girl in the school" (ibid., 2). "From a child," she reported many years later,

> *the bent of my mind has been one of extreme practicality. . . . I have never been able to enter into the prejudices of the centuries past, that have had no foundation in reason, in nature, or in nature's laws, nor to discover that the limitations of woman's sphere as heretofore dictated by the customs of society were worthy of serious consideration. . . . I have not raised the dead, but I have awakened the living (Lockwood, 220).*

Lockwood's faith in herself and in the ultimate rational justice of natural law brought her into direct conflict with many firmly entrenched prejudices and myths of Victorian America. Fearless, principled, logical, turning her frustration into the weapon of sarcastic humor, Lockwood repeatedly waged war against the ignorance and arrogance of her society. In the course of her battles she overcame seemingly insurmountable obstacles and changed the legal landscape for all women who came after her.

Belva Ann Lockwood
Courtesy, Niagara County Historical Society.

The Niagara frontier, where Belva Ann Bennett was born in 1830, was a harsh and demanding environment. Always hungry for learning, Belva attended local schools while carrying her share of the endless burden of farm chores. Her father saw no use for her education and refused to pay for it, forcing her to leave school at the age of fifteen. When she won a local declamation contest a year later, one of the judges commented, "That effort is worthy of a man." Belva mused that since she had always been academically ahead of the boys in her class, she could not see the comment as a compliment. After teaching school herself for three years, she married Uriah McNall, a young neighbor; their daughter, Lura, was born the following year. Only two years later, weakened by injuries in a sawmill accident, McNall died. Widowed at the age of twenty-one, Belva was alone with her infant daughter.

For a short period after McNall's death, Belva ran the sawmill herself, but she realized that teaching offered her a more secure path. Recognizing that her own education was incomplete, she enrolled in Gasport Academy in nearby Gasport, where she studied geography, geometry, German, and physiology while raising her daughter and running a small boarding house. After graduating in 1854, Belva taught at Gasport for two years. At that point, she discovered that the male teachers on staff were being paid twice as much as she was. Her reaction was characteristically direct. She confronted her superiors with the inequity. "I kicked to the school trustees," she was quoted years later. "I went to the wife of the Methodist minister. The answer I got opened my eyes and raised my dander. 'I can't help you; you cannot help yourself, for it is the way of the word.' " She remembered her anger, not only at the injustice itself but at the other woman's passivity before it. "I have never stopped fighting. My cause was the cause of thousands of women" (*New York Times*, 23).

Belva quit her job, left her small daughter with her parents, and traveled sixty miles to Lima, New York, to complete her college education at Genessee College (later Syracuse University). Her tuition was $8.50 a term. Granted junior standing, Belva insisted on taking the "Scientific Course." She studied electricity and magnetism, chemistry and geometry, international law, political economy, and the United States Constitution.

In June of 1857, Belva McNall received her Bachelor of Science degree with honors. Reunited with the daughter she had not seen for two years, Belva accepted the position of principal of the Lockport Union School. For the next nine years she administered and taught in several schools in upstate New York. Active in a variety of relief efforts throughout the Civil War, she was a widely known and respected figure in the region.

Her pastor recalled, "Such was the spirit and manner in which she performed her work that she secured the respect and good will of the entire community" (Winner, 5).

In 1866, feeling that she needed broader horizons and sensing the possibilities as well as problems that the postwar era offered, Belva moved to Washington, D.C. She opened a school with her younger sister, whose education she had guided; seventeen-year-old Lura was also enlisted as a teacher. At the same time they were initiating the school project, Belva was exploring the Constitution more deeply and studying German and Spanish independently.

Inevitably, Belva was drawn to reform enterprises in the turbulent city. Within a year she had become the vice-president of the Universal Franchise Association and was a frequent speaker at public meetings. In March of 1868 Belva married Ezekiel Lockwood, a tall, older dentist who fully endorsed her views on women's rights. But Belva did not seem destined for domestic bliss; a second daughter, Jessie, born in 1869, died at twenty months. Devastated, Lockwood focused all her tormented energies on the struggle for women's suffrage.

In the fall of 1869 Lockwood applied to the law school of Columbian College; despite her honors degree from Genessee, her application was rejected. As the president of the college wrote to her, the professors thought that "the attendance of ladies would be an injurious diversion of the attention of the students" (Stern, 210). Georgetown and Howard universities also believed their students could not resist the distracting charms of a demure thirty-nine-year-old woman. Finally, in 1871, the National University Law School agreed to accept women. Lockwood was among fifteen women matriculating in that first class; she was one of only two women who completed the course two years later.

Responding to angry protests from some of her male classmates, the university refused to grant Lockwood her diploma. Typically, Lockwood fought back. Since President Ulysses S. Grant was titular president of the National University Law School, she wrote directly—and scathingly—to him on September 3, 1873:

> You are, or you are not President of the National University Law School. If you are its President I wish to say to you that I have been passed through the curriculum of study of that school, and I am entitled to, and demand my Diploma. If you are not its President then I ask you to take your name from its papers, and not hold out to the world to be what you are not (Stern, 211).

While Lockwood never received a direct reply from President Grant, she did, a week later, receive her diploma, signed by the National University Law School faculty and its president. At the age of forty-three Belva

Lockwood had conquered one more bastion of prejudice and intolerance. She was now better equipped to fight further battles.

Lockwood's private law practice soon focused on citizens' claims against the federal government. When one of her cases came before the Federal Court of Claims in early 1874, the court denied her the right to argue before it. As Lockwood, with her characteristic biting humor, described the moment,

> There was a painful pause. Every eye in the court-room was fixed first upon me, and then upon the court; when Justice Drake, in measured words, announced, *"Mistress Lockwood, you are a woman."* For the first time in my life I began to realize that it was a crime to be a woman; but it was too late to put in a denial, and I at once pleaded guilty to the charge of the court. . . . On the following week, . . . [w]hen the case of Lockwood was reached, and I again stood up before that august body, the solemn tones of the chief justice announced, "Mistress Lockwood, you are a *married woman!"* (Lockwood, 218).

Lockwood refused to accept defeat. She submitted a sophisticated brief to both Houses of Congress, asserting that the right to practice law was a privilege of citizenship. At the same time, she applied for admission to the United States Supreme Court. During the October, 1876 term of the court, Lockwood's application was heard, no doubt with consternation, and promptly denied. The Supreme Court declared that it had never admitted women and that until so required by statute, it had no intention of doing so. Lockwood reported the incident before a convention of Washington suffragists, and flung out her challenge: "It is the glory of each generation to make its own precedents" (Stern, 216).

Lockwood accepted the Supreme Court's insistence on statutory action. She drafted a bill according the right to practice before the Supreme Court to any woman lawyer of good moral character and three years' experience. The bill, entitled "A Bill to Relieve the Legal Disabilities of Women," was introduced in the House of Representatives in November, 1877, where it passed only after three readings and considerations in the Judiciary Committee. The Senate proved even more resistant. Some senators insisted that no law specifically denied women the right to practice before the Supreme Court, and therefore legislative redress was inappropriate. It took the courageous and outspoken support of several suffragist senators, Aaron A. Sargent of California and George Hoar of Massachusetts, to convince their colleagues. "In this land," commented Senator Sargent, "man has ceased to dominate over his fellow—let him cease to dominate over his sister" (Stern, 218). Finally, in February, 1879, while Lockwood and her friends watched from the gallery, the bill was passed in the Senate. More than five years had passed since her original rejection before the Court of Claims. During the protracted struggle, elderly Dr. Lockwood had died, but Lockwood had refused to let grief overwhelm her. On March 3, 1879, Lockwood was admitted to the Bar of the United States Supreme Court. Three days later, cornered at last, the recalcitrant Court of Claims admitted her. Fittingly, it was Lockwood who, less than a year after her own admission, sponsored Samuel Lowery of Alabama, the first Southern black lawyer admitted before the Supreme Court. Once again, Lockwood's determination, energy, intelligence, and perseverance had achieved what no one before her thought possible.

Throughout her long career, Lockwood worked effectively for women's rights. She had helped found the Universal Franchise Association in 1867, and throughout the 1870s and '80s she was active in the National Woman Suffrage Association. She was the author of an 1870 petition to Congress that demanded equal pay for female federal employees; the petition resulted in legislation in 1872 guaranteeing pay parity.

By 1880, when she addressed the annual convention of the National Woman Suffrage Association, Lockwood was beginning to weave more closely the two major causes of her life, women's rights and international peace. She believed that women, armed with the vote and moving broadly in positions of authority, could help soften the tone of international relations. "We have the woman merchant, the lawyer, the doctor, the correspondent, the editor," she declared.

> We want great statesmen in this country rather than great generals. . . . We hope that with the experience this nation has had in the war of the rebellion and in all of the train of evils that has followed in its wake, we are educated out of war; and that reason and the pen will be the controlling influence of the future (Winner, 42).

In 1884 Lockwood wrote a bitter letter to *Woman's Herald of Industry*, the organ of a California women's rights organization. She had attended the Republican National Convention in Chicago to urge the inclusion of a women's suffrage plank in the platform, and she felt she had been dismissed with derision. She was outraged, and she was furious that leading suffragists like Elizabeth Cady Stanton and Susan B. Anthony still urged women to support the Republican candidate, James Blaine. Typically, Lockwood cut right to the core of the issue:

> Why not nominate women for important places?. . . . *If women in the States are not permitted to vote, there is no law against their being voted for.* . . . We shall never have rights until we take them, nor respect until we command it. Reforms are slow, but they never go backwards (Stern, 223).

Marietta B. Snow, a leading West Coast feminist and a past independent candidate for the governorship of California, recognized the daring and logic of Lockwood's declaration. The National Equal Rights Party, meeting in San Francisco, responded by nominating Lockwood for U.S. President.

When Lockwood accepted the nomination of the Equal Rights Party, she knew she had no chance of winning the election. She knew she would be the object of ridicule and vituperation. Yet she did accept, willingly. She believed the gesture itself was the opening wedge in a long-term campaign to render the *un*thinkable thinkable. "Like all candidates, we of course claim everything with confidence," she told a reporter in Cleveland, "but I tell you confidently that our work will begin when the campaign closes" (Winner, 62). She was the primary author of the party's platform, which called for women's suffrage; labor reform, especially protection for working women and children; formation of a Peace and Arbitration League with a court for settling international disputes; elimination of business monopolies; equal justice for every citizen without regard to color, sex, or nationality; full citizenship for Indians; and temperance. Lockwood was especially determined to nominate qualified women for federal judgeships—including the Supreme Court. The *Washington Gazette*, analyzing her platform in September, 1884, commented disapprovingly, "Her Indian policy would consist in paying the Indians what we owe them, making them citizens, and treating them justly" (Winner, 55).

Campaigning vigorously, Lockwood pointed out that the country held 10.5 million male voters—and 12.5 million taxpaying women who were denied the vote. How, she demanded, could this lead to government by the will of the majority? She called on all "noble, free-minded men" to support women's rights—and the only party that endorsed those rights.

Lockwood did not win the election. She did win more than four thousand male votes, which gave her the electoral vote of Indiana, half the electoral votes of Oregon, and respectable showings in New Hampshire and New York. Unfortunately, other leading suffragists continued to see the campaign as an embarrassment, and a bitter rift grew between Lockwood and her former companions. Although she did accept a second nomination from the Equal Rights Party in 1888, she seemed to be less committed to the campaign, and the party did not achieve the level of support it had had in the previous race.

From the mid-1880s on, Lockwood moved farther away from the center of women's rights agitation and devoted most of her energies to the cause of international peace. She became an officer in the Universal Peace Union and served as a delegate to every International Peace Congress from 1889 until 1911, when she attended the conference in Rome at the age of eighty-one. Her major goal was always binding arbitration to resolve international confrontations without resort to force. An officer of the International Bureau of Peace, Lockwood was also a member of the Nobel Peace Prize nominating committee.

Throughout her other involvements, Lockwood maintained a large private law practice. She took divorce cases, child support cases, discrimination cases of all sorts, and above all, she took claims cases. In 1905 she handled a major, controversial claims case on behalf of the Eastern Cherokee Indians, in a case dating back to 1828 and the forced removal of the Cherokee from North Carolina. The purchase of the Cherokee's ancestral lands had first been mandated by a treaty in 1835 and confirmed by another treaty in 1891. The total capital owed to the Cherokee was not in dispute; rather, the issue was the accumulated interest on parts of the principal that had not yet been paid. When Lockwood, representing the Cherokee, argued the case successfully before the Supreme Court, she must have felt a special satisfaction. The decision against the federal government awarded the Cherokee a five million dollar judgment—by far the largest claim award to date.

Lockwood's courageous spirit seemed unquenchable despite great personal sadness. Her beloved daughter Lura, her partner in the law practice, died unexpectedly in 1894, and her later years, though filled with activities and with numerous awards, were emotionally deprived. Nonetheless, she told the New York *World* in 1912 that her message to women was "Fight, fight, fight everlastingly—not with your claws and fists, but with your wits" (Whitman, 529). In her eighties, having unwisely succumbed to the flattery of "an unscrupulous admirer," Lockwood found herself in severe financial difficulties; she was dispossessed from the home that had been her personal and professional base for thirty-five years. Having campaigned hopefully for Woodrow Wilson, Lockwood was deeply saddened to see the country slide toward the morass of World War I. In the midst of the nation's increasingly hysterical patriotism, 86-year-old Belva Lockwood, who had fought so hard for equality, rationality, and peace, stopped fighting. She died in Washington on May 19, 1917.

Lockwood provided her own most eloquent eulogy, responding to a journalist's 1897 inquiry whether she considered herself a "New Woman." "As a rule," she wrote,

> I do not consider myself at all. I am, and always have been a progressive woman. . . . I do not believe in sex distinction in literature, law, politics, or trade; or that modesty and virtue are more becoming to women than to men; but wish we had more of it everywhere.
>
> I was new about 60 years ago, but did not then appreciate my privileges (Lerner, 419).

References

James, Edward T., ed. *Notable American Women*. Cambridge, MA: Harvard University Press, 1971.

Kennedy, Patricia Scileppi and Gloria Hartmann O'Shields, eds. *We Shall Be Heard: Women Speakers in America, 1828–Present*. Dubuque, IA: Kendall/ Hunt Publishing, 1983.

Lerner, Gerda, ed. *The Female Experience: An American Documentary*. New York: Oxford University Press, 1977.

Lockwood, Belva. "My Efforts to Become a Lawyer." *Lippincott's Monthly Magazine*, February, 1888: 215–220.

Marlow, Joan. *The Great Women*. New York: Galahad Press, 1979.

Morris, Charles. *The World's Great Orators and Their Orations*. Philadelphia: John C. Winston, 1917.

New York Times. Obituary, May 20, 1917, p. 23.

Stern, Madeleine. *We the Women: Career Firsts of Nineteenth Century America*. New York: Schulte Publishers, 1963.

Whitman, Alden, ed. *American Reformers*. New York: H. W. Wilson Co., 1984.

Winner, Julia Hull. *Belva A. Lockwood*. Lockport, NY: Niagara County Historical Society, 1969.

SETH LUTHER

(1795–1863)

Labor Organizer

Seth Luther was a dangerous man. He was one of those rare individuals whose words inspire others—to think, to hope, to act. What Thomas Paine did for the American Revolution, Seth Luther did for the first generation of the labor movement in America: he articulated a coherent, irresistible moral vision; he delineated intolerable conditions; he proposed a sound, humane set of goals; and he called for immediate mass action. It should come as no surprise that both Paine and Luther were ill-treated by many contemporaries and betrayed by history; they both used their gifts in the service of the lowly, and they both demanded more honesty than the powerful could allow.

Seth Luther was born in 1795 in Providence, Rhode Island. His father, a poor tanner, had fought with the Continental Army during the Revolution. Seth was brought up in a working-class home that treasured the ideals of unalienable rights and natural equality; the Revolution was a source of inspiration for him, and a great deal of his moral outrage was grounded in the betrayal of its goals. The Luther family was deeply religious, not with the comfortable, genteel deism of the Founding Fathers or the formal Anglicanism of the upper classes, but with a passionate, intense, severe faith focused more on sin and retribution than on grace and salvation. This belief in the very palpable reality of sin and evil in the world is another major element of Luther's rhetorical power.

As a poor child, Luther received a minimal elementary education and was at work in the lumber mills at an early age. His impassioned advocacy of working women and children, his descriptions of the terrible costs of early, heavy labor, are undoubtedly based on his own experiences. Given his almost total lack of formal education, Luther's broad reading and familiarity with history are evidence of tremendous native intelligence and determination.

Restless, imaginative, hungry for the unknown, and unwilling to let himself be crushed and shaped by the deadening mill labor, 22-year-old Seth Luther escaped in the quintessential American way: he went west. For fifteen years, Luther wandered throughout the West—down the Ohio River on an eight-foot-long pine skiff to Cincinnati, out further through Indian territories, and south through the slave states. His experiences during these years confirmed in him a total faith in the "common man," an awareness of human relatedness that transcended the artificial barriers of race and class, and a direct, challenging approach to problem-solving—what has been referred to as "a pugnacious individualism" (Hartz, 402). Tall, long-limbed, and deliberately inelegant, Luther consciously assumed the persona of the frontiersman; he saw himself offering the renewed freshness and hope of the frontier to an industrialized East that had become as corrupt and decadent as Europe.

When Luther returned to New England sometime in 1831, he found a vastly changed situation. The working conditions he had experienced paled in comparison to the factory system now firmly entrenched in Rhode Island, Massachusetts, Maine, and New Hampshire. New England's major towns were now dominated by huge cotton and woolen mills. Uncontrolled industrialization devastated thousands of lives and altered the shape of society. Mill workers—men, women, and children as young as six—labored thirteen to fifteen hours a day under appalling conditions for pennies per hour. A minute's lateness could be penalized by the loss of half a day's wages. Workers, especially the children, were so tired and poorly fed that disastrous accidents and mutilations were common; the thick dust and fiber content in the air represented major health hazards, and factory workers' life expectancy was low.

Luther returned to the work he knew—lumber milling and carpentry. He soon became involved in the growing labor unrest of the time. In 1831 Luther helped organize the New England Association of Farmers, Mechanics, and Other Workingmen, which concentrated its energies on a campaign for a ten-hour working day. Luther was appointed a "traveling agent" for *The New England Artisan*, a newspaper that soon became the official organ of the New England Association. In this role, Luther traveled throughout industrialized New England, addressing workers' groups on the Association's goal of a ten-hour day. At the same time he began writing for the *Artisan*, developing his fundamental themes: that the Revolution guaranteed working people decent lives; that the fourteen-hour day denied working children and adults any chance to better themselves through education; that group solidarity in support of political and economic reforms was essential.

In 1832, frustrated by the defeat of a Boston ship carpenters' strike, Luther published his best-known pamphlet, *An Address to the Working Men of New England*. It is a ringing model of his passionate, broad-ranging, stunningly well-informed voice. In it, Luther noted that American manufacturers were frequently urged to emulate the "splendid British system." Citing parliamentary reports, medical surveys, and other evidence from a range of British sources, Luther drew a devastating picture of the true condition of the British industrial worker. Is this, he asked, a system worthy of emulation? One of Luther's fiercest charges against the factory system was that it denied education to the workers:

> Our wish is to show that education is neglected, and that as a matter of course, because if 13 hours actual labor is required each day, it is *impossible* to attend to education among children, or improvement among adults. . . . The mills *generally* in New England run 13 hours the year round. . . . At the Eagle mills, Griswold, Connecticut, 15 hours and 10 minutes actual labor in the mill are required; at another mill in the vicinity, 14 hours of actual labor are required. It needs no argument, to prove that education *must* be, and is almost entirely neglected. Facts speak in a voice not to be misunderstood or misinterpreted. In 8 mills all on one stream, within a distance of two miles, we have 168 persons who can neither read nor write . . . and to add to the darkness of the picture, . . . in all the mills which the enquiries of the committee have been able to reach, books, pamphlets, and newspapers are *absolutely prohibited* (Luther, 21).

In addition, Luther declared, many workers were forced to contribute to the support and to attend the church services of factory-appointed clergymen, in direct violation of constitutionally guaranteed freedom of conscience. "It seems," he wrote angrily, "the owners of Mills wish to control their men in all things. To enslave their bodies and souls, make them think, act, vote, preach, pray, and worship, as it may suit 'We the Owners' " (Luther, 28).

Luther recognized the special horrors to which the young mill girls were exposed, and he explicitly supported the role of women within the labor movement. "It is quite certain that unless we have the female sex on our side, we can not hope to accomplish any object we have in view" (Whitman, 549). Luther's detailed, unvarnished revelations of the conditions and treatment of women and children in the factories affected a broad audience. The *Hampden Whig* of Springfield, Massachusetts, scarcely a sympathetic organ, called his stories "not only alarming but absolutely shocking to the mind of every free and patriotic man." The *Boston Post* expressed the hope that his pamphlet would have "a salutary effect on the community" (Hartz, 405).

Luther's vivid, anguished imagery anticipates Marx's descriptions of class struggle. He consistently referred to workers as "the producing class" and to the factory owners and the rich as "the idle class"; he saw one large group being sacrificed to the selfish demands of the smaller group:

> The whole system of labor in New England, *more especially in cotton mills*, is a cruel system of exaction on the bodies and minds of the producing classes, destroying the energies of both, and for no other object than to enable the "rich" to "take care of themselves," while "the poor must work or starve" (Luther, 28).

Outraged but realistic, Luther acknowledged that manufacture and industry could not be eliminated; he insisted without compromise, however, that they must be reformed. He had never learned, he wrote, "that it is necessary, or just, that manufactureres must be sustained by injustice, cruelty, ignorance, vice, and misery; which is now the fact to a startling degree." He went on:

> If what we have stated be true, and we challenge denial, what must be done? . . . Let the word be—Onward! Onward! We know the difficulties are great, and the obstacles many; but, as yet, we "know our rights, and knowing, dare maintain." We wish to injure no man, and we are determined not to be injured as we have been; we wish nothing, but those equal rights, which were designed for us all. And although wealth, and prejudice, and slander, and abuse, are all brought to bear on us, we have one consolation—WE ARE THE MAJORITY. . . . Let us awake. Our cause is the cause of truth—of justice and humanity. *It must prevail.* Let us be determined no longer to be deceived by the cry of those who produce *nothing* and who enjoy *all*, and who *insultingly* term us—the *farmers, mechanics and labourers*, the LOWER ORDERS—and *exultingly* claim our homage for

themselves, as the HIGHER ORDERS—While the DECLARATION OF IN-
DEPENDENCE asserts that "ALL MEN ARE CREATED EQUAL" (Luther,
32).

Within weeks of its original publication, Luther's *Address* had been
reissued in New York and Philadelphia, where it helped launch a massive strike for the ten-hour day.

Luther's moral passion was contagious. He evoked the country's revolutionary heritage to people whose fathers had fought the war; he insisted that the Revolution was incomplete—even betrayed—as long as
gross inequalities existed in the lives of American citizens:

> The Workingmen bared their arms and bosoms in '76, and they are about
> to do it again in '36. The Workingmen of '76 stood on our battlefields,
> scorning the mercy and defying the power of foreign tyrants; and we of
> '36 despise the power of domestic foes. . . . The minions of domestic tyr-
> anny must be made to know and feel that a people to be free have but to
> will it. We will try the ballot box first; if that will not effect our righteous
> purpose, the next and last resort is the cartridge box (Gersuny, 243).

This sort of inflammatory rhetoric exposed Luther to condemnation in
the mainstream press. He was called a "natural radical," an "Apostle of
Sedition," a "Disturber of the Peace," a "disorganizer," and even a spy
(Luther, i). But no one could question his sincerity. His ethical standards
influenced many men to look beyond the competition from more poorly
paid women and to see rather that their best interests lay in uniting
against common exploitation. When the Ladies' Shoe Binders in Lynn,
Massachusetts, struck for higher wages in 1834, they were fully supported by the men's Cordwainers Union, which offered financial support and resolved not to work for any shoe manufacturer who refused
to meet the women's demands. In 1836 the same two unions in Philadelphia coordinated a strike. The men announced, "Although they [the
employers] may forget that they have mothers, we have resolved to
take them under our protection, to flourish or sink with them" (Foner,
111).

In a similar spirit, Luther insisted that factory workers and skilled
mechanics faced a common enemy and that class solidarity was utterly
essential to any protest or strike. When the Boston Trades Union, of
which Luther was secretary, called a general strike in 1834, Luther's fiery
words illuminated their struggle:

> We have been too long subjected to the odious, cruel, unjust, and tyrannical
> system which compels the operative mechanic to exhaust his physical and
> mental powers. We have rights and duties to perform as American citizens
> and members of society, which forbid us to dispose of more than ten hours
> for a day's work (Foner, 116).

In keeping with Luther's faith in Jeffersonian ideals was his belief in the power of education. To Luther, greed—in his term, "Avarice"—was the real Original Sin, "the mainspring of crime, in all its thousand shapes and forms." He blamed defective moral education for the prevalence of greed, and with the optimism of the Enlightenment, he trusted that intense early character education and an exposure to healthy manual labor could create citizens imbued with love and respect for one another. The problem for him was forcing the corrupt minority to provide the necessary education; his logical solution was to eliminate the disproportionate power of the minority by establishing universal suffrage.

The Constitution of the United States did not stipulate universal suffrage. The states were left to legislate their own qualifications; in many cases, the property requirements completely and intentionally disenfranchised the vast majority of laborers. Throughout the 1830s, Luther was active in the struggle for equal manhood suffrage in Rhode Island. In 1833 he served on the Rhode Island Committee for the Extension of Suffrage; that year he published *An Address on the Right of Free Suffrage*, in which he advocated passive resistance among the disenfranchised to the collection of taxes and to serving in the militia.

In 1840 the Rhode Island Suffrage Association was founded, and despite the apprehension its middle-class leaders may have felt, Luther became its most eloquent spokesman. The increasingly agitated demands for equal suffrage escalated in 1842 with the almost spontaneous formation of the People's Party, which framed a constitution based on universal manhood suffrage and submitted it directly to the populace instead of to the legislature. Declaring that "the people" had ratified their constitution, the People's Party elected an entire new administration, with Thomas Dorr as governor. As crudely armed men flocked to support the rebel government, Luther became a major organizing and coordinating figure.

The rebellion was short-lived; Dorr, Luther, and several other leaders were arrested, imprisoned, and charged with treason. There is little doubt that Luther was subjected to especially brutal treatment in prison while awaiting trial; he later described beatings, shackling, and other cruelties. At one point, desperate, he set fire to his cell and attempted to escape; he was soon recaptured. Finally, in August, 1843, a year after the rebellion, the state attorney general quietly decided not to proceed with the case against Luther. The year's imprisonment had been damaging to Luther in many ways. He wrote to a friend that "my mind has been extremely impaired by my confinement" (Gersuny, 245).

In poor health and impoverished, Luther threw himself back into the ten-hour movement. In the spring of 1846, while planning strategy for a major new ten-hour campaign, Luther seems to have suffered what may have been an emotional collapse. He was arrested in a bizarre, theatrical attempt to rob a Boston bank and was committed to a lunatic asylum in Cambridge. The final seventeen years of life were spent in various mental institutions. The records of the Vermont Asylum in Brattleboro, where he was transferred in 1858, described him as "much known as a noisy politician. Demented when he entered. Not violent, nor mischievous but occasionally noisy. . . . Probably has some friends in Providence but if so they have never visited him" (Gersuny, 248). Alone, broken, isolated, and abandoned, Luther died on April 29, 1863; no one claimed his body, and he was buried at public expense.

Luther was a brilliant, dedicated orator and reformer. He advocated a progressive reform program including universal suffrage, the abolition of child labor, universal free public education, a system of adult education, the elimination of debtors' prison, and the abolition of capital punishment. Outspoken, controversial, and courageous, Seth Luther paid a fearful price for his unflinching attack on an inhumane and demeaning system.

References

Foner, Philip. *History of the Labor Movement in the United States.* New York: International Publishers, 1982. Vol. 1.

Gersuny, Carl. "A Biographical Note on Seth Luther." *Labor History* 18 (Spring, 1977): 239–248.

Hartz, Louis. "Seth Luther: The Story of a Working-Class Rebel." *New England Quarterly* 13 (1940): 401–418.

Luther, Seth. *An Address to the Workingmen of New England.* Boston, 1832.

Whitman, Alden, ed. *American Reformers.* New York: H. W. Wilson, 1982.

VITO MARCANTONIO

(December 10, 1902–August 9, 1954)

Civil Rights and Freedom of Conscience Advocate

Vito Marcantonio, perhaps the most fiercely independent con-
gressman of the 20th century, was the child of an Old World
arranged marriage and for almost twenty years the represen-
tative of an intensely conservative constituency. His fierce ad-
herence to the dictates of conscience frequently left him a
lonely figure in Congress: the only member to vote against
American participation in the Korean War, in many cases the
only member voting against the flood of congressional con-
tempt citations initiated by the House Un-American Activi-
ties Committee against a wide assortment of intellectuals and
liberals during the McCarthy years. In many ways it seems
as if both Congress and the American sense of national honor
and decency have had to grow into positions Marcantonio
assumed.

Vito Marcantonio
Courtesy of the Library of Congress.

In 1902, when Vito Marcantonio was born on East 112th Street in East Harlem, this New York City neighborhood was the largest Italian community in America. Marcantonio was an eager student; his father, a skilled carpenter, was able to support his family alone, so that Vito could stay in school. Life was always precarious, however; when his father was killed by a streetcar, the family could not afford the twenty-five-dollar fee for a funeral mass, and Marcantonio's mother took in washing to keep him in school. At DeWitt Clinton High School, Marcantonio acquired a socialist perspective on history from a dynamic teacher, Abraham Lefkowitz, a leader of the teachers' union. Lefkowitz also introduced Marcantonio to two life-long inspirations: Jefferson and Lincoln. (Years later, Southern civil rights activist Virginia Foster Durr called Marcantonio "the most perfect Jeffersonian I have ever known. He would work with anybody, but he was a Jeffersonian if there ever was one.") A teacher described Marcantonio's "unswerving fidelity, his fine zeal in the performance of his duties, his tenacity of purpose, his initiative, his courage, and his innate leadership" (Meyer, 8).

A major influence on Marcantonio was Leonard Covello, a gifted teacher dedicated to broadening the educational goals of his first-generation Italian students within the context of family and community loyalty. Covello founded the first settlement house in Harlem; Marcantonio was deeply involved in this effort and in the "Circolo Italiano," the Italian cultural study club Covello originated. From Covello Marcantonio learned to speak correct Italian, to be proud of his heritage, and above all to commit himself to his community. Marcantonio never abandoned his neighborhood. He was born on East 112th Street, and at the time of his death he lived on East 116th Street; his New York City residence was never more than four blocks from his birthplace. He never considered himself superior to his neighbors, and his first concern was always for their day-to-day survival.

Marcantonio attended law school at New York University in the early 1920s, a period disfigured by the harsh, paranoid government overreaction to the Russian Revolution. Attorney General A. Mitchell Palmer launched hundreds of blatantly unconstitutional raids against socialists and labor organizers in general and most specifically against foreign-born reformers; he called for a permanent sedition act to eliminate "the real menace of evil thinking." Thousands were illegally arrested, held without bail, and deported without due process. Marcantonio clerked for a firm that specialized in civil liberties and labor disputes—clients included anarchists Emma Goldman and Alexander Berkman and many other aliens facing deportation during this "Red Scare."

Marcantonio was also profoundly affected by the case of Sacco and

Vanzetti, which united radicals and the Italian community. In 1920 an armed robbery at a shoe factory in Braintree, Massachusetts had resulted in the deaths of the payroll clerk and his guard. On evidence that was circumstantial at best and rigged at worst, Nicola Sacco and Bartolomeo Vanzetti were arrested and tried for the crime. The two men, Italian nationals, were prominent local philosophical anarchists who had criticized America's role in World War I. Presiding Judge Webster Thayer was openly biased against the defendants, as were most of the jurors, it seemed clear to many throughout the country that Sacco and Vanzetti were really tried and convicted for their radical political and economic beliefs. They became the first major national *cause célèbre*; numerous appeals were filed and support for them was growing when they were executed in 1927. Marcantonio never forgot what he saw as the total subservience of the legal system to the interests of capitalism. In 1937 he wrote a pamphlet entitled "Labor's Martyrs: Haymarket 1887, Sacco and Vanzetti, 1927." He drew parallels between Sacco and Vanzetti and the earlier anarchists, also largely foreign-born, who had been hanged for murder as the result of a bomb explosion during a workers' protest meeting in Chicago. In the case of the Haymarket anarchists, the court acknowledged that none of the seven men tried had thrown the bomb that killed a policeman (the real culprit was never found), but held that their words—their speeches and writings—had incited the workers and that they were therefore responsible for the officer's death. To thoughtful people, it seemed clear that the anarchists, who were agitating for an eight-hour work day, were feared, hated, and eliminated for their beliefs rather than for the crime of which they were convicted.

In 1924 Marcantonio became education director of Haarlem House, a settlement house dedicated to community organization and self-improvement; the same year, Congressman Fiorello LaGuardia appointed him his liaison for East Harlem, initiating Marcantonio's intense involvement in politics.

Marcantonio married Miriam Sanders, a social worker whom he had met at Haarlem House, in 1925. She was eleven years older than he, a good bit taller, and a New England Protestant; it was by all accounts an unorthodox marriage, but one that provided support and stability for them both.

At DeWitt Clinton, Marcantonio had also first met his other, more famous mentor, then Alderman Fiorello LaGuardia; LaGuardia nurtured and guided Marcantonio's early career; a childless widower, he came to regard Marcantonio as his son. In 1934, when LaGuardia left his congressional seat to become mayor of New York, Marcantonio ran for—and won—his mentor's old seat as a nominal Republican. (Marcantonio did not fit easily into any of America's conventional political categories. He frequently received endorsements from both major parties, although for most of his House career he served as a member of the newly formed American Labor Party.) As a freshman in the House, he was outspoken, direct, and eloquent. He waded willingly into controversial areas; within months he was taking a leading role in the defense of alien Communists threatened with deportation—in this case, Mexican miners and union organizers in New Mexico. Marcantonio focused on the First Amendment as the cornerstone of the Constitution:

> I maintain that the moment we deprive those with whom we extremely disagree of their right to freedom of speech, the next thing that will happen is that our own right of freedom of speech will be taken away from us. Freedom of speech, if it means anything, means freedom of speech for everyone and not only for those who agree with us or who are in the majority (May 16, 1935, Rubenstein, 49).

Marcantonio's insistence on the absolute integrity of the Bill of Rights never varied. In the anguish of the Depression, labor conflicts were especially bitter and the suppression of unions was merciless. Marcantonio defended the right of the unemployed, the nonunionized, the ethnic, religious, and political minority or outcast to speak out, to assemble, to petition for redress of grievances. As a devout student of American history, he was always able to reinforce his position on a current issue with vivid historical analogies; his speeches are peppered with references to the despised Alien and Sedition Laws enacted by the Federalists under John Adams (and he never failed to point out that the popular reaction to those laws effectively killed the Federalist Party).

Marcantonio's commitment to the working people of the country led him to focus on occupational hazards, especially in the mining industry. In 1936 he introduced pioneering studies on the devastation of silicosis—black lung disease—and produced clear evidence that most silicosis could be prevented by adherence to simple safety procedures; his work resulted in tighter safety standards for mines, an improved inspection system, and an understanding that led to numerous legal judgments favorable to afflicted miners.

Throughout his career, Marcantonio confronted issues of racial oppression head on. He supported strong federal anti-lynching legislation; he introduced the first House anti-poll tax bill and personally maneuvered it safely out of committee, where Southern members had tried to kill it. (Despite Marcantonio's superb parliamentary skills in shepherding the bill to the floor of the House, he was unable to prevent repeated Southern filibusters, and the discriminatory poll tax was not outlawed at the federal level until 1964.) In 1938, when race riots in East Harlem pitted Italian teen-agers against blacks and Puerto Ricans, Marcantonio rushed throughout his district to restore peace. "He was most forceful in condemning violence on the part of Italians," an aide remembered years later, "reminding them constantly that they too had once been the butt of violence, segregation, and discrimination, and it was particularly shameful for them to indulge in such tactics against others" (Meyer, 77). Marcantonio also championed the cause of Puerto Rican independence; he urged an end to segregation and discrimination in the armed forces; he repeatedly called on Congress to eliminate the shame of school segregation in the nation's capital. He introduced an amendment to an appropriations bill that would have denied federal funds to any educational institution that discriminated racially. Decades before the rest of the country was able to, he saw racial oppression and race relations as a major issue that was ignored at grave national peril. As *Collier's* reported in 1944,

> In Congress, Mr. Marcantonio has invited and received the deep disregard of all Southern Members. His fight to abolish poll taxes, to strengthen the Fair Employment Practices Committee and to enact tough anti-lynch legislation has made him so many enemies (October 14, 1944).

Marcantonio returned to the House in 1938—his vehement opposition to fascism and especially to Mussolini had cost him the 1936 election, but two years later, enough East Harlem Italians were also uncomfortable with Mussolini. Marcantonio turned his attention to the newly formed Dies Committee, the direct ancestor of the House Committee on Un-American Activities (HUAC). He was appalled to watch self-righteous patriotism and fear of communism utilized to derail reform. He lashed out at his colleagues in the House:

> If communism is destroyed, I do not know what some of you will do. It has become the most convenient method by which you wrap yourselves in the American flag in order to cover up some of the greasy stains on the legislative toga. . . . You do not have to defend yourselves to the country and to the unemployed, to labor or to the farmer. All you have to do is stand up here and say, "I am opposed to communism. Let us destroy communism." What are you going to do when there is no more communism in this country? (January 23, 1940, Rubenstein, 111)

Repeatedly, Marcantonio fought against the concept, mission, and funding of HUAC. The vision of government increasingly operating in secrecy horrified him; the inevitable abuse of power struck him as fatal to true democracy. As early as 1940, he urged legislative restraints on the FBI. He cited testimony from FBI director J. Edgar Hoover about the Bureau's new division assigned specifically to investigate "individuals, groups, and organizations engaged in . . . any activities that are possibly detrimental to the internal security of the United States." Appalled, Marcantonio responded with astounding contemporary relevance:

> The creation of a super secret service body in a democracy is injecting our democratic institutions with the virulent toxin of an anti-democratic activity under the guise of so-called protection of so-called national defense. Himmler's super secret service in Germany has kept Hitler alive and German democrats dead or dying in concentration camps (January 11, 1940, Rubenstein, 110).

Similarly, Marcantonio opposed the 1949 creation of the Central Intelligence Agency:

> As a result of the hysteria under which this bill is being passed I suppose a majority of the House will vote for this bill, even though in doing so you are suspending your legislative prerogatives and evading your duty to the people of this Nation. . . . Hysteria is used to undermine the civil liberties of the people and to extend the military control—military control—I emphasize that, over the lives and thinking of the people of these United States (March 7, 1949, Rubenstein, 282).

Marcantonio, convinced that the Korean War was essentially a civil war on which the United States sought to impose unfair influence, cast the only vote in the House against America's entry into the war in 1950. That stand, embellished and distorted by both major parties, cost him the upcoming election, as he probably knew it would. "It is best to live one's life with one's conscience," he said at the time, "rather than to temporize or accept in silence those things which one believes to be against the interests of one's people and one's nation" (June 27, 1950).

After his defeat, Marcantonio returned to private law practice. He successfully defended W.E.B. Du Bois, a founder of the NAACP, against charges that he was an agent for a foreign power; he represented the American Communist Party before the Subversive Activities Control Board. In August of 1954, while organizing his campaign for reelection, Marcantonio died in the street of a sudden heart attack. Because he was wearing a crucifix, a neighborhood priest administered last rites, but Francis Cardinal Spellman, a rabid red-baiter, claimed that Marcantonio, who hadn't attended church in years, wasn't "reconciled" to the Church and denied him a Catholic burial. At his wake, a black father lifted his small son up to the coffin, saying, "I want you to say goodbye to the best friend the Negro people ever had" (Meyers, 182). Eulogies were delivered by W.E.B. Du Bois; Nicolo Notar, a Methodist minister; and Luigi Albarelli, Marcantonio's barber. He is buried in Woodlawn Cemetery, beside Fiorello LaGuardia.

Marcantonio's entire life was guided by the primacy of conscience, the inviolability of human dignity, and a total commitment to his community. He spent every weekend in his local offices in East Harlem, seeing as many as four hundred distressed constituents in a single day, responding as needed in Italian, Spanish, English, or Yiddish. In many cases, he alleviated their immediate crises—doctors' bills, overdue rent, emergency expenses—from his own funds. He left his wife almost penniless. Virginia Durr reported, "After Marc died I went up to see Miriam. What a hell of a time she had after he died. She couldn't find a job. McCarthyism was in full stride. She finally took a job in Bellevue Hospital under another name" (Durr, 169). Marcantonio had lived a life of tenacious honor. He defended views and confronted abuses no one else in Congress was willing to face. He earned the epitaph on his tombstone: "Vito Marcantonio: The People's Congressman."

References

Brandeis, Louis D. *The Case of Sacco and Vanzetti*. New York: Universal Library. 1962 [1927].

Durr, Virginia Foster. *Outside the Magic Circle*. New York: Simon & Schuster, 1985.

Meyer, Gerald. *Vito Marcantonio, Radical Politician*. Albany, NY: SUNY Press. 1989.

Rubenstein, Annette, ed. *I Vote My Conscience: Debates, Speeches, and Writings of Vito Marcantonio*. New York: Vito Marcantonio Memorial, 1956.

Whitman, Alden, ed. *American Reformers*. New York: H. W. Wilson, 1985.

Tanya Zolotoroff Nash

(May 10, 1898–July 10, 1987)

Activist for Deaf Rights

Tanya Nash's long life encompassed several different worlds. In a reverse Cinderella story, she moved from the elegance of a townhouse in Odessa, Ukraine, to the poverty of an immigrant Jewish neighborhood in turn-of-the-century Brooklyn. An assimilated child who before school spoke only Russian, she discovered in herself a life-long fascination with all language; she learned Yiddish, excellent English, and, in addition, American Sign Language—for Tanya Nash became one of this century's strongest advocates for the Deaf and for the utter centrality of Sign—known in this country as Ameslan—for Deaf culture. (The accepted practice of scholars is to distinguish between "deaf" and "Deaf": "deaf" refers merely to a physical limitation; "Deaf" indicates an entire culture and the self-identified members of it.)

Tanya Zolotoroff Nash
By permission of Julia Mallach, executrix for the estate.

In Odessa, Tanya Zolotoroff Nash's father was a prosperous manufacturer of expensive fur hats. The family lived well, with numerous servants and a constant stream of guests, many of whom were socialists; Nash's parents had "revolutionary sympathies." In 1904, as war with Japan seemed imminent, Nash's father, fearful of being drafted into the army, decided to emigrate to America. (In czarist Russia, drafted Jews served longer terms and were frequently assigned specifically to hazardous duty.) The move to Brooklyn plunged the family from security and wealth into poverty, confusion, and, for some, life-long frustration. Nash's father was never able to regain the status he had held in Russia. He got a job in a cap factory, but never really supported his family. Nash's mother was a woman of indomitable spirit, humor, and determination. While raising five children (and enduring twelve abortions), she raised money selling baked sweet potatoes in Borough Park. Nash saw her mother as a heroine, a woman who seemed able to give and support others endlessly without bitterness.

The child Tanya was hungry to absorb what the new country had to offer. She convinced two young aunts to take her along to night school in English, although she was technically too young to be enrolled. She haunted the Brooklyn Public Library, studying nursery rhymes to teach herself English poetic forms. The family, dedicated socialists, all learned English by attending the free socialist lectures available during the Progressive Era. A sixth-grade teacher complimented Tanya on her excellent English, and she was thrilled and inspired. At thirteen, she won a city-wide spelling contest; she recalled being unable to attend the award ceremony because her shoes were too ragged.

Nash was forced to leave school at fifteen to go to work. For the rest of her life, she regretted this premature truncation of her formal education. Like many older immigrant children, she worked and contributed to the family's support while the younger children were allowed to stay in school. Although she resented never having gone to college, she declined the offer of an honorary degree from Columbia University because she felt it was inappropriate for someone who had never even completed high school.

Although forced out of school, Nash never stopped seeking education. She joined a "self-culture club," a group of other young working people, most of them socialist radicals, who met to discuss pertinent topics and to hear speakers; she joined the Brooklyn Philosophical Society.

In a debate offered by her local library, she confronted a young rabbi, Felix Nash. Rabbi Nash, a committed socialist, had studied at Hebrew Union Seminary in Cincinnati. His socialist convictions drew him away from the traditional rabbinical role, and in his tragically brief life, he never led a congregation. Tanya and Nash, on opposite sides of the debate, continued their argument on the street outside after the library had closed. Debating seems to have led to other shared interests; the two were married in 1927. Irreverently, Tanya recalled, "I no more wanted to marry a rabbi than to fly off the house" (Tanya Nash File).

Young Rabbi Nash was drawn to social work; in 1929 he assumed the leadership of the Society for the Welfare of the Jewish Deaf, the ancestor of the New York Society for the Deaf. (The name was changed in 1966.) The stock market crash that year created special hardships for the Deaf, who had traditionally found work largely in the hard-hit printing and needlework industries. Tanya quit her job in a newspaper clipping service to work as a volunteer with her husband. She was so eager to learn Ameslan that she described struggling to speak it with Rabbi Nash even in bed. "That I should learn sign language, which is a silent language, is another magical thing in my life," she later commented (Nash, 10). At the age of twenty-nine, Rabbi Nash died of a brain tumor. Widowed and stunned with grief, Tanya took over the agency he had worked so hard for.

In many unexpected ways, the history and struggle of the Deaf in America parallels that of African Americans. They have had to resist powerful negative images from the majority culture; to insist on their integrity and legitimacy in the face of a power structure that has defined them as aberrant and defective; to demand the right to participate fully in the educational, political, and social life of their country. For the Deaf, much of this struggle is epitomized by the conflict between oral and manual (signed) education.

From the late 18th century, when enlightened educators in France codified a sign language and opened the National Institution for Deaf-Mutes, the Deaf had been perceived more or less as a special class of citizens, as different but not necessarily deficient, as a linguistic minority. Humane signed education produced remarkably well-read, articulate advocates for the Deaf, like Laurent Clerc, who profoundly influenced the American Thomas Gallaudet. Gallaudet, in turn, opened his first school for the Deaf in Hartford, Connecticut, in 1817. In 1864 Congress authorized a National Deaf-Mute College in Washington, run by Gallaudet's son Edward. It offered a rigorous academic curriculum and grew to include a successful teacher-training institute. Schools for the Deaf, taught manually, were founded throughout the country. In 1880 the National Association of the Deaf was organized.

Ironically, that same year saw the Milan Conference, organized by Alexander Graham Bell. Bell, revered by most people for his inventions, is despised among the Deaf. He was a strong proponent of Social Darwinism and eugenics; he perceived deafness as an imperfection that must be isolated and bred out of the human race. At Milan, he demanded that

sign language be totally outlawed, that deaf teachers of the deaf be removed, that younger deaf children be isolated from the "corrupting"
influence of older children who already signed, and that all education
be conducted by the "pure oral" method. The five American delegates
at the conference included the *only* Deaf delegate; unanimously, they
opposed Bell's resolution, but it passed overwhelmingly. From that point
on, the Deaf felt themselves, their language, and their culture, under
virulent attack. One deaf leader commented:

> 1880 was the year that saw the birth of the infamous Milan Resolution that
> paved the way for foisting upon the deaf everywhere a loathed method;
> hypocritical in its claims, unnatural in its application, mind-deadening and
> soul-killing in its ultimate results (Lane, 394).

The unavoidable truth was that, despite years of intensive, exhausting
oral education, very few Deaf ever learned to read lips well or to speak
intelligibly. The form of their "education" completely subsumed any
content, and they were left bitter, isolated, ashamed, and ignorant. Mainstream society misunderstood and feared them, tried to force them out
of their "difference," assumed a level of stupidity among them, and
doomed them to unskilled menial labor. Their experiences resembled
those of many Native American children, until recently forced into residential schools and forbidden to speak their own languages or to wear
their own costumes.

By the turn of the century, Deaf leaders were rallying to assert the
validity of Ameslan. Gallaudet College (formerly the National Deaf-Mute
College) had never abandoned Sign, and soon other schools were taking
tentative steps to preserve Ameslan. In this atmosphere, around 1906,
the Hebrew Congregation of the Deaf was founded in New York to provide religious instruction for Deaf Jews. In 1911, the Society for the Welfare of the Jewish Deaf (SWJD) was formed; by 1917 it had absorbed the
Hebrew Congregation and opened expansive new headquarters on West
115th Street.

The organization that Rabbi Nash headed briefly and Tanya Nash directed for thirty-five years provided a variety of services to the Deaf
community: social gatherings, dances, and plays (in Sign); lectures (in
Sign) on a wide range of topics—usually on Deaf concerns, Jewish issues,
or world politics; basketball, baseball, wrestling, boxing, and gymnastics;
a large lending library; an employment bureau; religious services (in
Sign) on Friday nights and all Jewish holidays, with a social hour afterward. In addition, it published *The Jewish Deaf*, a lively monthly newsletter that tried to connect Deaf Jews who might be isolated by distance,
disability, or poverty.

When Nash took over, the SWJD was desperate for funds. "I liked the challenge despite so little money," she reminisced years later.

In fact, when I didn't have enough money to meet the agency's expenses, I paid the fare of the deaf who went to jobs, after I found them. If a deaf person owed the union money, I contacted relatives and we got enough money for them to clean their record up with the union and to be able to get a job (Nash, 19).

Nash helped steer the SWJD in a broader, nonsectarian direction. She greatly expanded the scope of services provided by the society; she reached out to embrace the deaf-blind and the deaf-disabled. She forced municipal and state governments into a totally new level of awareness of the Deaf and their needs. A woman of immense energy and humor, Nash was only four feet, ten inches tall; she loved to surprise people with her size and her paradoxically commanding presence. In the early years, during the Depression, she would scour the garment district in person, seeking jobs for the Deaf, working to convince employers of the intelligence and reliability of her clients.

Much of Nash's work was with recent immigrants. The Deaf were always vulnerable to misunderstanding and confusion with the police—frequently being mistaken as drunk when their speech was unintelligible—and Deaf immigrants were especially at risk. Nash had printed a sort of calling card for Deaf immigrants, identifying the holder as Deaf and urging the police to contact her directly so that she could interpret. At any time, at any hour, she would respond to one of these calls. She developed an international reputation among the immigrant Deaf and those contemplating immigration. The word was out: if you're Deaf and you emigrate to New York City, find Tanya Nash. She interpreted for them in the courts, with doctors, and with lawyers. She tramped through the immigrant neighborhoods, seeking out deaf women and informing them of health benefits and birth control availability. (She never forgot the nightmare of her mother's multiple abortions.) She assisted hundreds of Deaf immigrants as they applied for citizenship, and she interpreted at their citizenship examinations. She was known to cheat for her beloved clients. One of the routine questions asked of prospective citizens was: Who was the third president of the United States? No matter what a confused or anxious Deaf immigrant might sign to her, Nash always turned to the presiding judge and said distinctly, "Thomas Jefferson, Your Honor." Once, when Helen Keller had an ulcerated toe amputated, Nash visited her in the hospital and, with her ever-present humor, signed to Keller, "I'm so glad it was your toe and not your thumb, because if it were your thumb, you would have had a speech defect" (Nash, 24).

Nash was always concerned with the dignity and self-esteem of the Deaf. During the Depression she was known to take homeless Deaf women into her home until she could find shelter for them. She worked hard to find summer camp placements for Deaf children, and she would frequently spend time at the camps beforehand, teaching the hearing children elementary Sign and preparing them to accept the Deaf children. She understood the isolation, frustrations, and pressures experienced by the Deaf. In 1955 she helped plan and initiate the New York State Mental Health Services for the Deaf, the first such state-funded agency. John Rainer, the psychiatrist with whom she designed the service, recalled years later, "Through those early years I would go to her for advice, and to listen to her stories and absorb some of her dedication" (Tanya Nash File). The NYSD is still the only agency that provides psychological testing for the profoundly deaf.

Perhaps Nash's most enduring achievement is Tanya Towers, a ten-story apartment building on East 13th Street in New York City. Tanya Towers represents the embodiment of Nash's deep love and concern for the Deaf—especially the elderly Deaf. "I knew that some of my deaf people were alone," she recounted,

> and their friends didn't want to walk all those stairs to go see them, and take trains or subways to see them. They were alone. So the idea of Tanya Towers occurred to me, and I said, "Well, this is what I've got to do before the agency gets rid of me. I've got to do it." Now there's a ten floor house. I didn't want it to be an institution; I said, "This must be a house, where hearing people can also live." And it worked out beautifully. They have parties, they invite each other, and they play games with each other. Marvelous. That's Tanya Towers (Nash, 33).

Nash began orchestrating the massive project in 1968. With her driving determination, expertise, and irresistible personal style, she managed to steam-roll through the initial stages of paperwork—licensing, zoning, financing. The $5.5 million project received 100% mortgage financing and a fifty-year mortgage at 1% interest, allowing them to offer exceptionally low rents to the intended tenants. Nash's dream was to provide mixed housing for the hearing, deaf, and deaf-blind elderly. By the time she retired at the end of the year, the dream was well on its way to reality.

Tanya Towers opened in 1974. It was the first and only public building in New York named for a living private citizen. Even Nash was impressed: "If I had known from the start that buildings were not named after women who were still living, I would have been exhilarated sooner" (Tanya Nash File). Tanya Towers provides 137 units. It is outfitted with a visual alarm system, doorbell lights, closed-circuit television in the apartments monitoring the entrance, on-site social services, and pay phones in the lobby that are equipped with a teletypewriter, allow-ing phone communication with the residents. Sign language classes are offered to hearing tenants.

Nash continued to spend long hours as a consultant and fundraiser for the NYSD after she retired. During the 1980s her health deteriorated steadily and she found herself increasingly restricted. She died at home in July of 1987. "She wasn't only a social worker," a Deaf friend com-mented at a memorial service. "She acted as a speaker, a P.R. person, a guidance counselor, and also a jill-of-all-trades" (Tanya Nash File). She was lovingly eulogized for her commitment, generosity, sensitivity, and humor. She was so beloved by the Jewish Deaf that even before her final illness, several Deaf rabbis representing different congregations argued over whose cemetery she should honor by being buried there. Amused, Nash suggested they cut her in half and each take a piece. In reality, the solution was much more appropriate. Tanya Nash was cremated, and her ashes are buried at Tanya Towers.

References

Berson, Jessica. "Deaf Education and the Milan Conference." Unpublished paper, 1989.

Gannon, Jack R. *Deaf Heritage: A Narrative History of Deaf America*. Silver Spring, MD: National Association of the Deaf, 1981.

Interview. Robert Caress, Board Member, NYSD, July 1992.

Interview. John Rainer, MD. New York State Psychiatric Institute, July 1992.

Interview. Joel Ziev, Director, NYSD. June 1992.

Jewish Deaf. Monthly Publication of SWJD. New York, 1915–1925.

Lane, Harlan. *When the Mind Hears: A History of the Deaf*. New York: Vintage Books, 1989.

Nash, Tanya. *Oral Memoir*. New York. United Jewish Philanthropies Oral History Project, 1982.

Tanya Nash File. NYSD.

MARY WHITE OVINGTON

(April 11, 1865–July 15, 1951)

Civil Rights Activist

Mary White Ovington was a quiet crusader. As a privileged white woman in a society of violent, hateful stereotypes, she countered ignorance with methodically gathered data; in a class insulated by distance, she sought direct experience and open-mindedness and demanded nothing less of others; in an arena mined by explosive animosities and conflicts, she soothed, cajoled, and nurtured the infant National Association for the Advancement of Colored People into one of the major forces for justice in 20th-century America. In his preface to her 1947 autobiography, The Walls Came Tumbling Down, *NAACP director Walter White called her "a fighting saint."*

Mary White Ovington
Courtesy, National Association for the Advancement of Colored People.

Mary White Ovington may have seemed like an outrageous iconoclast to many of her contemporaries, but she was in reality the honorable harvest of seeds sown through several generations of her family. As a child in Connecticut, her grandmother had heard the abolitionist Unitarian minister Samuel J. May and had become a confirmed abolitionist herself. Ovington's parents were deeply sympathetic to the abolitionist cause, and their home library was stocked with the works of escaped slaves like Josiah Henson, Henry "Box" Brown, and Anthony Burns. While Mary had no direct contact in childhood with African Americans, she did hear Frederick Douglass speak at Plymouth Church in Brooklyn Heights. Her family minister, John White Chadwick of the Second Unitarian Church in Brooklyn Heights, nurtured Mary's vision of social justice with readings on women's rights, social reform, and social gospel. At Radcliffe College she was exposed to a more radical interpretation of history by the economic historian William J. Ashley. When the depression of 1893 disrupted her father's business and forced her to leave college, Ovington was well prepared to face her world with an unusual degree of honesty.

Ovington worked briefly as registrar of the Pratt Institute in Brooklyn; while there, she engineered a grant from Frederick Pratt himself and opened the Greenpoint Settlement in an immigrant neighborhood of Brooklyn. During her eight years as head social worker there, the settlement grew from a five-room house to a forty-room multifaceted social service agency. At the same time, Ovington became vice-president of the Brooklyn Consumers League (see Florence Kelley*) and assistant secretary of the Social Reform Club in New York. While she was consolidating invaluable experience in social work and in sociological analysis, her involvement was still more specifically with the European immigrant poor than with New York's black population. It took a chance encounter to change the focus and direction of her entire life.

During the winter of 1903 Ovington served on the Social Reform Club committee planning a dinner to honor Booker T. Washington. His speech that night dealt with the hardships facing the black community in New York. It was a revelation to Ovington. She left Greenpoint Settlement and went to live and work at Greenwich House in lower Manhattan; with the help of the pioneering head social worker there, Mary Simkhovitch, Ovington received a fellowship from Columbia University to study conditions among New York's sixty thousand black residents. The project, begun in 1904, drew her deep into the black community and led to her long association with W.E.B. Du Bois, then a fiery professor of history and sociology at Atlanta University. A hard-headed reformer, Ovington was determined to prove empirically what she believed idealistically.

Confronted with the widely held belief that blacks—especially black youths—had a racial tendency toward criminality, she undertook a detailed statistical analysis of New York's Children's Court records by race, ethnicity, and category of crime. She was able to demonstrate convincingly that black children were actually *less* likely to be brought into court than were white children. The major problem for black children, she declared, was "improper guardianship," the result of so many black mothers working long hours as domestics in distant white homes. Examining chiefly housing and employment discrimination through years of exhaustive interviews and research, her work was finally published in 1911 under the title *Half a Man: The Status of the Negro in New York*. One of her conclusions speaks directly to the present: "If there is an increase in discrimination against the Negro solely because of his color, it is a serious matter to the city as well as to the race. Every community has its social conscience built up of slowly accumulated experiences, and it cannot without disaster lose its ideal of justice or generosity" (Ovington, *Half a Man*, 215).

Well before then, the structure of Ovington's life-work was clearly delineated. In the spring of 1904, Du Bois invited her to attend a conference at Atlanta University; it was her first exposure to the degradation of Southern segregation. In 1906 Ovington, on assignment for the *New York Evening Post*, covered the second annual meeting of Du Bois's proud and assertive African American Niagara Movement at Harpers Ferry, Virginia; she was deeply moved by his total commitment to an unconditional demand for total equal rights. One month later Ovington met with Du Bois again, in Atlanta shortly after the horrifying race riot in that city. The data she gathered on this trip through the rural South convinced her that the escalating level of violence and injustice against blacks was a national nightmare. In 1907 Du Bois invited her to be the first white member of the all-black Niagara Movement. Ovington was willing, but only "if the members really want me."

Ovington had already determined to act on the outrageous facts she had uncovered on the horrendous housing shortage among African Americans. With her friend and fellow socialist, John Milholland, she approached philanthropist Henry Phipps and convinced him to fund a model tenement for blacks in New York City. The Tuskegee Apartments opened on West 63rd Street in 1907—fireproof, steam-heated, properly plumbed, with a roof garden—and Ovington was for some time the only white resident.

Ovington's reform zeal on behalf of blacks was perceived as less radical—and less threatening—than her calm, respectful associations with them. Early in 1908, the Cosmopolitan Club, an interracial social reform organization of which Ovington was a member, held a public dinner with invited nonmembers at a restaurant on Fulton Street. The affair was invaded by a gang of newspaper reporters, and the scandal of blacks and whites—more specifically, of black men and white women—sitting at the same table made major news throughout New York the next day: "Social Equality!" blared one headline, "Intermarriage Advocated! White Women and Negro Men Dine Together!" *The New York Times* reported the incident as a secret socialist plot to encourage intermarriage. Wild, lurid accounts of the "depraved" dinner circulated throughout the South: "Worst of all was the high priestess, Miss Ovington, whose father is rich and who affiliates five days a week with Negro men and dines with them at her home in Brooklyn. . . . But the horror of it is she could take white girls into that den. That is the feature that should arouse and alarm northern society" (Ovington, *Walls*, 46); the reports occasioned a condemnation from the floor of the United States Senate, and engendered such hate mail to Ovington that she was forced to take refuge with her sister's family in Brooklyn. Ovington's response to the vituperation resonates with a poignant immediacy:

> We shall not be discouraged in our purpose to bring men and women together who need to learn of one another's problems, and we believe that the meal we shared was a pleasant bond that will make us a little kinder to one another, a little less ready to look for faults, as we work upon the great problem of helping the two dissimilar races to dwell together in the United States (Foner, 193).

In truth, while the infamous Cosmopolitan Club dinner was the first public interracial dinner in New York City, it was far from the last, and no further controversy was created. "We at the Cosmopolitan Club were pioneers," Ovington commented later. "We suffered the notoriety of pioneers, but we did a good piece of work."

In the summer of 1908, Springfield, Illinois endured a sickening explosion of racial violence, involving the lynching of two black men, six other blacks killed, fifty wounded, and two thousand black refugees seeking shelter from the rage of whites. Covering the story for the newspaper *Independent* was William English Walling, socialist scion of a Southern gentry family. Appalled by what he saw, Walling compared the riot to the anti-Semitic pogroms of Russia. (Walling and his Russian-born wife, Anna Strunsky, had recently spent time in Russia; his analogy was not offered carelessly.) Walling concluded his article with an impassioned plea for responsible, powerful citizens to support blacks in their struggle for survival and justice. Ovington, reading this, wrote to him and they arranged a meeting in his apartment in New York. Also present was Henry Moskowitz, a Jewish social worker and leader in the progressive Ethical Culture Society. They were joined by Oswald Garrison Villard, editor of the *New York Post* (and grandson of William Lloyd

Garrison), who issued his stirring "Call" on February 12, 1909—the hundredth anniversary of Lincoln's birth. The "Call" summarized the current situation of blacks in America and concluded, "Silence under these conditions means tacit approval. . . . Hence we call upon all believers in democracy to join in a National Conference for the discussion of present evils, the voicing of protests, and the renewal of the struggle for civil and political liberty" (Hughes, 22).

The document was signed by sixty people whose names are an honor role of the best hopes of the Progressive era, among them Jane Addams, founder of Hull House; Francis Grimké, militant black minister; philosopher John Dewey; Alexander Walters, bishop of the African Methodist Episcopal Zion Church; philanthropist J. Phelps Stokes; muckraking journalist Lincoln Steffens; Mary E. Woolley, president of Mount Holyoke College; Mary Church Terrell, women's and civil rights activist; reform author Ray Stannard Baker; John Lovejoy Elliott* and William Salter of the Ethical Culture Society; Mary White Ovington*; labor reformer Florence Kelley*; Lillian Wald, founder of the Henry Street Visiting Nurses; and W.E.B. Du Bois.

The conference that resulted from the call was held that spring at Henry Street Settlement in New York; it produced an organization called the National Negro Committee, which held public meetings throughout the following year. By May of 1910 a new name had been chosen for the growing organization: The National Association for the Advancement of Colored People. Typically, Ovington was modest and capable of wry humor in recalling those early days; twenty-five years later, she reminisced, "We started without money, unpopular (those were the days when you must talk not of 'rights' but of 'duties'), in a tiny office on Vesey Street. The only thing pretentious about us was our newly adopted name" (Ovington, "The Year of Jubilee," 7).

The fledgling organization's goals were to eradicate racial discrimination and segregation and to promote full legal, civil, and educational rights. These goals were radical by contemporary standards, and a direct challenge to the accommodationist views of Booker T. Washington. Ovington, a founding member, served on the Board of Directors; Du Bois became director of publications and research, and launched the dynamic journal *The Crisis*. Response to the superbly edited journal was overwhelming: within two years circulation was over 24,000, and it was so feared in the South that several states forbade its sale or distribution.

By 1913 the NAACP had twenty-four branches, growing in response to an escalating incidence of brutal lynchings: 63 in 1912, up to 79 in 1913. The new organization hastened to support blacks in a wide range of struggles, and to provide sympathetic publicity and legal representation when charges were brought prejudicially. It succeeded in several cases in having blatantly unjustified charges dropped; it secured the release of a black soldier court-martialed in a racially tainted incident; it organized the first mass protests against discrimination in employment; it published the voting records of all congressmen on racially significant bills. Throughout this early period, Ovington mediated among the difficult personalities and disparate dreams of the various key figures: Villard and Du Bois were frequently close to blows, and Du Bois regarded Ovington as one of the few whites he could really trust.

Ovington always believed in the power of education to dispel mistaken images and impressions; she took literally the notion that the truth was liberating. In the tempest caused in 1915 by the release of the virulently racist film *Birth of a Nation*, Ovington became deeply angered by its mocking depiction of the African American Reconstructionist legislators in South Carolina. Typically, her anger led to practical investigation. Unable to find the relevant records in the New York Public Library or the Library of Congress, she determined to search for documentation in South Carolina. William Sinclair, an NAACP board member whose father (later lynched) had been a member of that legislature, warned Ovington that the state had tried to destroy all official records of the proceedings and that his father's own copies had been forcibly removed from his home by a mob. Persistent as usual, Ovington was able to track down some of the proceedings in a Washington library; she could thereafter demonstrate that the black legislators' ideas had been progressive, well-wrought, and humane, involving far-reaching programs for public education and the care of the elderly.

When Ovington took over as chairman of the board in 1919, the NAACP had 44,000 members in 165 branches and had won a number of symbolically important cases before the Supreme Court. In 1921, at the organization's request, Missouri Representative L. C. Dyer introduced a House bill to make lynching a federal offense; the bill passed the House but was unable to survive repeated Southern filibusters in the Senate. With the publication of its groundbreaking, horrifying pamphlet "Thirty Years of Lynching in the United States, 1889–1918," the NAACP became a leader in the struggle for federal anti-lynching legislation. "Thirty Years of Lynching" analyzed the lynchings during that time of 3,224 men, women, and children; one section of the study detailed, graphically and sickeningly, one hundred of the most horrifying incidents. Justifying such a jolting publication, Ovington wrote:

> I can think of no more nauseating work for a kindly set of people than this task of setting forth brutality. We felt that it was the only way to end a method of community life in which a dark-skinned group was denied education, economic opportunity, and a full cultural life, while another group, the poor whites, also ill-educated and penniless, were encouraged to consider themselves inherently superior to the blacks because their own

skin was white—or, more accurately, sallow. This second group was never punished for violence against the first, and so it indulged in brutalities partly for the fun of it, as boys torture animals (Hughes, 37).

That same year, Ovington reported significant and exciting shifts within the organization:

> We white delegates were working *with* the people we were trying to help, were discussing not their economic problems but their status as citizens, and were constantly learning from them. Time has shown that white direction was short-lived. . . . White people were interested in a story of distress . . . but philanthropy and justice often stand apart. The very recognition of the need of philanthropy denies justice. So the NAACP, started by whites, was being organized all over the United States by Negroes (Ovington, *Walls*, 168).

In 1923, in an atmosphere of despair and discouragement over the defeat of the Dyer Bill, Ovington mobilized her own innate optimism and convinced the NAACP board to shift its focus and pour renewed energy into securing equal federal aid for blacks as well as white school systems. While seeming to operate within the framework of "separate but equal" articulated in the 1896 Supreme Court case *Plessy v. Ferguson*, the strategy was actually laying a carefully constructed foundation for the eventual triumph of *Brown v. Board of Education* thirty years later.

Ovington resigned as chairman in 1932 and became treasurer. Throughout the 1930s she fought to maintain the integrated character of both the organization itself and its stated goals. Still a socialist at heart, she urged moderation in order to avoid alienating the black middle class. She maintained close relations with her family, traveling frequently with her mother. Mrs. Ovington's death in 1927 left Mary briefly wealthy, but the stock market crash devastated her income; she was forced to move in with her brother and sister-in-law. After retiring in 1947, Ovington lived with a sister in Massachusetts; she died in 1951. By the time Ovington retired, the NAACP had 530,000 dues-paying members, a paid staff of sixty, 1,100 branches, and Eleanor Roosevelt on its board. Some ultimate goals were still distant dreams—as they are even today—but Ovington's cherished, bold organization was thriving and willing to face the challenge. As Walter White wrote when she retired, "She has marched serenely ahead armed with the assurance that the fight she was making was as much . . . to save white America's soul as it was to save black America's body" (Ovington, *Walls*, vii).

References

Foner, Philip. *American Socialism and Black Americans*. Westport, CT: Greenwood Press, 1977.

Hughes, Langston. *Fight for Freedom: The Story of the NAACP*. New York: W. W. Norton, 1962.

Ovington, Mary White. *Half a Man: The Status of the Negro in New York*. New York: Longmans, Green and Co., 1911.

―――. *Walls Came Tumbling Down*. New York: Harcourt Brace & Co., 1947.

―――. "The Year of Jubilee." *Crisis* 41 (January 1934): 7.

Ross, B. Jocelyn. *J. E. Spingarn and the Rise of the NAACP, 1911–1939*. New York: Atheneum, 1972.

Sicherman, Barbara, ed. *Notable American Women: Modern Period*. Cambridge, MA: Belknap Press. 1980.

JEANNETTE RANKIN

(June 11, 1880–May 18, 1973)

Women's Rights Activist, Pacifist

Jeannette Rankin was born a pioneer in the wild hills of Montana. She lived her long life in constant fidelity to a pioneering spirit of reform, justice, and practical idealism. Rankin was the first woman elected to the United States Congress—in actuality, she was the first woman in the world ever elected to a national legislature. She holds a unique distinction as the only congressperson to vote against American entry into both world wars. Far beyond her moments of incandescent courage and notoriety, Rankin was a serious, committed, insightful reformer, feminist, and pacifist. It is altogether fitting that in her last years she became a role model and icon for a new generation of human rights activists.

Jeannette Rankin
Courtesy, Montana State Historical Society.

Jeannette Rankin was born on a ranch outside Missoula, Montana, nine years before the territory achieved statehood. The atmosphere on the frontier was one of shared responsibility, risk, and reward. Women knew that their contributions in skill and knowledge were essential; they tended to be independent and assertive to a degree almost unthinkable in the more civilized East. Jeannette was the oldest of seven children born to an educated Scots-Canadian immigrant father and a school-teacher mother. The family was close-knit; although discipline was strict, the children were respected as individuals and encouraged to follow their own interests. The regimen of affection, responsibility, and challenge produced a remarkable family: Jeannette's sister Harriet became the dean of women at the University of Montana; Mary taught English at the university; Edna became a lawyer and a leading advocate of birth control; and Wellington, the only son, became one of the state's most prominent lawyers and Jeannette's major political adviser.

As the eldest child, Rankin bore early and heavy responsibilities. Her father relied heavily on her and taught her always to trust her own judgment. She was an active, vigorous child, physically fearless, aware of her own competence and strong in her self-confidence. The Rankins instilled a large degree of wary skepticism in their children. The family was not religious in any conventional sense; the children were offered a vision of an inclusive human family that embraced the nearby Indian tribes with acceptance and compassion. Rankin recalled her parents' outrage at the unprovoked massacre of several Native American families at a nearby mission. Years later, she traced the roots of her pacifism to the great Nez Percé Chief Joseph's outmaneuvering of the local army commander: without firing a shot, Chief Joseph had saved his band from imminent massacre through sheer stealth and daring. As a result, Montanans tended to view the military as both incompetent and self-righteous; for the rest of her life, Rankin always searched behind pronouncements and propaganda to find the real intentions and capacities of the armed forces.

In 1898 Rankin entered the newly established University of Montana. She was a young woman of tremendous energy, practicality, humor, and confidence, open to any interesting challenge. Unfortunately, formal education seemed not to engage her; she always considered herself an indifferent student, and her graduation in 1902 with a bachelor's degree in biology meant little to her. She taught school for several years in the small towns of Montana, but the work did not fulfill her; she was restless, bored, and frustrated.

Rankin's world changed forever in 1904 when her father died suddenly of Rocky Mountain spotted fever. Without his interest and encouragement, she felt staggeringly alone; she recognized the need to accept total responsibility for her life. That same year, Rankin visited her younger brother Wellington at Harvard, her first trip outside Montana. Wandering the streets of Boston with him, she was transfixed by the images of squalor, degradation, and starvation in the slums; nothing in her life had prepared her for the realities of urban poverty.

Ever sympathetic to the underdog, Rankin was drawn into the Progressive reform movement. She spent four months in a settlement house in San Francisco, where she was deeply affected by the desperate conditions of poor women and children; she decided to try a career in social work, and in 1908 enrolled in the New York School of Philanthropy (later the Columbia School of Social Work). She used her social work degree only briefly in Missoula, placing children in foster homes, but she still felt frustrated and unconnected.

In 1910 Rankin accepted a position in a children's home in Spokane, Washington. Quickly disillusioned by her powerlessness to effect meaningful change, she came to realize that much more massive societal and institutional changes were called for, and that achieving such changes required more complex skills. Determined to equip herself for the work she now saw as necessary, she enrolled in the University of Washington, studying sociology, economics, and public speaking.

In 1910 the state of Washington was in the midst of a tempestuous campaign for women's suffrage. Rankin was drawn into the suffragists' ranks, where she worked under the dynamic, determined Abigail Scott Duniway, gaining invaluable experience in grassroots organizing and campaign methodology. The suffrage amendment passed; Washington became the first state with any large cities to give women the vote. Previously, only four sparsely populated Western states had accepted women's suffrage: Wyoming, Colorado, Idaho, and Utah. Nonetheless, the National American Woman Suffrage Association, led by the charismatic Carrie Chapman Catt, was a growing, vital organization determined to push its agenda on the state as well as the federal level. Rankin's energy, imagination, and spirit were welcome.

Rankin finally felt that she had found a sense of purpose and direction to sustain her. She went home to Missoula, eager to focus attention on women's suffrage in Montana. With typical directness and daring, Rankin notified the Montana state legislature that she wished to address them on the suffrage question as a representative of the Equal Franchise Society; only after her request was accepted did she set about organizing the until-then fictitious Equal Franchise Society. Rankin's speech to the state legislature sounded themes that would dominate her public life: in addition to the justice and practicality of women's suffrage, she emphasized the broader issue of direct participatory democracy, demanding that the voters, not the legislators, of a society should make any such crucial decisions. This vision of direct voter responsibility underlay much of Rankin's philosophy and her hopes for a more humane society. The women's suffrage amendment passed the legislature but fell short of the two-thirds majority needed to call for a referendum. It would be another three years before Montana granted its women the vote.

Rankin was galvanized by the suffrage movement. For the next several years she traveled from New York to California, participating in numerous organizing and lobbying campaigns for the Progressive Party as well as for suffrage. She became adept at street-corner oratory, literally standing on soap boxes and learning how to debate resiliently, to present complicated data succinctly, and to handle hecklers with skill and humor. When she was past ninety, she confided to an interviewer, "And when the men make fun of you, that's when you know you're getting on well" (Frappollo, 65). In 1913 alone Rankin addressed legislatures in Delaware, Florida, Alabama, Nebraska, Michigan, and South Dakota.

The constant lobbying and outreach campaigns of the National American Woman Suffrage Association were increasingly effective. In 1913 the Montana legislature passed the suffrage amendment with only two dissenting votes; after an imaginative, well-run campaign by the Equal Franchise Society, women's suffrage carried the state-wide referendum by a solid majority.

As the world descended into the madness of World War I, Rankin discovered the other governing passion of her life: she came to believe that women held a special responsibility for ending the institutionalized violence of war. With other prominent women like Jane Addams and future Nobel laureate economist Emily Greene Balch, she helped found the Women's Peace Party. Although American public opinion was deeply divided in the early years of the war, powerful business interests were profiting from war orders from all the combatants; any pretense of neutrality was flawed long before formal American entry into the war. Despite the almost mystic martyrdom of the *Lusitania*, sunk by German submarines in 1915 with a heavy loss of American lives, research has revealed that the ship had been well warned and was indeed carrying munitions that were not on its manifest.

In this atmosphere of tension and rapid change, Rankin felt herself at a career crossroads. With the support of numerous other suffragists, she decided to run for Congress from Montana. The idea was audacious. Montana had a notoriously corrupt, violent political life, dominated by the copper bosses of the monolithic Anaconda Copper Mines—"the company," as it was known. Since Montana's sparse population justified only one congressional district, the campaign would be state-wide. With a majority of the women's vote behind her, Rankin won the Republican nomination easily. She called for a federal women's suffrage amendment, for legislation to protect working children and women, and for continued

American neutrality in the war; as always, she argued for reform of congressional procedure in order to hold legislators more directly responsible to their constituents. In lumber camps, mines, private kitchens, and public street corners, Rankin campaigned tirelessly. Her reform ideas and prolabor stance earned her the outspoken hostility of the Anaconda bosses, which in the past would have guaranteed her defeat. To everyone's astonishment, despite the multiple handicaps of being both female and in disfavor with Anaconda, Jeannette Rankin carried the election by an agonizingly slim margin. Suddenly, at the age of thirty-six, she became a national celebrity.

With a long history of lobbying and negotiating for women's suffrage, Rankin was better acquainted with Washington and legislative procedures than most other new congressmen. She was eager to work on legislation to protect children and to promote full equality for women; in addition, she espoused a visionary program of electoral reform, calling for direct primaries, presidential elections by direct popular vote, and proportional representation in state legislatures. She was given virtually no opportunity to deal with these issues: by the time she was installed as the nation's first congresswoman on April 2, 1917, everyone recognized that America was on the brink of war.

In a special session on April 2, President Woodrow Wilson addressed the Senate and called for a declaration of war. In the ensuing debate, Wisconsin Senator Robert LaFollette argued that both sides of the conflict were equally criminal and undemocratic; a citizens' referendum on going to war would be defeated. Fired by passions and propaganda, the Senate voted 82 to 6 to declare war; there were eight abstentions.

The House of Representatives was due to debate the war resolution next. Rankin, whose pacifism was well known, was under enormous pressure from friends as well as from antagonists. Her brother Wellington visited her offices to urge her to cast "a man's vote" for war; leading suffragists, fearful that she would discredit the entire suffrage movement, begged her to vote for war. "It was a very difficult and emotional time for her," a close colleague recalled. "I could not imagine her voting for war; neither could I imagine her letting her friends down" (Winestine, 75). Despite the mounting pressure and the obvious consequences, Rankin never wavered in her convictions. "Never for one second could I face the idea that I would send young men to be killed for no other reason than to save my seat in Congress," she wrote years later (Josephson, 74).

At the first roll call on the war resolution on the evening of April 6, Rankin did not respond. A senior representative, a war supporter, leaned forward and whispered to her, "Little woman, you cannot afford not to vote. You represent the womanhood of the country" (Zinn, 363). At the last minute on the second roll call, Rankin cast her vote against entry into the war. Sentimental newspapers popularized a totally false image of her weeping as she voted; "I had wept so much that week that my tears were all gone by the time the vote came," she recalled (Josephson, 76). A female constituent of Fiorello LaGuardia, freshman representative from New York City, demanded angrily whether Rankin had indeed wept as she voted. "Dear Madam," LaGuardia responded, "I am sorry, but my own eyes were so full of tears, I couldn't see how Miss Rankin voted" (Winestine, 76).

The final House vote was 374 for the resolution, 50 against, and 9 abstentions. Of the fifty antiwar voters, only Rankin was subjected to individual vilification and slander. She was declared "a disgrace to all womanhood" and a prime example of women's general incompetence to hold public office. But Rankin was at peace with her conscience, and she expected to be at peace with her constituents; at the time of the vote her mail from home had been running sixteen-to-one against the war.

During the next two years, Rankin supported the war effort and sought to protect civil liberties from the ruthless demands of crisis. She never turned her attentions from the concerns of workers, especially working women and children. Her undercover investigation revealed gross abuses of young women workers in the Treasury Department, which was operating around the clock to print Liberty Bonds; under great pressure, the poorly paid women were working twelve-hour shifts, suffering from stress, emotional breakdowns, and frequent accidents. Confronting Treasury Secretary William McAdoo himself and threatening to open congressional hearings, Rankin was able to force a restoration of the eight-hour day, sick leave, and the right to request a transfer; as usual, her abrupt, uncompromising approach caused consternation. "You can't do that in Washington," McAdoo's assistant remonstrated feebly. "It's a government bureau. Things take time. You're new here. It takes months to reorganize things and change schedules. You'll learn when you're here for a while" (Winestine, 78). LaGuardia saw her in a different light: "This woman has more courage and packs a harder punch than a regiment of regular-line politicians" (Josephson, xii).

Rankin helped establish the congressional Women's Suffrage Committee, of which she was a member. She introduced into Congress the bill that would become the Nineteenth Amendment, and she lobbied eloquently for it. She spoke of the United States as a democratic role model for the emerging nations of the world, insisting that the validity of that role model stature depended on the full enfranchisement of women. The bill passed the House but failed in the Senate; in 1919 it passed in both houses, and by 1920 the requisite two-thirds of the states had ratified it. All American women were now constitutionally guaranteed the right to vote.

Rankin tried to run for reelection in 1918. Her antiwar vote was far less damaging to her than the implacable hostility of the Anaconda bosses, who never forgave her the massive publicity she had mustered in support of a doomed 1917 miners' strike. The state legislature, controlled by Anaconda interests, gerrymandered Montana into two congressional districts designed to rob Rankin of a Republican majority. Recognizing the futility of that race, she turned instead to the senatorial race, where a dirty campaign of red-baiting defeated her bid.

In 1919, out of office and out of a job, Rankin turned her full energies to the peace movement. The negotiations in process at Versailles seemed to many thoughtful people a corrupt and opportunist display of national selfishness and short-sightedness. Rankin joined forces with such formidable American reformers as Lillian Wald, founder of the Henry Street Settlement; Jane Addams, founder of Hull House in Chicago; Florence Kelley,* director of the National Consumers League; and Emily Greene Balch, political economist and later Nobel Peace Prize laureate. They were all delegates at the Women's International Conference on Permanent Peace in Zurich, where more than two hundred highly qualified women from thirteen countries analyzed the Versailles Treaty. They pointed out the grotesque reparation and indemnity clauses; both of which Wilson had sworn to eliminate; they suggested that the arbitrary nature of new national boundaries would lead inevitably to increased ethnic tensions; they insisted that the proposed League of Nations would be ineffectual as designed, and that the punitive arrogance behind the treaty would foster resentment, rage, and poverty in Germany and encourage further armed conflict within a generation. Although they were right on all counts, and although Wilson agreed with them, their suggestions were ignored at Versailles. The real product of the women's conference was a new organization, the Women's International League for Peace and Freedom (WILPF), currently the longest-lived peace organization in the world.

After Zurich, Rankin worked with Kelley's National Consumers League, lobbying in Washington for social welfare legislation. In 1925 she became a field secretary for WILPF, but she found it difficult to function administratively within the loose, somewhat chaotic organization. She retreated to Georgia, where in 1923 she had bought a small, rustic farm near Athens; in 1928, with her farm as its base, she founded the Georgia Peace Society. Throughout most of the 1930s Rankin worked as a lobbyist for the National Council for the Prevention of War, which had been founded in 1921 to facilitate communication and coordinate the efforts of various other peace groups. She campaigned devotedly for United States membership in the World Court, testifying before congressional committees and visiting senators personally. Despite her efforts, right-wing opposition from the Hearst tabloids and the strong current of isolationism led the Senate to reject the World Court in 1935.

The major achievement of the American peace movement in the 1930s was the Nye Commission of 1934–35. Chaired by Senator Gerald Nye of North Dakota, this commission investigated the collusion of "merchants of death"—arms and munitions manufacturers, bankers, and propagandists—in manipulating and profiting from America's entry into World War I. The country was shocked and revolted by the evidence uncovered by the Nye Commission; one result was a neutrality bill that prohibited any United States commerce with combatants. The bill passed in the Senate, but was frozen in the House by Congressman McReynolds of Tennessee, the chair of the Foreign Affairs Committee. Rankin, direct as always, launched a frontal assault on McReynolds in his home state. In twelve days she toured ten counties in Tennessee, lobbying and speaking over twelve hours a day, going directly to the ultimate source of democratic power—the people. She was able to generate enough pressure on McReynolds to make him release the bill for a House vote, where it passed.

With the outbreak of the Spanish Civil War in 1936 and the escalating violence in Asia and Ethiopia, anguished pacifists joined forces for a nation-wide educational drive. Rankin was a passionate campaigner, her idealistic vision always suffused with an understanding of human nature and the grim surety that the alternatives to peace would be beyond conventional imagination. "The fact that we have never had peace need not deter us," she exhorted her audiences. "Every day we see things we have never seen before. . . . There was a time when cannibalism, parricide, and dueling were not even against the law. War can likewise be outgrown" (Josephson, 143). Throughout the late 1930s Rankin traveled widely, desperately trying to alert the people to the country's drift toward war.

She was so confident of a strong antiwar sentiment among private citizens that she decided to run for Congress again. She returned to Montana, where she ran her campaign largely through local high schools, urging activism and awareness on a new generation. Despite a twenty-year absence from the state, she won the Republican nomination easily. Since Anaconda disliked Rankin's liberal Democratic opponent almost as much as it did her, the contest was allowed to progress relatively free from corruption. Rankin won the election and reported to Washington in January of 1941.

The atmosphere in the capital was hauntingly reminiscent of early 1917. Once again, the other major powers were at war, while the United States was not—yet. Once again, the United States was supplying England; once again, the country's comatose economy was revived and stimulated by war-generated orders. During the year, Rankin submitted several bills designed to discourage any commitment of American troops except for defense; she tried to force propagandists to identify themselves as such. All her efforts were defeated.

On December 7, 1941, the Japanese air force bombed Pearl Harbor. America reacted with rage, revulsion, and hysteria; President Roosevelt called for a declaration of war. Rankin was convinced that Roosevelt's policies had forced Japan into a desperate position; she was still unwilling to bear responsibility for sending thousands of young men to their deaths. This time, Rankin bore the anguish of her decision alone. The vote for war in the House was 388 to 1. Rankin was subjected to such open hostility and abuse that she was forced to lock herself in her office. Journalist William Allen White stood alone in the respect he accorded her:

> Probably 100 men in Congress would have liked to do what she did. Not one of them had the courage to do it. The *Gazette* [White's newspaper, the *Emporia Gazette* in Kansas] entirely disagrees with the wisdom of her position. But Lord, it was a brave thing! . . . When in one hundred years from now, courage, sheer courage based on moral indignation, is celebrated in this country, the name of Jeannette Rankin . . . will be written in monumental bronze not for what she did but for the way she did it (Josephson, 163).

For all practical purposes, Rankin's political career was over, and she knew it. Her attempts to introduce reform legislation were sidetracked by the war-driven agenda that dominated Congress. After her term was over, she retreated to Montana, where she cared for her elderly mother, spent time with her family, and sought to recoup her energy and spirit.

The renewal she longed for came to her through travel, especially to India, where she was drawn by her study of Mohandas Gandhi. Over the next two decades she made seven trips to India. She thus took her place in a peculiarly satisfying cycle: Henry David Thoreau, America's greatest early proponent of nonviolence and civil disobedience, had studied Indian philosophy; Gandhi himself studied the writings of Thoreau; and Gandhi was a profound influence on Rankin and, shortly later, on Martin Luther King, Jr. Rankin's wide travels served to confirm her pacifism. She was convinced that ordinary people across the globe had the capacity to find common ground; moreover, she believed the needs and problems facing the world are so massive that only a supranational attention on equity rather than competition can offer any hope of solution.

After years of relative obscurity and virtual poverty in Georgia, Rankin responded to the national crisis of the Vietnam War. In May, 1967, at an antiwar meeting in Atlanta, she suggested that if ten thousand women—the number of American casualties in Vietnam at that moment—were willing to go to jail, they could stop the war. The organization Women's Strike for Peace accepted her challenge. In January of 1968 a somber delegation of over five thousand women, dressed in black, marched through Washington to the Capitol Building; they called themselves the

Jeannette Rankin Brigade, and 88-year-old Rankin marched at their head. Rankin remained a driving force in the antiwar movement for the rest of her life.

For her ninetieth birthday, Rankin was honored by a huge celebration at the Congressional Office Building. Lee Metcalf, the junior senator from Montana, listed her goals and achievements, cited her constant courage and the inspiration she offered to the contemporaneous peace movement:

> We honor tonight a woman young at heart, who not only has survived a generation gap but has jumped over a couple of generations and is now shoulder to shoulder with the youngsters of today who are seeking peace. ...She is...a saver with a great heart, a builder, a trail-blazer and an example to all legislators who would have the courage of their convictions (Josephson, 193).

Although Rankin fully intended to run for office again, she was prevented from doing so by a debilitating neurological inflammation, tic douloureux. Despite increasing pain and limitation, she remained an active figure in the antiwar movement throughout 1972. Above all, she urged women to seek political power and to use it for the inclusive, healing, cooperative agenda she believed in so fervently.

Weakened by her disability to the point where swallowing was difficult, Jeannette Rankin died in her sleep shortly before her ninety-third birthday. She had grounded her life's work in a vision of a just, peaceful society built on equity and mutual responsiveness. She had sacrificed a political position of great moral value to her for the greater moral integrity of her conscience. She knew clearly that her vision of a world at peace would not be fulfilled in her lifetime, but she also recognized that the struggle to come closer to that vision was an honorable goal in itself. "You take the people as far as they will go," she mused, "not as far as you would like them to go" (Josephson, xii).

References

Alonso, Harriet Hyman. *Peace as a Woman's Issue: A History of the U.S. Movement for World Peace and Women's Rights.* Syracuse: Syracuse University Press, 1993.

Foster, Catherine. *Women for All Seasons: The Story of the Women's International League for Peace and Freedom.* Athens: University of Georgia Press, 1989.

Frappollo, Elizabeth. "At 91, Jeannette Rankin is the feminists' new heroine." *Life* 72, 8(March 3, 1972): 65.

Josephson, Hannah. *Jeannette Rankin: First Lady in Congress.* Indianapolis: Bobbs-Merrill Co., 1974.

Sicherman, Barbara, ed. *Notable American Women: The Modern Period*. Cambridge, MA: Belknap Press, 1980.

Symes, Lillian and Travers Clement. *Rebel America: The Story of Social Revolt in the United States*. Boston: Beacon Press, 1934.

Whitman, Alden, ed. *American Reformers*. New York: H. W. Wilson, 1984.

Winestine, Belle Fligelman. "Mother was Shocked." *Montana: The Magazine of Western History* 24, 3(July, 1974): 70–79.

Zinn, Howard. *A People's History of the United States*. New York: Harper & Row, 1980.

JOHN SWETT ROCK

(October 13, 1825–December 3, 1866)

Abolitionist, Civil Rights Activist

John Rock was a man of rare intelligence and skill. Endlessly thirsty for knowledge, he seemed able to absorb learning almost effortlessly and to excel at whatever he tried. He became a dentist, a physician, and a lawyer—all despite overwhelming prejudice and discrimination. Rock was an early and eloquent exponent of racial pride for African Americans. His short life is a paradigm of individual achievement exquisitely balanced with a profound and active commitment to his entire community. At the dramatic climax of his public life, Rock became a vital symbol of perseverance and promise for all African Americans.

John Swett Rock
Courtesy of the Library of Congress.

John Swett Rock was born in southern New Jersey in the small town of Salem. His parents, recognizing early his eagerness to learn, worked hard to keep him in school as long as possible. By the time he was nineteen, Rock had taken advantage of whatever education was available to him, and he became a teacher in the local public schools. Rock was already a recognized and respected young figure in Salem; two white doctors in the town opened their private libraries to him so that he could study medicine in the evenings after school was dismissed. Despite his preparation, no medical school would admit him. Undaunted—or, at the least, flexible—Rock apprenticed himself to a local dentist, and after more than a year's study he felt ready to open his own practice.

In 1850 Rock moved to Philadelphia, hoping to build a practice among the city's large free black population. But Philadelphia was a harsh home for free African Americans. There had been five major, lethal antiblack riots in the city in the previous twenty years. African Americans, largely employed in menial functions, were economically marginal and severely segregated. An English Quaker, visiting the city in 1843, believed there was no other city "where dislike, amounting to hatred of the coloured population, prevails more than in the city of brotherly love" (Litwack, 102). Barely surviving, Philadelphia's African Americans could not afford the luxury of dental care.

Within a year, Rock had abandoned dentistry and had become the director of Apprentice's High School, an evening school for blacks. The evening hours gave him the flexibility to resume his medical studies. Through the influence of white colleagues, he was permitted to enter the American Medical College, from which he received his medical degree in 1852. His teachers there remembered him as "favorably known and much respected"; a professor who had observed Rock in surgery reported, "It gives me great pleasure to bear . . . testimony to his superior abilities" (Levesque, 328).

Armed with his medical degree and a determined spirit, 27-year-old John Rock relocated to Boston. The African American community there was small—scarcely more than two thousand—but cohesive, sophisticated, and active. This was the community that had supported the earlier radical abolitionist David Walker.* Although Massachusetts blacks retained full suffrage, they faced the same prejudices that other free African Americans did. In 1831, Boston Mayor Harrison Gray Otis described the city's blacks as "a quiet, inoffensive, and in many respects a useful race," but remarked that "repugnance to intimate social relations with them is insurmountable" (Litwack, 104).

When Rock arrived in Boston, the African American community was deeply involved in a lengthy struggle to integrate the school system.

When the city school committee rejected a protest against school segregation signed by over two hundred citizens, angry African Americans turned to the courts for redress. In 1849 one Benjamin Roberts sued the committee on behalf of his small daughter, who had to trudge past five white schools each day before reaching one where she was welcome. The family's lawyer was Charles Sumner, a young liberal white with abolitionist sympathies, who would go on to a prominent role in the United States Senate and in the life of John Rock.

Although Sumner lost the case, the publicity surrounding it seemed to energize the black community. Agitation and political pressure for integration mounted, and white public sentiment began to shift. John Rock, who had achieved a name in Philadelphia as a public speaker on temperance and slavery, joined the battle wholeheartedly. By 1855, when the state legislature prohibited the exclusion of any child from a school because of race, color, or religion, Rock was a respected figure; he was appointed to the African American planning committee charged with monitoring implementation of the new law. More significant for his own future, Rock had made the acquaintance and gained the respect of Charles Sumner.

During his early years in Boston, Rock maintained a practice in both medicine and dentistry. Increasingly concerned with the cause of abolitionism, Rock provided medical care to fugitive slaves through the Boston Vigilante Committee. He became a frequent public speaker throughout New England, lecturing on such topics as "Races and Slavery" and "The Unity of the Human Races." His speech on the unity of all races was a frontal assault on the popular racist theories of the day, which suggested "polygenesis"—a separate Creation of blacks as a totally different species from whites. This lecture was so well received that Rock was invited to present it to the Massachusetts legislature in the spring of 1856. No text of this speech has survived, but press reviews deemed it a masterpiece. *The Liberator*, William Lloyd Garrison's abolitionist newspaper, declared of Rock, "if he was white, there would not be honors enough in the state to confer upon him." Even the staid *Boston Daily Bee* hailed Rock as "an original thinker . . . of superior mental and oratorical powers" (Levesque, 330).

The free African Americans of Boston had sought to keep alive the memory of Crispus Attucks, the escaped slave who was the first fatality in the Boston Massacre of 1770; they had established the anniversary of the massacre, March 5, as an evening of speeches and exhortation. The Attucks Day celebration in 1858 bore a special, bitter character to protest the recent, despised Dred Scott decision, in which the United States Supreme Court had denied the full citizenship of any African American. At Faneuil Hall that night, the most militant speaker on the platform was John Rock. He was enraged by the intimations, even from sympathetic white abolitionists, that blacks were somehow responsible for the continuation of slavery because they lacked the courage to resist:

> Our true and tried friend, Rev. Theodore Parker, said . . . that "the stroke of the axe would have settled the question long ago, but the black man would not strike." Mr. Parker makes a very low estimate of the courage of his race, if he means that one, two or three millions of these ignorant and cowardly black slaves could, without means, have brought to their knees five, ten or twenty millions of intelligent, brave white men, backed up by a rich oligarchy. . . . But when he says that "the black man *would not strike*," I am prepared to say that he does us great injustice. The black man is not a coward. . . . The history of the struggles for the liberty of the United States ought to silence every American calumniator (*The Liberator*, March 12, 1858).

Rock was unsparingly blunt about the inescapable consequences of continued slavery. He anticipated not only the Civil War, but the controversy over the military role of African Americans:

> I would have all men free. We have had much sad experience in this country, and it would be strange indeed if we do not profit by some of the lessons which we have so dearly paid for. Sooner or later, the clashing of arms will be heard in this country, and the black man's services will be needed. . . . Will the blacks fight? Of course they will. The black man will never be neutral. He could not if he would and would not if he could (ibid.).

Rock was fierce in his insistence on racial pride. He ridiculed not only the myth of black inferiority, but also the myth of white superiority:

> White men may despise, ridicule, slander, and abuse us; they may seek as they have always done to divide us, and make us feel degraded; but no man shall cause me to turn my back upon my race. With it I will sink or swim. . . . I will not deny that I admire the talents and noble characters of many white men. But I cannot say that I am particularly pleased with their physical appearance. . . . When I contrast the fine tough muscular system, the beautiful, rich color, the full broad features, and the gracefully frizzled hair of the Negro, with the delicate physical organization, wan color, sharp features and lank hair of the Caucasian, I am inclined to believe that when the white man was created, nature was pretty well exhausted—but determined to keep up appearances, she pinched up his features, and did the best she could under the circumstances (ibid.).

Rock was willing to use sharp humor as a weapon, but the situation facing African Americans was far too grave to sustain any levity. Rock saw with painful clarity that education and economic security were the real prerequisites to racial uplift; he knew intimately how strenuously whites would resist any efforts toward black self-betterment:

> In this country, where money is the great sympathetic nerve which ramifies society and has a ganglia in every man's pocket, a man is respected in proportion to his success in business. When the avenues to wealth are opened to us, we will then become educated and wealthy. . . . We do not expect to occupy a much better position than we do now, until we shall have our educated and wealthy men, who can wield a power that cannot be misunderstood. Then, and not till then, will the tongue of slander be silenced and the lip of prejudice sealed. Then, and not till then, will we be able to enjoy true equality, which can exist only among peers (ibid.).

Rock's health had always been fragile, and by 1857 he was beginning to exhibit symptoms of the tuberculosis that would destroy him nine years later. Weak and exhausted, Rock closed his medical office and underwent several surgical procedures, possibly aimed at facilitating breathing or strengthening his lungs. In despair, Rock decided to seek more sophisticated medical relief in Paris. But his application for a passport was denied by Secretary of State Lewis Cass. Cass notified Rock that a passport was "a certificate of citizenship," and that no person of color was regarded as a citizen—especially after the Dred Scott decision. The incident caused a public controversy and seemed to provoke feelings of injured Massachusetts pride that transcended the problematic detail of Rock's race. After extensive protests, the state legislature authorized the secretary of state to grant passports to any citizen of Massachusetts; thus armed with a passport of sorts, Rock sailed for France in May of 1858.

Rock spent almost a year in France, undergoing undisclosed medical treatment and studying French language and literature. When he returned to Boston, he was still not strong enough to resume his medical practice, and he turned of necessity to the lecture circuit in New England. One of his most popular lectures was on "The Character and Writings of Madame de Stael," in which he emphasized that women were the intellectual equals of men. When Rock was again invited to address the Massachusetts legislature on this topic, Boston's German-language newspaper was ecstatic. This "thinking, educated, German and French speaking negro," *Der Pioneer* declared, was "as learned in German as he is in French literature. . . . [He] converses and instructs a select American audience on female intelligence and literature . . . in the Hall of the House of Representatives of one of the first states in the Union! What is to become of such?" (Levesque, 332).

Rock felt frustrated and purposeless without his medical practice. Ever restless and eager to be challenged, he began to study law with Robert

Morris, a highly respected black lawyer who had been a member of the Massachusetts Bar since 1847. In September of 1861, Rock was admitted to the Massachusetts Bar; a week later he was commissioned as a justice of the peace for Boston and Suffolk County.

Thus armed with knowledge and cloaked with respectability, Rock turned his attention toward a truly daring private dream. Within free blacks' anguished awareness of slavery and white prejudice, a special rage was reserved for the Dred Scott decision, by which the Supreme Court had stripped all African Americans of the assumption of citizenship—and of full humanity itself. With the audacity and fierce pride so typical of him, Rock determined to refute the poisonous implications of the decision: he launched a campaign to be admitted to practice before the Supreme Court.

His ally and mentor in the process was Charles Sumner, the Massachusetts senator who had been attacked on the floor of the Senate in 1856 and severely beaten because of his antislavery position. Sumner was so badly injured in the attack that he was forced to withdraw from the Senate for four years; he did not return until the summer of 1860. Rock and Sumner had known and respected each other since the days of the Boston school desegregation struggle. Rock turned to Sumner for support in this new battle. Sumner expressed concern that any such attempt was bound to fail as long as Chief Justice Roger Taney, architect of the Scott decision, controlled a majority on the high court.

Impatient with the delay, and well aware that his physical condition was steadily deteriorating, Rock continued to offer his passion and intelligence as a lecturer. When he addressed the West India Emancipation Day celebration in the summer of 1862, Rock looked beyond the controversial issue of emancipation itself and focused on the rights and needs of freedmen. He was probably the first public speaker to demand land compensation for freed slaves and to insist that the moral obligations of white America would merely *begin* with the act of emancipation.

Why talk about compensating masters? Compensate them for what? What do you owe them? What does the slave owe them? What does society owe them? Compensate the master? No, never, it is the slave who ought to be compensated. The property of the South is by right the property of the slave. You talk of compensating the master who has stolen enough to sink ten generations, and yet you do not propose to restore even a part of that which has been plundered. This is rewarding the thief. . . .

Emancipation will entirely revolutionize society. . . . This will be no child's play. When the government has been brought to the saving knowledge of emancipation, then the antislavery work will have but fairly commenced. I hope our friends will not stop here and think their work is done. The slaves have toiled for you for more than two centuries. It is but right that you should do something for them. They have a heavy claim against you—a long catalogue of outrage and oppression. You must not forsake them now. The slaves are to be educated for a higher civilization. They need your friendship and we ask you to cooperate with us, and help clear the way. All I ask for the black man is an unobstructed road and a fair chance (*The Liberator*, August 15, 1862).

Roger Taney died in October, 1864; the new chief justice was Salmon Chase of Ohio, a member of Lincoln's cabinet and a man with an anti-slavery reputation. Rock and Sumner saw their opportunity. Sumner approached Chase, describing Rock as "an estimable lawyer, who, as you will see, is cordially recommended by [Massachusetts] Governor [John A.] Andrew and others in the public service. He is one of several colored lawyers in Massachusetts, who practise in all the courts, and are always received with courtesy" (Levesque, 334). The correspondence between Sumner and Chase went on for several months. Finally, by early 1865, the stage was set and all the players were ready for one of the most dramatic moments in American legal history. The scene that took place on February 1, 1865, was vividly recorded by a reporter for *The New York Tribune*:

The black man was admitted. Jet black with hair of an extra twist—let me have the pleasure of saying, by purpose and premeditation, of an aggravating "kink"—unqualifiedly, obtrusively, defiantly "Nigger" . . . this inky hued African stood, in the monarchical power of recognized American Manhood and American Citizenship, within the bar of the Court which had solemnly pronounced that black men had no rights which white men were bound to respect; stood there a recognized member of it, professionally the brother of the distinguished counsellors on its long rolls, in rights their equal, in the standing which rank gives their peer. By Jupiter, the sight was grand. . . . Immediately the Senator from Massachusetts arose, and in composed manner and quiet tone said: "May it please the Court, I move that John S. Rock, a member of the Supreme Court of the State of Massachusetts, be admitted to practice as a member of this Court." The grave to bury the Dred Scott decision was in that one sentence dug; and it yawned there, wide open, under the very eyes of some of the Judges who had participated in the judicial crime against Democracy and humanity (Brown, 172).

His admission to the Bar of the Supreme Court was the crowning achievement of Rock's hectic, difficult life. Rock never actually argued a case before the Supreme Court. In truth, his health was deteriorating so rapidly that it soon dominated and limited his activities. On December 3, 1866, John Rock died of the tuberculosis that had stalked him throughout his life.

John Rock believed passionately in equal opportunity—in the "unobstructed road" he had demanded for freedmen. He accepted a stern vision of individual responsibility and an even more exacting standard of responsibility to one's race. But Rock knew from his own bitter experience how obstructed the road really was, how frustrating the African American's struggle for self-betterment. In reality, any sign of meaningful improvement in the free black community elicited a hostile response from most whites. Popular "scientific" racist theories could accommodate the idle, shiftless, childish, slovenly black. When African Americans challenged this image by organizing their communities and churches, by fighting for the vote and for their children's education, they aroused resentment, fear, and anger among whites. In the thirty years before the Civil War, free African Americans were active and articulate on their own behalf in ever greater numbers, and the response of their white neighbors was only too predictable. As Rock himself described conditions in Massachusetts,

> To be sure, we are seldom insulted by passers-by, we have the right of suffrage, the free schools and colleges are open to our children, and from them have come forth young men capable of filling any post of profit or honor. But there is no field for these young men. Their education aggravates their suffering. The more highly educated the colored man is, the more keenly he suffers. . . . You can hardly imagine the humiliation and contempt a colored lad must feel by graduating first in his class and then being rejected everywhere else because of his color. . . .
>
> Nowhere in the United States is the colored man of talent appreciated. Even in Boston, which has a great reputation for being antislavery, he has no field for his talent (*The Liberator*, August 15, 1862).

The life and career of John Rock are a paradigm of individual excellence and effort. By any standards, his achievements were outstanding. He sought to demonstrate that prejudice against African Americans was grounded in their condition, not in their color; with a deep faith in rationality, he set out to prove that the miserable conditions of his people could be ameliorated by principled determination, and that a strengthened, enriched American society could then live in harmony. Ironically, his own life seemed to betray his faith. Ultimately, individual effort alone could not eradicate deeply held racial attitudes. To achieve that admirable goal, all the varied components of American society would have to be better educated.

References

Berry, Mary Frances and John W. Blassingame. *Long Memory: The Black Experience in America*. New York: Oxford University Press, 1982.

Brown, Charles Sumner. "Genesis of the Negro Lawyer in New England." *Negro History Bulletin* 22(May, 1959): 171–176.

Levesque, George A. "Boston's Black Brahmin: Dr. John S. Rock." *Civil War History* 25,4 (December, 1980): 326–346.

The Liberator, March 12, 1858; August 15, 1862.

Link, Eugene P. "Civil Rights Activities of Three Great Negro Physicians." *Journal of Negro History* 52, 3 (July, 1967): 169–184.

Litwack, Leon T. *North of Slavery: The Negro in the Free States, 1790–1860.* Chicago: University of Chicago Press, 1961.

Logan, Rayford W. and Michael R. Winston, eds. *Dictionary of American Negro Biography.* New York: W. W. Norton Co., 1982.

McPherson, James M. *The Negro's Civil War: How American Blacks Felt and Acted During the War for the Union.* New York: Ballantine Books, 1991.

Pease, Jane and William H. Pease. *They Who Would be Free: Blacks' Search for Freedom, 1830–1861.* New York: Atheneum, 1974.

ERNESTINE LOUISE ROSE

(January 13, 1810–August 4, 1892)

Abolitionist, Women's Rights Activist, Free-thinker

As Ernestine Rose described herself, she was "a rebel at the age of five, a heretic at fourteen." Rose's spirit and integrity moved her through vastly different worlds and thrust her into the forefront of the momentous reform struggles of the 19th century. Even among the ranks of pioneering reformers, Rose was an anomaly: In movements dominated by native-born small-town Protestants, she was a sophisticated, urbane immigrant Jew; her Judaism would have been difficult enough for her companions to deal with, but they could more easily have accepted a pious Jew than the outspoken atheist and free-thinker Rose was. To complicate matters even more, Rose was an avowed socialist with a vision of social and economic justice that went far beyond the immediate goals of both the abolition and women's rights movements. Her very existence was a challenge to the status quo.

Ernestine Louise Rose
Courtesy of the Library of Congress.

Ernestine Rose's tumultuous life began in the ghetto of Piotrkow, Poland, where her father was a highly revered rabbi. Blessed with a wealthy wife, Rabbi Potowski was able to hold himself above the venality and corruption that tainted the difficult, precarious life of Jews in Poland. He never accepted a fee for his religious work; he was widely seen as a champion of justice, willing to stand up to oppressive authorities. Disappointed that his only child was a girl, he nonetheless devoted himself to her education, exposing her to a depth of Hebrew and Torah learning usually forbidden to women. He was at first delighted and then increasingly dismayed by her capacity for logic and clarity and her refusal to be intimidated by dogma. When he warned her that "little girls must not ask questions," her inevitable response was "Why must little girls not ask questions?" When Ernestine asked her father why he fasted rigorously several days a week, he replied that his fasting pleased God. Having observed that the fasting was difficult for her thin, ascetic father, Ernestine declared, "If God is pleased in making you sick and unhappy, I hate God" (Stanton, 1:95). Her heresy, as she herself termed it, was never doctrinal. It was broadly humane, grounded in what she perceived as a sacred right to ask questions, to investigate the unknown with the tools of logic, to base her life on reason. There was no room in Ernestine's mind for the idea of woman's inferiority to man; her rejection of secondary status was central to her ultimate rejection of Judaism.

When Rose was sixteen, her mother died and left her a substantial inheritance. Her father, offering her inheritance as a dowry, betrothed her without her knowledge to an older man. Appalled, Ernestine refused to honor the arrangement; her angry suitor declared that she would forfeit her inheritance as a result. But Ernestine, already poised and articulate, petitioned the Polish secular court, testified in her own behalf, and won a judgment returning her inheritance to her control. Shortly thereafter, her father married a young woman no older than she, and Ernestine knew there was no place for her in that household. At the age of seventeen, alone, she traveled to Berlin.

Rose's journey to Berlin was the first brave stage of an epic quest for justice and for rational truth. In Berlin, happily, her curiosity led her to the leaders of the Jewish Enlightenment (*Haskalah*); these liberal protesters criticized and satirized the passionate superstitions of Hassidism, a poor people's movement that emphasized rigid piety, fervor, and miracle-prone rabbis at the expense of learning and any hint of secular flexibility. In this challenging, exciting environment, Rose was nurtured and strengthened by the companionship of other inquiring, literate, liberal Jews.

Rose spent two years in Germany. She traveled throughout the coun-

try, observing firsthand official oppression, censorship, political persecution, poverty, and hypocrisy. Touring Holland and Belgium as well,
she arrived in France during the revolt of 1830 that deposed Charles X
and brought Louis Philippe to power. Hearing of a popular uprising in
Poland, Rose tried to get back home to fight; she was stopped and ques-
tioned by Austrian border police at Coblenz and was unable to continue
her journey—which may have saved her life, since the Polish revolt was
brutally crushed.

Permanently cut off from her roots, Rose turned west and arrived in
London. She supported herself teaching Hebrew and German while she
herself learned English; in addition, she marketed a deodorant paper
wick she had invented in Germany. England was in a state of great social
and economic turmoil. Reformers were agitating for universal suffrage,
improved working conditions, the rights of labor unions, protection of
child laborers, and other humanitarian causes. Within a few years of
arriving in England, Rose was introduced to the leading social reformer
of the day, Robert Owen. Owen, forty years her senior, became a second
father figure for Rose. In his utopian socialism she found a focus and
coherent direction that sustained her the rest of her life.

Robert Owen was already a legend in England and America. He believed that people were totally the products of their environment, and
that a good environment could be expected to produce good people. In
1800, as a successful cotton manufacturer, he took over the Scottish mill
town of New Lanark and set out to demonstrate the validity of his theories. The average mill town of England's industrial revolution was a
brutal world of poverty and degradation; alcoholism, illiteracy, disease,
and prostitution were rampant; children as young as five or six might
work fourteen or fifteen hours a day. Instead, Owen built decent housing
in New Lanark, stocked its markets with good produce at reasonable
prices, cut working hours, improved working conditions, and established
a "rational infant school." In a major depression in 1806, when mills
throughout England shut down, Owen paid his laid-off workers at full
salary and still showed a profit. Owen's trip to America in 1824 saw the
founding of New Harmony, an Owenite community in Indiana; New
Harmony spawned more than a dozen other communities, none of which
was able to sustain itself long in the mercurial economic environment of
America. Returning to England, Owen threw his support behind the burgeoning labor union movement; it was at a workers' meeting that he met
Rose. The rapport between the two was intense; for the rest of his life,
Owen referred to Rose as his daughter.

In 1836, through her activities with Owen, Rose met William Rose, a
silversmith and a like-minded Owenite. The two were married in a civil
ceremony; committed to taking an active part in the constant struggle
for wider justice and human happiness, they decided to emigrate to

America. The young couple arrived in New York City in May of 1836. They were among 16,000 new immigrants in that month alone. New York, a city of over a quarter million residents, was already experiencing urban problems. It was hideously filthy, overcrowded, noisy, and notoriously dangerous. It was also, even then, the scene of a vibrant cosmopolitan cultural vanguard. William and Ernestine made it their home for the next thirty-three years.

The United States of 1836 was a country of profound contrast and contradiction. The optimism of the Jacksonian era was still strong, industry was expanding rapidly and fortunes were easily made in Western land speculation. Almost universal (white) male suffrage created the illusion that anything was within reach. Concomitantly, rapid industrialization created massive rural displacement, inhuman working conditions, rising child labor and prostitution, an atmosphere officially hostile to labor unions.

In addition, the Roses were for the first time exposed to an environment of which chattel slavery was an integral part. Both abolitionist agitation and reaction against it were intensifying. William Lloyd Garrison's American Anti-Slavery Society was founded in 1833, the first of the abolitionist societies to accept African-American members. The following year the Female Anti-Slavery Society was founded in Boston. By 1836, agitation and petitions to Congress had reached such a pitch that Congress resolved to table *without printing* all further petitions or resolutions relating in any way to slavery; in what was no doubt a violation of the constitutional right of petition, they voted to take no notice of these petitions whatsoever.

Rose's first campaign, and her major crusade in America, was for the rights of women. At the time, the status of married women was based on the 1760s' jurist William Blackstone's *Commentaries on the Laws of England*: "By marriage, the husband and the wife are one person in law; that is, the very being or legal existence of the woman is suspended during the marriage, or at least, is consolidated into that of her husband, under whose wing, protection, and cover, she performs everything" (Suhl, 49). Thus legally classified with children and idiots, a married woman lost all control of any property she brought to the marriage and of any wages she earned during the marriage. She could not sign a contract; she could neither sue nor be sued in court; she had no voice in the educational, marital, and career choices made for her children. In the rare instance of divorce, she automatically lost custody of her children. When her husband died, she was not permitted to function as the guardian for her own children; her husband was free to name whatever guardian he chose in his will. Only chattel slaves had fewer rights and less control over their lives than did married women.

Shortly before the Roses arrived in 1836, a state legislator named Thomas Herttell introduced a controversial bill entitled "An Act for the Protection and Preservation of the Rights and Property of Married Women." Understandably, Rose was quickly drawn into the struggle and spent weary days trudging the streets of New York soliciting signatures for an independent petition in support of the bill. This first petition, after a grueling five months, carried a total of six signatures, one of them Rose's own. As she recalled years later,

> After a good deal of trouble I obtained five signatures. Some of the ladies said the gentlemen would laugh at them; others, that they had rights enough; and the men said the women had too many rights already. . . . I continued sending petitions with increased numbers of signatures until 1848 and '49, when the Legislature enacted the law which granted woman the right to keep what was her own. But no sooner did it become legal than all the women said: "Oh! that is right! We ought always to have had that!" (Stanton, 1:99)

The bill would endure a horrible twilight limbo-like existence for twelve years; when Herttell lost his seat in the legislature in 1840, the bill was still "under discussion" in committee. And Rose, refusing to abandon the effort, was still circulating petitions at her own expense and lecturing in an effort to reach the minds of her sisters. By 1840 she had found two allies who would become invaluable life-long friends and stalwarts in the struggle: Paulina Wright Davis and Elizabeth Cady Stanton. The three went to Albany to address the legislature directly; they were beginning to draw support from the conservative, wealthy Dutch patroons of the Hudson Valley, who did not want to lose control over their daughters' substantial dowries. By 1845 the campaign in support of the bill was state-wide. In 1846 and 1847 the legislature was presented with four separate property rights bills, and Rose's lonely first petition had engendered a torrent of furious letters and petitions.

Finally, after twelve years of unrelenting pressure, lobbying, and education, the "Act for the More Effective Protection of the Property of Married Women" passed the legislature in April of 1848. It would take another twelve years of strenuous agitation before the "Act on the Rights and Liabilities of Husband and Wife" established the wife's financial and legal autonomy and her equal right to the children of the marriage. Half a century later, the writer Lillie Devereux Blake commented, "The liberal laws which we now live under are due to the tireless exertions of this gifted woman, and never ought the women of New York to forget the debt of gratitude they owe to Ernestine L. Rose" (Suhl, 278).

Through the 1830s and '40s Rose was deeply involved with a freethought organization called the Society for Moral Philanthropists. The group sponsored lectures and debates on moral philosophy, with a large component of biblical skepticism; their events were always well attended, and Rose became a leading speaker. The clergy and the proslavery press feared and ridiculed the group and labeled them "infidels"—a serious, potentially damaging charge in pious, righteous, Protestant America. In defiant response, the group held a highly publicized "infidels' convention" in Coliseum Hall, New York, in May of 1845. Over two hundred free-thinking delegates and hundreds of guests attended from as far away as Alabama, Indiana, and Vermont. The support and solidarity these radicals experienced in each other's company was intoxicating. The high point of the event was an address by the venerable 74-year-old Robert Owen, joined by his beloved protegé, Ernestine Rose. Their guiding axiom, Rose declared, was: "Unlimited and inviolable freedom of thought alone can prevent prejudice and insure peace and harmony of mind" (Suhl, 88). The renamed Infidel Society held an annual celebration of Thomas Paine's birthday; Paine himself had been labeled an infidel and an atheist and had been shunned by more middle-class revolutionaries because of his profound radicalism. Ernestine Rose became a favorite keynote speaker at these Tom Paine birthday dinners, at which she exhorted her audience to honor Paine's memory by opposing error and falsehood fearlessly and by never sacrificing their principles to popularity.

In the summer of 1848, the first conference anywhere in the world to discuss women's rights was held in the small upstate New York town of Seneca Falls. It grew out of the contentious circumstances of the 1840 World Anti-Slavery Convention in London: the women delegates, led by Lucretia Mott, found that their credentials as delegates were not honored and they were initially denied access to the hall; when the issue was put to a floor vote, the majority ruled against the women, who were segregated in a crowded upper gallery behind a curtain. When the renowned William Lloyd Garrison, the keynote speaker, arrived late, he insisted on sitting in the gallery with the women, despite embarrassing pleas from his colleagues to take his "proper" place on the floor. The implications of this tangible, painful demonstration of their true status were not lost on the women. Mott and a young protegé, the newly wed Elizabeth Cady Stanton, formed an alliance forged in the humiliation and rage of this experience. When they orchestrated the meeting at Seneca Falls eight years later, they based their protests on the Declaration of Independence, which they amended to read, "We hold these truths to be self-evident, that all men and women are created equal." Their first demand was for the right to vote.

The movement begun that summer faced a difficult and tortuous future. Hostility, rage, and ridicule from the clergy and the press were vicious and unrelenting. In October 1850, in a society bruised and divided by the infamous Fugitive Slave Law, the first National Women's

Rights Convention met in Worcester, Massachusetts. Garrison hailed the meeting as launching the most important movement in the destiny of the human race. Most of the press disagreed. Headlines in the *New York Herald* blared, "Awful Combination of Socialism, Abolitionism, and Infidelity! Bible and Constitution Repudiated!" The newspaper described the convention as "that motley mingling of abolitionists, socialists, and infidels . . . this hybrid, mongrel, piebald, crackbrained, pitiful, disgusting, and ridiculous assemblage. . . . May God have mercy on their miserable souls" (Gurko, 139). The group thus pilloried included Rose, Frederick Douglass, Lucretia Mott, Sojourner Truth, Abby Kelley Foster, William Lloyd Garrison, Lucy Stone, and Wendell Phillips. Over one thousand delegates packed the conference hall; hundreds were turned away.

By this time, Ernestine Rose was widely acknowledged as "the Queen of the Platform." Her colleague L. C. Barnard recalled,

> She had a rich musical voice, with just enough foreign accent and idiom to add the charm to her oratory. As a speaker she was pointed, logical, and impassioned. She not only dealt in abstract principles clearly, but in their application touched the deepest emotions of the human soul (Stanton, 1:100).

A Boston newspaper called her "an excellent lecturer, liberal, eloquent, witty, and decidedly handsome" (Gurko, 88). The convention resolved unanimously that they bore a special responsibility to the million and a half abused slave women. Rose added, "We are not contending here for the rights of the women of New England, or of old England, but of the world" (Suhl, 112).

At the next year's convention, Rose exploded in anguished eloquence against the artificial image of fragility and incompetence forced on women:

> Do you not yet understand what has made woman what she is? Then see what the sickly taste and perverted judgment of man now admires in woman. Not health and strength of body and mind, but a pale delicate face; hands too small to grasp a broom, for that were treason to a lady; a voice so sickly, sentimental and depressed, as to hear what she says only by the moving of her half-parted lips; and, above all that nervous sensibility that sees a ghost in every passing shadow—that beautiful diffidence that dare not take a step without the arm of a man to support her tender frame, and that shrinking modesty that faints at the mention of the leg of a table. . . . Oh! the crying injustice towards woman! She is crushed in every step she takes, and then insulted for being what a most pernicious education and corrupt public sentiment has made her. . . .
>
> But it will be said that the husband provides for the wife, or in other

words, he feeds, clothes, and shelters her! I wish I had the power to make every one before me realize the degradation contained in that idea. Yes! he *keeps* her, and so he does a favorite horse; by law they are both considered his property. . . .

Carry out the republican principle of universal suffrage, or strike it from your banners and substitute "Freedom and Power to one half of society, and Submission and Slavery to the other." Give women the elective franchise. . . .

No! there is no reason against woman's elevation, but there are deep-rooted, hoary-headed prejudices. The main cause of them is, a pernicious falsehood propagated against her being, namely, that she is inferior by her nature. Inferior in what? What has man ever done, that woman . . . could not do? (Stanton, 1:237–242).

As the woman's movement grew, the opposition of the clergy turned more active. They invaded women's conferences, interrupting and shouting biblical verses and St. Paul's well-worn admonition to women to be silent in church and not to teach. This focus on the Bible almost destroyed the 1852 convention when the Reverend Antoinette Brown Blackwell, the first ordained woman, determined to reconcile the Bible with the concept of women's rights. Rose saw grave danger in the effort and sensed once again the unwelcome tyranny of religion. She fought back and managed to rally the general convention behind her:

For my part, I see no need to appeal to any written authority, particularly when it is so obscure and indefinite as to admit of different interpretations. When the inhabitants of Boston converted their harbor into a teapot rather than submit to unjust taxes, they did not go to the Bible for their authority; for if they had, they would have been told from the same authority to "give unto Caesar what belonged to Caesar." Had the people, when they rose in the might of their right to throw off the British yoke, appealed to the Bible for authority, it would have answered them, "Submit to the powers that be, for they are from God." No! on human rights and freedom, on a subject that is as self-evident as two and two make four, there is no need of any written authority. . . . We ask not for our rights as a gift of charity, but as an act of justice. . . . For it is in accordance with the principles of republicanism that, as woman has to pay taxes to maintain government, she has a right to participate in the formation and administration of it . . . and any difference, therefore in political, civil, and social rights, in account of sex, is in direct violation of the principles of justice and humanity, and as such ought to be held up to the contempt and derision of every lover of human freedom (Stanton, 1:537).

Rose was evidently the rare orator who could appeal to both emotion and logic. Her eloquence and total dedication illuminated her addresses. The English reformer Joseph Barker considered her "the most perfect specimen of intellectual and moral excellence I have had the happiness to know. . . . To hear her reason you might fancy she was all intelligence; to hear her plead you would think her an incarnation of benevolence" (Suhl, 138).

Throughout the 1850s, Rose traveled throughout the Midwest and East lecturing for women's rights, free thought, and abolition. As an atheist, a foreigner, and a Jew by birth, Rose was the occasional object of overt hostility even within her own ranks. When she was slated to preside at the women's rights convention in 1854, conservatives within the movement urged her removal; Susan B. Anthony, a devoted friend, stood staunchly behind her, and Rose was able to assume her scheduled role. Anthony mused in her private diary, "Mrs. Rose is not appreciated, nor cannot be by this age" (Du Bois, 75).

As a Garrisonian abolitionist, Rose believed that Abraham Lincoln behaved dishonorably by sidestepping the issue of slavery in the early years of the Civil War. When Lincoln delivered the Emancipation Proclamation in 1863, Rose, Stanton, and Anthony worked with the Women's Loyal National League to keep generating abolitionist awareness and sympathy. To Rose, the Proclamation was a feeble compromise, since it "freed" slaves in the rebel states (where the federal government had no impact) and neglected to free slaves in either the Unionist Border states or the District of Columbia. Like many others, Rose felt misled and manipulated. She addressed the convention of the National Loyal League in May of 1863:

> And now we have got all around us Loyal Leagues. Loyal to what? What does it mean?. . . . I know not what others mean by it, but I will give you my interpretation of what I am loyal to. . . . I am loyal only to justice and humanity. Let the Administration give evidence that they too are for justice to all, without exception, without distinction, and I, for one, had I ten thousand lives, would gladly lay them down to secure this boon of freedom to humanity. . . . I am not unconditionally loyal, until we know to what principle we are to be loyal. Promise justice and freedom, and all the rest will follow. . . . Free the slaves in the Border States, in Western Virginia, in Maryland, and wherever the Union flag floats, and then there will be a consistency in our actions that will enable us to go to work earnestly with heart and hand united, as we move forward to free all others and crush the rebellion (Stanton, 2:78).

The years after the Civil War were a dark and bitter period for the women's rights movement. The Fourteenth Amendment specifically extended suffrage to any "male citizen"; this was the first time that gender had been designated in the Constitution, and it was a sour sign of things to come. In the effort to keep their party alive, Republicans appealed to the freedmen's vote and turned their backs on women. The Fifteenth

Amendment stipulates that rights shall not be abridged because of "race, color, or previous condition of servitude"; sex was very deliberately excluded as a protected category. Garrison, Phillips, even Frederick Douglass all threw their energies into Reconstruction and abandoned their female colleagues; the women's movement itself was torn by anguished division over how far the women were willing to subsume their own agenda within the program of Reconstruction. Rose, Anthony, and Stanton insisted that women must not be expected to wait any longer for the vote; they and their followers broke away from the abolitionist wing and formed the American Equal Rights Association. Women who had worked together for years were drawn into vicious attacks on each other; frustrated and demoralized, the women's movement faltered for years.

Tired, ill, and bitter, Rose and her husband left the United States for England in 1869; they returned only for a brief visit in 1873, during which Rose made one last appearance at the convention of her suffrage association. Settling in London, Rose inevitably became involved with the suffrage struggle in England. During the late 1870s she corresponded regularly with Anthony and Stanton as they compiled their monumental *History of Woman Suffrage*; astonishingly, Rose reported that she never spoke from notes and had no records of her own speeches. Modestly, she reflected, "All that I can tell you is that I used my humble powers to the uttermost and raised my voice in behalf of Human Rights in general, and the elevation and Rights of Woman in particular, nearly all my life" (Stanton, 1:99). In 1882 William Rose, who had been a gentle, generous, unfailing support to his wife, died. Shortly afterward, Anthony and Stanton visited the widowed Rose and urged her to come back to America with them, but she was determined to be buried next to William. Her last years were burdened by the deaths of most of her old friends—Lucretia Mott, Garrison, and Phillips among them. When she died at the age of eighty-three, she was buried beside her husband in Highgate Cemetery, as she had wished. At her funeral, she was eulogized fittingly: "Mrs. Rose took truth for authority, not authority for truth" (Suhl, 274).

References

Anderson, Judith, ed. *Outspoken Women: Speeches by American Women Reformers, 1635–1935*. Dubuque, IA: Kendall/Hunt Publishing, 1984.

Barry, Kathleen. *Susan B. Anthony: A Biography of a Singular Feminist*. New York: New York University Press, 1988.

Du Bois, Ellen Carol, ed. *Elizabeth Cady Stanton/Susan B. Anthony: Correspondence, Writings, Speeches*. New York: Schocken Books, 1981.

Gurko, Miriam. *The Ladies of Seneca Falls: The Birth of the Woman's Rights Movement*. New York: Macmillan, 1974.

James, Edward T., ed. *Notable American Women*. Cambridge, MA: Harvard University Press, 1971.

Kraditor, Aileen S., ed. *Up From the Pedestal: Selected Writings in the History of American Feminism*. Chicago: Quadrangle Books, 1968.

Stanton, Elizabeth Cady, Susan B. Anthony, and Matilda Joslyn Gage. *A History of Woman Suffrage*. 6 vols. New York: Fowler & Wells, Pub., 1881.

Suhl, Yuri. *Ernestine L. Rose: Women's Rights Pioneer*. New York: Biblio Press, 1990.

ROSE SCHNEIDERMAN

(April 6, 1882–August 11, 1972)

Labor Organizer

Diminutive Rose Schneiderman was a towering figure in some of industrial America's most significant, divisive moral challenges. She served a unique mediating role between inarticulate laboring women and the middle-class women who wanted to help them, between men and women within the trade union movement, between the socialists who inspired her and the New Deal Democrats she helped educate. She combined passion and pragmatism in the finest moments of Progressivism. Like so many others within these pages, she identified pressing human problems, analyzed their causes unflinchingly, and fought for realistic, humane solutions.

Rose Schneiderman
Courtesy of the Library of Congress.

Rose Schneiderman, the oldest of four children, spent her first eight years in Russian Poland, where her parents both worked in the needle trades. Her mother, a strong-willed, determined woman, had taught herself to read Hebrew; at her insistence, Rose had two years of Russian-language school as well as two years of religious education before the family emigrated in 1890. Her father, a self-taught intellectual, read to his daughter constantly and emphasized to her the primacy of education; his dream was that she become a schoolteacher. For the rest of her life, Schneiderman treasured the image of this gentle, dignified, warmly supportive man.

The family settled on New York's teeming Lower East Side. Less than two years later, Samuel Schneiderman was dead of meningitis, leaving his wife, Deborah, destitute and pregnant with their fourth child. Deborah took in boarders and tried to find work as a seamstress, but she could not care for her small children at the same time. For the better part of a year, Rose and her two younger brothers were placed in different Jewish orphanages. Rose never forgot the isolation, loneliness, and deprivation of that time. Regimented, kept under severe discipline, shorn of her flaming red hair, she felt robbed of her identity. "The shame of that experience is very real even now. To say it was humiliating is to put it mildly," she wrote seventy-five years later (Schneiderman, 31).

While Deborah was able to reclaim her children, she frequently depended on Rose to stay home from school and care for her baby sister while her mother worked. Despite the irregularity of her attendance and the stresses at home, Rose completed ninth grade before permanently leaving school at the age of thirteen. To help support her family, the child worked as a cash girl at Hearn's Department Store, where she earned $2.16 for a 64-hour week. After three years that brought her wages up to $2.66 per week, she decided to seek better-paying work in a factory.

As a seamstress in a cap-lining shop, she earned the grand sum of $6.00 a week. From that was deducted money for the electricity consumed by her sewing machine—which she had had to buy. In addition, workers were expected to supply their own thread, needles, and scissors. Employers ran their shops under a system of capricious and arbitrary rules: five minutes' lateness might cost the worker an hour's pay; minor stitching irregularities could be fined at the full retail cost of the item— often an entire week's wage for the worker. Sanitary and safety conditions were appalling. Despite all of this, Schneiderman settled into the routines of working life. She attended night school briefly, but found the teacher boring and turned instead to the culture club of the local settlement house. She went to neighborhood socials, danced with boys she found immature and dull, and dreamed of a romantic marriage. She knew nothing of women's rights, socialism, or unionism; she seemed indistinguishable from thousands of other immigrant girls.

In 1902 Deborah Schneiderman took her family to Montreal to spend time with a sister who had settled there. The visit lasted a full year and proved a turning point in Rose's life; she was befriended there by a neighboring family who introduced her to trade unionism and socialism. Rose returned to New York a different person. She was alert to disparities between the women's working conditions in her shop and those of the men, who were unionized. In 1903, with two friends, she organized the twelve women in the shop and approached the United Cloth Hat and Cap Makers Union for a charter. She was told that they needed twenty-five women before a charter could be granted; within days, Schneiderman returned with the required signed membership cards and received the union charter. As secretary of the new local, Schneiderman nurtured it through a successful infancy. Within two years it had grown to several hundred members and was strong enough to negotiate a Saturday half-day.

Schneiderman's life was transformed. The union movement offered her intellectual challenges she had missed since leaving school; it provided warm companionship and offered support and exhilarating approval. Through the union she was drawn into the exuberant, tumultuous political and cultural life of the East Side. "It was such an exciting time for me. A new life opened up. All of a sudden I was not lonely any more. It was the beginning of a period that molded all my subsequent development" (Dye, 49).

By 1904 Schneiderman had been elected to the general executive board of her local's parent union. She had become the ranking woman in the American labor movement, a fact that was as indicative of organized labor's wariness of women as it was of Schneiderman's undeniable competence. Although union leaders like Terrence Powderly and Samuel Gompers claimed to welcome women into the ranks of organized labor, the rank-and-file in most trades was distinctly hostile. Women were viewed as cheaper competition for scarce jobs, as potential strikebreakers rather than potential allies. The language of distrust and disrespect used in the shops and factories against women carried the same fearful, vicious undertones as the language aimed at African American workers. Even as increasingly sophisticated women recognized the advantages of unionizing, they learned that they needed to rely on themselves and that male-dominated unions were willing to abandon and betray them. During the cap makers' strike of 1905, married men received $6.00 a week in strike benefits; women, even when they had numerous dependents, received nothing.

Early in 1904 Rose Schneiderman attended a meeting of the recently formed Women's Trade Union League (WTUL), a group then dominated by upper- and middle-class reform-minded women eager to improve the lives of working women. At first, she was skeptical. "I could understand why working women . . . joined, but I could not believe that men and women who were not wage-earners themselves understood the problems that workers faced" (Dye, 50). The following winter, when Schneiderman organized and led a long, bitter, industry-wide cap makers' strike, she came to appreciate both the depth of commitment in many WTUL members and the value of the publicity and assistance they could provide. When the thirteen-week cap makers' strike concluded in victory, Schneiderman joined the WTUL.

The relationship between Schneiderman and the WTUL was pure symbiosis. Schneiderman was the first strike organizer and shop worker to devote herself to the League. Although well under five feet tall, she was already an orator of enormous power and presence, and she was fluent in Yiddish. She represented a crucial direct link to the disaffected, distrustful, insular working girls the League was so eager to reach. In tacit exchange, the leaders of the League became major mentors for the young immigrant woman, molding her and honing her skills for battles she would wage long after the League had ceased to be effective. From the impassioned socialist Leonora O'Reilly, Schneiderman learned rhetoric and sophisticated political theory; wealthy Margaret Dreier Robins provided a model of femininity, grace, and poise; Robins's sister, Mary Dreier, offered an ideal of patience, compassion, and total dedication to the movement. They taught her superb English and exposed her to a broad, enriching panorama of culture.

By 1906 Schneiderman was vice-president of the New York League. A year later, a wealthy League "ally" (the term used to distinguish the non-working-class members of the League) offered Schneiderman a fellowship that enabled her to quit factory work, study organizing skills at the Rand School, and become a full-time organizer for the League. She had grown into a highly skilled, mesmerizing speaker, and the League recognized her value. "Dearest Rose," wrote Margaret Dreier Robins,

> go out among your fellow workers, speak to them on any street corner, fire them with your spirit and you will help give birth to the new world emerging. . . . It is because I remember your great gift of interpretation that I am so eager for you to be our interpreter to the great unknowing and unthinking world (Lagemann, 131).

When Rose accepted a job as a full-time organizer, her mother disapproved and warned her that she was risking her chances of marrying. In her autobiography, Schneiderman acknowledged the consuming, grueling, ultimately solitary nature of the path she had chosen:

I found out that organizing is a hard job, too, and often very frustrating. You work and work and seem to be getting nowhere. Just when you feel that it is no use going on, something happens.

You organize a group and set up a local. Then you have to nurse the members along so they won't get discouraged and quit before the union is strong enough to make demands on the employers. All this could be terribly discouraging if you didn't have faith in trade unionism and didn't believe with every cell in your body that what you were doing in urging them to organize was absolutely right for them . . . and on top of all this, you never have a life of your own, for there is no limit to the time you can put into the job (Schneiderman, 111).

In 1909 spontaneous strikes broke out in a number of shirtwaist shops throughout the East Side. The League quickly moved to support the strikers, providing bail money, emergency food and fuel, and sophisticated legal advice. The youth and idealism of the overwhelmingly female waistmakers and the degrading conditions under which they worked elicited fervent support and drew hundreds of new members to the League. Within weeks twenty thousand young women were out of the shops, the first great strike of women in American history. Police reaction was swift and brutal. In the month before Christmas, 723 women and girls were arrested. Wealthy allies like Mrs. Henry Morganthau, Mrs. O.H.P. Belmont, and the youthful Carola Woerishoffer* picketed with the girls, went into the jails to post bail—as much as $2,500 a day— arranged crucial sympathetic press coverage and publicity, and involved prominent lawyers in the strikers' defense, among them the dean of Columbia University Law School. Mary White Ovington,* a founder of the NAACP, worked through the interracial Cosmopolitan Club to ensure that African American women would not be used as strikebreakers. The strike dragged on to an inconclusive end in February of 1910; despite many disappointments, strikers in a vast majority of shops won many of their demands.

One of the major shops that refused to negotiate with the waistmakers' union was the Triangle Shirtwaist Company, located on the upper floors of the Asch Building on Greene Street in Greenwich Village. Two key unmet demands of the Triangle workers had been for sturdy fire escapes and for accessible, unlocked doors to the stairwells. Late in the afternoon on Saturday, March 25, 1911, one of the few male workers at Triangle dropped a cigarette into a pile of remnants, setting off one of the great disasters of American labor history. As the factory floors erupted in searing flames, terrified young women found that the fire doors were locked, to keep union agitators out as well as to keep workers in; the girls who managed to reach them discovered a single fire escape so old and poorly maintained that it twisted and collapsed under the strain. The Fire Department's ladders, fully extended, stopped two floors short of the trapped women. With no hope of rescue, girls made the agonizing decision to jump to their deaths rather than endure the flames. While horrified thousands watched helplessly below, body after body thudded broken and lifeless to the street. By the final count, 146 young women had either plunged to their deaths or been incinerated at Triangle. A United Press reporter in the crowd recalled,

> The floods of water from the firemen's hose that ran into the gutter were actually stained red with blood. I looked upon the heap of dead bodies and I remembered these girls were the shirtwaist makers. I remembered their great strike of last year in which these same girls had demanded more sanitary conditions and more safety precautions in the shops. These dead bodies were the answer (Shepherd, 193).

An unprecedented wave of rage and revulsion swept New York City. By Monday morning a Red Cross emergency committee was set up with over $5,000 in funds for affected families; contributions ultimately topped $120,000. But the devastated families, largely Jewish and Italian, had no prior experience with charities; at first, no one applied for emergency aid, and Schneiderman had to lead Red Cross workers into the tenements of the East Side to seek out the bereaved survivors.

On April 2 the WTUL rented the Metropolitan Opera House for a mass memorial meeting. Prominent public figures deplored the loss and offered resolutions for improved safety regulations and inspection. The workers in the audience were enraged by what they saw as pious platitudes; angry shouts erupted throughout the hall. The meeting was on the verge of disintegrating when Rose Schneiderman took the podium. Her vibrant voice hovering at a whisper, she sliced through the layers of compromise and sanctimony:

> I would be a traitor to those poor burned bodies if I were to come here to talk good fellowship. We have tried you good people of the public—and we have found you wanting. . . .
>
> This is not the first time girls have been burned alive in this city. Every week I must learn of the untimely death of one of my sister workers. Every year thousands of us are maimed. The life of men and women is so cheap and property is so sacred! There are so many of us for one job, it matters little if 140-odd are burned to death.
>
> We have tried you, citizens! We are trying you now and you have a couple of dollars for the sorrowing mothers and brothers and sisters by way of a charity gift. But every time the workers come out in the only way they know to protest against conditions which are unbearable, the strong hand of the law is allowed to press down heavily upon us. . . .
>
> I can't talk fellowship to you who are gathered here. Too much blood

has been spilled. I know from experience it is up to working people to save themselves. And the only way is through a strong, working class movement (Shepherd, 145).

As a direct result of the protests, the state created a Factory Investigating Commission. New York WTUL President Mary Dreier was the only woman on the commission; field investigators included Rose Schneiderman and Frances Perkins, later secretary of labor under Franklin Roosevelt.

Even as the commission began its investigations, the owners of the Triangle Company, Isaac Harris and Max Blanck, reopened in a nearby building under almost identical conditions. Indicted for first- and second-degree manslaughter, the two men did not go on trial until December, when most middle-class memory of the carnage had dimmed. An all-male, middle-class jury acquitted the two men. One juror, a businessman, commented comfortably,

I cannot see that anyone was responsible for the disaster. It seems to me to have been an act of the Almighty. . . . I paid great attention to the witnesses while they were on the stand. I think the girls who worked there were not as intelligent as those in other walks of life and were therefore the more susceptible to panic (Wertheimer, 315).

In the years after the Triangle fire, Schneiderman began to recognize the limitations of the strike as a tool of widespread industrial reform, and she placed increasing faith in reform legislation. Concomitant with her interest in legislation was a new emphasis on the necessity of women's suffrage. In 1912 she offered her services to the women's suffrage campaign. "I wasn't going to parade under false colors," she recalled, "so I told [them] that I was a socialist and a trade unionist who looked on the ballot as a tool in the hands of working women with which through legislation, they would correct the terrible conditions existing in industry" (Kessler-Harris, 168).

Schneiderman was a tireless and effective suffrage worker. A local suffrage campaigner reported on Schneiderman's efforts for the 1912 Ohio state suffrage bill:

Here in Cincinnati everyone I think who is interested at all is working like a Trojan. But no one has ever touched the hearts of the masses like Miss Rose Schneiderman. . . . We have had splendid speakers here but not one who impressed people as she did. Strong men sat with tears rolling down their cheeks. Her pathos and earnestness held the audiences spellbound (Wertheimer, 284).

From her experiences with the WTUL, Schneiderman brought to her suffrage work a passionate belief that middle-class women had a profound
moral responsibility to reach out to their laboring sisters. She constantly
sought to remind the more comfortable women of the daily realities the
working woman faced:

> I want to say to you suffragists, especially to some of you who are saying
> that the working women are not taking part in this great suffrage move-
> ment, and that they are not coming to the fore as they should, how can
> they? Working nine, ten hours a day and then on their return home at-
> tending to their home duties, where is the time for them to take active part
> in even a suffrage movement? . . . it seems to me that it is up to the women
> of leisure who are working in some way in the suffrage movement not to
> cry out or protest against the working woman's indifference to suffrage
> but to recognize her distinct contribution as an organized worker and to
> be ready to stand by her in her heavily handicapped struggle to better her
> conditions. . . . I call upon you women to stand ready to help the working
> woman. Not to ask her to come out and help you get woman suffrage but
> to go to her and offer her your help to win woman suffrage. Show her that
> you understand her difficulties, are in sympathy with her struggle, eager
> to help her when the opportunity offers; that you want woman suffrage to
> give the working woman the much needed weapon to the end that all
> women together may work for the common good of mankind (Anderson,
> 157).

In 1918 Schneiderman was elected president of the New York WTUL;
the following year she became vice-president of the national WTUL,
served as a delegate to the Paris Peace Conference, and helped organize
the International Congress of Working Women. Increasingly, Schneiderman placed her faith in the power of education. She encouraged a growing emphasis within the WTUL on workers' education, working to set
up small schools that would train young women as activists and union
organizers. Elected to the board of Bryn Mawr College, Schneiderman
helped to design the experimental Bryn Mawr Summer School for
Women Workers; the school, which functioned from 1921 until 1939, was
the first of its kind in the country. It offered seventy-five working women
between the ages of eighteen and thirty-five a free eight-week summer
program that combined academic courses with classes in union organizing and participatory democracy. Schneiderman related proudly that
the first group of students promptly organized in behalf of the college's
nonunionized dormitory housekeeping staff. They demanded—and
got—an eight-hour day for the school's domestic workers. College President M. Carey Thomas was so impressed by their unified, forceful
presentation that she instituted an eight-hour day for the entire non-
academic staff. In addition, Schneiderman served on the boards of the

Brookwood Labor College in Katonah, New York, the Pioneer Youth of America, and the Manumit School for workers' children.

One of the major pleasures of Schneiderman's life was her deep friendship with Eleanor Roosevelt, who had joined the WTUL in 1922. Schneiderman became a frequent guest of the Roosevelts, both in New York City and Hyde Park. Her thoughtful, honest companionship offered the Roosevelts a totally frank, unsparing perspective on labor history they might never otherwise have gained. Years later, First Lady Eleanor Roosevelt commented to an AFL-CIO convention that Rose had taught her all she knew about trade unionism. "It was one of the very proud moments of my life," wrote Schneiderman (Schneiderman, 257).

In 1933 Franklin Roosevelt named Rose Schneiderman to the labor advisory board of the National Recovery Administration, the only woman so appointed. For two years, until the NRA was declared unconstitutional, she concentrated on designing wage and hour codes for various industries in which the workforce was predominantly female. In 1935 Schneiderman returned to New York and to the WTUL, reinvigorating the League's organizing work among exploited laundry workers. A confirmed believer in the necessity of protective legislation, she lobbied powerfully for the eight-hour day and the minimum wage, both of which measures became New York law during the 1930s. In addition to her work with the League, Schneiderman served from 1937 to 1943 as the secretary of the New York State Department of Labor; ultimately, this administrative job proved too remote and antiseptic for her, and she resigned.

An active member of the New York League until it disbanded in 1955, Schneiderman retired to a quiet, possibly lonely private life in Manhattan. She dictated her autobiography when she was eighty-five years old. That same year she entered the Jewish Home for the Aged in New York, where she died five years later.

Rose Schneiderman grew from a solemn, hesitant, poorly educated thirteen-year-old laborer into the most influential woman in the American labor movement, the confidante of presidents. In the process she learned to balance her early socialist dreams against New Deal realities, to withstand prejudice and outright abuse from union men without losing her belief in the union movement. Her unwavering faith in the dignity and capability of the community of women illuminated her entire life.

References

Anderson, Judith, ed. *Outspoken Women: Speeches by American Women Reformers, 1635–1935*. Dubuque, IA: Kendall/Hunt Publishing, 1984.

Dye, Nancy Schrom. *As Equals and Sisters: Feminism, the Labor Movement, and the*

Women's Trade Union League of New York. Columbia: University of Missouri Press, 1980.

Eisenstein, Sarah. *Give Us Bread But Give Us Roses: Working Women's Consciousness in the United States, 1890 to the First World War*. London: Routledge & Kegan Paul, 1983.

Jacoby, Robin Miller. "The WTUL and American Feminism." In Milton Carter and Bruce Laurie, eds. *Class, Sex, and the Woman Worker*. Westport, CT: Greenwood Press, 1977.

Kessler-Harris, Alice. "Rose Schneiderman and the Limits of Women's Trade Unionism." In Melvyn Dubovsky and Warren Van Tine, eds. *Labor Leaders in America*. Urbana: University of Illinois Press, 1987.

Lagemann, Ellen Condliffe. *A Generation of Women: Education in the Lives of Progressive Reformers*. Cambridge, MA: Harvard University Press, 1979.

Schneiderman, Rose. With Lucy Goldthwaite. *All for One*. New York: Paul S. Eriksson, 1967.

Shepherd, William. "Eyewitness at Triangle." In Leon Stein, ed. *The Triangle Fire*, Philadelphia: J. B. Lippincott Co., 1962.

Sicherman, Barbara, ed. *Notable American Women: The Modern Period*. Cambridge, MA: Belknap Press, 1980.

Stein, Leon. *Out of the Sweatshop: The Struggle for Industrial Democracy*. New York: Quadrangle Books, 1977.

Stein, Leon, ed. *The Triangle Fire*. Philadelphia: J. B. Lippincott Co., 1962.

Wertheimer, Barbara Mazer. *We were There: The Story of Working Women in New York*. New York: Pantheon Books, 1977.

Whitman, Alden, ed. *American Reformers*. New York: H. H. Wilson, 1985.

Tye Leung Schulze

(1887–1972)

Chinese American Community Activist

Tye Leung Schulze was born in San Francisco's Chinatown, into a world that held a deeply hostile image of her and offered rigid, limiting expectations for her. She repeatedly defied the limitations imposed on her, transcending barriers, achieving a self-created life of honor, dignity, and service. No national organization or major legislation bears her name. Her legacy is one of determined belief in human worth, in a kinship that transcends artificial borders, in the steady, dedicated assault on prejudice and bigotry.

Tye Leung Schulze
Courtesy, Louise Schulze Lee.

The California into which Tye Leung Schulze was born was roiling with anti-Asian hostility. A generation before, the first Chinese immigrants had been welcomed as a source of inexpensive labor and praised for their docility, industriousness, and politeness. The Burlingame Treaty of 1868 guaranteed their right to immigrate. But the very virtues for which they had been praised began to be perceived as threats to American labor, and anti-Chinese rhetoric soon spewed from newspapers and politicians. In a telling phrase, the Chinese were declared "morally a far worse class to have among us than the negro" (Low, 2). Local and statewide agitation by groups like Dennis Kearney's infamous Asiatic Exclusion League culminated in 1882 with the passage of the federal Chinese Exclusion Act. Ten years later the Geary Act finalized what had been a temporary prohibition on immigration, stripped Chinese in California of the protection of the courts, required all resident Chinese to carry certificates of legal residency, and denied them bail in *habeas corpus* cases. When the Supreme Court found all these measures consistent with the Constitution, the bitter phrase "not a Chinaman's chance" became popular (Low, 75). The Panic of 1893 and the consequent depression and unemployment added a desperate, violent tone to the well-established anti-Asian sentiment on the West Coast.

Into this atmosphere, in 1887, Tye Leung was born. Her family, which included her parents, eight children, and the elderly aunt and uncle who had brought her father from China, were crowded into two rooms. Her father, a shoemaker, earned twenty dollars a month. Shortly before Tye's birth, the city of San Francisco, to avoid having Chinese children attend white schools, had created a separate, segregated elementary school for "Mongolian" children. There was no provision for the higher education of any nonwhite children. Although most of her siblings had no chance to attend school, Tye Leung seems to have been more determined. She was allowed to attend English classes at the Presbyterian Mission on Stockton Street, where her eagerness and intelligence attracted the kind attention of several teachers. Years later, Tye recalled, "The teacher, who was Miss Wesley, later Mrs. Cook, was very fond of me. She took a liking to me and got me clothes, bathed me, took me to different church meetings, and showed me off." Tye calculated that she had had the equivalent of a sixth-grade education (Tye, n.p.).

When Tye's oldest sister was thirteen years old, her parents arranged her marriage to a much older man living in Butte, Montana. The sister eloped with a boy her own age instead, and Tye's parents expected Tye, then no more than twelve years old, to take her place. Horrified, Tye also resisted; she turned for support to the only place where she had felt valued and encouraged as an individual: the Presbyterian Mission.

At this point Tye's life intersected with one of the most colorful, controversial figures of Chinatown history, Donaldina Cameron. Cameron, a Scot born in New Zealand, had come to San Francisco in 1895 to teach sewing at the Presbyterian Mission. She became obsessed with the appalling situation of young girls and women brought from China and sold into slavery in Chinatown, and she launched a life-long personal mission to rescue the girls and eradicate slavery. She regarded Tye Leung as another rescued slave; Tye regarded Cameron as her savior and benefactress. Tye stayed for years at the mission. She perfected her English and became an invaluable aide and interpreter for Cameron, accompanying her on daring rescue raids and dealing with police departments and the courts. Cameron reported:

> Her greatest success in dealing with and winning these unfortunate Chinese girls she has helped to rescue lay in the fact of her keen appreciation of their ignorance and helpless condition, and a loving sympathy which is ever reaching out to help and save them. There is hardly a court in San Francisco or Oakland where Tye Leung is not known and welcomed as an excellent interpreter. The police departments on both sides of the bay recognize her efficiency and honesty. There is no one better known and respected by the officers of the immigration service than is this small, winsome Chinese girl. All Chinatown knows her well, and strangest of all, nearly all Chinatown loves her, though it is well known that Tye leads nearly every rescue party from the Mission which finds and seizes slaves worth three thousand dollars and then follows the rescue, with the strongest evidence in court to convict the owners.
> "Ah Tye does not take bribes," is the talismanic password that saves her. No wonder the Occidental Board [in charge of Presbyterian missionary activity] holds very dear this "child of its love and care" (Cameron, n.p.).

Cameron was famous for her dedication, courage, and devotion to the young women she rescued; however, she was limited by a rigidly doctrinal Christianity and implicitly racist assumptions that viewed all of Chinese culture with contempt and abhorrence. Perhaps one of the greatest proofs of Tye Leung's strength is her ability to retain a sense of loving identity with her community despite overwhelmingly negative messages from her beloved teacher at the Presbyterian Home.

In 1910 Tye Leung became the first Chinese American to pass the civil service examinations. She was appointed an interpreter at Angel Island, San Francisco's equivalent of Ellis Island. Two years later, shortly after the state of California granted women the vote, Tye Leung received nation-wide news coverage as the first Chinese woman to vote. "Celestial Maid cast her vote," declared the *San Francisco Call*. Newspapers on both coasts, many of them mangling her name, managed simultaneously to congratulate her and to condescend to her. ("Ah Tie is a very human little girl, one of the cleverest and prettiest children of her race that have ever grown up in America" [*The Daily News*, May 20, 1912].) One quoted her glowingly:

> My first vote?—Oh, yes, I thought long over that. I studied; I read about all your men who wished to be president. I learned about the new laws. I wanted to KNOW what was right, not to act blindly. . . . I think it right we should all try to learn, not vote blindly, since we have been given this right to say which man we think is the greatest. . . . I think too that we women are more careful than the men. We want to do our whole duty more. I do not think it is just the newness that makes us like that. It is conscience (*ibid.*).

"Epoch in the Sex's Emancipation," crowed the *San Francisco Examiner*, proudly calling Tye Leung's vote "the last word in the modern movement for the complete enfranchisement of women. . . . It was the latest achievement in the great American work of amalgamating and lifting up all the races of the earth" (*San Francisco Examiner*, May 15, 1912).

For Tye Leung, there might have been a certain bitter irony in such declarations of "amalgamating and lifting up all the races." Working at Angel Island, she had met and come to love an immigration official, Charles Frederick Schulze. California was one of fifteen states that legally prohibited a Caucasian from marrying a person of Asian descent; the young couple faced disapproval from both families as well. Years later, Tye commented gently, "When two people are in love, they don't think of the future or what happens." In October of 1913, Tye Leung and Schulze traveled to Vancouver, Washington state, to be legally married. The occurrence was rare enough to be newsworthy. "Little Dan Cupid does strange tricks," "White Man Weds Chinese Maiden," read the headlines.

When they returned to San Francisco, both Schulze and Tye Leung lost their jobs, as they had no doubt known they would. Schulze struggled for years with a variety of jobs until he finally found a decent position as a telephone repairman. He died in 1935. Tye herself, while raising two sons and two daughters, worked wherever she could, spending several years as a bookkeeper at the Chinese Hospital. Her linguistic gifts and compassion drew her into social work with the patients, where her knowledge and skill were invaluable.

In 1926 Tye launched a new career as a phone operator for the Pacific Telephone's China Exchange. Service was very direct and personal. There were few phones, no dials, no prefixes. Tye knew where everyone lived, and where they probably were if they weren't at home. For almost twenty years, until the phone company modernized during World War II, Tye was a Chinatown institution.

During and after the war, Tye found her language skills in great demand again. And again, she was always willing, always giving. "The thing I remember about my mom," her son recalled years later, "she was always asked to interpret. GI brides, immigration, court cases. She never refused to help" (Wong).

Throughout her life, Tye Leung Schulze was a committed, selfless presence in her community. She did not see herself as a hero or martyr. She believed in each individual's dignity and worth, and she lived her life unflinchingly according to that belief. After her death at the age of eighty-four, her son Frederick commented, "My mother was an unusual woman" (Wong).

References

"Ah Tie, Once a Slave Girl, the First Chinese Woman to Vote in America for a President." *The Daily News*, May 20, 1912.

Cameron, Donaldina. "Tye Leung, Interpreter of the Presbyterian Mission Home, Appointed to a Government Position." *Pacific Presbyterian*, February 24, 1910.

Hogan, Mary Ann. "Breaking Stereotypes of Chinese Women." *The Tribune* (Oakland, CA), August 18, 1983.

Low, Victor. *The Unimpressible Race: A Century of Educational Struggle by the Chinese in San Francisco*. San Francisco: East/West Publishing, 1982.

"San Francisco has Only Chinese Woman Voter in History." *San Francisco Examiner*, May 15, 1912.

Schulze, Tye Leung. Autobiographical Sketch. Unpublished.

Wong, Ken. "Tye Leung Schulze: A Heroine Among Bay Area Women." *San Francisco Examiner*, April 2, 1980, p. A-2.

Yung, Judy. *Chinese Women in America*. Seattle: University of Washington Press, 1986.

DAVID WALKER

(1795[?]–August 6, 1830)

Abolitionist

David Walker, the child of a slave father and a free mother, lived a life of paradox, dedication, and defiance. In an environment that denigrated and humiliated him daily, he grew up with an unshakable sense of pride in himself and in his race. Despite almost insurmountable obstacles, he managed to educate himself and to mature into an articulate, erudite activist. Shunned at first by many African Americans as well as by white abolitionists, he emerges from history as the architect of militant abolitionism. His uncompromising, unflinching depiction of the realities of American slavery set off storms of panic across the South and changed forever the language of the antislavery movement.

David Walker was born in Wilmington, North Carolina, sometime in the late 18th century. Henry Highland Garnet, who interviewed Walker's widow years after his death, gave his birth date as 1785, but also stated that he was thirty-four years old at the time of his death in 1830. Subsequent secondary sources such as the *Dictionary of American Negro Biography* have all drawn their information from Garnet. However, recent research casts strong doubt on the accuracy of the original date: three contemporaneous newspaper accounts of Walker's death—in the *Boston Daily Courier*, the *Boston Daily Advertiser*, and the *New England Palladium*—all list his age as thirty-three at the time of death. It is highly probable that Garnet's original date is in error, and that Walker was actually born in later 1795 or early 1796.

Legally, Walker was assigned the free status of his mother. In reality, in North Carolina as throughout the South, the conditions of free African Americans were so difficult that they were scarcely distinguishable from slaves. The free black had always been an anomaly within the ideological constellation of America. Unlike earlier Spanish slavery in the West Indies and South America, English slavery depended heavily for justification on theories of profound racial inferiority and on the concomitant notion that Africans were simply unable to take care of themselves alone. The free black community represented a constant contradiction to these concepts and was indeed perceived as a dangerous threat to the existing power structure. As a result, they were closely monitored and severely restricted. A 1785 law in North Carolina required all free blacks to wear a distinctive badge on the left shoulder, embroidered with the word "FREE." Their contacts with slaves were held at an absolute minimum; free blacks convicted of "idleness" or other minor crimes could be sold into lifetime bondage. The successful Haitian revolt in 1791 caused panic in the South and further convinced slaveowners of the need to control all Africans. From 1800 on, an increasing number of slave rebellions in Virginia, North and South Carolina, and elsewhere generated an atmosphere of unremitting fear and anxiety; the result for both slave and free black was an ever more hostile and repressive environment.

Walker survived in these surroundings into young adulthood, but he knew that he could not endure his entire life in constant fear and danger. He described his decision to leave:

If I remain in this bloody land, I will not live long, as true as God reigns, I will be avenged. This is not the place for me, no, I must leave this part of the country. It will be a great trial for me to live on the same soil where so many men are in slavery, certainly I cannot remain where I must hear their chains continually, and, where I must encounter the results of their hypocritical enslavers. Go I must (Aptheker, "Militant," 53).

Walker's later writings offer evidence of wide travel. He mentions intimate contact with the free black communities in Philadelphia, New York, and Baltimore. During his time in Philadelphia, he was deeply impressed by the fervor and integrity of Richard Allen, the founder of African Methodism; throughout his adult life Walker remained a passionate Christian, convinced that the slave's sufferings paralleled the Crucifixion and indicated a special, higher moral understanding among African Americans.

Sometime before 1825, Walker joined the tiny community of free blacks in Boston; a business directory in that year lists "David Walker, clothes dealer." The free black community in Boston numbered fewer than two thousand, only 3% of the population. They suffered from the generally pervasive racist attitudes of white Americans, as did free African Americans across the North. "Though they have long since ceased to be slaves," commented a New Yorker in 1853, "they are still a wholly-distinct and an outcast class in the community." An English laborer in New York before the Civil War reported, "I have met with a few well-conditioned men who look upon the blacks as rational beings; but the strongly expressed opinion of the majority was, that they are a soulless race . . . some of these people would shoot a black man with as little regard to moral consequences as they would a wild hog." From Philadelphia, another English visitor declared, "Only the warmly philanthropic view them as men" (Curry, 83).

In the face of this widespread hostility, and despite the resultant discrimination in employment, education, and housing, the black community of Boston retained a remarkably cohesive sense of identity and pride. David Walker came to play a prominent role in shaping and directing the energy and pride of free black Boston. Walker was a tall, slender, graceful man with an intensity and dedication that were contagious. He was "possessed of a noble and courageous spirit . . . ardently attached to the cause of liberty" (Garnet, vii).

In 1826 Walker was among the founders of the General Coloured Association of Massachusetts, which organized to address issues of concern to African Americans. As a frequent speaker at meetings, Walker articulated the themes that drove him all his life: the absolute evil of slavery, the righteousness of race pride, and the overriding need for unity. He continued to emphasize this message as a contributor to and agent for the first newspaper published by African Americans, *Freedom's Journal*. The editors, John Russwurm and Samuel E. Cornish, sympathized with Walker's insistence on unity and self-reliance. Their first editorial, on March 16, 1827, declared, "We wish to plead our own cause. Too long have others spoken for us. . . . The civil rights of a people being of the greatest value, it shall ever be our duty to vindicate our brethren, when oppressed" (Aptheker, *Documentary*, 82).

By 1828 Walker was a well-known figure in the African American community. He was respected for his learning and his unstinting generosity; his impassioned speeches were an anticipated part of many public gatherings within the community. His used clothing business was doing well, he had recently married, and his life was relatively secure and prosperous. He turned all his considerable energy and passion to what would be his life's work, the summation of all he had observed and studied and believed—the 76-page antislavery tract known as *Walker's Appeal*. Walker completed his *Appeal* late in 1829. His full title was *David Walker's Appeal, in Four Articles; Together with a Preamble, to the Coloured Citizens of the World, but in Particular, and Very Expressly, to Those of the United States of America*. Walker printed the pamphlet at his own expense and arranged for its secret distribution, especially in the South. Within a year it had gone through three editions.

There had been condemnations of slavery in America ever since the mid-17th century; perhaps the best-known of these early protests was that of the Germantown Friends, dating from 1688. Throughout the Revolutionary period, there were always people of conscience who recognized the discrepancy between the rhetoric of the Revolution and the reality of slavery. In 1764, Bostonian James Otis affirmed blacks' inalienable right to freedom; six years later, again in Boston, Isaac Skillman demanded the immediate liberation of all slaves and asserted their right to rebel. When the Haitian Revolution occurred, Bostonian J. P. Martin viewed it as a logical continuation of the American and French revolutions: "Let us be consistent, Americans, if we justify our own conduct in the late glorious revolution; let us justify those who, in a cause like ours, fight with equal bravery" (Aptheker, "Militant," 51). And especially in Massachusetts, there was a long history of protesting petitions addressed to various legislative bodies from individual African Americans, both slave and free.

Walker's *Appeal* represented a radical departure from these antecedents. For the first time, an African American addressed other African Americans, not whites. He did not apologize, petition meekly, or humbly assure his "betters" that he had no desire for economic and social equality. Rather, he appealed to "the revolutionary consciousness of the oppressed, not to the Christian conscience of the oppressor" (Bennett, 74). In dense, astringent prose heavily laced with learned allusions from the Bible and from ancient history, Walker outlined the condition of Africans in America; he discussed the origins of the situation, and he offered a solution. He described his own motivation:

> Having travelled over a considerable portion of these United States, and having, in the course of my travels, taken the most accurate observations of things as they exist—the result of my observations has warranted the

full and unshakable conviction, that we (coloured people of these United
States) are the most degraded, wretched, and abject set of beings that ever
lived since the world began. . . . I appeal to Heaven for my motive in writing—who knows that my object is, if possible, to awaken in the breasts of
my afflicted, degraded, and slumbering brethren, a spirit of inquiry and
investigation respecting our miseries and wretchedness in this *Republican
Land of Liberty!!!!!* (Walker, 2).

Walker delineated four basic sources for his people's wretchedness: slavery, ignorance, the hypocrisy of white Christians, and the "colonizing
plan." One of his major aims was to refute any claims of lesser humanity
for Africans. He cited examples of white rapaciousness and cruelty
throughout history and claimed a moral superiority for blacks. He raged
against the viciousness of white prejudice, against the inadequate education available to most black children, against the discrimination that
condemned most free blacks to menial occupations. As always, his underlying message was a call for racial unity and shared responsibility. It
was the inescapable duty of blacks to take responsibility for freeing all
their people:

I advance it therefore to you, not as a *problematical,* but as an unshaken
and for ever immovable *fact,* that your full glory and happiness, as well as
all other coloured people under Heaven, shall never be fully consummated,
but with the *entire emancipation of your enslaved brethren all over the world.*
. . . Our greatest happiness shall consist in working for the salvation of our
whole body (Walker, 30).

Throughout, Walker remained firmly convinced of the love and righteousness of God. "I ask every man who has a heart, and is blessed with
the privilege of believing—Is not God a God of justice to *all* his crea-
tures?" (Walker, 5).

Walker was especially outraged by what he deemed the perversion of
Christian doctrine that both justified slaveowners and denied slaves access to true Christianity. All unsupervised slave gatherings worried
slaveowners, and slave preachers were considered potential troublemakers. If slaves frequently resonated with the revolutionary egalitarian implications of Christianity, their masters were only too aware of the fact.
Walker described slave prayer meetings violently terminated by whites:

[T]yrants, calling themselves *patrols,* would also convene and wait almost
in breathless silence for the poor coloured people to commence singing
and praying to the Lord our God, as soon as they had commenced, the
wretches would burst in upon them and drag them out and commence
beating them as they would rattlesnakes (Walker, 37).

Walker, a profoundly religious man, believed in both human sinfulness and the possibility of human redemption. For him, the original sin was avarice. He could find no other ultimate explanation for the existence of slavery; he insisted that all other explanations—theories of racial inferiority, of dependence, of civilizing the savage—were nothing but *a posteriori* rationalizations:

> I have been for years troubling the pages of historians, to find out what our fathers have done to the *white Christians of America*, to merit such . . . punishment as they have inflicted on them, and do continue to inflict on us their children. . . . I have come . . . to the immovable conclusion, that they (Americans) have, and do continue to punish us for nothing else, but for enriching them and their country, for I cannot conceive of anything else. Nor will I ever believe otherwise, until the Lord shall convince me (Walker, 14).

Walker reserved a special contempt for the American Colonization Society, founded in 1817, which was dedicated to shipping as many blacks as possible to Liberia. He insisted that African Americans had built America and had as much right—if not more—as whites to be here. "America is more our country, than it is whites—we have enriched it with our *blood and tears*. The greatest riches in all America have risen from our blood and tears:—and will they drive us from our property and homes, which we have earned with our blood?" (Walker, 76). Hauntingly, this passage resonates with Paul Robeson's angry declaration before the House Committee on Un-American Activities in 1947. As the Cold War hysteria mounted, Robeson's socialism and his continuing condemnation of segregation exposed him to the wrath of HUAC, where he was asked why he did not leave the country, since he was so critical of much in American society. Robeson exploded, "Because my father was a slave, and my people died to build this country and I am going to stay here and have a part of it just like you" (Robeson, 205).

The most radical element in Walker's *Appeal* was his direct call for armed revolt. To Walker's mind, the original violence lay in the fact of enslavement itself and in the brutality it engendered; he could see no immorality in a violent act aimed at the overthrow of unspeakable evil and injustice. He recognized the numbing effect of prolonged oppression and deprivation, the sense of helplessness and ultimately of a distorted affection for the oppressor; he urged slaves to overcome this deadening hopelessness and to retrieve their dignity in rebellion:

> Now, I ask you, had not you rather be killed than to be a slave to a tyrant, who takes the life of your mother, wife, and dear little children? Look upon your mother, wife and children, and answer God Almighty! and believe this, that it is no more harm for you to kill a man, who is trying to kill

you, than it is for you to take a drink of water when thirsty; in fact, the man who will stand still and let another murder him, is worse than an infidel, and, if he has common sense, ought not to be pitied (Walker, 74).

Despite this call for violent rebellion, Walker held on to a thin, fragile hope for the possibility of white repentance. He still believed that reconciliation was possible:

> Treat us like men, and there is no danger but we will all live in peace and happiness together. . . . Treat us like men, and we will be your friends. And there is no doubt in my mind, but that the whole of the past will be sunk into oblivion, and we yet, under God, will become a united and happy people. The whites may say it is impossible, but remember that nothing is impossible with God (Walker, 70).

The reaction to the *Appeal* was thunderous and vitriolic. Across the South, state legislatures met to consider ways to prevent its distribution. The mayor of Savannah wrote to Boston's mayor, Harrison Otis, demanding that Walker be arrested. (Otis replied that, although all decent people in Boston despised the *Appeal*, Walker had broken no laws and unfortunately couldn't be arrested.) The governor of North Carolina, with unintentional irony, condemned the pamphlet as "an open appeal to [slaves'] natural love of liberty . . . and throughout expressing sentiments totally subversive of all subordination in our slaves" (Litwack, 234). Fearfully, the Charleston *Gazette* queried, "Will these wretches never be quiet? Have they no apprehensions that they may be destroyed in the very flames they are looking to enkindle?" (Pease and Pease, 288). In Georgia, South Carolina, and Louisiana, men found with multiple copies of the pamphlet were convicted of distributing seditious literature, fined $1,000, and sentenced to a year in prison. Georgia forbade black sailors from coming ashore in its ports, while South Carolina allowed them ashore but imprisoned them while their ships were in harbor. North Carolina made it a criminal offense to teach slaves to read. Throughout the South, slaveowners who insisted vehemently that their slaves were simple and content took desperate measures to keep those happy slaves from any contact with Walker's inflammatory pamphlet.

The *Appeal* caused consternation even among white abolitionists. One of the leading Quaker abolitionists, Benjamin Lundy, condemned its call to violence. His protegé, William Lloyd Garrison, was ambivalent: while he considered it a "most injudicious publication," he acknowledged that it contained "many valuable truths and seasonable warnings." Only a few years later, one of the first issues of Garrison's newspaper, *The Liberator*, reprinted entire sections of the *Appeal*. Samuel May, perhaps the most widely respected abolitionist of the period, declared that "the excitement which had become so general and so furious against the Abolitionists throughout the slaveholding states was owing in no small measure to David Walker" (Quarles, 17). Walker's radicalism frightened even some blacks; Garnet reported, "He had many enemies, and not a few were his brethren whose cause he espoused. They said he went too far and was making trouble" (Garnet, vi).

Walker was infamous; a group of Georgia slaveholders put a $1,000 price on his head—the price allegedly increased tenfold if Walker were delivered alive. Friends urged Walker to take refuge in Canada, but he refused. At a dinner in Boston celebrating the *Appeal's* publication, Walker declared, "I will stand my ground. Somebody has to die in this cause. I may be doomed . . . but it is not in me to falter if I can promote the work of emancipation" (Katz, 128). His premonition proved only too accurate: in the summer of 1830, shortly after the *Appeal* had gone into a third edition, Walker was found dead on the street near his clothing store. Although no hard evidence has been discovered, his friends were convinced that he had been poisoned.

Walker redefined the shape of American abolitionism. His own merciless appraisal of slavery and of the hypocrisy that perpetuated it set a standard for other abolitionists, black and white. Despite his Quakerism, Garrison admitted, "Of all men living, however, our slaves have the best reason to assert their rights by violent measures, inasmuch as they are more oppressed than others" (Aptheker, "Militant," 55). In 1833 Garrison's American Antislavery Society became the first such organization to welcome both blacks and women; within five years, it had 1,346 branches nation-wide and one quarter of a million members. In Boston, addressing a meeting of African Americans in 1833, the reformer and educator Maria W. Stewart exhorted her audience in Walker's name: "Where is the man that has distinguished himself in these modern days by acting wholly in defense of African rights and liberty? There was one; although he sleeps, his memory lives" (Stuckey, 137).

References

Aptheker, Herbert, ed. *Documentary History of the Negro People in the United States.* New York: Citadel Press, 1969. Vol. I.

———. "Militant Abolitionists." In Sebastian O. Mezu, ed. *Black Leaders of the Centuries.* Buffalo, NY: Black Academy Press, 1970.

Bennett, Lerone, Jr. *Pioneers in Protest.* Chicago: Johnson Pub., 1968.

Curry, Leonard P. *The Free Black in Urban America, 1800–1850: The Shadow of the Dream.* Chicago: University of Chicago Press, 1981.

Garnet, Henry Highland. *Walker's Appeal, with a Brief Sketch of his Life.* New York: J. H. Tobitt, 1848.

Jacobs, Donald M. "David Walker: Boston Race Leader, 1825–1830." *Essex Institute Historical Collections* 107, 1 (1970): 94–107.

Katz, William Loren. *Breaking the Chains: African-American Slave Resistance*. New York: Atheneum, 1990.

Litwack, Leon. *North of Slavery: The Negro in the Free States, 1790–1860*. Chicago: University of Chicago Press, 1961.

Pease, William H. and Jane H. Pease. "Walker's Appeal Comes to Charleston: A Note and Documents." *Journal of Negro History* 59(July, 1974): 287–292.

Quarles, Benjamin. *The Black Abolitionists*. New York: Oxford University Press, 1969.

Robeson, Susan. *The Whole World in His Hands: A Pictorial Biography of Paul Robeson*. Engelwood, NJ: Citadel, 1981.

Stuckey, Sterling. *Slave Culture: Nationalist Theory and the Foundations of Black America*. New York: Oxford University Press, 1987.

Walker, David. *David Walker's Appeal, in Four Articles: Together with a Preamble, to the Coloured Citizens of the World, but in Particular and Very Expressly, to Those of the United States of America*, 3rd ed. Boston, 1830.

GEORGE HENRY WHITE

(December 18, 1852–December 28, 1918)

Civil Rights and Anti-lynching Activist

George Henry White was the last survivor of a small, brave, honorable fraternity—African Americans who served in the United States Congress in the decades after Reconstruction. From 1870 to 1901 twenty-two African American men were elected to Congress throughout the South. Half of them were former slaves; amazingly, half of them also had some college education, and several of them had completed degrees. Republican congressman, senator, and presidential candidate James G. Blaine, who had worked with a number of these men, described them later: "The colored men who took seats in both the Senate and the House did not appear ignorant or helpless. They were as a rule studious, earnest, ambitious men whose public conduct . . . would be honorable to any race" (Katz, 265). In the last quarter of the century, the black congressmen faced a rising, acid tide of racism and white supremacist ideology. By the time George White took his House seat in 1897, the current throughout the country seemed to be running swiftly against African Americans, who responded sometimes with desperate, self-demeaning attempts at conciliation. To his credit, George White unfailingly assumed his dignity and worth as a human being. He accepted the role of lone spokesman of his people in the Congress, and he consistently functioned as an insistent moral compass in a period of exceptional brutality, corruption, and ethical amnesia.

George Henry White
Courtesy of the Library of Congress.

The task of supporting four million newly liberated slaves in their difficult evolution into citizenship was the greatest challenge American society faced in the late 19th century. Tragically, the absence of an underlying moral consensus and of a humane, rational understanding of race created divisions, fears, hypocrisy, and misunderstandings that haunt us today. Shortly after the Civil War, Southern legislatures enacted "black codes" designed to keep the former slaves subservient and disenfranchised. In response, Congress imposed military control over the entire South and encouraged active black participation in all the functions and levels of government. One of the definitive public articulations of radical Northern ideals was the 1875 Civil Rights Act, which guaranteed African Americans equal enjoyment of public conveyances, theaters, and restaurants, among other things. This was the final Reconstruction legislation to protect civil rights.

In 1876 Rutherford B. Hayes was elected president in a controversial campaign in which his Democratic opponent, Samuel Tilden, actually won the popular vote in a number of key Southern states. In a remarkably cynical deal, Hayes promised to withdraw all federal troops from the South in exchange for the electoral college votes of the states in question. The agreed-upon withdrawal of the troops in 1877 signaled the formal end of Reconstruction and initiated a long, painful, shameful period of corruption, violence, betrayal, and virulent racism in the North as well as the South.

The 1880s saw a deliberate, concerted campaign in the national popular press arguing that Southerners understood their "Negro problem" in ways that Northerners could not and that the region should be left alone to achieve its own solutions to the "problem." In the era before radio or television, these magazines, with national circulations, exerted enormous influence over public opinion. At the same time, the scientific community obliged with racial theories and grotesquely distorted Darwinian "survival of the fittest" (by which Darwin had referred to entire species). It seemed as though all sectors of American society were being educated to accept doctrines of divinely ordained white supremacy, cultivated from the seed of earlier expansionist "Manifest Destiny" and bearing, logically, the poisoned fruit of imperialism. In 1883 the Supreme Court declared the Civil Rights Act unconstitutional. From that point on, African American citizens were increasingly stripped of their rights and officially denied access to any legal protection. Their prominent leaders were under terrific pressures and faced unbearably painful ethical dilemmas in trying to decide how best to serve their people.

White Southerner apologists created, embellished, and actively promulgated a distorted image of ignorant, lazy, incompetent, vulgar black politicians who had no right to the offices they occupied. This vicious caricature was never more mistaken than in the case of George Henry White. White, born a slave in Rosindale, North Carolina, was always eager to learn. While working on the family farm and as a cask-maker, White struggled after emancipation to take full advantage of local public schools. He attended Howard University for four years, supporting himself by teaching school during the summers. At first he studied medicine, but turned from that to liberal arts and law, and graduated with a teaching certificate. After graduation, he taught school in New Bern and Raleigh, while reading law with a superior court judge. Two years later, he passed the Bar examination and opened an office in New Bern. Mixing teaching and a small law practice, he became increasingly involved in local Republican politics.

In 1880 White was elected to the North Carolina house of representatives, where he agitated successfully for more support for public education and better training for black teachers. Elected to the state senate in 1884, he continued to stress the need for improved educational facilities, especially for black children. He urged federal support for education and also served on committees dealing with treatment of the mentally ill, insurance, and judicial reform. White was known and respected throughout the state; in 1885 he was elected solicitor and prosecutor for the Second Judicial District in North Carolina, an office he held until 1894. Two years later, White won a seat in the United States House of Representatives.

When George White, tall, dark-skinned, and confident, walked into the House in January of 1899, he was the only African American in the room. If he found this daunting, he never showed it. On the contrary, from the beginning he was outspoken, assertive, demanding, proud, and utterly beyond apologetics. Confronting an early boast of white superiority from the Mississippi delegation, he declared:

> Yes, by force of circumstances, we are your inferiors. Give us 240 years the start of you, give us your labor for 240 years without compensation, give us the wealth that the brawny arm of the black man made for you, give us the education that his unpaid labor gave your boys and girls, and we will not be begging, we will not be in a position to be sneered at as aliens or members of an inferior race (Christopher, 164).

White refused to accept the genteel conventions and euphemisms of the decade. He spoke with unflinching directness of race relations and racism, and he demanded a corresponding honesty from others. On the issue of racial injustice, he announced to his colleagues, "You will have to meet it. You have to get this problem settled, and the sooner it is settled the better it will be for all concerned. I speak this in all charity. I speak this with no hostility" (Katz, 320).

By the time White was elected, most Southern states had adopted constitutional amendments and a variety of devices to deny African American citizens the vote; these included utterly unrealistic literacy requirements, property requirements in the form of stiff poll taxes, and the infamous "grandfather clause," which exempted men from the other requirements if they or their grandfathers had voted on January 1, 1867—before the Fourteenth Amendment gave blacks the vote. African Americans, while totally disenfranchised themselves, found their population statistics still used to apportion congressional representation, a situation that they resented and one that White repeatedly decried. The greatest sense of rage and betrayal stemmed from the realization that the Fourteenth Amendment incorporated penalties for states that denied full rights to any of their citizens, and that one major penalty was proportionately reduced representation in Congress. Repeatedly, White demanded that the stipulations of the Fourteenth Amendment be acted upon:

Here's the plain letter of the Constitution, the plain, simple, sworn duty of every member of Congress; yet these gentlemen from the South say, "Yes, we have violated your Constitution of the nation; we regard it as a local necessity; and now, if you undertake to punish us as the Constitution prescribes, we will see to it that our former deeds of disloyalty to that instrument, our former acts of disfranchisement and opposition to the highest law of the land will be repeated many fold" (Woodson, 407).

Sounding uncannily like Martin Luther King, Jr. would sixty years later, White condemned those who urged patience and docility on blacks. "We are taunted with being uppish," he declared, "we are told to keep still; to keep quiet. How long must we keep quiet?" He continued:

We have kept quiet while numerically and justly we are entitled to fifty-one members of this House; and I am the only one left. . . . We are entitled to thirteen United States Senators, according to justice and our numerical strength, but we have not one and possibly never will get another; and yet we keep quiet. . . . We have kept quiet while hundreds and thousands of our race have been strung up by the neck unjustly by mobs of murderers. If a man commits a crime he will never find an apologist in me because his face is black. He ought to be punished, but he ought to be punished according to the law as administered in a court of justice. But we keep quiet; do not say it, do not talk about it. How long must we keep quiet, constantly sitting down and seeing our rights one by one taken away from us? (Christopher, 165)

Here, White touched on what was for him a major issue: the horrifying surge of violent mob action against African Americans. The number of lynchings had risen steadily since records were first kept in the early 1880s. By the end of that decade, the victims were overwhelmingly black; in 1892, 162 African Americans were lynched, and from 1893 through 1904 every year saw more than one hundred blacks tortured and murdered—an average of over two a week. The great crusading African American journalist Ida B. Wells compiled detailed statistics on the circumstances behind these atrocities. She was able to demonstrate the falsity of white claims that rape and assault against white women were a major factor in lynching. Of the hundreds of cases she investigated, charges of rape or attempted rape were mentioned in only 15%; other "crimes" included threatening to sue a white man, trying to collect back wages from a white employer, trying to register to vote, expressing interest in labor unions, or being disrespectful to a white man. Bluntly, lynching was used throughout the South as the instrument of a conscious policy of intimidation and demoralization.

George White certainly saw it as that; in a situation where local authorities were frequently either active participants or tacit accomplices, White became the first person to demand federal intervention. On January 20, 1900, he introduced the first congressional bill to make lynching a federal crime. He cited the shameful statistics on recent lynchings and described the unwillingness of local officials even to investigate the murders. Once again, he took pains to refute the negative stereotyping of his race then so virulent and casually accepted.

> It is rather hard to be accused of shiftlessness and idleness when the accuser of his own motion closes the avenues for labor and industrial pursuits to us. It is hardly fair to accuse us of ignorance when it was made a crime under the former order of things to learn enough about letters to read even the Word of God.
>
> While I offer no extenuation for any immorality that may exist among my people, it comes with rather poor grace from those who forced it upon us for two hundred and fifty years to taunt us with that shortcoming (*Congressional Record*, 56th Congress, 1st Session, 2153).

White's bill equated lynching with treason and established equivalent penalties for those convicted as "principals, aiders, abettors, accessories before or after the fact." He concluded, "I have simply raised my voice against a growing and, as I regard it, one of the most dangerous evils in our country. I have simply raised my voice in behalf of a people who have no one else to speak for them here from a racial point of view" (ibid., 2154).

Although White received thousands of letters and petitions in support of his bill, it received virtually no congressional support and was never even brought to a vote. The lingering economic effects of the Panic of 1893 had absorbed much of the energy and attention of the North. The growing influx of southern and eastern European immigrants coincided with the American annexation of Hawaii and the Philippines to produce a smug attitude of vast white superiority and contempt for "primitive" dark-skinned peoples.

By 1900, the disenfranchisement of the African American in the South was almost complete. The blatant, contemptuous racism of Southern spokesmen met with polite approval from their Northern counterparts. James K. Vardaman, running for the Senate from Mississippi in 1900, declared, "We would be justified in slaughtering every Ethiop on earth to preserve unsullied the honor of one Caucasian home." Earlier he complained bitterly that education ruined blacks and led them to demand equality; as governor he saw to it that funding for black schools was almost totally eliminated. In a similar vein, Senator Ben Tillman of South Carolina vowed that he would not let the Constitution stand in the way of lynching rapists: "To hell with the Constitution" (Gossett, 271). In this atmosphere of hatred and violence, with Southern states denying more and more rights to African American citizens, the *New York Times* editorialized sympathetically, "Northern men . . . no longer denounce the suppression of the Negro vote in the South as it used to be denounced in the reconstruction days. The necessity of it under the supreme law of self-preservation is candidly recognized" (May 10, 1900).

Not surprisingly, White concluded that he had no chance of winning another term in office, and he decided not to seek reelection. On January 29, 1901, he made his final speech in the House. He used the occasion to summarize the growth and achievements of African Americans in the thirty-five years since emancipation: the illiteracy rate cut by almost 50%; schools, colleges, and seminaries established and funded; scholars, doctors, lawyers, and ministers trained; banks and businesses owned. "All this was done under the most adverse circumstances," he reminded his colleagues. "We have done it in the face of lynching, burning at the stake, with the humiliation of Jim Crow laws the disfranchisement of our male citizens, slander and degradation of our women. . . . You may tie us and then taunt us for a lack of bravery, but some day we will break the bonds." He concluded:

> Now, Mr. Chairman, before concluding my remarks I want to submit a brief recipe for the solution of the so-called American Negro problem. He asks no special favors, but simply demands that he be given the same chance for existence, for earning a livelihood, for raising himself in the scales of manhood and womanhood, that are accorded to kindred nationalities. . . . Treat him as a man; go into his home and learn of his social

conditions; learn of his cares, his troubles, and his hope for the future. . . .

This, Mr. Chairman, is perhaps the Negro's temporary farewell to the American congress; but let me say, phoenixlike he will rise up some day and come again. These parting words are in behalf of an outraged, heartbroken, bruised and bleeding, but God-fearing people, faithful, industrious, loyal people, rising people, full of potential force. . . .

The only apology that I have to make for the earnestness with which I have spoken is that I am pleading for the life, the liberty, the future happiness, and manhood suffrage for one eighth of the entire population of the United States (*Congressional Record*, 56th Congress, 2nd Session, 1638).

White was right. Congress would not see another African American member until Oscar DePriest was elected from Illinois in 1928.

White moved his family to Washington, D.C., and opened a law office there. He became deeply involved with a project to establish an all-black town in New Jersey. In 1899 he had formed a consortium with several of the most respected black businessmen in Washington; they purchased almost two thousand acres of land in Cape May County, New Jersey, and began to urge persecuted Southern African Americans to come north to safety. By 1903, a small number of black families had built homes and begun farming the land. Two years later, White moved to Philadelphia and established the People's Savings Bank, which provided low-cost mortgages and financed small businesses within the black community. With the generous and understanding support of the People's Bank, Whitesboro developed further: by 1906 the population was over eight hundred, with three hundred single-family homes. Businesses included numerous farms, fishing concerns, a sawmill, and a number of retail stores.

Ever a committed race man, White served on the boards of the Frederick Douglass Hospital, the Home for the Protection of Colored Women, and the Berean Schools in Philadelphia. In 1906 he lent his legal expertise to the defense of African American soldiers in Brownsville, Texas, who had retaliated against especially brutal abuse from local authorities and had been unjustly punished by mass dishonorable discharge. Defense groups nation-wide cut across racial lines, but President Theodore Roosevelt was adamant in his severe condemnation of the men; it finally took an act of Congress to address the situation more reasonably and to rescind many of the dishonorable discharges.

African American intellectual life in the early 20th century was largely dominated by the ongoing ideological war between Booker T. Washington and W.E.B. Du Bois. Washington advocated a subservient demeanor, modest expectations, and an industrial education suited to the menial functions in society he publicly deemed proper for blacks. Du Bois, who held the first history Ph.D. from Harvard University, was an abrasive, fiercely proud, uncompromising figure who demanded full rights and unrestricted academic and professional horizons for his people. White America was, as might be expected, much more comfortable with Washington; Washington became the sole conduit through whom Northern white philanthropies dispensed their funds, the one black man whose recommendation could assure another of an appointment within the segregated political employment market. White threw his considerable prestige and reputation behind Du Bois. With Du Bois, he became active in the NAACP and served on the executive committee of the Philadelphia branch.

During World War I, White's health deteriorated. He was further dispirited by the collapse of his bank in 1918, and he died that same year at the age of sixty-six. He had lived and spoken with remarkable constancy to his principles of justice, decency, and equality. During long, dark years when struggling African Americans found virtually no support, understanding, or compassion among white Americans, George White continually insisted on the rights and dignity of all people. His immediate practical impact on federal legislation may in the short run have seemed negligible, but his vision was clear and his voice was raised in honor and courage. If American seemed to lose sight of its own moral imperatives and potential, it was in defiance of the prophetic call of George White.

References

Bennett, Lerone, Jr. *Before the Mayflower: A History of Black America*. New York: Penguin Books, 1984.

Christopher, Maurine. *America's Black Congressmen*. New York: Thomas Y. Crowell, 1971.

Congressional Record. 56th Congress, 1st and 2nd Sessions.

Edmonds, Helen A. *The Negro and Fusion Politics in North Carolina*. Chapel Hill: University of North Carolina Press, 1951.

Gossett, Thomas E. *Race: The History of an Idea in America*. New York: Schocken Books, 1965.

Katz, William Loren. *Eyewitness: The Negro in American History*. New York: Pittman Publishing Corp., 1967.

Logan, Rayford W. *The Betrayal of the Negro from Rutherford B. Hayes to Woodrow Wilson*. New York: Collier Books, 1965.

Logan, Rayford W. and Michael R. Winston, eds. *Dictionary of American Negro Biography*. New York: W. W. Norton & Co., 1982.

Meier, August. *Negro Thought in America from 1880–1915: Racial Ideologies in the Age of Booker T. Washington*. Ann Arbor: University of Michigan Press, 1963.

Woodson, Carter. *Negro Orators and Their Orations.* New York: Russell & Russell, 1969.

Woodward, C. Vann. *The Strange Career of Jim Crow.* New York: Oxford University Press, 1966.

CAROLA WOERISHOFFER

(August 1885–September 11, 1911)

Women's and Labor Rights Activist, Philanthropist

Few people have traveled as far from their "proper" places in society as did Carola Woerishoffer in her tragically brief life. The child of astonishing wealth and privilege, she committed herself with passionate intensity to the most devastated, deprived members of society. While she was endlessly generous with the vast wealth at her disposal, her commitment went far beyond the condescension of conventional philanthropy. As the Board of Managers of Greenwich House Settlement mourned her loss, "Her generosity was boundless, yet her other qualities so overshadowed her generosity that her gifts were the least of her contributions" (Bryn Mawr College, 119). Woerishoffer played a vital role in the exhilarating world of the Progressive reform movement. She worked undercover as a laundress to gather data for the Consumers League; she kept the Women's Trade Union League alive and became an almost mythic figure of support and guidance to hundreds of immigrant sweatshop girls in the great Shirtwaist Strike of 1909. Mary Kingsbury Simkhovitch, founder of Greenwich House, called Woerishoffer "a knight errant of industrial democracy, without fear and without reproach, seeking opportunities to protect the weak, never hesitating to oppose the powerful" (Bryn Mawr College, 119).

Carola Woerishoffer
Courtesy, Bryn Mawr College Archives.

Unlike most children of her social class, Carola Woerishoffer was always made aware of the responsibilities her wealth imposed on her. Her family was part of the intense, deeply committed world of German-American socialism. Her grandmother, Anna Uhl Ottendorfer, had come to New York from Germany in 1836. She and Jacob Uhl, Carola's grandfather, published the *New-Yorker Staats-Zeitung*, the leading German language socialist daily newspaper in the country. Widowed at the age of thirty-seven, she managed to raise six children and to develop the newspaper into a national voice for reform and progressivism. Carola's step-grandfather, Oswald Ottendorfer, was a courageous socialist and crusading journalist. Her father, Charles Woerishoffer, was a stunningly successful banker who died when his daughter was barely eight months old; Carola inherited over one million dollars from him.

The child grew up in a secure, loving home steeped in traditions of active, radical socialism. Her mother agitated for a progressive income tax, knowing full well how heavily it would affect her. Her step-grandfather, whom she adored, provided a heady home life in which leading socialists were frequent visitors and the atmosphere was charged with passionate political and ethical discussions. Carola was encouraged to inquire, to challenge authority, to seek rational answers. She grew into a passionate, adventurous, open-minded, and eager child.

A student at the prestigious Brearley School, Carola was driven to school in an elegant coach; she made the footman sit in the coach so that she could sit up on the box with the coachman and feel more direct contact with the city. Even as a small child, she was hungry for adventure: Angry because she was not permitted to go to school alone, she was told that, unattended, she might "meet with some very unpleasant experience." Her response, "But I want to meet a very unpleasant experience!" is almost a paradigm for the rest of her life (Bryn Mawr College, 96). The headmaster of Brearley recalled, "Carola was a person at ten years of age, full of honor.... She had no care whatever for making a good impression.... She was a good citizen, but careless of fame" (Bryn Mawr College, 56).

Woerishoffer entered Bryn Mawr College in 1903. Bryn Mawr, founded by Quakers in 1885, had a reputation for uncompromising academic rigor and intellectual excellence; even then, it sent an astonishing proportion of its women on to graduate and professional schools. The president of Bryn Mawr, M. Carey Thomas, remembered Woerishoffer as a determined young woman who came to college with the goal of working for social justice firm in her mind, "already touched by the flame of this vision of helping to improve present social conditions." Carola was so eager, so daring, that Thomas recalled, "Her mother told me that she wondered whether Carola could ever be tamed sufficiently to live any life" (Bryn Mawr College, 44). Woerishoffer chose her curriculum carefully to provide her with the tools she would need for effective social work: she managed a double major in economics and philosophy, taking in addition extra courses in politics and psychology; she seemed especially gifted in foreign languages, a skill that would prove immensely useful working with immigrants.

Woerishoffer's intensity, directness, and unconventionality seem to have awed—and intimidated—many of her classmates. Comfort Dorsey, a close friend, commented after her death,

> It would be difficult to convey to one who did not know her a notion of how different she was from the ordinary run of girls entering college. She fell into no type or class. She was, to use her own words, an experiment. Many of her fellow-students will remember her as eccentric and unapproachable. But those of us who came under the spell of that brilliant and powerful personality will always feel that to have known her was a privilege of incalculable significance. She was indeed a figure to fire the imagination, sound of body, of incredible physical endurance, and with such a mind, so clear, so receptive, so vigorous, so unfettered by convention and tradition! . . . And as for her humor, which was indeed the fine flower of her whole personality, who can forget it? . . . She had a fine scorn of the obvious, of pretense, sentimentality, and affectation. . . . The humor of a situation never escaped her, and she could render it with a crude directness of which she alone was master (Bryn Mawr College, 120).

In 1907 Woerishoffer moved directly from the idyllic green campus of Bryn Mawr to the tumultuous slum streets of New York. She became a member of the board of managers of Greenwich House, the settlement house founded by Mary Kingsbury Simkhovitch in 1901; more significant for the future course of her life, she also became a resident of Greenwich House. Her whole vision of social change hinged on understanding through direct experience of workers' living conditions. Abstract theory

had no meaning for her; ideologies did not attract her. As Helen Marot of the WTUL recalled, "She never called herself anything, and we need not name her faith, for she lived it" (Bryn Mawr College, 73).

The president of Greenwich House, Edwin Seligman, admitted later that the rest of the board had initially doubted Woerishoffer's commitment and usefulness; she soon laid all doubts to rest. At the time Woerishoffer came to Greenwich House, the settlement was in the midst of coordinating a major, pioneering exhibition on urban population density. In the course of her struggles against sweatshop and child labor, Florence Kelley* had come to realize that overcrowding itself caused many of the slums' horrifying problems. In 1907 she approached other reformers, including Lillian Wald of Henry Street Settlement and Mary Simkhovitch of Greenwich House, and they formed a Committee on the Congestion of Population; with the faith of Progressives, they believed that education—presenting irrefutable data to the middle and upper classes—would inspire legislative reform. They planned a massive multimedia exhibit featuring dioramas of existing and ideal low-income housing, maps, photographs, charts, and diagrams. Seriously exceeding its budget, the exhibit seemed doomed when Carola Woerishoffer quietly provided enough funds to keep the project alive. The New York Congestion Exhibit, the first of its kind anywhere, opened to considerable fanfare at the Museum of Natural History in the spring of 1908. The following year cities across the Northeast mounted similar exhibits, and the mayor of New York appointed a City Commission on Congestion. The original Committee on Congestion organized the first national conference on city planning in Washington, D.C. in May, 1909; the National Association of City Planning grew out of this national conference. Carola Woerishoffer, who had "seeded" the project at a crucial moment, took no credit whatsoever.

Woerishoffer joined the Women's Trade Union League in the fall of 1908, at a time when the infant organization was weak and dispirited. With her standard two-dollar membership fee she enclosed a check for five thousand dollars. She joined an intense, highly self-selected corps—the "allies" of the WTUL. The WTUL, founded in 1903, tried to bridge the gap between working-class women and their middle- and upper-class sisters, to foster a recognition of shared needs that would transcend class divisions and benefit all parties. The allies were the wealthier part of the team; they were an exceptional band of women. Of the twenty-seven allies active with the League before World War I, twelve were college graduates, two had had some college, and several held law degrees—at a time when some doctors and professors were still warning that higher education atrophied the uterus. These highly educated allies were almost all financially independent and unmarried—on one hand, they were free from the distractions and burdens of family, and on the other, they may have especially needed the support and comradeship the League work provided. These were practical, clear-eyed activists, and Woerishoffer was comfortable in their midst. She offered herself and her resources freely; when the League was forced to relocate and could not meet the rent at the new site, Woerishoffer quietly provided the funds. Her donations, large or small, were always made as anonymously as possible.

Woerishoffer was an active member of the New York Consumers League, a reform organization working to eliminate sweatshops through the power of enlightened consumer pressure. Within months of moving to New York, Woerishoffer had taken over the operation of the League's Label Shop, a store that sold only those goods bearing trade union and Consumers League labels, which certified that the goods had been produced under hygienic, humane conditions. Woerishoffer's involvement with the League led her into one of her most memorable and daring experiences: During the summer of 1909 Woerishoffer posed as a poor working girl to gather irrefutable data on working conditions in the city's laundries. For four months she took various menial, difficult, dangerous jobs, changing every week or so in order to observe a wide range of situations; before the summer was over she would work in sixteen different laundries. She found the working conditions appalling: days as long as twelve hours or more with no provision for rest periods; unventilated laundries saturated with choking steam; dangerous machinery without appropriate shields and guards; disgusting sanitary facilities. In one shop she was told by a more experienced girl, "You didn't get burned today or yesterday, but you will some time, everyone does." In all these situations Woerishoffer offered herself as an equal and was accepted as such. Her report to the Consumers League stated, "Upon entering a new place the investigator found, as a rule, a spirit of friendly interest and cordiality, expressed occasionally in the accepted formula, 'Say, you got a feller?' 'Sure, ain't you got one?' 'Sure' '' (Tarbell, 284).

Woerishoffer conducted her investigation objectively and professionally, but she was deeply shaken by the experience. Florence Kelley* recounted how Woerishoffer had come to her office early one afternoon that summer. The young woman stated that she had been fired for defending an old woman who was being abused by the laundry foreman; as a consequence, she had no money for lunch. She was determined to live totally on the earnings of a laundry worker; she was not willing to go to her mother's mansion to eat graciously, but she was hungry enough to suggest that Kelley take her to lunch. Kelley was awed by the younger woman's dedication and intensity:

> We went to luncheon at one o'clock, and she talked to me until about five, almost uninterruptedly, about the perfectly needless hardships of the people among whom she worked. I don't think she knew at all what she was eating. I do not think she realized when we walked back to the office. I do not think she knew that it was five o'clock, until the cleaners came to close the office. She talked all those hours, perfectly absorbed. I have been haunted by that conversation. I have thought of it innumerable times, and the memory of her is always the memory of an unsmiling young face, of one absorbed, aflame with the passion of living and changing the things that ought to be changed. I cannot imagine saying anything that day that could possibly have made her smile (Bryn Mawr College, 63).

That fall (1909) Carola Woerishoffer testified about her work before the New York State Commission on Employer Liability and Labor Legislation. The members of the commission were stunned by her evidence and by her total dedication. As one of them recalled at her memorial service,

> Here was a girl who had every temptation, every inducement, to follow the conventional lines—youth, attractiveness, wealth, everything to lead her away from social service. That on leaving college . . . she was filled with the generous desire to do something for the unprivileged classes was perhaps to be expected; that is becoming a common thing. The remarkable thing about Carola Woerishoffer was that this desire seemed to crowd everything else out of her mind. I have never known anyone who seemed to be consecrated with such singleness of purpose to the various kinds of social service to which she devoted herself (Bryn Mawr College, 82).

Later that fall, Woerishoffer became involved in the epic Shirtwaist Strike, the first mass strike of women in American history. Wages in New York's garment industry had been falling since the depression of 1908, despite an economic recovery early in 1909. By the fall of 1909, wages averaged only $5.00 for a fifty-six to sixty hour week. Workers were charged for needles and thread, for the electricity used by their sewing machines (which they had to buy themselves), for the use of chairs and lockers; they were fined heavily for the slightest lateness and for any minor imperfections in their work. Throughout the summer and early fall, sporadic, spontaneous small strikes began to coalesce into momentum for a coordinated general strike. On November 22, union leaders and strikers addressed a mass meeting at Cooper Union, a site emblematic of freedom since Abraham Lincoln spoke there during the Civil War. The catalyst for action was twenty-year-old Clara Lemlich, a striker newly released from the hospital after a savage beating on the picket line. Lemlich's inspiring call to action brought the huge crowd to its feet. The next day almost twenty thousand shirtwaist makers walked off the job; within days there were close to thirty thousand workers on strike.

The industry was stunned. Most of the strikers were very young, female, and foreign-born. They were uneducated, unskilled workers at the bottom of the pay scale. No one—not even the major unions—had thought them capable of the coordinated, sustained action they now undertook so competently. Within a week, numerous smaller shops capitulated totally to the strikers' demands: the right to a union shop, a 52-hour week, a limit to overtime, and the provision of machines and supplies by the employer. Almost ten thousand satisfied young strikers returned to work.

The larger shops were better able to resist the strike pressure; the owners formed an association to coordinate their war against the unions. They hired eager strikebreakers to keep their shops open and, assisted by the police, launched a campaign of terrorism and intimidation against the strikers. Girls on the picket lines were insulted by prostitutes hired for that express purpose; they were provoked and openly assaulted by the police. In response, the WTUL established a corps of forty-eight upper- and middle-class volunteers to walk the picket lines with the girls and try by their protective presence to soften the rage of the police. League volunteers provided reputable witness, legal services, bail money, and invaluable publicity. They were soon joined by student volunteers from Bryn Mawr, Barnard, Vassar, and Wellesley.

In the month before Christmas, 1909, over seven hundred strikers were arrested and dragged before blatantly biased magistrates. "You are on strike against God and nature," one such judge pontificated, "whose prime law is that man shall earn his bread by the sweat of his brow." When a League volunteer cabled this incident to George Bernard Shaw, he shot back, "Delightful. Medieval America is always in the most intimate personal confidence of the Almighty" (Foner, 139).

Woerishoffer was in her element. Every day for eleven weeks she came to court with the accused strikers, haunting the Jefferson Market and Essex Street courthouses, providing bail money for young girls who would otherwise rot in prison awaiting trial. Rose Schneiderman* estimated that Woerishoffer paid over $29,000 in bail for more than two hundred strikers, not one of whom failed to return for her trial. In one instance an arrogant judge refused to accept cash for bail and insisted instead on real estate. Woerishoffer, with her mother's proud and loving collusion, promptly bought from her real estate worth $75,000 for a token single dollar. Her entrance into the court, armed with the property deeds, was highly dramatic. Helen Marot, executive secretary of the League, recalled the scene vividly:

> There was a sensation in the court-room when she appeared with her $75,000 bond. . . . There she was by all precedent the heroine of the hour, a romantic personage, her bond a veritable fairy wand, releasing the girls from the dreaded confinement of prison walls and evil association. But Carola's integrity was greater than her romanticism. Before the first day was over, by sheer force of character she had turned the attention from herself to the strikers. . . . She even performed a superhuman feat with the press. Without exception every reporter sacrificed an opportunity to turn in "copy," and copy which every reporter knew would have first place and several days' run. They took from her instead stories about the strike, and during the thirteen weeks she promised and gave them material, telling them if they published her name they would never have another story from her, but if they would be good, she would keep them well supplied (Bryn Mawr College, 70).

The scope of the assault on the strikers convinced Woerishoffer that ad hoc measures could not meet the challenge. Anonymously, she donated $10,000 to establish a permanent strike benefits fund; the source of the gift was disclosed only after her death. Woerishoffer could never forget the desperate situation of the young strikers; until her death, she let it be known within the unions that she was always available, day or night, to post bail for any striker. She never refused such a summons.

The massive strike spread to Philadelphia, but the major manufacturers were too well organized and too well connected to be defeated. By mid-February the strike was over. Available strike benefits had been exhausted, the strikers themselves were tired and discouraged, and many of the wealthy allies had begun to lose interest in the sustained struggle. Still, some real benefits and some intangibles had been won. Women of various classes had witnessed the power of unity; the shame of their working conditions had been thrust irrevocably before the city's public conscience; poor immigrant women had demonstrated their capacity for unionization and collective action. Woerishoffer herself had come to see the strike as an inadequate, reactive, ad hoc weapon in the war for industrial democracy and decency. She came away firmly convinced that only vigorously enforced legislation could improve the lives of the working poor.

Funded in part by anonymous contributions from Woerishoffer, the New York State Bureau of Industries and Immigration was created in 1910 to monitor and regulate the circumstances of immigrant workers. Woerishoffer applied for and won a position with the Bureau as a special investigator of conditions in the isolated labor camps of upstate New York. Simkhovitch remembered, "She was very proud of the fact that she had passed the Civil Service examination and was earning her own living" (Simkhovitch, 162). Her annual salary was $1,200. She lived entirely on what she earned. Other income—dividends and interest from her huge trust fund—was reserved exclusively for carefully designated, anonymous contributions to important purposes, both institutional and individual; even personal gifts were paid for from money she had earned and saved herself.

Woerishoffer drove herself relentlessly in her new job. The roads were poor, traveling conditions difficult, and the work in the camps draining. She was emotionally and morally assaulted by the shocking circumstances in the labor camps, although she apparently tried never to let her exhaustion and despair reach her friends. After a warm, relaxing visit with the Simkhovitch family, she wrote to them, "Oh, how I hate these lonely roads. Camping with you people is quite a different story from the Italian labor camps!" Recalling that letter, Mary Simkhovitch's husband, Victor, commented, "It was the only plaintive note that either we or any of her intimate friends ever heard her utter about her work. She was a soldier of the cross without ever admitting or even knowing it" (*Bryn Mawr Alumnae Quarterly*, 117). Driving to a labor camp on the night of September 10, 1911, Woerishoffer was unable to control her car on a rain-slicked, pitted dirt road; the car overturned, pinning the 26-year-old woman beneath it. She died of her injuries the next morning.

The outpouring of grief, affection, and deep respect was remarkable. A memorial service held for her at Greenwich House on October 30 featured eulogies by such leading figures as Florence Kelley* of the National Consumers League; Helen Marot of the WTUL; Mary Simkhovitch of Greenwich House; M. Carey Thomas, president of Bryn Mawr College; and George McAneny, borough president of Manhattan. This dedicated young woman had clearly had a significant impact on the Progressive movement in New York City. "I can tell you," McAneny reported, "that this girl has led the city of New York to do things that will last for many and many a year, and that will continue to grow and to expand and to represent the beautiful things for which she stood" (Bryn Mawr College, 40). Florence Kelley* spoke:

> She was so honest and so modest that it was a test of everyone who worked with her, and now that she has gone, it seems to me that we are, all of us, whoever had the privilege of working with her at all, immeasurably richer, because she existed (Bryn Mawr College, 65).

The great muckraking journalist Ida Tarbell described her as "one who refused the weapons those in authority put into her hands, refused the place in life they wished her to take, refused to march in the way they ordered her to go" (Tarbell, 286). The sense of personal loss resonates in Mary Simkhovitch's final comment: "We miss this striving, planning, buoyant, gallant girl" (Bryn Mawr College, 89).

Woerishoffer willed almost all of her remaining estate to Bryn Mawr College. The unrestricted bequest of $750,000 was the largest the school had ever received. In recognition of the passionate commitment of the donor, Bryn Mawr used the funds in 1915 to establish the Carola Woerishoffer Graduate Department of Social Economy and Social Research, the first such professional school affiliated with a college or university. Woerishoffer would have been pleased; the school would further the mission to which she had dedicated her brief, shining life.

References

Bryn Mawr Alumnae Quarterly, November 1911.

Bryn Mawr College Class of 1907. *Carola Woerishoffer: Her Life and Work*. Bryn Mawr, PA, 1912.

Davis, Allen F. *Spearheads for Reform: The Social Settlements and the Progressive Movement, 1890–1914*. New Brunswick, NJ: Rutgers University Press, 1984.

Dye, Nancy Schrom. *As Equals and as Sisters: Feminism, the Labor Movement, and the Women's Trade Union League of New York*. Columbia, MO: University of Missouri Press, 1980.

Foner, Philip S. *Women and the American Labor Movement from the First Trade Unions to the Present*. New York: Free Press, 1982.

Schneiderman, Rose. With Lucy Goldthwaite. *All for One*. New York: Paul S. Ericksson, 1967.

Simkhovitch, Mary Kingsbury. *Neighborhood: My Story of Greenwich House*. New York: W. W. Norton & Co., 1938.

Stein, Leon. *The Triangle Fire*. Philadelphia: J. B. Lippincott Co., 1962.

Tarbell, Ida. "A Noble Life: The Story of Carola Woerishoffer." *American Magazine* 74 (November 1911): 281–287.

MINORU YASUI

(October 19, 1916–November 12, 1986)

Civil Liberties Activist

On the night of Saturday, March 28, 1942, a young man walked the streets of Portland, Oregon, determined to get arrested. It wasn't easy. "I had my secretary call the police . . . and report that "There's a Japanese walking up and down the streets, arrest him," he recalled. "I had an awful time getting arrested, and I was getting tired walking around town" (Irons, War, 84). Finally, at eleven o'clock, the young man approached a policeman and explained why he should be arrested; somewhat rudely, the officer refused. The young man went into a police station and insisted on being arrested. What had brought him to that point, what drove him further, and what happened afterward is a story of one lone individual's determination to see the Bill of Rights brought to life in the courts of his native land.

Minoru Yasui
Courtesy, True S. Yasui.

Being of Japanese ancestry had never been a totally safe or comfortable experience on the West Coast of America. The pattern of nativist and racist discrimination against the Japanese closely paralleled the treatment of the Chinese a generation earlier. The anti-Asian campaigns of the leading nativist demagogue, Dennis Kearney (himself an Irish immigrant) culminated in 1882 with the passage of the Chinese Exclusion Act. A decade later, Kearney turned his venom against the Japanese. Early Japanese immigrants were hated not because they were indolent, troublemakers, or a welfare burden on the state. Quite the contrary, it was their highly disciplined, efficient, meticulous habits that earned the envy and hatred of Caucasians throughout the farming regions of the West Coast. (By 1919, although Japanese owned only 1% of the cultivated land in California, they produced over 10% of the cash value of produce.)

By 1905 an expanded Oriental Exclusion League focused heavily on the Japanese. A federal law that same year limited naturalization to "free white persons" or "persons of African descent." President Theodore Roosevelt had argued for the inclusion of Japanese, but pressure from California politicians overrode him. In 1906 the San Francisco School Board transferred all Japanese students—ninety-three children—to the already segregated Chinese school. The segregation of the Japanese children caused a major international incident, especially since Japan at the time enjoyed "most favored nation" status. One result, a careful diplomatic compromise, was the "gentlemen's agreement" of 1908, in which Japan agreed to withhold passports to the United States from all except men who had already lived there and their families; this compromise still permitted the immigration of an additional 118,000 Japanese between 1908 and 1924, and racist groups were outraged.

In 1913 California passed an Alien Land Law, which barred further purchases by Japanese aliens (who were legally barred from applying for citizenship) and limiting farm leases by aliens to a maximum of three years. *Issei* (first-generation Japanese) circumvented the law by transferring titles and deeds to their American-born citizen children, the *Nisei*. The festering American version of rising world-wide racism triumphed with the 1924 Immigration Restriction Act, which established rigid quotas based on ethnic representation in the 1890 census. The act was aimed primarily at Italians and Eastern European Jews, but because any substantial Japanese immigration had begun after 1890, the Japanese now found themselves totally excluded.

Nisei moved in an uneasy balance of acceptance and bigotry. In 1922, thirteen-year-old John Aiso was elected student body president at predominantly white Le Conte Junior High School in Hollywood. Although he had won by a landslide, his election precipitated a major community crisis involving angry white parents, jingoistic local newspapers, and the eager participation of anti-Asian pressure groups. The school principal suspended all student government until Aiso graduated (Daniels, 179).

Ironically, Minoru Yasui grew up in an idyllic all-American setting and seems to have experienced a fairly idyllic all-American childhood. His parents were Christian, prosperous, and well respected by both Japanese and Caucasian neighbors. His family was large—seven children survived—and active, affectionate, and assimilated. Minoru's father, Masuo Yasui, had come to the United States in 1903 at the age of sixteen. He worked for several years as a house boy in the Pacific Northwest; he dreamed of becoming a lawyer but learned that his Japanese birth barred him forever from both citizenship and qualifying for the Bar. In 1906 Masuo and an older brother opened a small dry goods store in Hood River, Oregon. In 1912 Shidzuyo Miyake came from Japan to marry Masuo Yasui. A college graduate herself, she had taught at a woman's school in Japan before marrying, and saw to it that all her children attended college. Slowly and carefully, Yasui Brothers Company acquired shares in many farms and orchards surrounding the picturesque town. By 1940 the brothers owned hundreds of acres outright and owned shares in other rich farms and orchards amounting to over one thousand acres. Masuo was a member of the Rotary Club, on the board of the local Apple Growers Association, and the recognized leader of the roughly six hundred local Japanese.

Both Masuo and Shidzuyo were devout Methodists. Masuo was a founder of the Hood River Japanese Methodist Church, where the entire family was active. Both parents were determined that their children would take full advantage of their American citizenship without losing their Japanese heritage. The Yasui children attended Japanese-language school as well as the local public schools. Minoru spent three summers in Japanese school, but he was a restless, independent, outspoken boy who had a hard time with the exquisite politeness and deferential attitude expected of him. "I was kicked out before I finished Book Three for being a bad boy," he commented years later (Irons, *War*, 82).

Yasui entered the University of Oregon in 1933. He completed the two years of basic Reserve Officers Training Corps (ROTC) required, then volunteered for an additional two years of advanced training. He received his army commission as a second lieutenant on December 8, 1937, shortly after his twenty-first birthday. At the University of Oregon Law School, Yasui studied under Wayne Morse, then the youngest law school dean in the country and later the leading maverick senator opposing the Vietnam War. In 1943, after Yasui had earned his notoriety, Morse admitted to ACLU founder Roger Baldwin that he had frequently noted "a streak of blind stubbornness in him" (Irons, *War*, 82).

Minoru Yasui was the first Nisei to graduate from the university's law school; he passed the Bar and became the only Nisei lawyer in the entire state of Oregon. He was unable to find a job. Through his father's commercial contacts and longstanding friendship with the Japanese consul in Portland, Yasui found work as an attaché with the Japanese consulate in Chicago. As required, he registered with the State Department as an American working for a foreign government. He later described his job at the consulate as basically clerical, although he did give occasional speeches to local civic groups; he found he had a good deal of free time. Yasui ran a local Boy Scout troop and got involved with various community activities. He also led, by his own description, "a hyperactive social life . . . playing poker all night and generally running around too much" (Tateishi, 65).

On December 7, 1941, Yasui's easygoing world fell apart. The next morning he resigned his consular position. Masuo cabled him: "Now that this country is at war and needs you and since you are trained as an officer, I as your father urge you to enlist immediately" (Irons, *War*, 82). A few days later Yasui received orders from the United States Army requiring him to report to Camp Vancouver in Washington state by January 19, 1942. Even these official army orders couldn't convince the ticket agent in Chicago to sell a railroad ticket to a "Jap"; Yasui had to confront the Union Pacific attorney and threaten legal action before he was able to buy a ticket home. During an overnight stop in North Platte, Nebraska, he was harassed in his hotel room by a plainclothes policeman, and his wild, defiant streak erupted under the strain. "You're a Jap, aren't you," the officer challenged, and Yasui, tired and angry, snapped back, "No I'm bog-Irish." The officer was not amused, and only Yasui's army orders prevented his arrest (Tateishi, 66).

On December 13, 1941, Masuo was arrested as an enemy alien; for weeks his family had no word of his condition or whereabouts. Their situation was further complicated because, as was done to all Issei, Masuo's assets were frozen and family finances were suddenly chaotic and precarious. In the midst of the crisis, Second Lieutenant Minoru Yasui reported for duty at Camp Vancouver; he was told that he was unacceptable and was ordered off the base. Yasui went back, offering to serve, eight more times and was rejected each time. Almost three years later, with no explanation, he received his official discharge papers; he had never been permitted to serve. Forty years later, both his characteristic dry humor and his pain were evident as he commented, "It occurred to me that was probably just as well, because the outfit to which I would have been assigned was a detachment from Texas. If we had gone into any active combat situation, I'd probably have been shot in the back" (Tateishi, 66).

Masuo Yasui had been sent to a Justice Department internment camp in Missoula, Montana. In February, 1942 Minoru asked for permission to represent his father and other Issei from the Portland area at their loyalty hearings. The Justice Department had no intention of conducting these hearings with legal counsel, and Minoru's petition was denied; he was allowed to attend his father's hearing as a private citizen. At the hearing, the official for the Enemy Control Unit cited Masuo's local prominence; his visit to Japan with his family (in the summer of 1925); and his Japanese medal, awarded by the emperor for promoting good relations between the two countries, as evidence of his subversive intentions. Finally, the official produced several children's crayon drawings of the Panama Canal, seized from the Yasui home. Despite Masuo's fervent denials, these were submitted as evidence that he was plotting to blow up the Panama Canal. In a total perversion of the assumption of innocence, the official challenged Masuo: "Prove that you didn't have such an intention." Unable to prove what he hadn't intended, Masuo Yasui was classified as disloyal and interned until 1945.

Minoru was shocked and disgusted by the hearing. He believed in the rule of law; he believed in the objectivity and honor of the law. Deeply shaken, he returned to Oregon "utterly repulsed by the kangaroo-court proceedings of the United States Department of Justice" (Tateishi, 68).

On February 19, 1942, Executive Order 9066 authorized the military to designate zones "from which any or all persons may be excluded." The initial response to the plight of the Nisei after Pearl Harbor had been balanced and even sympathetic; on December 8, 1941, the *Los Angeles Times* declared most Japanese Americans "good Americans, born and educated as such," and urged "no precipitation, no riots, no mob law" (Irons, *War*, 6). But within the next few months, as the war news was grim and pressure mounted from established anti-Asian sources, public perceptions shifted. Government policy at the highest levels was consciously manipulated and deliberately distorted to accommodate the rolling racism on the West Coast. Plans were laid for the evacuation of the entire Issei and Nisei populations of the West Coast, although Attorney General Francis Biddle urged that the evacuation of the Nisei would be unconstitutional and both General Mark Clark and Admiral Harold Stark argued that complete evacuation was simply not justifiable militarily.

One of the preliminary stages preparatory to evacuation was the establishment of curfews for certain elements of the population. Military Proclamation #3, promulgated by General John L. DeWitt, the commander of the West Coast military operations, applied an all-night curfew to German enemy aliens, Italian enemy aliens, and *all* persons of Japanese ancestry.

This inequity drove Yasui beyond the point of helpless anger. He could accept the notion of the curfew itself, but not lopsided application.

> It was my feeling and belief . . . that no military authority has the right to
> subject any citizen to any requirement that does not equally apply to all
> other United States citizens. . . . If we believe in America, if we believe in
> equality and democracy, if we believe in law and justice, then each of us,
> when we see or believe errors are being made, has an obligation to make
> every effort to correct them (Tateishi, 71).

Yasui was determined to challenge the curfew. Methodically, he con-
sulted beforehand with both the Portland FBI agent (a law school classmate) and the U.S. Attorney, discussing options, penalties, and possible
government responses. He conferred with other Portland Nisei to plan
a strategy and to select an appropriate sacrificial lamb for the test case.
Yasui was not his own first choice for martyr:

> We were going to find a Nisei who'd served in the Army and had an
> honorable discharge, with two or three little kids, and we thought that
> would be an ideal test case. So I talked to my friends, but none of them
> were [sic] willing to undertake it. . . . I knew I was not an ideal test case,
> but somebody had to do it (Irons, *War*, 84).

Public Law 503, establishing a 6:00 P.M. curfew in conformity with
Military Proclamation #3, went into effect at midnight, March 28, 1942.
The very next evening, Minoru Yasui argued his way into a jail cell at
the Second Street station house. Of the almost 120,000 people of Japanese
descent affected by the curfew and eventual relocation, only twelve
sought any legal redress; four cases—Yasui, Hirabayashi, Korematsu,
and Endo—reached the Supreme Court. Minoru Yasui's arrest and trial
were the first.

The largest Japanese American organization, the Japanese American
Citizens League, was desperately careful, compliant, and determined to
prove Nisei loyalty. Yasui was an intense embarrassment to them, and
they disowned him angrily. Although Roger Baldwin was concerned
about Yasui's test case, a frightened ACLU board voted to steer clear of
involvement, precipitating bitter fights within the ACLU. Yasui was in
effect "a Lone Ranger, without the backing of any person or organization, challenging the power and authority of the United States government" (Hosokawa, 176).

As soon as his lawyer bailed him out, Yasui telephoned his mother to
reassure her he was safe. Hesitantly, he asked if she was worried. "Non-
sense!" she retorted, "I encourage you." Forty years later, Yasui reflected,
"We have never given our Issei mothers enough credit for having
brought up a generation of Nisei strong enough to endure and prevail
in a hostile environment" (Tateishi, 72).

Yasui's case finally came to trial in Portland in November, 1942. Since

Yasui never denied violating the curfew, there was no jury and the case was heard directly before the judge, Alger Fee. Lawyers for the War Relocation Authority argued that "racial characteristics" of Japanese Americans predisposed them to subversive acts; they claimed that the lack of evidence of any subversive actions was merely proof of how devious and well organized the subversion was. The judge's 10,000-word decision was actually two separate findings: first, that DeWitt's curfew could not constitutionally be applied to citizens; and second, that Yasui, by working for the Japanese consulate, had forfeited his citizenship, and so was guilty despite the ruling on constitutionality. During the trial, Yasui had cited his military oath in the Army Reserves, his admittance to the Bar of Oregon, and his registration with the State Department before working for the Japanese consulate, as evidence of his decision to maintain American citizenship. Judge Fee disregarded all of the above. Fee sentenced Yasui to the maximum allowed: one year in prison and a $5,000 fine. Proud and defiant, Yasui declared, "I can say that I have never and will never voluntarily relinquish my American citizenship." Yasui's case went into appeal, while Yasui himself went into a harsh and unwarranted solitary confinement.

While Yasui was outraged at the slur on his patriotism and citizenship, the United States government was trying to cope with Fee's declaration that the curfew—and by extension the scheduled evacuation—could not legally apply to citizens. The Ninth Circuit Court of Appeals received the case in February, 1943 and decided literally to pass the hot potato, sending it directly on to the Supreme Court in a little-known maneuver called "certification." The Supreme Court ordered the case before it for full review.

Judge William Denman of the Ninth Circuit Court reminded the Supreme Court of "the admission by the Government, at the time of hearing here, that not one of these 70,000 Japanese-descended citizen deportees [has been charged] with espionage, sabotage, or any treasonable act" (Irons, *War*, 183). Defense lawyers argued that the delegation of legislative powers to General DeWitt was too vaguely worded and that military necessity had never been demonstrated. (In fact, as lawyers discovered in 1983, DeWitt had known that there was no sabotage threat from the Nisei; he had been fully informed by military intelligence units and had chosen, with the collusion of the FBI, the Department of Justice, and the FCC, to suppress that information [Irons, *Delayed*, 168].) The court appeared hostile to the defense lawyers; unanimously, it upheld Yasui's conviction. To do so it had to reverse Fee on both his points: first, it declared that the curfew law could constitutionally apply to citizens; and second, it graciously restored Yasui's citizenship to him. The court did imply that the sentence was too harsh, and it remanded the case to the lower courts for resentencing. Yasui's sentence was reduced to time already served: at that point, a full nine months in solitary confinement.

Yasui spent the next year in Minidoka Camp. He never denounced the Japanese American Citizens League (JACL) for abandoning him; quite the contrary, he worked with Joe Grant Masaoka, brother of the JACL executive secretary, touring other detention camps and urging angry young Nisei to comply with draft registration laws. (By late 1943, even Nisei bodies were welcome in the armed forces.) Critics have accused Yasui of inconsistency in this urging of patriotic duty on others, but Yasui's ethical position was remarkably consistent: he had defied the curfew as a violation of a citizen's rights, and he supported the draft as a fulfillment of a citizen's responsibility.

In June, 1945 Yasui took the Colorado Bar examination. He received the highest test score in the state, but was nonetheless rejected by the Bar: its committee on ethics informed him that his criminal conviction disqualified him. With the help of Samuel L. Menin, an ACLU lawyer, Yasui convinced the Colorado Supreme Court to reverse that decision. He settled in Denver, married, and plunged into a hectic existence juggling family life, private practice, and an extensive community volunteer commitment.

Throughout his life, Yasui remained not only a loyal member of the JACL but also one of its most prominent, articulate spokesmen. In the 1950s he campaigned across the country to obtain long-denied citizenship for the Issei and to secure rights for the thousands of Japanese war brides. He was an early leader in the Committee for Redress, which sought both official recognition and reparations for the victims of the evacuation. (Sadly, he did not live to see the passage in 1988 of the Redress Act.)

In 1967 Yasui was appointed executive director of the Commission on Community Relations for the city and county of Denver, a position he held for sixteen years. In 1976, a monthly award for community volunteers that Yasui had initiated was renamed the Minoru Yasui Community Volunteer Award, in recognition of his own "consummate volunteerism" (Yasui, n.p.).

In 1981 Congress launched an investigation into the mass relocation of Japanese Americans. Predictably, the men who had been involved in the decision exhibited varying degrees of remorse and arrogance. Belatedly, the ACLU called the detention program "the greatest deprivation of civil liberty by government in this country since slavery" (Irons, *War*, 349). In February 1983 a report of the Commission on Wartime Relocation found unanimously that Executive Order 9066 was not justified by military necessity but was prompted by "race prejudice, war hysteria, and a failure of political leadership (Irons, *War*, 362). In that atmosphere of greater sensitivity and understanding, Yasui, Hirabayashi, and Korematsu were encouraged to file a renewed appeal of their cases. Yasui's driving goal was to see the slander against his honor and citizenship eradicated, but even in 1986 the federal judiciary could not acknowledge the enormity of the wrong done. Acting on a government motion, Judge Robert Belloni vacated—voided—Yasui's conviction and simultaneously dismissed his petition, thus refusing to confront the real issues. Yasui commented scathingly on the ethical implications of the decision:

> I'm not satisfied. Forty years later, it isn't crucial whether I was convicted or not; it just isn't important any longer. I want a declaration from the Court that the United States government committed misconduct and that therefore the case is vacated. This should never be done to anyone else, but the sad thing is it could happen again. If we have a court record saying the government was wrong, the government officials will be less apt to repeat it. But if you say, "Well, forty years have gone by, and we'll forget about it," they can intern others and forget about *that* too. Unless we are all vigilant to protect the rights of others, it can happen to us (Schultz and Schultz, 359).

On November 12, 1986, while further appeals were tangled in legal maneuvers, Minoru Yasui died. A few years earlier, Yasui described a conversation he had had with an old friend, who had declared he would barricade himself in his home and fight rather than be interned ever again. Yasui reflected sadly:

> As for myself, I believe I would passively resist again, protesting all the way, but I cannot possibly conceive of taking the lives of other people to protect and preserve my rights. It would be far better to be killed than to kill, because the person who might kill me might just as fervently believe that he's doing his duty as I would believe it to be wrong. . . . Perhaps in that kind of death, rather than killing or being killed, there would be a far more principled dying (Tateishi, 93).

References

Daniels, Roger. *Asian America*. Seattle: University of Washington Press, 1988.
Hosokawa, Bill. *JACL in Quest of Justice*. New York: William Morrow & Co., 1982.
Irons, Peter. *Justice at War*. New York: Oxford University Press, 1983.
———. *Justice Delayed*. Middletown, CT: Wesleyan University Press, 1989.
Schultz, Bud and Ruth Schultz. *It Did Happen Here: Recollections of Political Repression in America*. Berkeley: University of California Press, 1989.
Tateishi, John. *And Justice for All: An Oral History of the Japanese American Detention Camps*. New York: Random House, 1984.
Yasui, True S. Unpublished correspondence, 1994.

INDEX

Abolitionists, 73, 113–25, 195–201; African American, 258–62, 269, 296–301
ACLU. *See* American Civil Liberties Union
Addams, Jane, 100, 127, 140, 158, 161, 166, 239, 250
Adler, Felix, 98–101, 104
African Americans: after Reconstruction, 37–39; after Reconstruction in Atlanta, 130–34; after Reconstruction in Chicago, 129; disenfranchisement, 307–12; education, 75–85, 188–93; free, before Civil War, 257, 295; free, in Boston, 257–58, 296–301; in Georgia, 47–49, 54, 188–93; legislators, 303–12; in Massachusetts, 109–10; in New York City, 236–38; in North Carolina, 77
Alexander, Will, 132, 141
Allotment (Native American), 89–90; and Dawes Act, 184
American Civil Liberties Union (ACLU), 102, 330, 332
American Liberty League, 29–30
American Sign Language (Ameslan), 226, 229–33

Anarchism, 58, 61–63
Anthony, Susan B., 274
Anti-Asian movement (California), 290, 326–27
Apess, William, 1–11; childhood, 3–4; "Eulogy on King Philip," 9–10; "Indian Nullification of the Unconstitutional Laws of Massachusetts Relating to the Mashpee Tribe; or the Pretended Riot Explained," 8; "An Indian's Appeal to White Men of Massachusetts," 7–8; "An Indian's Looking-Glass for the White Man," 9; in Mashpee, 5–8; religion, 4–5
Ashley, John, 108, 110–11
Association of Southern Women for the Prevention of Lynching, 133
Atlanta Baptist College (later Morehouse College), 130–33
Atlanta, GA, 130–34, 237
Atlanta University, 188

Baker, Sara Josephine, 12–19; childhood, 12, 14–15; education, 15; public health career, 15–18; socialism, 18

Barbados, slavery in, 122–23, 198
Bethune, Mary McLeod, 133, 144, 192
Bevel, James, 145
Blackwell, Antoinette Brown (Rev.),
    273
Blue, Arthur, 101–2
Boxer Rebellion, 23
Brackenridge, Henry (Judge), 173
Brandt, Joseph, 91–92
Brown, Charlotte Hawkins, 133, 192
Bryn Mawr College, 315, 320, 322
Bryn Mawr Summer School for
    Women Workers, 285–86
Bureau of Child Hygiene (New York
    City), 16–17
Butler, Smedley Darlington, 20–32;
    anti-imperialism, 28, 30–31; back-
    ground and education, 22; early
    military career, 22–27; fascist plot,
    29–30; Mussolini controversy, 26

Cable, George Washington, 33–43;
    "The Freedman's Case in Equity,"
    38–39; on "race question," 38–42;
    research on jails and asylums, 36–
    37; "The Silent South," 40; youth,
    35–36
Cameron, Donaldina, 291
Campbell, Tunis G., 44–55; on Belle-
    ville Plantation, 50; political career,
    51–54; in prison, 52–53; racial
    attitudes, 46; on Sea Islands, 47–50
Capetillo, Luisa, 56–66; background
    and education, 58; *Ensayos Libertar-
    ios*, 61; labor career, 59–65; anar-
    chist philosophy, 61–65; *Mi Opinión
    sobre las Libertades, Derechos y De-
    beres de la Mujer como Compañera,
    Madre, y Ser Independiente*, 63
Chandler, Elizabeth Margaret, 115
Child labor, 162–66, 212–14; New
    York Child Labor Committee, 164
China, 23, 26
Choctaw (tribe), 88–89
Citizenship schools, 145–47
Civil rights: Civil Rights Act of 1875,
    38, 305; George Washington Cable
    on, 38–41; Highlander Folk School,

144–47; Mexican Americans, 152;
    NAACP, 239–41
Clark, Septima, 145
Club movement (African American
    women), 80, 127, 129
Coit, Stanton, 100
Coles, Edward, 67–74; attitude toward
    slavery, 69–70, 73–74; background,
    69; move to Illinois, 70–72; political
    career, 72–74
Congress of Industrial Organizations
    (C.I.O.), 143–44
Convict lease system, 37; Tunis
    Campbell, 52–53
Cooper, Anna Julia, 75–85; back-
    ground, 77; confrontation with
    Board of Education, 82–83; doctoral
    studies, 83; organizational role, 80–
    85; teaching career, 78–85; *A Voice
    from the South*, 79
Cornell University, 97–98, 160
Council for Interracial Cooperation
    (later Commission on Interracial
    Cooperation), 132–33, 141
Covello, Leonard, 220
Creek (tribe), 89, 92
La Crónica, 152–54, 156
La Cruz Blanca, 155
Curtis Act (1898), 89–90

Dale, Edward Everett, 88
Danish Folk Schools, 140
Dawes, Henry (Sen.), 183
Dawes Act (1887), 89, 184
Deaf: definition, 226; education and
    history, 229–30; as immigrants, 231
Debo, Angie, 86–94; activism, 92–93;
    *And Still the Waters Run: The Be-
    trayal of the Five Civilized Tribes*, 91–
    92; background and education, 88–
    89; *Geronimo: The Man, His Time,
    His Place*, 93; publishing contro-
    versy, 91–92
DeWitt, John L. (Gen.), 329, 331
Dombrowski, James, 141
Dorr, Thomas, 216
Du Bois, W.E.B., 130, 165, 224, 236–39,
    310–11

Dundy, Elmer S. (Judge), 181–82
Dyer Anti-lynching Bill, 240–41

Eastland, James (Sen.), 145
Elliott, John Lovejoy, 95–105; background and education, 97–98; educational and housing reforms, 103–4; Hudson Guild, 100–105; NAACP, 102, 239; with Society for Ethical Culture, 98–105
Ethical Culture, Society for, 98–105
Etting, Solomon, 171

Factory system (New England), 212–13
Fairbanks, Calvin, 117, 119–20
Farmer, John, 122, 199
Fascists, in the United States, 29–30. See also American Liberty League
Feminism: Anna Julia Cooper, 78–81; Ernestine Rose, 269–75; in Mexican American community, 153–54; in Puerto Rico, 62–64; Fish, Phineas (Rev.), 6–8
Five Civilized Tribes, 86, 89
Freedmen, 47–49; conditions, 118–20; Freedmen's Aid Commission, 118–20; Freedmen's Bureau, 47, 49
Freedom's Journal, 296
Freeman, Elizabeth, 106–12; background, 108; court case, 108–9, 111; later life, 111–12
Freire, Paulo, 148
Frelinghuysen University, 83–84
Fugitive Slave Law (1850), 116

Garrison, William Lloyd, 269, 271–72, 300–301
Ghost Dance Uprising (1890), 184
Gompers, 60, 280
Greenwich House, 313, 316–18

Haines Institute, 190–93
Haiti, 24–25
Hallett, Benjamin Franklin, 8
Harlem (New York City), 220, 222–23
Haviland, Laura, 113–20; activities with freedmen, 118–20; activities with Underground Railroad, 115–17; background, 115
Hayes, Rutherford B. (Pres.), 305
Haymarket martyrs (1887), 221
Hazard, Thomas, 121–26; abolitionism, 123–25; background, 121–22
Highlander Folk School (now Highlander Research and Education Center), 135–48; and CIO, 143–44; and Civil Rights, 144–47; environmental activities, 147–48; organization, 141–42; persecution of, 145–47
Hope, John, 129–31, 134, 192
Hope, Lugenia, 127–34; background, 129; Council for Interracial Cooperation, 132–33; national activities, 133–34; Neighborhood Union, 131–34; YWCA, 132
Horton, Myles, 135–49; background and education, 137–38; in Denmark, 140–41; at Highlander, 141–48; philosophy, 140–43, 145–48; Union Theological Seminary, 139–41
Horton, Zilphia Johnson, 143
House Committee on Un-American Activities, 223–24, 299
Hudson Guild, 100–105
Hull House, 100, 127, 158, 161–63

Idar de Juarez, Jovita, 150–57; background and education, 152; career as journalist, 152–56; La Liga Feminil Mexicanista, 154; in Nuevo Laredo, 155–56
Idar, Nicasio, 152–54
Iglesias, Santiago, 60
Ingersoll, Robert, 97, 99

Jackson, Helen Hunt, 89, 183
Japanese American Citizens League (JACL), 330, 332
Japanese Americans, 328; relocation, 329–33
Jefferson, Thomas, 67, 70
Jenkins, Esau, 145
"Jew Bill" (Maryland), 171–75
Jews: Deaf, 230–31; in Maryland,

170–75
Johnson, Andrew (Pres.), 47

Kelley, Florence, 158–67; background
    and education, 160–61; Committee
    on Congestion of Population, 316–
    17, 322; at Hull House, 161–63; with
    NAACP, 164–65, 239; with National
    Consumers League, 163–66, 318;
    with Women's International League
    for Peace and Freedom, 166, 250
Kennedy, Thomas, 168–75; back-
    ground, 168, 171; and "Jew Bill,"
    171–75; religious beliefs, 172
King, Martin Luther, Jr. (Rev.), 147
King Philip's War (1675–1676), 6, 10–
    11
Ku Klux Klan, 51, 120

Labor: in Appalachia, 141–44; in New
    England, 212–17; in Puerto Rico,
    60–65; in sweatshops, 161–65, 279–
    84, 316–21
La Flesche, Francis, 176, 182, 185
La Flesche, Joseph (Iron Eye), 176, 178
La Flesche, Marguerite, 176
La Flesche, Susan, 176
La Flesche, Susette (Inshtatheamba
    [Bright Eyes]), 176–85; background
    and education, 176–79; Ponca re-
    moval and trial, 181–82; speaking
    tour, 182–85
La Guardia, Fiorello, 221, 248
Laney, Lucy Craft, 186–94; education,
    188; educational philosophy, 189–
    92; Haines Institute, 190–93;
    teaching career, 188–93
Lathrop, Julia, 163
Lay, Benjamin, 122, 195–201; in Barba-
    dos, 198; on capitol punishment,
    200–201; in Philadelphia, 198–201;
    youth, 197
La Liga Feminíl Mexicanista (Mexican
    Feminist League), 154
"Little Mothers Leagues," 17–18
Lockwood, Belva Ann, 202–10; before
    Supreme Court, 206–9; confronta-
    tion with federal courts, 206–7; edu-

cation, 204–5; political career, 208
Luther, Seth, 211–17; An Address to the
    Working Men of New England, 213–
    15; background, 212; as labor
    leader, 213–16; and suffrage rebel-
    lion, 216
Lynching, 39, 133, 152, 154, 222;
    George White's fight against, 307–9;
    NAACP's fight against, 239–41

MacCormack, John (Rep.), 29–30
Magon, Ricardo Flores, 153
Marcantonio, Vito, 218–25; back-
    ground and education, 220–22; and
    civil rights, 223–24; political career,
    221–25; and labor rights, 222
Marine Corps, 22–23
Maryland, 170; religious test in, 170–
    71
Mashpee (Massachusetts), 5–8
Mashpee Resolutions, 6–7
Massachusetts, constitution, 108
Methodism, 4–5
Mexican Americans, 152–56
Mexico, 24; revolution, 153–56
Mitchell, John G., 117
Moskowitz, Henry, 102, 238
Mott, Lucretia, 271
M Street School, 78, 81–83
Mussolini, Benito, 27

Nash, Felix (Rabbi), 228–30
Nash, Tanya Zolotoroff, 226–33; back-
    ground and education, 228; work
    for Deaf rights, 229–33
National Association for the Advance-
    ment of Colored People (NAACP),
    102, 133, 144, 164–65, 238–41
National Child Labor Committee,
    164–65
National Children's Bureau, 165
National Consumers League, 163–66
National Equal Rights Party, 208
National Woman's Suffrage Associa-
    tion, 207
Native Americans: colonial perception
    of, 3; European impact on, 3; his-
    tory, via Apess, 9–11; nineteenth

century Anglo attitude toward, 179, 184; in Oklahoma, 86–93. *See also under names of specific tribes*

Neighborhood Union Association, 131–34

New York City: Chelsea, 105; in 1830s, 269; Hell's Kitchen, 16; infant mortality, 17

New York Consumers League, 317–18

New York Society for the Deaf (formerly Society for the Welfare of the Jewish Deaf), 229–33

Niagara Movement, 237

Niebuhr, Reinhold, 139–41

Nightingale, Abram (Rev.), 139, 141

Nixon, E. D. (Rev.), 144

Northwest Ordinance (1787), 72

Nye Commission, 251

Oberlin College, 77–79, 82

Omaha (tribe), 176–80, 184–85

Ovington, Mary White, 164–65, 189, 234–42; background and education, 236; *Half a Man: The Status of the Negro in New York*, 237; NAACP, 239–41; and Women's Trade Union League, 282

Owen, Robert, 268, 271

Pacifism, 102, 247–48, 250–53

Paine, Thomas, 271

Parks, Rosa, 144

Pequot (Tribe), 3, 5

Phillipines, 23

Ponca (tribe), removal of, 179–83

El Primer Congreso Mexicanista (First Mexican Congress), 154

Puerto Rico: history, 58–59; labor movement, 60–61; status within United States, 59

Quakers (Religious Society of Friends), 22, 73; abolitionism, 122–25, 160, 197–201

Racism: against Native Americans, 3, 9–11, 179; against free African

Americans, 257–63, 295–301, 303–12; against African Americans after Reconstruction, 33, 36–38, 130–34; against Mexican Americans, 152–54; against Asians, 290, 326–28; against immigrants, 38, 41, 326; Haviland on racism, 115, 120; Cooper and racism against African American women, 78–84

Raisin Institute (Haviland Home), 115–17, 119–20

Rankin, Jeannette, 243–54; background and education, 245–46; first election to Congress, 247–48; pacifism, 247–48, 250–53; second election to Congress, 251; vote against entry into World War I, 248–49; vote against entry into World War II, 252

Reconstruction (1865–1877), 37–38, 41, 49–50, 120, 303

Rhode Island, 121–26, 216

Rhode Island Suffrage Association, 216

Robeson, Paul, 299

Robinson, Bernice, 146

Rock, John Swett, 255–264; abolitionist career, 258–62; admitted to Supreme Court, 261–63; background, 257

Roosevelt, Eleanor, 286

Rose, Ernestine Louise, 265–276; background, 267; free thought, 267, 270–75; in London, 268–69; and Married Woman's Property Bill, 269–70; as orator, 272–75

Sacco, Nicola, and Bartolomeo Vanzetti, 221

Sandiford, Ralph, 199

Schneiderman, Rose, 277–87; background, 279; as labor organizer, 280–89, 320; national role, 284–86; Triangle Fire, 283–84

Schulze, Tye Leung, 288–93; background, 290; civil service, 291; first vote, 291–92; marriage, 292

Sea Islands (Georgia), 47–49

Sedgwick, Theodore, Jr. 111
Sedgwick, Theodore, Sr. 108–11
Segregation: in Atlanta, 130–34; in
    Boston, 257–58; in California, 326-
    27; in Georgia, 188; in New Or-
    leans, 39–40, 42; in Tennessee, 138–
    39, 144; in Texas, 152–53; in YWCA,
    80–81, 1342
Settlement houses, 100–101, 161, 220–
    21, 313, 316–17. See also Greenwich
    House; Hudson Guild; Hull House;
    Neighborhood Union Association
Sheffield Declaration (1773), 108
Shirtwaist Strike (1909), 319–321
Simkhovitch, Mary Kingsbury, 236,
    313, 316, 321–22
Sioux (tribe), 178–79, 185
Slavery: early condemnations, 297;
    Coles, Edward, 69–74; in Massachu-
    setts, 109–10; in Pennsylvania, 198–
    201; in Rhode Island, 121–25;
    Rock's condemnation, 259–60
Social Darwinism, 81, 184, 305
Socialism: Christian socialism, 139–40;
    in health care, 18; Kelley Florence,
    161, 166, 228; Partido Liberál Mexi-
    cano (Mexican Socialist Party), 153;
    in Puerto Rico, 61–62, 65
Society for Moral Philanthropists
    (freethinkers), 270–71
Southern Christian Leadership Con-
    ference (SCLC), 146
Springfield, IL, race riot, 238
Standing Bear, 180; trial, 181–83
Stanton, Elizabeth Cady, 271
Student Nonviolent Coordinating
    Committee (SNCC), 147
Sumner, Charles, 258, 261–62
Sweatshops, 161–65, 317–18
Syndicalism, 61–62

Tanya Towers (New York City), 232–
    33
Terrell, Mary Church, 79, 239
Thomas, Martha Carey, 160, 285, 315,
    322
Thompson, John, 141–42
Tibbles, Thomas, 180–85

Triangle fire, 282–84
Triangular trade, 121–22

Underground Railroad, 77, 115–16
Union Theological Seminary (New
    York City), 139–41
Universal Peace Union, 208–9

Vaux, Roberts, 73–74, 197, 201
Veterans' Bonus, 28
Villard, Oswald Garrison, 238, 240
Villegas de Magnon, Leonor, 155–56

Wald, Lillian, 166, 239, 250, 316
Walker, David, 294–302; background,
    295–96; Walker's Appeal, in four arti-
    cles, 297–301
Walling, William English, 238
Wampanoag (tribe), 36
Washington, Booker T., 82, 189, 236,
    310–11
Wells, Ida B., 308
White, George Henry, 303–12; anti-
    lynching bill, 307–9; background,
    306, Congressman, 306–10; founds
    Whitesboro, 310
Woerishoffer, Carola, 313–23; back-
    ground, 315; at Bryn Mawr College,
    315–16; memorial service, 322; re-
    form activities, 318–21
Women: African American, club
    movement, 80, 127, 129; African
    American, education of, 79–80; in
    Mexican American community,
    153–54; in New England factories,
    214–15; in New York City labor
    movement, 280–86, 316–21; nine-
    teenth century legal status, 269–72;
    in Puerto Rico, 60, 62–63
Women's International Conference on
    Permanent Peace (1919), 250
Women's International League for
    Peace and Freedom (WILPF), 250
Women's rights, 207–9, 249, 269–75
Women's suffrage, 166, 207–8; Mon-
    tana, 246–47; national, 247–49, 272–
    75; Ohio, 284–85; Puerto Rico, 64,
    80; Washington state, 246

Women's Trade Union League
  (WTUL), 281–86

Yasui, Minoru, 324–33; arrest, trial,
  and appeal, 330–33; background
  and education, 327–28; later career,
332–33; and the United States
  Army, 328
Young, Andrew, 146
YWCA, segregation within, 80–81,
  132

About the Author

ROBIN KADISON BERSON is Director of the Upper School Library of Riverdale Country School in New York City. A graduate of Bryn Mawr College, she was a Woodrow Wilson Fellow at New York University, where she received a Master of Arts degree in history; she holds a Master of Science degree from Columbia University School of Library Service. She has taught secondary school history in a variety of settings, and spent seven years as Managing Editor of *History of Education Quarterly*.